Liberty without Anarchy

*A History of the
Society of the Cincinnati*

Liberty without Anarchy

›› ‹‹

*A History of the
Society of the Cincinnati*

MINOR MYERS, JR.

University of Virginia Press   Charlottesville and London

University of Virginia Press
© 1983 by the Rector and Visitors of the University of Virginia
Foreword © 2004 by the Rector and Visitors of the University of Virginia
All rights reserved

First published 1983
First University of Virginia Press paperback edition published 2004
ISBN 0-8139-2311-5 (paper)

9 8 7 6 5 4 3 2 1

The Library of Congress has cataloged the hardcover edition as follows:

Library of Congress Cataloging-in-Publication Data

Myers, Minor, 1942-
    Liberty without anarchy.

    Includes index.
    1. Society of the Cincinnati—History. I. Title.
E202.1.A7M93   1983   369'.13   83-5764
    ISBN 0-8139-0993-7

Frontispiece: Colonel Benjamin Tallmadge (1754–1835) and son, William Smith Tallmadge (1785–1822); painting by Ralph Earl; Litchfield, Connecticut, 1790; oil on canvas. (Collection of the Litchfield Historical Society, Litchfield, Connecticut)

To
my father
and
the memory of my mother
who first taught me of
General Washington and the Founding Fathers

Contents

Foreword to the 2004 Edition   ix
Preface   xiii
Acknowledgments   xv
Short Titles and Abbreviations   xvii

1. A Mutiny Transformed into One Society of Friends   1
2. The Institution   23
3. A New and Strange Order of Men   48
4. Facing the Threat of Anarchy   70
5. The Cincinnati and the Politics of a New Constitution   91
6. The Original Members   120
7. The French Society   145
8. A New Government: Some Compensation for the Toils and Dangers   177
9. Frustration, Success, and Decline   205
10. Rebirth   226
11. *Esto Perpetua*   245

Appendix
The Institution of the Society of the Cincinnati   258

Index   267

Illustrations follow page 144

Foreword to the 2004 Edition

On July 22, 2003, the Society of the Cincinnati lost one of its leading historians and most admired members. Minor Myers, jr., was admitted to membership in the Rhode Island society in 1976 in the right of Lieutenant Silas Devol, a Continental marine. Minor soon demonstrated his dedication to the society, and served as assistant secretary general from 1983 to 1986, secretary general from 1986 to 1989, and president of the Rhode Island society from 1992 to 1995.

He will be remembered as a warm and generous friend by those who knew him, and by the society at large as one of its foremost historians. His research on the history of the Cincinnati consumed several years and culminated in 1983 with the publication of this book. It was, and remains, the finest history of the Society of the Cincinnati yet written.

Minor Myers, jr., was born in Akron, Ohio. He earned a bachelor's degree in 1964 from Carleton College and went on to Princeton University, where he earned a doctoral degree in politics and political philosophy in 1972. The next year he joined the faculty of Connecticut College, where he ultimately became department chair in government. In 1984 he was named provost and dean of faculty at Hobart and William Smith Colleges in Geneva, New York, where he served for five years before being appointed president of Illinois Wesleyan University in 1989.

He was something of a Renaissance man. He found time in the busy life of a college administrator to be married and raise two sons and to write on a diverse range of subjects. We knew him as the historian of the society, but he also wrote extensively on early American furniture. He wrote about baseball and Roman coinage. He played the piano and the harpsichord. He even wrote a musical for the stage. He collected meteorites. In recent years he was working on a study of multitalented people, which makes perfect sense. He was one of them.

All the while he maintained a zest for learning. "The greatest teachers," he wrote, "are the ones who are inspired from the inside because they are asking interesting questions to which they are finding answers, and in doing so they pass along a real and authentic enthusiasm for discovery." That very enthusiasm for discovery drove him forward.

His work focused critical attention on what the founders of the society intended. He could find no evidence ("not one shred," he wrote) that they sought to create an American nobility, as some of their critics charged. He quite rightly identified European orders of merit as a precedent for the Cincinnati.

He saw the society as a reminder of the road the American revoluionaries avoided—the road that led from revolution to army coup to military dictatorship—a road taken by most of the armed revolutions of the past two hundred years. The society, as he saw it, was a testament to the patriotism of the officers and their dedication to the principles of constitutional government and civilian rule in the face of what he called "sharp provocation."

He was a modest and gracious scholar who had a deep appreciation of the unique character of the society. He understood that the society is very different from the lineage organizations founded in the late nineteenth and twentieth centuries. He was fascinated by the way the Cincinnati's eighteenth-century origins projected themselves into our time, giving the society its peculiarly federal character.

Liberty without Anarchy was originally published to commemorate the society's bicentennial. Minor Myers focused much of his attention on the founding and early years of the Cincinnati. But he did not neglect the society's modern history. He recognized that recent presidents general—including Frank Anderson Chisolm, Armistead Jones Maupin, Harry Ramsay Hoyt, John Taylor Gilman Nichols, and John Sanderson du Mont—each made essential contributions to the life of the society. The passage of time has magnified their accomplishments.

In the twenty-one years since *Liberty without Anarchy* was first published, the Society of the Cincinnati has grown and prospered. Under the leadership of a succession of remarkable presidents general— Catesby Brooke Jones, Reuben Grove Clark, Jr., Frank Mauran, Frederick Lorimer Graham, William McGowan Matthew, and my predecessor, William Russell Raiford—the society has committed itself with increasing dedication to promoting the memory of the American Revolution and the heroic American and French officers who secured American independence.

In those years the society's library, which Minor Myers used extensively in researching this book, has grown at an extraordinary pace. It now houses the archives of the general society as well as the records of many of the state societies. It also maintains one of the world's finest collections of printed materials on the art of war in the age of the American Revolution. The society's programs in history and education are also growing, as the society works to remind Americans of the debt they owe to the heroes of the American Revolution.

The last decade has seen a thorough restoration of Anderson House, the magificent mansion given to the society by Mrs. Larz Anderson in 1938 in honor of her late husband, Ambassador Larz Anderson, a member of the Virginia society. Anderson House is now almost a century old, but it remains one of most beautiful buildings in Washington and a landmark of which every member of the society can be proud. With its eclectic collection of decorative arts and artifacts of the Revolutionary War, the mansion attracts thousands of visitors every year. Every one of those visitors has an opportunity to learn about the history of the Cincinnati.

For tracing that history with such skill and grace we all owe a great debt to Minor Myers. His passing was a great loss to our "One Society of Friends." But his life and work enriched and inspired us all, and they will undoubtedly inspire and challenge historians of the Society of the Cincinnati for generations to come.

Jay Wayne Jackson
President General
The Society of the Cincinnati
January 2004

Preface

IN A DARWINIAN ERA there is a propensity to think that things were destined to be what they have become. Probably as a consequence of such assumptions, many a modern historian has ignored the Society of the Cincinnati completely or simply treated it as the early incarnation of a modern patriotic society.

Such treatment has appeared so commonly that historians appear to imply that the fears of Aedanus Burke, John Adams, Elbridge Gerry, and most notably Thomas Jefferson were essentially groundless. These critics consistently asserted that this group of former Revolutionary officers aimed at becoming a hereditary nobility that might well transform a republic into a monarchy. Curiously, no historian seems to have asked whether the society had such goals in mind. My conclusion is that during the critical years of 1786 and 1787 some of the leaders, and possibly some of the state societies in New England, did contemplate constitutional changes, and certainly some Cincinnati by that point *were* advocates of monarchy. Needless to say, plotters do not leave a rich documentary trail, and thus the evidence is somewhat sketchy, yet the patterns give Jefferson's doubts about the society, expressed as late as 1794, more plausibility than they are usually accorded.

I have not found, however, one shred of evidence to suggest that the society aimed to set itself up as an American peerage. Some members, many critics, and a few of the societies themselves referred to the organization as an "order" as opposed to a "society," its official name except in France. While some of the founders may have seen it as comparable to one of the orders of merit which flourished in Europe during the century, an order was not to be equated with nobility.

Another point often ignored is that the Cincinnati was America's first nonclerical pressure group with a national scope. When newspapers carry reports of coups almost every month in Latin America, Asia, and Africa, it bears asking why there was no coup in America in 1782 or 1783. The government was powerless against fiscal chaos, army officers had not been paid for four years, and there was a perception in the army that civil officials at Philadelphia were not only paid but living in considerable luxury. Whether the Newburgh Addresses might have led to a full-scale coup will be debated for generations, but the Society of the Cincinnati, as a national organization, offered the moderate, law-abiding patriot a peaceful alternative to express grievances that otherwise might have fired a coup. It is an enduring testimony to the patriotism of the army that it remained loyal to constitutional principles despite sharp provocation.

The pressure for ordered liberty runs through the whole early history of the society. The officers of the army were not about to see eight years of war transformed into anarchy, and support for a stronger central government than the confederation followed naturally from that outlook. The Federalists and the Cincinnati were natural allies. Given that some Cincinnati claimed credit for the society in suppressing Shays's Rebellion and that the Cincinnati met just before the constitutional convention of 1787 (some delegates were accredited to both sessions), the role of the Cincinnati at the constitutional convention deserves an examination it has seldom had, especially since Cincinnati comprised 38 percent of the delegates.

In the 1790s the society generally remains a staunch ally of Federalism, but by Jefferson's second administration the partisan aspects of the society in the previous decade are all but gone. And with the final funding of pensions for surviving veteran officers in the 1820s, the original needs that gave rise to the society had been met. Thereafter follow several decades of decline, until the Cincinnati reemerged as the model for the dozens of hereditary societies that spring up in the late nineteenth century. Today it continues, maintaining the fellowship its founders intended, enhancing the nation's historical heritage, and nurturing a warm affection for France. The following chapters tell of its transformation over two centuries. The emphasis is on the critical early years, up to the final funding of pay for life in the 1820s. The remaining chapters offer a summary overview of what the society has done subsequently.

Acknowledgments

IN WRITING THIS HISTORY I have been privileged to draw on the work of many others. Anyone researching the history of the Cincinnati is much indebted to the research of Asa Bird Gardiner and Edgar Erskine Hume, pioneer editors and publishers of the society's records in the nineteenth and twentieth centuries. In the current era, Mr. Stephen C. Millett's knowledge of the society and its history is encyclopedic, and Mr. Clifford Lewis 3d has developed an extraordinary fund of observations on the whole society based on his extensive work with the Pennsylvania society. Likewise, Mr. James Risk, C.V.O., F.S.A., has been most generous in providing background on European orders. Masterful with ready information, references, and suggestions about the whole society within its national context was Mr. John D. Kilbourne, director of the Library and Museum at Anderson House. To all four I am much obliged.

I am indebted also to those who gave this project birth. Professor Alpheus T. Mason of Princeton many years ago called my attention to the historical significance of the society, and Mr. Frank Mauran and the Reverend Mr. DeWolf Perry, chaplain general of the society, urged me to pursue this history in its present form. I am deeply indebted to Professor Carl Bridenbaugh of Brown University for a critical reading of several chapters. The full support of Mr. John Sanderson du Mont, president general of the society, and Mr. Harry Ramsay Hoyt, past president general, has been vital to moving the project ahead. I am grateful too for the support the general society has provided throughout the research, and the efforts of Dr. Walker Cowen and his colleagues at the University Press of Virginia have been unparalleled in transforming copy into a printed volume.

Others too deserve special thanks for sharing ideas and references, and here I would name Messrs. John Absalom Baird, Jr., Henry Lyman Parson Beckwith, Scott D. Breckinridge, Jr., John P. Burnham, Robert Girard Carroon, Virginius Dabney, Curtis Carroll Davis, David W. Dumas, William L. Hires, James E. Mooney, William Russell Raiford, George A. Seymour, Richard J. Sommers, William Stephen Thomas, and Rhys Williams. I am thankful too for the generous help from the staffs of the libraries at Connecticut College, Brown University, Yale University, the Rhode Island Historical Society, and the Massachusetts Historical Society. Needless to say, I am supremely grateful for the assistance I was given at Anderson House by Mr. Kilbourne, Mr. Gallatin de Knox, and the entire staff there.

Thanks would be incomplete without acknowledging my wife's help in going over the manuscript. Whenever there was a moment of discouragement, she and our sons Minor III and Joffre soon had my spirits revived.

As always, an author may be eager to share credit through his thanks, but responsibility for errors, and for the opinions expressed, remains his own.

Short Titles and Abbreviations

Adams, *Works*. John Adams, *The Works of John Adams*, ed. Charles Francis Adams (Boston: Little and Brown, 1851).

Adams, *Writings*. Samuel Adams, *The Writings of Samuel Adams*, ed. Henry Alonzo Cushing (New York: Putnam's, 1908).

Bancroft, *History*. George Bancroft, *History of the Formation of the Constitution of the United States of America* (New York: Appleton, 1882).

Burnett, *Letters*. Edmund C. Burnett, *Letters of Members of the Continental Congress* (Washington: Carnegie Institution, 1934).

Documents Illustrative of the Union. *Documents Illustrative of the Formation of the Union of the American States* (Washington: Government Printing Office, 1927).

GW. George Washington.

Hamilton, *Papers*. Alexander Hamilton, *The Papers of Alexander Hamilton*, ed. Harold C. Syrett et al. (New York: Columbia University Press, 1961-).

Hume, *Virginia Documents*. Edgar Erskine Hume, ed., *Papers of the Society of the Cincinnati in the State of Virginia, 1783-1824* (Richmond: Virginia Society, 1938).

Hume, *Virginia History*. Edgar Erskine Hume, *Sesquicentennial History and Roster of the Society of the Cincinnati in the State of Virginia, 1783-1933* (Richmond: Virginia Society, 1938).

Hume, *Washington Correspondence*. ed. Edgar Erskine Hume, *General Washington's Correspondence concerning The Society of the Cincinnati* (Baltimore: Johns Hopkins University Press, 1941).

JCC. *Journals of the Continental Congress, 1774-1789*, ed. W. C. Ford (Washington: Government Printing Office, 1904).

Jefferson, *Papers*. Thomas Jefferson, *The Papers of Thomas Jefferson*, ed. Julian P. Boyd (Princeton: Princeton University Press, 1950-).

Madison, *Papers*. James Madison, *The Papers of James Madison*, ed. W. T. Hutchinson, W. M. E. Rachal et al. (Chicago: University of Chicago Press, 1962-).

Proceedings. *Proceedings of the General Society of the Cincinnati*, vol. 1: Philadelphia: Review Printing House, 1884, vol. 2: N.p.: General Society, 1928, vol. 3: N.p.: General Society, 1930.

Washington, *Writings*. George Washington, *The Writings of George Washington*, ed. John C. Fitzpatrick (Washington: Government Printing Office, 1931-44).

Liberty without Anarchy

*The History of the
Society of the Cincinnati*

Chapter One

A Mutiny Transformed into One Society of Friends

THE SOCIETY OF THE CINCINNATI began as a mutiny moderated into an organization. It offered a constructive alternative to the desperate measures contemplated by some officers of an impoverished army in a week that might have transformed the Revolution into a civil war. The immediate history of the Cincinnati begins with the Newburgh Addresses and the fact that many officers had not been paid for four years.

It was March 10, 1783. Washington had known that something was afoot, and now the details were beginning to take shape in the army's regular winter quarters at Newburgh, New York. The anonymous documents now known as the Newburgh Addresses had just been distributed among the officers.

"The army has its alternative." What did it mean? Was a successful revolution now to be transformed into a military coup? Washington, the generals, and junior officers all studied the documents, which were perhaps all too persuasive. Who was the "fellow soldier" who wrote them and how would the officers respond? When would their patience and their patriotism run out?

"He has felt the cold hand of poverty without a murmur." Many officers could have said that about themselves. They had, all of them, left their private stations, devoted themselves to the cause of independence in hopes that when the war ended "gratitude would blaze forth" on those who had upheld the nation. Washington knew as well as any that Congress had not treated the army well, but this writer was taunting his fellow officers: "To be tame and unprovoked when injuries press hard on you, is more than weakness; but to look up for kinder usage, without one manly effort of your own, would fix your character, and show the world how richly you deserve those chains you broke."[1] The next day, in that mood, the author called the officers to draft still another letter to Congress about their pay. Or would it now be more than a letter? Would the army produce instead an ultimatum? A mutiny? A coup? Here within the army camp were sentiments that might stir up the sedition Washington had learned to fear as early as 1777.

The minuteman of 1775 had grown into the underfed, unpaid veteran, and, with his plow left behind, many a crop had been neither sown nor reaped. Congress and the states were perpetually slow in paying the troops, and if the army complained about not being paid, it was caustic about those rare moments when it was paid. Printing paper money both by the states and the Continental government had become a minor industry. When they first appeared, Continental bills passed at par with silver coins, but by March 1780 it took forty dollars in paper to equal one silver dollar. Virginia's paper was even worse. By the end of 1781 its ratio to specie was 1000 to 1.[2] Given the depreciation, being forced to accept paper at par was almost worse than not being paid at all.

By 1783 Washington realized that mutiny was no impossibility. There had already been outbreaks in 1777, 1778, two incidents in 1779, and two more in 1781.[3] Pay had often been the central issue, and each year the question of pay strained relations between Congress and the army further.[3]

During the hard winter at Valley Forge many unpaid officers simply resigned and went home. On December 23, 1777, Washington wrote Henry Laurens, president of Congress, about the "necessity of some better provision for binding the officers by the tie of interest to the service."[4] He had reluctantly concluded that the British practice of half pay for life was that better provision. Each officer who served to the end of the war would receive half his monthly army salary for the rest of his life.[5] A Congressional committee supported the plan, but to many the half-pay scheme seemed to advocate what the Revolution was trying to defeat: a political system taxing its people to support a vast hoard of pensioners and officeholders. Governor William Livingston of New Jersey, for example, opposed the plan: "It is a pernicious precedent in republican states; will load us with an immense debt, and render the pensioners themselves in great measure useless to their country."[6]

Philosophy explains only part of Congress's reluctance to fund half pay. With no power to tax, Congress lacked the means to pay for the program. Congress therefore did nothing, and in March 1778 Washington reported another rash of resignations. "Since the month of August last, between two and three hundred officers have resigned their commissions, and many others were with great difficulty dissuaded from it."[7] Despite Washington's steady stream of letters, Congress narrowly defeated half pay in April. In May, however, the delegates accepted a modified proposal promising half pay for seven years after the conclusion of the war, with no one to receive more than the half pay of a colonel. Initially Washington was delighted, but six months later he advocated half pay for life anew. Seven years were not enough to bind the interests of the officers to the army. In a confidential letter he was quite open: "Officers, unable any longer to support themselves in the army, are resigning continually, or doing what is worse, spreading discontent, and possibly the seeds of sedition."[8]

In summer 1779 Congress finally voted half pay for life, only to change its mind instantly. The original vote was rescinded, and Congress voted the states the burden of funding half pay for life, or any other formula, to provide the officers "adequate compensation" for the dangers they had endured.

Sensitive as always to political nuance, Washington had advised the delegates not to vote on half pay at all unless the prospects for passage were good. For army morale, rejection would be worse than inaction,[9] and the rejection only added to the growing alienation between civil authority and military power.

In that same month, August 1779, Congress also managed to provoke the generals themselves to organize as a pressure group. Responding to pleas from the army, Congress had granted a subsistence allowed to officers up to the rank of colonel, but the generals got nothing additional. When the generals met in September, probably at West Point, they drew up a protest which eleven major generals and fifteen brigadier generals signed, with the tacit approval of Washington himself. Only Maj. Gen. Robert Howe refused. Maj. Gen. Nathanael Greene, for one, was convinced that Congress was "determined to keep the general officers poor, to prevent their obtaining an extensive influence."[10]

By the early months of 1780 some generals began to sound as though the enemy were Congress rather than the British. Maj. Gen. Alexander McDougall wrote in February that the country expected "rigid virtue" from a starving army, while others were free to "pursue property as the primary object." The judgment of his brother officers was that "one or the other must give way" where constitution and manners did not accord. Increasingly, the officers were determined that it was the constitution which had to go.[11]

Disillusionment grew in 1780, especially among the generals. Congress had not even responded to their memorial of September 1779, and when the generals gathered at Preakness, New Jersey, in July 1780 they were determined not to be ignored again. They now demanded additional pay to compensate for inflation, increased living expenses, and a pension system for families of those who had died in the war. Should Congress not comply, they threatened to resign en masse.[12] This petition would not be sent but delivered, and Maj. Gen. Alexander McDougall could be counted upon to put the case to Congress with force.

At fifty, the same age as Washington, McDougall, despite his stuttering, would mince no words. He had, after all, earned a jail term for shaking his fist in and at the New York legislature in 1770, yet he was not so uncontrollably radical as to be ineffective. He could speak for the suffering and commitment of the army's leaders. He had taken a personal loan of £1,000 to finance the original organization of his regiment, and his devotion to the revolutionary cause saw him ignore his own financial interests to the point of reducing the formerly prosperous merchant to near bankruptcy.

McDougall arrived in Philadelphia on July 31 and spent the next seven weeks lobbying. He wasted no time on subtlety. While the army was suffering and dying, others were getting rich. The Revolution, McDougall said, had become a war "for Empire and Liberty to a people whose object is Property." Crudely put, the generals and the rest of the army wanted their share of the spoils: "the army expects some of that property which the citizen seeks, and which the army protects for him." Large land grants and half pay for life, he suggested, were only the generals' due.[13]

Washington seconded these arguments. To Samuel Huntington, president of Congress, Washington wrote of the complaints which pervaded the army because of variations in state funding. Pennsylvania *had* provided its troops half pay for life, but other states were unable, or unwilling, to send even adequate clothing. A *national* policy of half pay for life would silence discontent, and unless Congress acted decisively, half the army might go home at the end of the year. "The dissolution of the Army" was a real possibility. By October he had facts to support earlier predictions. In the five months since Pennsylvania's decision to offer half pay, only one Pennsylvania officer had resigned.[14]

Congress stood by its earlier recommendation that the states, and not the national government, establish a system of half pay for seven years, at least until Gates's defeat at Camden and Arnold's treason convinced the delegates that the army was not invincible and that the generals might really resign or, worse, go over to the British. On October 21, 1780, with no prospect of funding the measure, Congress voted half pay for life for officers who continued in service to the end of the war.[15]

The struggle for half pay had made the officers critics of the Confederation and advocates of stronger central government. McDougall's visit to Philadelphia produced a deep impression as he saw those who had risked little well fed, housed, and *paid* in the splendor of Philadelphia Georgian. He returned to an army of men who had left all to serve their country and led a squalid, unpaid existence in camp. Over a year before McDougall had asked Greene, "Can the country expect Spartan virtue in her army while the people are wallowing in all the luxury of Rome in her declining state?" Ominously, he had provided his own answer: "If they do, they are novices in the science of Human Nature."[16]

The twentieth century knows the surrender at Yorktown as the end of the Revolution, but then it merely seemed the end of the Campaign of 1781. The British still held New York, Charleston, and Savannah, and through most of 1782 Washington still feared that they would mount a new campaign. By fall the army was once more settled in its winter quarters along the Hudson. West Point was under the command of Maj. Gen. Henry Knox. Stationed there were three Connecticut regiments under Brig. Gen. Jedediah Huntington, Knox's own Continental artillery, three companies of Sappers and Miners, and the Corps of Invalids under their imaginative colonel Lewis Nicola.

Further north at Newburgh were Washington's headquarters,

three Massachusetts brigades, two New York regiments, and detachments of troops from New Hampshire, New Jersey, and Maryland. The composition of the camp is worth noting, since these men were the founding nucleus of the Cincinnati. The southern regiments were in the south with Greene, and not even all the New England units were at Newburgh. The cavalry was in Connecticut, and the Rhode Island regiment was at Albany. The Canadian regiment was in Pompton, New Jersey.

That fall the officers were more concerned with politics than the British. Massachusetts officers, realizing that Congress lacked resources to support half pay for life, directed their energies toward Boston and asked the state to make good the Congressional promise of half pay for life voted by Congress. Or, and here was a new option, they asked for a large lump sum as they left the army. For men with no cash, the prospect of commutation, as it was called, was more appealing than a lifetime of smaller payments.

Once again officers were not content to commit a petition to the mails, and Massachusetts men selected four prominent officers to deliver their demand: Maj. Gen. Knox, Col. Rufus Putnam, Lt. Col. John Brooks, and Lt. Col. William Hull. Washington refused to let Knox go, but the colonels headed east. By September 9 they were in Boston, where they found the senate and the representatives of the seacoast towns inclined to support half pay or commutation. However, when it appeared that Congress would take up the question anew in January, the legislature found a compelling reason for inaction, and a disgruntled delegation returned to Newburgh. Who supported the army? It seemed neither the states nor Congress.

Washington's letters are a revealing barometer of discontent. By October 1782 he knew that he must stay in camp all winter "to try like a careful physician to prevent if possible the disorders getting to an incurable height." By December the army was more irritable "than at any period since the commencement of the war." There had been proposals among officers to resign in groups until Congress complied with their demands, but "by some address and management" their plan had been transformed into yet another address to Congress.[17]

That "address and management" had been then, as it would be later, the work of Henry Knox. Probably under his guidance three delegates from each regiment of the Massachusetts line, except the Second, had met with representatives of the artillery and the hospital department on November 16. That group invited regiments of all the lines in camp to submit written grievances to be synthesized into a memorial to Congress. As Knox's aide-de-camp, Maj. Samuel Shaw, later recorded events, another meeting on November 24 brought forth a "full representation of the whole army" and a committee to draft the memorial.[18] On the committee were Knox, Huntington, Col. John Crane of the Continental Artillery, Col. Philip van Cortlandt of New York, and Hospital Surgeon William Eustis.

When the regimental delegates reassembled on December 1, they heard a draft which was respectful but eminently firm. The officers recognized Congress as "our head and sovereign," but it was a sovereign that had failed its soldiers. The army saw itself as enduring hardships "exceedingly disproportionate to any other citizens of America." Soldiers had not been paid for four years, or they had received paper money "worth but little indeed." The army suffered while speculators in currencies stood to make large profits: "We complain that shadows have been offered us, while the substance has been gleaned by others." An ominous undercurrent pervaded the document, suggesting that dire consequences might follow if Congress did not make good on its promises: "Our distresses are now brought to a point. We have borne all that men can bear; our property is expended, our private resources are at an end, and our friends are wearied out and disgusted with our incessant applications. We therefore most seriously and earnestly beg that a supply of money may be forwarded to the army as soon as possible. The uneasiness of the soldiers, for want of pay is great and dangerous; any further experiments on their patience may have fatal effects."[19]

Once more a committee would present the pleas in person, and the procedures for choosing that committee reveal Knox's direction of a growing representative political organization in the army. Each line would nominate a field officer, and the officer corps as a whole would then elect two of those nominees. Officers would also elect a general who would become the third member of the group and certainly its leader. When the ballots were opened on December 5, two veteran lobbyists were chosen: Lt. Col. John Brooks and Maj.

Gen. McDougall. The third member of the committee was Col. Matthias Ogden of New Jersey.

The memorial itself was signed on December 7. Knox signed first followed by four Massachusetts officers and four Connecticut officers. Col. Philip van Cortlandt signed "on part of N. York line," and in the same manner Lt. Col. John Noble Cummings signed for New Jersey, and Maj. William Scott for Massachusetts. William Eustis signed for the General Hospital, and Moses Hazen signed for his Canadian Regiment. This orderly representation of opinion, by regiment and state line, was in no small sense the prototype of the Cincinnati, and of the signers only Major Scott did not join the society.

Another aspect of the December petition merits attention. How could impoverished officers send a delegation to Philadelphia? In 1780 McDougall had paid for his own trip, but that was a luxury he and his colleagues could not now afford. After two weeks of collecting donations in the camp, the three had an adequate fund in hand and headed south.

In early 1781 Congress had sought to fund half pay through a 5 percent duty, or "impost," on imports. The approval of each state was required, and consent would, in effect, give the national government the power to tax. That change was both what the officers and a coalition of nationalists in Congress wanted and what those who opposed a strong national government feared.

In Philadelphia, Robert Morris, the superintendent of finance, Gouverneur Morris, and Washington's former aide-de-camp, Alexander Hamilton, were all convinced that the Confederation would amount to little until the central government had the power to tax. Robert Morris had spared no effort on behalf of the impost, arguing that any who resisted the impost prolonged the war and the sufferings of mankind. It was an argument harder and harder to make with each passing month after Yorktown, but by the end of summer 1782 only Rhode Island had not approved the new congressional power. Pressed by Congress, the Rhode Island legislature voted unanimously against the impost, and when Virginia in turn rescinded its approval in December, the impost seemed dead. With the impost seemed to die Congress's ability to make good its promise, and the army's hope of being paid appeared at an end.[20]

The arrival of the officers from Newburgh on December 29

offered the nationalist leaders in Philadelphia an opportunity for joint machinations between the army and the nationalists. For the nationalists, the army protest was a crisis that could be exploited to their benefit, and the army soon saw that what the nationalists wanted could lead to funded half pay or commutation. Morris spent the early days of January 1783 coaching the army delegates on how to make their case. He would help the army if they were willing to do what was necessary to get an impost established. That meant that McDougall during his talks with members of Congress was to emphasize the dangers of sedition, and he was to make sure that the army in Newburgh maintained a sufficiently threatening posture to scare the reluctant delegates into action. McDougall was no novice in Philadelphia, for in addition to his lobbying he had served in Congress in 1781 and 1782 while on leave from the army.

The three officers met a congressional committee on January 13. James Madison recorded the sometimes stormy, emotional session. Asking for an immediate advance of pay, McDougall emphasized the "sufferings & services" of the officers. Ogden said he did not want to return to the army if he were sent back with bad news. What would happen? One of the colonels answered that "at least a mutiny would ensue," and he was unable to assure Congress that the officers would struggle hard to put it down. Brooks added later that disappointment might throw the army "blindly into extremeties."

When the question of funding military pay came up, Morris's coaching came forth beautifully. The officers "animadverted with surprise and even indignation" at the reluctance of the states to support a national revenue system. "The ease not to say the affluence with which the people at large lived" proved resources were available, and if they were not forthcoming, the army's patience "would have its limits." McDougall digressed into a discussion of the confederacy, arguing that "the most intelligent and considerate part" of the army were highly critical of the constitutional system, particularly the unwillingness of the states to "cement & invigorate" the national government.[21]

McDougall, Brooks, and Ogden did a fine job of conveying a sense of desperation more severe than the real discontent at Newburgh. On January 25, Congress committed the question of current pay to Robert Morris to solve as he would, but the issue of commutation as a substitute for half pay remained unsettled. Three times in January and February the nationalists tried to put through a motion for commutation, but New England delegates refused their assent. The nationalists now revised their strategy. Rumors and a show of force might galvanize Congress into action.

McDougall hoped that the interests of the army could be joined with those of other public creditors in pressing for a new system of national finance, and he counted on Knox to crystallize sentiment in the army and bring pressure on Congress. McDougall's hope for a union of creditors was no original idea or chance rhetorical flourish, for Robert Morris had been attempting to create just such an organization since early summer 1782. At his urging, public creditors in Philadelphia had met, petitioned Congress to adopt national taxation, and taken steps to correspond with creditors in other states. Under the guidance of Alexander Hamilton, New York creditors met in Albany in September, also advocating national taxes, further communication between creditors themselves, and a national convention. Despite the efforts of Morris and Hamilton, no national organization of creditors appeared. The army now offered another chance, and as will be seen, the Cincinnati would become a national organization of one kind of creditor.[22]

To implement the new strategy, Colonel Brooks was dispatched from Philadelphia on February 8. Five days later he saw Knox and delivered a letter from McDougall asking for help. That letter was reinforced by another, also from McDougall, but written in disguised handwriting and signed with the pseudonym "Brutus." To force Congress to comply with demands, Brutus wrote, the army should mutiny and declare that it would not disband until paid. Knox was disgusted with congressional inaction, but he was not the man to lead a mutiny. He responded, "Much has been said about the influence of the army: . . . it can only exist in one point, that to be sure a sharp point, which I hope in God will never be directed but against the enemies of the liberties of America." The army's reputation was still "immaculate," and the army should endure wrongs to the "utmost verge of toleration." But even Knox confessed that "there is a point beyond which there is no sufferance." To Gouverneur Morris, Knox wrote that the pay question must be settled before peace was announced, or "we shall be in a worse situation than we were at the commencement of the war."

By mid-February all Philadelphia buzzed with rumors. Madison heard that it appeared the army would not disband until its pay had been secured, and Gouverneur Morris and Alexander Hamilton were spreading the same tale. The British too heard the story, as General Carleton's agents penetrated congressional circles. In February an agent reported that Congress had become "so very contemptible" in the eyes of the army that "the army is ripe for annihilating them." And in early March an informant reported that "a most violent political storm is gathering." He predicted that "it must and will produce an overthrow of our republican constitution."[23]

Washington heard these rumors not from officers in Newburgh but from reports emerging from Philadelphia, making him at once suspicious of their political origin. Had such rumors filled the camp in January, he would not likely have allowed construction of a meeting hall. Chaplain Israel Evans, Aaron Burr's Princeton classmate of 1772, had suggested the building as a place for holding divine services, but other officers saw it more in terms of dances and parties. As events would prove, "The Temple of Virtue" was also an excellent site for a protest meeting.[22]

Rebuffed by Knox, Morris and his fellow nationalists turned to Maj. Gen. Horatio Gates and his "family." Gates might be counted on to play the role Knox had spurned, for he was an old hand at intrigues. When Washington heard that there was scheming within the camp, he suspected, correctly, that the "old leven" was at work again. Basic to the smooth operation of the army was the "military family," the aides who worked with each general. These young men, a high percentage of them college graduates, prepared drafts of orders and letters. They were a receptive group on whom generals could try new ideas, and between aides and their general there was often a fierce loyalty that lasted many years after the war.

Col. Walter Stewart of Pennsylvania had been in Philadelphia and was ordered back as soon as health permitted. He arrived in Newburgh on March 8, carrying the strategy for the next step of what now amounted to a conspiracy. The next day he met with Gates and his aides. Assembled there with Gates were Maj. John Armstrong, Jr., age twenty-seven, a Princeton dropout who had been Gates's aide since 1777; Lt. Col. James Miles Hughes of New York, another aide, who was twenty-six; Surgeon William Eustis of Massachusetts, age twenty-nine, a Harvard graduate of 1772 who had served under Knox since 1775; and Maj. Nicholas Fish of New York, age twenty-four, another Princeton nongraduate. Also present were two officers whose precise identity is uncertain, a Maj. T. Stewart and a Major Moore.[25]

Stewart reported on the political situation, and with Gates's full approval the group decided to issue the statements subsequently known as the Newburgh Addresses. Armstrong wrote them, Capt. Christopher Richmond of Maryland made copies, and Maj. William Barber of New York carried the copies around the camp.[26]

Armstrong was the most forceful of the group. He would go on to become a United States senator, minister to France, minister to Spain, and secretary of war, with a common thread running through his entire career: he was never known to restrain a forthright expression of his opinions. Jefferson found him "cynical and irritable and implacable," and Martin van Buren described him as "eminently pugnacious."[27] How far he and Gates were willing to go in assembling the officers is still debated. Richard H. Kohn is convinced that Armstrong anticipated a full fledged coup, possibly replacing Congress and establishing a military dictatorship. Paul David Nelson, Gates's most recent biographer, however, holds that Gates would have had nothing to do with such an outlandish scheme.[28] And, needless to say, the participants were not eager to give a full public accounting.

Armstrong's call for the officers to meet to discuss their plight on March 11 was not unanticipated. Hamilton and Morris had worried that the plot might go too far, and Hamilton therefore set out subverting those who thought they were subverting Washington's moderate leadership. On February 13 Hamilton had written his old general a cryptic letter, commenting without explaining, "I am under injunctions which will not permit me to disclose some facts." He did, however, offer at least a broad hint of what was happening. The army thought Washington too moderate yet a "*complaining* and *suffering army*" would be useful in persuading Congress to take up half pay or commutation. Washington must let the army be heard, yet keep the protests "within the bounds of moderation." If possible he must take control of the protests through third parties, and Hamilton had a nominee: "General Knox has the confidence of the army & is a man of sense. I think he may be safely

A Mutiny Transformed

made use of."[29] Knox could keep discontent bubbling along, but under control.

On the very day Hamilton wrote Washington, Colonel Brooks returned from Philadelphia. He too probably briefed Washington, for John Armstrong was to state later that the "timid Wretch" had "betray'd" the plan rather than talk to those he was meant to incite.[30]

Well warned, Washington dealt with the conspiracy firmly once the Newburgh Addresses appeared. His general orders on March 11 forbade outright the meeting called for later that day. It was "irregular" and "disorderly." There was, however, to be a meeting on the fifteenth to hear the report of McDougall's committee. Generals and field officers were to assemble together with one representative from each company and a "proper representative from the staff of the army." Here again was the representative structure that had given rise to the petition to Congress. The senior officer present, sure to be Gates, would preside.[31]

Washington lost no time in sharing with the leaders in Congress his conviction that the trouble had been "digested and matured in Philadelphia." No sooner had Colonel Stewart arrived than "a Storm very suddenly arose with unfavorable prognostics."[32] Congress could not label whatever happened as a spontaneous outburst. On March 13 Washington reported to the camp the resolutions which the grand committee of Congress had adopted on January 25, promising to fund their obligations to the nation's creditors.[33] Here was evidence that Congress at least was trying. And perhaps worrying that things might get out of hand on Saturday, Washington named Brooks officer of the day for Sunday March 16.[34]

Tension was high on Saturday as the officers gathered in the Temple of Virtue. Gates was in the chair when Washington himself strode in and moved to the podium quickly. He had not intended to come to the meeting when he issued the orders of March 11, he said, but reflection convinced him to express his thoughts directly.

The anonymous call for a meeting was "unmilitary" and "subversive of all order and discipline." The anonymous proposals were neither prudent nor possible. Neither abandoning the country nor turning military power against Congress would be as effective as maintaining their loyalty to Congress. He closed with an extraordinary rhetorical exhortation: Follow the path of moderation "and you will, by the dignity of your Conduct, afford occasion for Posterity to say, when speaking of the glorious example you have exhibited to Mankind, 'had this day been wanting, the World had never seen the last stage of perfection to which human nature is capable of attaining.' "[35]

The prepared remarks finished, Washington sought to buttress his own thoughts by reading a letter from a member of Congress. He began haltingly, paused, and reached into his pocket for his spectacles, adding, "Gentlemen, you must pardon me. I have grown gray in your service and now find myself growing blind."[36]

The officers were stunned. Many of them stood with tears in their eyes, and that simple comment delivered the group into the hands of Washington and his allies. Within minutes the commander was gone.

Knox now took control, moving thanks for the commander's excellent address and assuring him of the officers' affection. Seconded by Gen. Rufus Putnam, the motion passed easily. Then followed the report on the mission to Congress, probably delivered by Brooks. Putnam then moved that Knox, Brooks, and another officer be a committee to draw up resolutions. That too passed, and a half-hour later the three presented five proposals. The first affirmed that the army would undertake no conduct which would sully its reputation. The second, carefully phrased, asserted that since the officers had confidence in Congress, they were sure Congress would not disband the army until accounts were settled in some way. The third exhorted Washington to renew the army's case with Congress, while the fourth rejected the Newburgh Addresses "with disdain." The fifth thanked McDougall's committee and urged it to continue its efforts.[37]

It was a total condemnation of the Gates-Armstrong group, and the grumbling that had pervaded the camp for four days was now dispelled, or at least overawed. Only Q.M. Gen. Timothy Pickering tried to keep that discontent alive. He rose, as he wrote a day later, and said it was shameful that the officers now "damned with infamy two publications which during the four proceeding [sic] days most of them read with admiration, and talked of with rapture."[38] But Pickering stood alone, and the opinion against the Armstrong addresses had been unanimous.

Shocked by the near mutiny, Congress adopted commutation on March 22, just a week later. There would be five year's pay for those previously entitled to half pay for life. And on April 18 Congress went on to propose what amounted to an amendment to the Articles, providing again for imposts. The future of that amendment, however, still lay with the states, for all had to approve it separately.[39]

Commutation had been voted, but would the officers accept it? Was it an adequate substitute for the half pay already promised? Years later survivors remembered with some bitterness that senior officers at Newburgh pressured their junior colleagues into a positive response to the polls which headquarters ordered in mid-April.[40]

Knox now had reason to mature a plan that had been on his mind for years. Peace was at hand and the disbanding of the army was inevitable. As the officers feared, and Congress hoped, a disbanded army would have little power to exert political pressure for an impost. Knox planned a national organization of officers that might maintain the political momentum requisite to protect the officers' interests, and thus shortly after the Newburgh Addresses the Society of the Cincinnati was born in the mind of the soldier-bookseller.

William Gordon was one of the first historians of the Revolution to interview or correspond with the subjects about whom he wrote, and in 1788 he recorded that Knox had projected such a society even before Armstrong's anonymous papers appeared. After March 15, however, Knox "imparted his proposals to certain officers," and then communicated with "the several regiments of the respective lines."[41]

Who were the "certain officers"? After the society became controversial, early planners chided one another on their roles. Knox wrote to Baron de Steuben, referring to "your Society," as though the whole had been the baron's idea. Steuben, on the other hand, wrote "this dangerous plan had its birth in the brains of two Yankees, Knox and [Jedediah] Huntington."[42]

As the senior officers at West Point, Knox and Huntington often appeared at Washington's headquarters together, an image that probably brought forth many barbs, for Knox tested the scales at a full 280 pounds while Huntington was a mere 132. But Huntington was no lightweight intellectually. He was one of the few generals who was a college graduate (Harvard, 1763). He and his classmates had shown a penchant for Latin drama, and much to the faculty's dismay they had acted out scenes from Terence. A prosperous Norwich, Connecticut, merchant, Huntington like McDougall had spent his own money ($1,500) to supply his regiment. In personality, as in size, he was the opposite of Knox. He was austere, reserved, taciturn, in many ways like Washington.[43]

Knox depended too on his aide-de-camp, Capt. Samuel Shaw. Both men had similar backgrounds. Both came from merchant families in Boston, and both had gone to the Boston Latin School before entering the world of commerce. Both were jovial bon vivants whose company and conversation were much valued by their fellows. Shaw was four years older than the major general he served.

There can be no doubt that Knox conceived of an organization, or at least of a badge, in the year of Independence itself. While traveling through Holland in 1788, Jefferson recorded a story he heard from John Adams. The events probably took place on September 10 or 11, 1776.

> Baron Steuben has been generally suspected of having suggested the first idea of the self-styled order of Cincinnati. But Mr. Adams tells me that in the year 1776. he had called at a tavern in the state of N. York to dine, just at the moment when the British army was landing at Frog's neck. Genls. Washington, Lee, Knox, and Parsons came to the same tavern. He got into conversation with Knox. They talked of antient history, of Fabius who used to raise the Romans from the dust, of the present contest &c. and Genl. Knox, in the course of the conversation, said he should wish for some ribbon to wear in his hat, or in his button hole, to be transmitted to his descendants as a badge and a proof that he had fought in defence of their liberties. He spoke of it in such precise terms as shewed he had revolved it in his mind before. Mr. Adams says he and Knox were standing together in the door of the tavern, and does not recollect whether Genl. Washington and the others were near enough to hear the conversation, or were even in the room at that moment.[44]

Discussions for an order of some sort had been underway by the fall of 1782, for on March 12, 1783, the *Gazette des Deux Ponts* in Deuxponts, or Zweibrücken, Germany, described a proposed Order of Liberty consisting of twenty-four knights. The account purported to have been prepared in Philadelphia on January 1, and given the detail, discussion had probably gone on some time. The head of the order would be the president of Congress, the Chancellor, Benjamin Franklin, and the patron, Saint Louis. Each of the knights would wear a uniform of scarlet and blue with a gold decoration suspended from a special ribbon with thirteen stripes.[45]

There is not a trace of the Order of Liberty in Knox's papers, but the account shows that Knox was not the only one thinking of a decoration. Knox's concept was broader. He envisioned a society not only with a badge but also with a membership of the whole officer corps. By April 15 he had produced an eight-page draft constitution, or "Institution," as it would always be called.

A similar proposal seems to have sprung up in Gates's circle at Newburgh. Capt. Christopher Richmond, the copyist of the Newburgh Addresses, broached an idea to Surgeon William Eustis, who recorded the following sometime in the late 1780s: Richmond "said that it was unhappy that such a band of friends and brothers should be separated perhaps never to meet again." Perhaps these old friends might assemble again in a few years. A day or two after that first discussion, he was back with an idea for a society and a general meeting "in some central place of the continent." Richmond had drafted a few ideas which he hoped Eustis might transform into a constitution. Eustis was still thinking about the project a week to ten days later when he heard that the officers at West Point were already planning a similar organization. Eustis recorded his memories to assert that "the Society grew naturally out of the affections of the officers from a desire to perpetuate their friendships."[46]

It was those very real affections which the early documents emphasized rather than the fiscal interest in commutation. Whether out of gentlemanly instincts or from a desire to avoid conflict, the early drafts of the Institution played down, as Eustis did, the idea that the Cincinnati was what modern writers would call a pressure group. Yet Eustis tips his hand, for the last line of his short letter about the army and the Society reads, "By the Congress they were styled the Patriot, and Posterity will call them the unpaid Army."

Knox planned a hereditary society in which the officers would be succeeded by "any of their oldest male posterity, who may be judged worthy of becoming its supporters and members."[47] He characterized the organization as "one Society of Friends," and his draft abounds with feeling for the "mutual friendships which have been formed under the pressure of common danger." But there was another purpose—charity for those who needed it. Each of the state societies would collect funds which could offer support to officers, widows, and orphans who "unfortunately may be under the necessity of demanding it." If Congress would not provide for the officers, they would do it themselves.

Criticism of the Articles of Confederation had been a basic theme in the army since Yorktown, but when it came to setting up their own organization, the officers invoked the logic of the Articles on almost every point. The Society would be divided into three levels, national, state, and county, and the state societies, which were to meet once a year, were supreme. They judged the qualifications for membership, they admitted, and they expelled. The function of the county societies, which were to meet every three months, was to receive contributions which could be used for support of the needy. In Knox's draft it was "perfectly optional to subscribe, or not, and such sums as each member shall think proper." General meetings of the society would occur every three years, and to them each member was to be invited, but the national officers were under "indispensable obligations to attend."

In his draft Knox said nothing about commutation or any other political question. Yet he did provide that the state societies would produce circular letters to all other state societies each year, concerning all such matters "as may conduce to advance the general intendments of the Society."

The name of the society came naturally. Educated men in the eighteenth century had been nurtured on the Latin classics, and Cincinnatus was the Roman model of the selfless patriot. He was living in poverty in 458 B.C. when he was called to lead a war against the Aequi. The Roman senate voted him dictatorial powers that gave him absolute authority for six months. Cincinnatus left his plow and went off to war, but victory came quickly, and in days he was back at his plow, having resigned his powers as soon as possible. That image, of course, fit the officers well as they contemplated returning to their own plows. Even more like Cincinnatus, these victors faced the prospect of poverty.[48]

Quite readily the educated of the eighteenth century saw themselves as playing classical roles. Addison's *Cato*, first performed in 1713, held up the model of another fierce republican patriot who would resist the growing power of Caesar. Washington knew the play, as did Nathan Hale, who probably saw himself as Cato in his final moments. His reputed last words were probably a remembrance of Cato's lines in Act 4 as he views the body of his son: "What a pity it is that we can die but once to serve our country."[49] And McDougall had used the pseudonym Brutus for both his newspaper essays and his secret correspondence.

In his original draft Institution Knox provided that the society would have an "order," or badge, a medal of "silver or gold" depicting on the one side Cincinnatus leaving his plow and on the other Fame crowning Cincinnatus. The foreign officers who had served with the army were "entitled to all the honors, rights and privileges of the Society," but it was not clear in Knox's draft whether the French were members or not. Nor had Knox made a fine distinction between a badge and a medal, for the society was to send Rochambeau "a gold medal, containing the order of the Society."

Exactly a month after the dramatic meeting at Newburgh, Knox had drawn up the basics of a society to continue the struggle for commutation or pensions after the army had disbanded. He had suggested it be hereditary, perhaps thinking that generations might be needed to settle the fiscal questions, and he had provided an "order." He had thus given the society a variety of images, for its friends and its critics. Some would see it as a pension fund, some as a political threat to the Articles, and some as a nascent hereditary aristocracy, an attempt to establish an American order of knighthood. As will be seen, some members accepted one image while rejecting others: General Heath asked that his name be erased when the French Revolution abolished decorations, yet he never withdrew his contributions to the pension fund.

Notes

1. For the text of the Newburgh Addresses, see *JCC*, XXIV, 294-97, 298-99. The addresses and Washington's response were printed quickly: *A Collection of Papers, Relative to Half Pay and Commutation of Half Pay* (Fish-Kill: Loudon, 1783).

2. On the comparative value of currencies see *Daboll's Almanack* (New London: Green, 1791), unpaginated; Eric P. Newman, *The Early Paper Money of America* (Racine: Whitman, 1967), pp. 359-60.

3. GW to Robert Howe, January 22, 1781, Washington, *Writings* XXI, 128; GW to William Livingston, January 23, 1781, ibid., XXI, 132-33.

4. GW to Henry Laurens, December 23, 1777, ibid., X, 192-98.

5. William H. Glasson, *Federal Military Pensions in the United States* (New York: Oxford, 1918), p. 25.

6. William Livingston to an unnamed correspondent, April 27, 1778, as quoted in Glasson, *Federal Military Pensions*, pp. 28-29.

7. GW to the President of Congress, March 24, 1778, Washington, *Writings*, XI, 137-40.

8. GW to Committee of Congress, January 20, 1779, Washington, *Writings*, XIV, 26-32; GW to John Armstrong, May 18, 1779, ibid., XV, 96-99.

9. GW to Committee of Congress, January 20, 1779, ibid., XIV, 26-32; Louis Clinton Hatch, *The Administration of the American Revolutionary Army* (New York: Longmans Green, 1904), p. 84.

10. Nathanael Greene to Alexander McDougall, February 1780, as quoted in Roger J. Champagne, *Alexander McDougall and the American Revolution in New York* (Schenectady: Union College Press, 1975), p. 159.

11. McDougall to John McKesson, as quoted ibid., p. 159.

12. Ibid., pp. 159-60.

13. McDougall, Notes Delivered to the Committee of Congress, August 1780, as quoted ibid., p. 162.

14. GW to Samuel Huntington, August 20, 1780, Washington, *Writings*, XIX, 405, 411-13; See also Glasson, *Federal Military Pensions*, pp. 32-33.

15. *JCC*, XVIII, 958-59.

16. McDougall to Greene, March 24, 1779, and August 15, 1780, as quoted in Champagne, *McDougall*, pp. 149 and 165.

17. GW to James McHenry, October 17, 1782, Washington, *Writings*, XXV, 269-70; GW to Joseph Jones, December 14, 1782, ibid., XXV, 430.

18. Hatch, *Administration of the American Revolutionary Army*, pp. 147-49; Samuel Shaw, *The Journals of Major Samuel Shaw* (Boston: Crosby and Nichols, 1847), p. 102.

19. See Hatch, *Administration of the American Revolutionary Army*, pp. 147-49; the Petition is reprinted in William Parker Cutler and Julia Parker Cutler, *Life, Journals and Correspondence of Rev. Manasseh Cutler, LL.D.* (Cincinnati: Clarke, 1888), I, 152-54.

20. E. James Ferguson, *The Power of the Purse* (Chapel Hill: Univ. of North Carolina Press, 1961), pp. 146-53.

21. January 13, 1783, *JCC*, XXV, 851-53.

22. Ferguson, *Power of the Purse*, pp. 149-52.

23. "Brutus" to Knox, February 12, 1783, Knox Papers, Massachusetts Historical Society, Boston. On the identification of McDougall as Brutus, see Richard H. Kohn, "The Inside History of the Newburgh Conspiracy: America and the Coup d'Etat," *William and Mary Quarterly*, 3d ser. 27 (1970), 187-220, especially p. 197n. See also generally on the conspiracy Paul David Nelson, "Horatio Gates at Newburgh, 1783: A Misunderstood Role," *William and Mary Quarterly*, 3d ser. 29 (1972), 143-58; C. Edward Skeen, "The Newburgh Conspiracy Reconsidered," *William and Mary Quarterly*, 3d ser. 21 (1964), 273-98. Knox to McDougall, February 21, 1783, Knox to Gouverneur Morris, February 21, 1783, Knox Papers;

Ferguson, *Power of the Purse,* pp. 158-59; unknown informant to Sir Guy Carleton, February 18, March 7, 1783, Bancroft, *History,* I, 296-97, 300.

24. Hatch, *Administration of the American Revolutionary Army,* p. 171; Edward C. Boynton, *General Orders of George Washington . . . Issued at Newburgh on the Hudson, 1782-1783* (Harrison: Harbor Hill Books, 1973), pp. 62, 65, 67.

25. Skeen, "Newburgh Conspiracy Reconsidered," pp. 275-76.

26. Horatio Gates to John Armstrong, June 22, 1783, Bancroft, *History,* I, 318.

27. As quoted in Skeen, "Newburgh Conspiracy Reconsidered," pp. 276-77n.

28. Kohn, "Inside History of the Newburgh Conspiracy," p. 200; Nelson, "Gates at Newburgh," pp. 143-46.

29. Alexander Hamilton to GW, February 13, 1783, Hamilton, *Papers,* III, 253-55.

30. Armstrong to Gates, April 29, 1783, Burnett, *Letters,* VII, 155n. Original in Gates Papers, hereafter quoted from microfilm edition.

31. GW, General Orders, March 11, 1783, Washington, *Writings,* XXVI, 208.

32. GW to Hamilton, March 12, 1783, ibid., XXVI, 216-17.

33. GW, General Orders, March 13, 1783, ibid., XXVI, 221-22.

34. GW, General Orders, March 15, 1783, ibid., XXVI, 227.

35. Ibid.

36. *Journals of Major Samuel Shaw,* pp. 103-7.

37. *JCC,* XXIV, 310-11. On the debate itself, see Kohn, "Inside History of the Newburgh Conspiracy," p. 211 and 211n.

38. Pickering to Samuel Hodgdon, March 16, 1783, Pickering Papers, Massachusetts Historical Society.

39. *JCC,* XXV, 962.

40. See William Heath to Henry Knox, April 16, 1783, Knox Papers. The Massachusetts line assembled to vote on commutation in the Temple at 10 A.M. on April 18.

41. William Gordon, *The History of the Rise, Progress, and Establishment of the Independence of the United States of America* (London: Dilly and Buckland, 1788), IV, 398.

42. Steuben to Knox, November 11, 1783, in Francis S. Drake, *Memorials of the Society of the Cincinnati of Massachusetts* (Boston: Massachusetts Society, 1873); Knox to Steuben, February 21, 1784, as quoted in John McAuley Palmer, *General von Steuben* (New Haven: Yale University Press, 1937), pp. 111-12.

43. On Huntington see Clifford K. Shipton, *Biographical Sketches of Those Who Have Attended Harvard College* (Boston: Massachusetts Historical Society, 1970), XV, 408-18.

44. Diary, March 16, 1788, Jefferson, *Papers,* XIII, 11.

45. *Gazette des Deux Ponts,* March 12, 1783, as copied in manuscript by Eugene du Simitiere, Photostat, New Hampshire Collection, Anderson House, Washington, D.C. I have not been able to find this report in the American press,

and one may wonder how it found its way to Deuxponts, a tiny German principality. Two connections are possible. The marquis and comte de Deux Ponts had both served in America, and the marquis had been born in Deuxponts. Steuben provides a second possibility, for Zweibrücken is not far from Hohenzollern-Hechingen. It is not likely, however, that Steuben would have sent a critique of his own plan, and I find no evidence placing him in Philadelphia on January 1, 1783. Simitiere thought the whole account fictitious, but it is too specific and too likely not to have some basis in fact.

46. William Eustis, "Statement concerning the Origin of the Cincinnati," Boston, undated, but surely in the 1780s while the society was still controversial. Eustis misdates the origin of the society as 1782, and thus a date close to 1790 is likely. James M. Bugbee, ed., *Memorials of the Massachusetts Society of the Cincinnati* (Boston: Massachusetts Society, 1890), pp. 531-32.

47. Knox's first draft is printed with the institution as adopted later in parallel columns in Hume, *Virginia History,* pp. 26-41. The manuscript itself is reproduced in Drake, *Memorials* between pp. 6-7.

48. Why did Knox pick Cincinnatus? There were many other Romans whose names might have been used, e.g., Brutus or Cato. It is interesting to speculate what this bookseller might actually have known of the history of Cincinnatus. Two sources provide some clues, the curriculum of Boston Latin and his own catalogue of the London Book Store, published in 1773.

The fullest story of Cincinnatus is to be found in Livy and Dionysius Halicarnassus, neither of whom was used as texts at Boston Latin. Cincinnatus does appear in John Clarke's *Introduction to the Making of Latin,* which was used as a text, but the story does not provide enough detail to have fixed an image capable of inspiring the society. The catalogue of his bookshop had a special section on classics, but Livy was not listed. He did offer Goldsmith's outline history of Rome, which does have a rather full account of Cincinnatus, but he sold another book worthy of special note, L. M. Stretch's *The Beauties of History.* First published in 1770 by an English vicar, *Beauties* was a series of moral lessons for youth. Organized basically in terms of virtues, each was outlined and historical exemplars given. Continence, for example, was personified by Alexander the Great and the Yeoman of the Guard to King Charles II.

Knox offered few comments about any books in his catalogue, but of this he said: "The laudable intention . . . is to collect the records of virtue, and virtuous Men; and to inspire young minds with the love of virtue, and to make them gloriously emulous of the best and greatest characters that have been exhibited among mankind."

Knox says nothing of Stretch in his later correspondence, but I present these details because Cincinnatus is included, not as the exemplar of patriotism, but as the model of "Disinterestedness." Stretch emphasized that the poor Cincinnatus had the opportunity on several occasions for great wealth but chose rather his simple life. If that was Knox's image of this classical hero, the general was surely surprised when criticism of the society began. The members were seen as anything but "distinterested." See *A Catalogue of Books imported and Sold by Henry Knox at the London Book Store.* (Boston N.p., 1773). The comment quoted is on page 8.; L. M. Stretch, *Beauties of History* (Springfield: Gray, 1794) I, 204-11.

49. George Dudley Seymour, *Nathan Hale* (New Haven: Privately printed, 1941), pp. 85-86, 376-82. Joseph Addison, *Cato* (London: Tonson, 1713), p. 53.

Chapter Two

The Institution

THE CONCEPT OF A SOCIETY would gain support as it spread through the encampments along the Hudson, but with the disbanding of the army inevitable, Knox and his associates had to press with vigor to see the society established before the regiments marched off. With persistent efforts in May and early June, Knox and his associates had the basic organization accomplished by mid-June, but only in November was the society organized in the last of the thirteen states.

On April 16, only a day after Knox drafted his constitution for the Cincinnati, word of a formal peace arrived in Newburgh. The news was kept confidential to allow a solemn proclamation on April 19, eight years to the day from the Battle of Lexington. Those who might see the hand of the Creator in such timing failed to discern the same guidance in the acts of Congress: commutation was still unfunded. Memories of the Newburgh Addresses and fiscal considerations led Washington, Knox, and even the nationalists in Congress to see the dissolution of the army as not only inevitable but desirable. Reporting "a general uneasiness in the army," Knox advised Washington, "I think the sooner we can begin to discharge the men the better." A nonpolitical justification was needed, and what was better than to suggest that the men needed to return to their farms in the spring? Washington said nothing about plowing when he wrote Alexander Hamilton that so long as the army remained intact, discontent would increase. He was equally insistent, however, that the army's claims be settled.[1]

Unable to provide all the army's back pay, Congress nonetheless voted the men three month's pay, essentially traveling money to see them home. Even for these small sums, Congress resorted to freshly printed promissory notes coming due in six months.[2]

The desirability of dispersing the army made a society like the Cincinnati all the more politically useful. The society would maintain the old fellowship of the war, to be sure. Yet an organization to endure for generations would allow the officers to retire from camp knowing that someone would speak for the economic interests of the army as a whole. It was a constructive alternative to an ultimatum from an army refusing to lay down its arms until paid.

At the same time Knox was urging Washington to find justifications to send the men home, he was also working to see the society organized before the inevitable departures began. In late April and early May, Knox depended most on three men to help further these plans, his own aide-de-camp, Capt. Samuel Shaw, Brig. Gen. Jedediah Huntington, and Maj. Gen. Friedrich Wilhelm von Steuben, the colorful German who had brought the Continental army needed discipline.[3]

By late April, Knox, Steuben, and Huntington had drafts of the institution circulating among regimental headquarters. Changes were made as the document was discussed, and in the Second New York Regiment Ens. Bernardus Swartwout transcribed a variant which stipulated that the national meetings would "always be holden on the 19th april, the day on which the war commenced, & on which peace was proclaimed in the army."[4] State societies would meet on July 4.

Finding favorable responses, Knox suggested a meeting of general officers and representatives of the state lines, a pattern already developed in planning petitions in the previous year. In preparation for that gathering, at least one line elected representatives at a meeting which was less than voluntary. Gen. William Heath ordered officers of the Massachusetts line to meet at the Temple on May 7 at 10 o'clock to select one delegate to go to Knox's meeting, tentatively set for May 8. Heath explained that the May 8 meeting was "for the purpose of considering the expediency of the officers of the army forming themselves into a military society."[5]

Generals and delegates, however chosen, assembled finally on May 10 to consider the draft institution. Steuben presided since he was the senior officer present, a fact which implies that Generals Washington, Horatio Gates, and William Heath did not attend. The gathering amended the institution further, probably striking out April 19 as the day for national meetings. Further revisions were put in the hands of a committee of four—Knox, Huntington, Shaw, and Brig. Gen. Edward Hand of Pennsylvania.[6]

On May 13 the delegates gathered again at the Verplanck House, Steuben's headquarters at Fishkill-on-Hudson.[7] This time General Heath presided, and with seemingly little debate the representatives adopted the committee's revisions of the institution. If the Society of the Cincinnati can point to one day as its birthday, it is May 13, 1783.

Almost every paragraph of the institution adopted that day was to be the subject of controversy over the next two years. (The whole text is printed as an appendix.) As would often be pointed out later, it was drawn up in haste and lacked the precision of language that lawyers might have introduced.

Revisions in Knox's first draft made the group more militantly political. Knox had provided that the general society meet every three years, but now the general society would meet "annually, so long as they shall deem it necessary, and afterwards, at least once in every three years." Political pressure, rather than fellowship, was the likely explanation for "necessary" annual meetings. And circular letters that each state society was to send to all the others each year were to concern not only the good of the society, but also the "general union of the states."

The political import of the institution was subtle but undeniable. The document's announcement of "an unalterable determination to promote and cherish between the states, that union and national honor so essentially necessary to their happiness, and the future dignity of the American empire" was little more than a call for a revision of the Articles of Confederation. McDougall had used almost the same words before Congress.[8] A national system of taxation would provide that cement the union needed, and promotion of the union was therefore promotion of national power sufficient to support commutation.

The institution likewise introduced a more formal means of building the charitable fund. Every member was to contribute one month's pay to the general fund of his state society. Thus, according to the pay scales, a major general would contribute $166, while a captain of infantry would donate $40 and an ensign $20. The founders did not demand cash contributions, but offered each new member the option of giving a voucher authorizing John Pierce, the paymaster general of the army, to deposit a month's pay in the society treasury when commutation funds were received. This credit arrangement was a wise organizational move, for many impoverished officers could not afford a cash contribution.

Membership criteria became more explicit in the final version of the institution. In large measure those eligible for the society were those eligible for commutation, that is, those officers who had served to the end of the war. Also eligible for membership were officers who had been "deranged" (declared no longer needed by acts of Congress), or who had served honorably for three years during the war. Further provision was made to admit the "eldest male branches" or children of officers who had died in service during the war. Foreign officers were now eligible for membership. Their names were to be listed in the records of the general society, but they were counted as members of the society in the states where they lived.

Designing a society at state and national levels was a stroke of political genius. The army had pressed both Congress and the states for their pay, and if the national organization or general society might not succeed with Congress, state societies might fare better at home. Washington presented similar logic in a letter to Hamilton in April, though he was not speaking of the Cincinnati. The commander was determined to see the army paid, and if Congress would not stand by its commitments he would turn to the states. That, he reminded Hamilton, was a strategy which might defeat what the nationalists had in mind when they tried to involve the army in politics.[9]

The Cincinnati was to become controversial, in part because of its scope. As Forrest MacDonald commented a few years ago, the society was "virtually the only national organization except for Congress itself," a fact which would lead some critics to imagine that the Cincinnati was trying to parallel, and eventually usurp, the place of Congress.[10]

Honorary memberships were an addition to Knox's original concept. So long as the ratio of honorary to hereditary members did not exceed one to four, states might admit men "eminent for their abilities and patriotism, whose views may be directed to the same laudable objects with those of the Cincinnati." Honorary memberships were not hereditary, nor were those elected obliged to contribute to the general funds. As will be seen, states varied on the question of whether the honorary members were fully members in every sense. In what became another controversial provision, the writers of the institution allowed donations from nonmembers who wanted to support the charitable aspects of the society.

The final version of the institution brought little change to Knox's concept of the medal beyond providing that it would be gold. New, however, was the provision for its suspension from "a deep blue ribbon, two inches wide, edged with white, descriptive of the union of America and France." Thus the medal was converted to a decoration.

Perhaps with that "union" in mind, the meeting of May 13 directed that seven French leaders be sent the medal. Two were diplomats (chevalier de La Luzerne, minister to the United States, and his predecessor, Sieur Conrad-Alexandre Gerard), four were admirals (d'Estaing, de Grasse, Barras, and Destouches), and the seventh went to General Rochambeau. The institution provided also for the admission of "the Generals and Colonels" of the French army, but any provision for the navy was ambiguous at best.

Having finished the institution, the meeting of May 13 turned to organization. The institution was to be copied on parchment, and Generals Heath, Steuben, and Knox were to wait on Washington with the parchment copy and ask him to "honor the Society by placing his name at the head of it." Other generals and delegates would then sign "for themselves and their constituents." The creation of the society was thus the act of representatives acting for the regiments which chose them. Individual officers would become members only when they in turn signed a copy of the institution.[11]

Also on May 13, General Heath, as second in command, was charged with transmitting copies of the institution to Maj. Gen. Nathanael Greene, commander of the southern army, to the commander of the Rhode Island troops, and to the senior officers of each state line from Pennsylvania through Georgia. Each commander in turn was to expedite the establishment of the society in his own state.

The selection of Heath for the task of principal organizer is highly ironic, for he was the one general in Newburgh who had doubts about the society. As Knox would write Lincoln about him on May 21, "With a sagacity peculiar to himself, he thinks through the mist he sees spirits and hobgoblins of hideous forms and no popularity."[12] Heath told the story of his doubts in his *Memoirs,* where he invariably refers to himself as "our General." Initially he had been opposed to "any thing that had any resemblance of an order, or any insignia or badge of distinction." He and another officer discussed the society and decided not to join.

The next morning, the officer called upon him, and observed that one consideration, not before mentioned, had occured to him, viz. that it might happen in the days of their posterity, in case they did not sign, that the descendent of one who was a member might happen to fall in company with the descendant of one who was not; that the latter, on observing the badge, might inquire what it was, and what its intention? upon his being answered, that it was the insignia of a Society, of which his ancestor, who had served in the American army, during the Revolution, was a member—the other might reply, my ancestor too served during that war, but I never heard any thing of such a badge in our family; to which it might probably be answered, it is likely your ancestor was guilty of some misconduct which deprived him of it. Upon this, our General broke out—"I see it, I see it, and spurn the idea," which led him to sign the general Institution.[13]

Most officers in the camp joined the society eagerly, but Heath at least was not alone in his doubts. Forty years later Timothy Pickering recalled, "I felt a solid objection to subscribe to the institution, because it assumed so much importance, when I saw it was really so insignificant." He thought it ludicrous that a small group of officers, who compared to "the great body of their republican fellow-citizens, were but a drop in the bucket, should arrogate to themselves the sublime duty of preserving the rights and liberties of human nature." But that, he recalled, well bespoke the hand of Knox. The institution "bore the marks of his pomposity, and assumed an importance—'*to preserve the rights and liberties of human nature*'—corresponding with his disposition." Why then did he sign? Fundamentally, for the same reasons which led Heath to subscribe. "Absolutely and purely to avoid the reproach of singularity, for I supposed *all* the officers of the army would become members."[14]

In late May, when Christopher Richmond, copyist of the Newburgh Addresses, sent Gates a copy of the institution, he added a note. "The new hampshire line Generally have refused to be of the Society—General Heath & Col. Vose & Col. Miller also refused. What the motives for all or either of these may be I know not."[15] There were two Colonels Vose, both from Massachusetts, and both joined in the end. Miller's identity is uncertain. Given Richmond's comment, it is probably significant that New Hampshire's was almost the last of the thirteen societies in America to organize.

While Heath hesitated, Knox took over organizational efforts. Aides copied the institution, and by May 19 Knox sent Steuben four copies for the baron to sign and forward to the New York, New Jersey, Connecticut, and New Hampshire lines.[16] Another copy would go to Col. Jean Baptiste Gouvion of the Engineers. To Maj. Gen. Benjamin Lincoln, the secretary of war, Knox sent the institution and assurances that "the intention is pure, and uncorrupted by any further design." What were the intentions of the society? The first draft of Knox's letter shows that he changed his mind as he spelled them out. He began, "The sole objects are the happiness of the officers," but switched to "The sole objects are the union of the states as far as the humble influence of the officers may intend—and to erect some lone shelter for the unfortunate, against the storms and tempests of poverty." Washington took no part in the organization of the society. He attended none of the meetings, and his own letters are mute on the society until September. However, the general staff surely discussed plans for the society, for Knox assured Lincoln that "the commander in chief and almost all the officers are warmly in favor" of the society.[17]

Organization was well advanced by late May when the dreaded orders came. Congress directed Washington to furlough noncommissioned officers and men who had enlisted for the duration of the war. Fundamentally, the only officers furloughed were those needed to march the men home. Other officers and men enlisted for three years or other specific periods were kept on for the time being. Washington issued the appropriate orders on June 2, and many were ready to perceive political motives in sending the army home quickly. When he heard the news of the furloughs, Heath noted in his diary, without adding further explanation, "This mode appeared to be marked with policy in several respects."[18]

There were no farewell parades, no ceremonies of departure. The Maryland battalion, first to go, marched off on June 5, the same day the generals and commanding officers of regiments met again to entreat Washington to suspend the furloughs. No man should be sent home against his will until he was paid. Writing for his fellow commanders, Heath wrote Washington that the men would be "no less exposed then to the insults of the meanest followers of the army, than to the arrests of the sheriff—deprived of the ability to assist our families."[19] But Washington's order stood. Someone proposed that the officers should dine together before separating, but opposition was strong. As Col. Walter Stewart wrote, it was an occasion "more adapted to sorrow, than to Mirth." By June 9 the men from New Jersey, New York, and New Hampshire were gone. At least some of them had received Robert Morris's freshly printed notes for three month's pay, but many left without them. In Stewart's words, "Your heart would have bled for the Poor fellows who were in so disgraceful a manner turn'd off."[20] In that orderly dissolution of the army, the real devotion and love of country once more suppressed the bitter sense of betrayal felt by officers and men alike.

As the units marched off, Knox pressed on with the organization of the Cincinnati. On June 8 Col. Henry Jackson assured him that additional copies of the institution were on their way to Massachusetts and New York regiments. Heath had now come to terms with his future descendants and the society, and at Jackson's suggestion he had ordered the Massachusetts men to meet on June 9 to begin the process of electing officers. On June 16 Knox wrote the chevalier de Chastellux, the vicomte de Noailles, and the marquis de Lafayette, informing them that the society had been established and that the founders had taken the liberty "to associate all the Generals and colonels of the French Army." Once more there was perhaps a story to be told but not committed to paper, for each was advised that Colonel Gouvion would offer more information. As Knox wrote Noailles, Gouvion would elaborate on "the nature and intent of this matter."[21]

His tone to Lafayette was optimistic, and he looked to a new era with a stronger national government: "Our system of policy will mend & become good—it is the growing sentiment that there will be no good dignity or safety but in a general government unfettered by local or state policy. We shall have general funds and we shall be a united people. Our esteem for France will be perpetual." One could conclude from this letter announcing a new organization that, at the minimum, the Cincinnati would be no impediment to constitutional change. Knox's letters to these three officers, who were not among the seven named in the institution, further insured the survival of the society. As was to be evident the following May, one could not disband a society which such distinguished French leaders had joined.

On June 19 generals and representatives of regiments gathered again with Steuben presiding. It was a smaller meeting than the gathering of May 13, but this was the first to record the names of those present. In addition to the loyal cadre of Knox, Steuben, Huntington, and Shaw, there were twelve others. From the generals there were Robert Howe, John Paterson, Edward Hand, and Rufus Putnam. Regimental representatives from Connecticut were Col. Samuel Blachley Webb of the Third Connecticut and Lt. Col. Ebenezer Huntington of the First. Five Massachusetts regiments sent delegates: Maj. Joseph Pettengill (First), Lt. John Whiting (Second), Lt. Col. William Hull (Third), Col. Henry Jackson (Fourth), and Lt. Col. Hugh Maxwell (Eighth). Of New York regiments only the second was represented, by Col. Philip van Cortlandt. Samuel Shaw was the delegate for the Third Regiment of Artillery, and Steuben's aide-de-camp, William North, may have been there in his capacity as secretary to the president. These few men were responsible for the primary organization of the general society, a fact of which they were highly conscious. The official minutes of the meeting conclude with a statement that they had acted only because of the "necessity of making some temporary arrangements, previous to the first meeting of the General Society," a gathering expected in May 1784.[22]

That most basic of temporary arrangements was the election of officers. It came as no surprise that Washington was elected president general, an election that added the commander's prestige to the society. Conversely, he was in a position to moderate any demands the organization might make, an option he would exploit well the following May. Washington thus became the first president general, yet before that election Steuben had functioned as a president de facto and more so than in the sense of one who "presides" at meetings. He signed copies of the institution, organized meetings in May, and even referred to himself as president. Writing to L'Enfant about the June 19 meeting, he thanked him for "designs laid before them by the president on that day," and the minutes refer to him as "president." Likewise, when Maj. Gen. John Sullivan ran newspaper advertisements calling together an organizational meeting in New Hampshire, he referred to papers he had received from "His Excellency the President of the Society," and Steuben was the writer whose letter he quoted.[23]

In addition to Washington, the convention of June 19 named Knox secretary general, and McDougall, who had returned from his mission to Philadelphia, treasurer general. The offices of assistant treasurer general and assistant secretary general were left vacant, perhaps understandable in this temporary organization, but so too was the vice presidency. Why not Steuben? Why not Gates, who was chosen for the post the following May? The records are mute.

June 19 was also the likely occasion on which the Parchment Roll was signed, though the minutes make no reference to it. All the men present were signers, save Captain North. The parchment was lightly scored for signing in two columns, and Washington's signature stood at the head of the left column as the others began to sign their names, generals on the left, others on the right. Some signed later, either where spaces had been saved for them (as in the case of Greene, then in the South) or in the margin, as did Armand de La Rouerie.[24]

The French were members of the society by the nineteenth, for on that day the delegates heard that the chevalier de La Luzerne had accepted membership and assured Steuben that "all of the officers of my nation" would be equally honored.[25]

The most controversial development to come from the June 19 meeting was a new conception of the medal. Following the ideas and designs of Maj. Pierre L'Enfant, the delegates transformed the medal into a badge, or decoration.[26] In so doing, at least to the eye of critics, they also transformed their charitable society into a group emulating a European order of knighthood. From the perspective of the twentieth century, however, one might well wonder why decorations for officers had not come earlier.

Americans had known of British orders for generations, and the alliance with France brought the officers into daily contact with men wearing French orders. The British Order of the Bath was used primarily to reward general officers of great merit, but the French orders of Saint Louis (for Catholics) and Mérite Militaire (for Protestants) rewarded long and faithful service as well as extraordinary merit. Officers who had served with credit for twenty-five years could expect the St. Louis almost as a matter of right.[27] Also notable in the American camp were the badge and star of Baden's Order of Fidelity as worn by Steuben.[28]

Americans had taken some steps toward decorations of their own. In August 1782 Washington established chevrons to distinguish the uniforms of noncommissioned officers and men who had served for more than three years "with bravery, fidelity, and good conduct." For noncommissioned officers and men who had shown "unusual gallantry" or "extraordinary fidelity" he ordered the award of "a heart in purple cloth, or silk" to be sewn on the uniform. This was the decoration revived in 1933 as the Purple Heart. Historian William Gordon, writing in the 1780s, noted that these distinctions had been useful in improving order and discipline.[29]

Congress had voted gold or silver medals for ten Continental officers who had led major victories, oval silver medals for the three captors of Major André, and presentation swords for fifteen officers of unusual distinction. Most of these awards were not prepared or delivered until the late 1780s. But there was no outward sign of recognition for the regular officer of long meritorious service. The badge of the Cincinnati in that sense might fill a void. Knox, after all, had been thinking about a ribbon since 1776.[30]

L'Enfant had written Steuben from Philadelphia shortly before the nineteenth.[31] A medal, he held, would not do, for in Europe it was considered "only as the reward of the laborer and the artist, or as a sign of a manufactory, community, or religious society." Even worse, German and Italian "mountebanks, dancers and musicians" frequently showed up in France wearing medals, and "a gentleman already invested with any European order would be unwilling to carry a medal." By a medal here, L'Enfant meant a large coin-shaped object suspended from a ribbon, the original idea adopted in the institution.

A badge modeled on European orders was needed, and L'Enfant offered two designs. The first had an eagle holding a star of thirteen points. The second, which he recommended, featured the eagle alone with the design planned for the medal on its breast. This badge was to be worn. He was equally enthusiastic about a silver medal, but that was a keepsake to be cherished but not worn. Both the eagle-shaped badge and the round medal, he recommended, should be the work of Paris craftsmen "capable of executing it to perfection."

Following these suggestions, the meeting of June 19 adopted L'Enfant's second design for the badge and directed that silver medals also be prepared and given to "each and every member."

Major L'Enfant was to have both orders and medals produced, and in the fall he would leave for France to carry out that mission. One document connected with his trip makes it clear that the Cincinnati was intended by some of its founders as a continuation of the army's earlier protests to Congress. Going to France was not cheap, and Generals Knox, McDougall, and Huntington agreed that L'Enfant could have the remaining $303 of the fund collected in December 1782 to send McDougall, Brooks, and Ogden on their lobbying mission to Congress. The generals wrote, "We may with propriety appropriate the said Sum, to the purpose of purchasing the diploma and dies for the medals of the Cincinnati." Should any officer object, however, he could apply for a refund, and there is no evidence that any refunds were given. Thus the fund that sent McDougall to Philadelphia for commutation now sent L'Enfant to Paris for eagles.[32]

When the meeting of June 19 disbanded, the new Society of the Cincinnati had an institution signed, officers elected, a badge and medal adopted, and, as will be seen later, three of the state societies already in the early stages of organization. Knox had succeeded in creating an organization of officers that would outlast the army itself.

Knox and those around him were not the only officers using the last days at Newburgh to promote plans that might bear fruit later. Timothy Pickering and others proposed that Congress grant the officers and men tracts of western land. The men could then migrate west to establish their own separate state. This was undoubtedly the scheme which Gates called "Utopian" when he heard of it, yet it was no chimera for the 285 officers who petitioned Congress for such grants on June 16, just three days before the regimental delegates elected Washington president general of the Society of the Cincinnati. Of those signers, 87 percent would become members of the Cincinnati, and the vision of western settlements persisted until 1788, when Rufus Putnam led the first settlements of the Ohio Company[33] (see chapter 5).

The identity of these petitioners and the members of the society is but the first instance in which an activity was carried out by a high proportion of Cincinnati. Yet one cannot say that the petition itself was a Cincinnati project, even though land grants would be a regular topic at many Cincinnati meetings. As will be seen, the distinction between members of the society and the society was often lost on a highly critical public, yet there certainly were instances in which membership provided a common bond for organizing activities outside the society.

Another event of that critical June was far removed from the camp along the Hudson yet closely parallel to what had transpired there earlier that spring. A mutiny in Pennsylvania reflected the same discontent that led to the Newburgh Addresses, and there is a hint that the later mutiny may have been spurred on by the same personnel.

Troops stationed in Pennsylvania were equally concerned about their financial futures, and led by Capt. Henry Carberry and Lt. John Sullivan, soldiers at Lancaster mutinied and marched toward Philadelphia, where they were joined by troops from the Philadelphia barracks. On June 21 they surrounded the statehouse where both Congress and the Executive Council of Pennsylvania were meeting. In effect, both bodies were held hostage, though the mutineers' demands for pay were directed at the council. Members of Congress urged the state to act decisively in putting the mutiny down, but General St. Clair and state leaders held back, uncertain whether they could rely on the state militia. Events ended quietly that day. Washington sent General Howe south with 1,500 dependable Continental troops, but Congress moved immediately to the greater security of Princeton.[34]

In the context of other events, the mutiny is curious. Washington himself observed that the mutineers were new recruits, not veterans with long overdue accounts.[35] Was the Pennsylvania mutiny another attempt by the same group to bring about what was stifled at Newburgh in March? The shreds of circumstantial evidence are interesting, to say the least.

Maj. John Armstrong, author of the Newburgh Addresses, had left the camp along the Hudson by mid-April. Later that month he was in Philadelphia, taking up duties as secretary to the Council of the state. Gates too had gone home to Virginia, where his wife was dying. But amid his distress he was in touch with Armstrong; in fact he directed that letters to him be addressed to Armstrong.[36] And Armstrong remained in regular correspondence with Christopher Richmond, still at Newburgh.

The conspirators of March showed no remorse. Richmond wrote

Gates on May 29 that the army "let slip the best opportunity, (I mean about the 10th of March) which could have presented itself to obtain that Justice their services certainly merit."[37] When Armstrong heard of the furloughs he saw them as a political move against the army: "The meaning is evident—wrest the instruments of Redress from the hands of the Officers—by removing the old soldiers from about them and then discharge the obligation to both with the dash of the pen."[38] McDougall's embassy had been useless, for he was but the "representative of fools and Rascals." Armstrong hinted, three weeks before the Pennsylvania uprising, that there were alternative ways to bring about a satisfactory resolution of the army's plight: "If the troops here had force, with Mad Anthony at their head, I know not where they would stop. They feel like Men and could they be brought to think like politicians, weak as they are, they might do some good." What America needed was a new constitution, quite probably a monarchy. He continued to Gates: "Before we arrive at any degree of stability and firmness, some new principle must be introduced—and our forms of Government, brought to conform to the Genius of the people. We have reasoned hitherto, I am afraid, from what mankind should be, to what they are. We forget that we were formerly a constituent member of a monarchy, which we lov'd and rever'd, and that with the inexperience of youth, we have all the corruption of old age."

"If the troops here had force . . ." Did they? Armstrong hoped they did, and he was quite possibly passing along suggestions to them. He certainly knew their mood, well before any public demonstration. On June 15 he wrote Gates from Philadelphia. Congress's resolution furloughing the army "was taken up very spiritedly by the little Corps at this place, consisting of but 300 men. They addressed themselves to Congress upon the occasion in language very intelligible—'We will not accept your furloughts & demand a settlement.' " Within days the mutiny came.[39]

When all was done William Clajon wrote Gates, his former commander, describing the mutiny and commenting, "Major Armstrong's silence is now accounted for." And Armstrong himself wrote on June 26, 1783, "After the hurry of a week, in which I have had my share of sweat, dust & watching—I have scarcely spirits to hold up my head." Reporting that the mutiny was over and order restored, he continued that a consequence was that "the grand Sanhedrin of the Nation, with all their Solemnity & emptiness—have removed to Princeton & left a state, where their wisdom has been long questioned, their virtue suspect, and their dignity a jest."[40] Whatever their part, the Newburgh group was not critical of the mutiny.

The punishments not meted out bear note. Even though the captured leaders were sentenced to death, the sentences were later commuted. The cases of Sullivan and Carberry are interesting. By some accounts, the two sailed to England, where they remained in exile. But in fact they were soon back in the United States. Sullivan went to Georgia, where he became a member of the Georgia Cincinnati, while Carberry returned to Pennsylvania. He was commissioned a captain in the regular army in the early 1790s, then went west to Kentucky and Ohio, where he was a naval agent. In the War of 1812 he served as an army colonel. Only after twenty-four years did he join the Cincinnati. David Zeigler interceded on his behalf from Cincinnati, Ohio, in 1805 and two years later he was admitted in Pennsylvania.[41] It seems odd that the acknowledged leader of the Pennsylvania mutiny—and Carberry had been identified and detained as such on his return—should be made an officer in the standing army. Was he being protected by senior government officials? The records are mute.

To defend the officers' interest, the group around Gates probably had more faith in military pressure than in a new, untried organization. They had followed the creation of the Cincinnati with interest. All of them joined, but they had no vision that it was the solution to the army's problems. On May 29, 1783, Richmond wrote Gates that the society had been formed, but of the institution he commented only "let it speak for itself."[42] Envy at the success of Knox since March 15 may explain the lack of enthusiasm about the society. Wrote Major Stewart, who had brought the Newburgh plan from Philadelphia: "Every step taken by K—— and the Junto in this Army is carried, and it would astonish you to see the ridiculous manner in which we are all danc'd about by a very few Characters. He has however fix'd Himself at West Point, and I believe will now leave Manouvering to some other People as his End is in a great degree Answer'd."[43] In writing to Gates, Armstrong referred to

Washington as "Illustrisimo" and possibly the "Knight of Malta," and Stewart gloated that addresses of thanks and congratulations had been sent from the New York and New Jersey lines to Steuben, "but it appears strange to me that none has been propos'd for the Commander in Chief."[44]

If the Pennsylvania mutiny was another organized attempt at a military solution to economic problems, it found little sympathy among officers generally: Knox and his Society of the Cincinnati fit the American temper far better than a coup.

From early June, Knox, Steuben, and to a lesser extent Heath worked to see that the society was organized in each state. Among officers from northern and middle states, organization proceeded generally quickly and with enthusiasm. In the South, however, among those men who had not been at Newburgh, organization in some instances took longer and there was at least a hint of hesitancy, if not skepticism, about the new society.

Though Knox, Steuben, and Heath carried on an active correspondence about their society, early plans were not widely broadcast to the public. In fact, though there is no official record of it, a mantle of secrecy was thrown over the whole project. In May, Capt. Constant Freeman wrote a captain who had left the Massachusetts line in 1778. He reported formation of the society with enthusiasm, adding that the society would become "the most respectful society in America." But, he continued, the details of the organization "I can't at present inform you of."[45] He regarded his friend as a future member, but he would send an account of what had been done only "if permitted," not a stipulation one includes about public information. Knox was equally circumspect. In May when he sent copies of the institution for Steuben's signature, he advised the baron "to prevent mistakes it will be well to send them by one of your aids."[46] And historian Mercy Otis Warren recalled in 1805 that knowledge of the society did not spread until after the Philadelphia mutiny.[47] As will be seen in chapter 3, it was not really until early fall that the country knew a society existed.

It was with such circumspection that Knox and Steuben pressed the state lines to organize. Massachusetts, New York, and New Jersey had been organized before the June 19 meeting at Newburgh. At Heath's command the Massachusetts officers assembled with Brig. Gen. John Paterson presiding. The prime function of that meeting was to select a committee to receive ballots, and on June 20 it was announced that Maj. Gen. Lincoln had been chosen president. Knox became vice president, Colonel Brooks was secretary, and Col. Henry Jackson was treasurer. The results in Massachusetts were a model followed in most other states. The president of the society was usually the ranking general officer of the state line, whether he was present at the meeting or not. Lincoln, of course, was at this time secretary of war in Philadelphia. The vice presidency likewise went to an officer of senior rank, though not necessarily the second in seniority. The other offices, however, went to men committed to the organization, almost regardless of rank. Henry Jackson would remain treasurer for the next twenty-six years.[48]

The small group of New York officers who had gathered on the ninth already considered themselves members and met only to empower Washington's aide-de-camp, Lt. Col. Benjamin Walker, to collect ballots. On July 5 Walker announced that General McDougall had been chosen president. Governor Clinton, who Henry Jackson had speculated might be named president, was elected vice president.[49]

On June 11 Brig. Gen. Elias Dayton assembled the officers of the New Jersey line in Elizabethtown just before the regiments disbanded. Unlike the New York and Massachusetts men, New Jersey officers did not consider themselves members of the society when they met, for they began by "considering" the institution. They soon resolved "unanimously" to become members, and after signing a copy of the institution they chose General Dayton as their president.[50]

Officers of the Rhode Island line gathered at Saratoga Barracks at Schuylerville on June 24, where they chose the ranking officer from the state, Maj. Gen. Nathanael Greene, as president. Brig. Gen. James Mitchell Varnum, who had left the service in 1780, was named vice president.[51]

Connecticut officers had been part of the society from its inception, but they did not meet to organize until they gathered at West Point on July 4.[52] As with New York and Massachusetts, they met to elect officers rather than debate the institution. Given his role in creating the society, it was no surprise that Brig. Gen. Jedediah Huntington was elected president. Delaware officers organized at

Wilmington, also on July 4, about a month before the Delaware units disbanded. At its largest the Delaware society numbered only thirty-eight members, making it the smallest of the fourteen societies. Delaware was the only state society not to choose a general as its president, undoubtedly because there were no generals from Delaware. Dr. James Tilton, however, may well have been chosen because he was the highest ranking officer, for as a hospital surgeon he contributed $90 as his month's pay, while a colonel paid $75.[53]

In mid-July organization of the states societies languished, and Steuben took it upon himself to send out encouragements. He wrote to Generals John Sullivan in New Hampshire, William Moultrie in South Carolina, William Smallwood in Maryland, Arthur St. Clair in Pennsylvania, and probably the ranking officers in other states where he and Knox had no report of organization.[54]

A Georgia society was already underway, even as Steuben's letters went out. Officers gathered on August 13 at Savannah. Brig. Gen. Lachlan McIntosh presided and read the letter from Heath and then the institution. The minutes reveal a slight uncertainty about the plan, for it was only after considerable discussion that those present voted unanimously to follow "the plan of their brother officers at the Northward." Likewise they accepted the institution, as the minutes record, "subject nevertheless to such future amendments as may be thought necessary." They gathered again the next day, and elected General McIntosh president.[55]

Curiously, the Georgians forwarded their roster of officers not to Heath or Knox but to General Moultrie in South Carolina. South Carolina was the next state to organize, and the same doubts reappeared there. As will be seen, General Moultrie's early discussions of the plans for the society with Judge Aedanus Burke would lead to Burke's major diatribe against the Cincinnati. Moultrie assembled the South Carolina officers in Charleston on August 29. No one knew anything of the society but what the mail had reported. As a result the South Carolinians were not sure what was going on, and some were probably skeptical. Others, however, had done considerable thinking about the questions involved, for the meeting of the twenty-ninth adopted both the institution and a full set of bylaws. The first bylaw, which accepted the institution, included this revealing caveat: should any mandate of the society interfere "in any shape what soever, with the Civil Policy of this, any other of the United States, or the United States in general, this Society will not deem itself bound thereby, they prizing too highly the CIVIL LIBERTIES of their country, and their own RIGHTS as CITIZENS, to consent that a Military Society should in any sense dictate to Civil Authority."[56]

General St. Clair reported why organization in Pennsylvania was delayed until October, and similar political concerns may explain timing elsewhere. Pennsylvania officers knew about the society and it was "generally approved." Yet St. Clair had not called a meeting: "They [the officers] had great Expectations from the present Session of Assembly, and I thought it best to let that pass before they came into the Society—You know how Jealous the People of this Country are of anything that looks like distinguishing the military Profession, more especially when they do not understand the grounds." On October 4, however, St. Clair assembled the officers, and the Pennsylvania society was formed at the City Tavern in Philadelphia.

As in other societies the election of St. Clair to the presidency was more a matter of deference to seniority than expectation of service. The minutes of the first meeting provided that Vice President Anthony Wayne would preside over the next meeting, "the President being at too great a distance to be notified."[57]

Virginia began organizing two days later. At the "order" of Brigadier General Muhlenberg, the officers met at the Town House tavern in Fredericksburg, as the minutes put it "for the purpose of taking into consideration, the principles upon which the Society of the Cincinnati is founded." Despite the order, few assembled, but another meeting two days later brought an extended discussion leading to "entire approbation" of the society. Brig. Gen. George Weedon had been chosen to preside on the first day of the meeting, but when the officers were elected on October 9, his three-day term came to an end, and Gates, the only major general present, was chosen president.

Early in the proceedings the Virginians raised a question being asked in other state meetings—were officers of the state troops eligible for membership? The general opinion of the Fredericksburg meeting was that they were not but that they should have been.

Many officers had served "with great reputation," bringing "extraordinary aid" to the Continental troops. They looked to the general meeting in May to correct the error."[58]

North Carolina organized on October 23, when the few who appeared at Hillsborough debated the institution and concluded, in the words of Brig. Gen. Jethro Sumner, who was elected president, "Not to support such an institution betrays, in their opinion, a want of public virtue." Sumner told Heath why North Carolina men supported the society readily: "Before any intimation had reached us of what had been done at Hudsons River the Officers of this line had it in contemplation to form themselves into a society, less extensive, but with views similar to those of the Cincinati. For this and many other reasons, that institution is extremely agreeable to them, and will meet with their most zealous support."[59]

That same October marked the beginning of Washington's personal involvement in the society. Knowledge that such a group existed began to spread in the fall, and the general's public connection with the society now found him uncertain of his role. He wrote Knox on September 23, asking him to report "in precise terms" what was expected of a president of the Cincinnati. He reminded Knox, "I never was present at any of your meetings." "Your meetings" is not a phrase which suggests a strong identity with a group, but the commander worried that he might "neglect some essential duty which might not only be injurious to the Society, but Mortifying to myself."[60]

Knox responded on September 28, and Knox's aide Samuel Shaw perhaps went to Rocky Hill to confer with Washington on matters pertaining to the society.[61] So briefed, Washington outlined a plan of his efforts. He would provide necessary documents to get L'Enfant on his way to France for the double purpose of having the eagles made and organizing the French society. The major would take with him letters from Washington to the French officers named in the institution and to Lafayette. Washington would also write to the senior officers in each state where he had not heard a society had been formed, and he made a personal contribution of $500 to the general society.[62]

Washington wrote senior officers of Maryland, Virginia, North Carolina, South Carolina, and Georgia on October 24. Reinforcing the letter to Georgia was a personal letter to General McIntosh.[63]

The Institution 43

Obviously Washington did not know that all of the southern states but Maryland had organized by the time he wrote, a fact which underscores his peripheral role in the initial organization of the society.

New Hampshire officers met for the first time on November 18 at Exeter. Brig. Gen. James Sullivan had received the institution which Steuben sent in July, but not until October did he publish a call for officers to assemble. Though the announcement ran intermittently in the *New Hampshire Gazette* for six weeks, only fourteen assembled. New Hampshire men had been notably hesitant about the society at Newburgh, yet the fourteen who appeared voted that they would "chearfully embrace the Opportunity of forming a Society in this State."[64] Following the usual pattern, Sullivan was chosen president.

The institution had directed that officers eligible for commutation ask the paymaster-general to deposit the equivalent of a month's pay in the accounts of the Cincinnati. But many New Hampshire men, however, determined that they were not eligible for commutation. Their society's treasury would therefore be based on the "public security of the State of New Hampshire" rather than the notes of the United States.[65]

New Hampshire organized after widespread public criticism of the society had begun. Yet the New Hampshire men directed that the minutes of their meeting be published in the *New Hampshire Gazette*. Under the circumstances, the organization was all but flaunted.

Last of the thirteen states to organize was Maryland. Heath's original letter had arrived in time for the Maryland officers to discuss the proposals when they gathered to celebrate the fourth of July, but there were too few, so they thought, to organize a state society. They determined to gather again on November 20, as Maj. Gen. William Smallwood would later report, "when we might also address the General Assembly upon the Subject of the Lands which have been pledged, the Redemption of our Depreciation Certificates, and Arrears of Pay & c." Accordingly, Smallwood ran notices in the newspapers, but when the twentieth came many officers were absent, including Smallwood. Those present determined to try the next day, when the sixty-five present proceeded to organize, "cheerfully concurring in the establishment of the said Order."[66] Elections took place the following day when General Smallwood, still absent, was chosen president.

At the close of the Maryland meeting, there were societies in all thirteen states, and a French society would be added to the roster in January. In short order this new creation was to be the subject of major national controversy.

Notes

1. Knox to GW, April 16, 1783, Knox Papers; GW to Hamilton, April 22, 1783, Washington, *Writings,* XXVI, 351.

2. See the Report of the Superintendent of Finance, July 18, 1782 (really 1783), *JCC,* XXIV, 449.

3. Steuben has generally been called "von Steuben" in American histories; in papers connected with the Cincinnati he signed himself "de Steuben," preferring in a new land a French variant.

4. Orderly Book of Col. Philip van Cortlandt's Second New York Regiment, kept by Ens. Bernardus Swartwout, undated entry in book no. 2, New York Historical Society.

5. Maj Gen Heath's Orders, May 3, 1783, Boynton, *General Orders of Washington,* p. 82.

6. The short official record of the May 10, 1783, meeting was made a preface to the institution. It is reprinted in full in the appendix.

7. The original house burned in 1931, but it was reconstructed during the late 1970s and early 1980s by the Mount Gulian Society of Beacon, New York.

8. *JCC,* XXV, 853.

9. GW to Hamilton, April 16, 1783, Washington, *Writings,* XXVI, 323-26.

10. Forrest McDonald, *E Pluribus Unum* (Boston: Houghton Mifflin, 1965), p. 33.

11. With the signing of the parchment institution came a formality that was followed through the eighteenth century and persists today in varying degrees of formality. An individual became a member of the society only when he had *signed* the institution. Some of the signatures on petition for land which emerged from Newburgh were filled with proxy signatures of officers who had retired months, even years, earlier. And there may have been a few instances of proxy signatures on copies of the institution which the state societies began to produce and sign, but, proxy or otherwise, membership was dependent upon signature, most often in person. Even honorary members signed, and the Massachusetts records are filled with examples of individuals who were elected to the society but who never became fully members because they failed to "qualify" by appearing at a meeting to sign.

12. Knox to Benjamin Lincoln, May 21, 1783, Drake, *Memorials,* p. 16.

13. William Heath, *Memoirs of the American War* (New York: Wessels, 1904), pp. 397-98.

14. Pickering's comments of 1823, as quoted in Charles W. Upham, *The Life of Timothy Pickering* (Boston: Little Brown, 1867), I. 523-24.

15. Christopher Richmond to Gates, comment on the end of an undated copy of

the institution, May or early June, 1783, Gates Papers. There is an additional comment there about Gates himself, which the general obliterated with great care and effectiveness. It defied all attempts to decipher it.

16. Knox to Steuben, May 19, 1783, Knox Papers.

17. Knox to Lincoln, May 21, 1783, Knox Papers.

18. *JCC*, May 26, 1783, XXIV, 364–65; Heath, *Memoirs*, p. 390.

19. Heath to GW, June 5, 1783, Heath, *Memoirs*, p. 391.

20. Walter Stewart to Horatio Gates, June 20, 1783, Gates Papers. See also Ferguson, *Power of the Purse*, p. 170.

21. Knox to vicomte de Noailles, June 16, 1783, Knox to chevalier de Chastellux, June 16, 1783, Knox to Lafayette, June 16, 1783, Knox Papers.

22. Hume, *Washington Correspondence*, p. 14. Hume includes the minutes of the meetings of May 10, May 13 (the institution), and June 19, 1783, pp. 1–15.

23. Steuben to Pierre L'Enfant, July 1, 1783, quoted in Elizabeth S. Kite, *L'Enfant and Washington, 1791–1792* (Baltimore: Johns Hopkins University Press, 1929), p. 5n; *New Hampshire Gazette*, October 4, November 1 and 29, December 6, 1783.

24. The original of the Parchment Roll is preserved at Anderson House.

25. La Luzerne to Steuben, June 3, 1783, Hume, *Washington Correspondence*, p. 10.

26. Col. John Trumbull also volunteered to develop designs for the badge, possibly with the aid of Benjamin West in London. "Perhaps we have been too hasty in the adoption of the medal," Knox responded. He urged Trumbull to forward any new designs, but apparently Trumbull let the matter drop. Knox to John Trumbull, July 5, 1783, Knox Papers; also in Drake, *Memorials*, pp. 16–17.

27. I have been able to identify at least 86 French officers serving in America who had received the Saint Louis by 1783. Many more would receive it after their American service, Lafayette among them. Most were chevaliers, but Rochambeau had been made Grand Croix in 1771. Two French officers serving in the American campaign had the Mérite Militaire. John Paul Jones was given the Mérite Militaire, with the approval of Congress, and a cross was offered to Col. Matthias Ogden. Franklin cautioned that congressional approval was required, and Ogden was given the "droit de tabouret" instead. In a word, he and his descendants could sit in the presence of the king. On the Saint Louis and the Mérite Militaire, see Hugh Clark, *A Concise History of Knighthood* (London: Strahan, 1784), I, 235; Louis de Meslin, *Mémoires historique concernant l'Ordre Royal et Militaire de Saint-Louis et L'Institution du Mérite Militaire* (Paris: Imprimerie Royale, 1785); *Exposition La Renaissance du Culte de Saint Louis au XVIIe Siècle: L'Ordre Militaire, La Maison Royale de Saint-Cyr* (Paris: Musée national de la Légion d'honneur et des Ordres de Chevalerie, 1970). On John Paul Jones see Janette Taylor, *Life and Correspondence of John Paul Jones* (New York: Chandler, 1830), pp. 322, 377–78.

28. For reactions to Steuben's impressive decorations, see William North, "Memoir of Baron Steuben," as quoted in J. Palmer, *Steuben*, p. 128; James Thacher, Military Journal for May 28, 1779, as quoted ibid., p. 210; Amos Stoddard, Manuscript Autobiography, as quoted ibid., p. 211.

29. GW, General Orders, August 7, 1782, Washington, *Writings*, XXIV, 487–88; see also General Orders, August 11, 1782, specifying that continuous service was required to merit the rewards, ibid., XXV, 7; Gordon, *History*, IV, 312; Washington, *Writings*, XXIV, 488.

30. On the medals see Thomas Wyatt, *Memoirs of the Generals, Commodores, and Other Commanders...* (Philadelphia: Carey and Hart, 1848); John Brewer Brown, *Swords Voted to Officers of the Revolution by the Continental Congress, 1775–1784* (Washington: Society of the Cincinnati, 1965).

31. L'Enfant to Steuben, June 3, 1783, Hume, *Washington Correspondence*, p. 10.

32. Certificate to Major L'Enfant from Alexander McDougall, Henry Knox, and Jedediah Huntington, October 15, 1783, L'Enfant Papers, Anderson House.

33. For the petition and the list of signers, see Cutler and Cutler, *Manasseh Cutler*, I, 159–67; Gates to Pickering, May 19, 1783, Massachusetts Historical Society.

34. For accounts of the mutiny, see Robert Levere Brunhouse, *The Counter-Revolution in Pennsylvania, 1776–1790* (Harrisburg: Pennsylvania Historical Commission, 1942), pp. 135–40; Edmund Cody Burnett, *The Continental Congress* (New York: Macmillan, 1941), pp. 575–80; see also James Madison's Notes on Debates for June 13, 19, 20, and 21, 1783, *Papers*, VII, 141, 141n, 165–70, 176–80. Virginia Delegates to Benjamin Harrison, June 24, 1783, Madison, *Papers*, VII, 189–91. Elias Boudinot's proclamation on June 24, 1783 moving Congress to Princeton may be found ibid., facing p. 196; see also Boudinot to GW, June 21, 1783, Burnett, *Letters*, VII, 193–94.

35. GW to Elias Boudinot, June 24, 1783, Washington, *Writings*, XXVII, 32.

36. Gates to Timothy Pickering, May 19, 1783, Pickering Papers; Brunhouse, *Counter-Revolution*, p. 135.

37. Christopher Richmond to Gates, May 29, 1783, Gates Papers.

38. John Armstrong to Gates, May 30, 1783, ibid.

39. Armstrong to Gates, June 15, 1783, ibid.

40. Armstrong to Gates, June 26, 1783, ibid. William Clajon was a Frenchman who had served as Gates's secretary and interpreter earlier in the war. See C. Edward Skeen, *John Armstrong, Jr., 1758–1843: A Biography* (Syracuse: Syracuse University Press, 1981), pp. 26, 235 n. 23.

41. *A Synopsis of the Records of the State Society of the Cincinnati of Pennsylvania* (Philadelphia: Pennsylvania Society, 1909) p. 87.

42. Richmond to Gates, May 29, 1783, Gates Papers.

43. Stewart to Gates, June 20, 1783, ibid.

44. Armstrong to Gates, June 9, 1783, Stewart to Gates, June 20, 1783, ibid.

45. Constant Freeman to John Winslow, May 30, 1783, Anderson House.

46. Knox to Steuben, May 19, 1783, Knox Papers.

47. Mercy Otis Warren, *History of the Rise, Progress and Termination of the American Revolution* (Boston: Manning and Loring, 1805), III, 280.

48. Charles Moorfield Storey, ed. *Minutes of all meetings of the Society up to and including the meeting of October 1, 1825* (Boston: Privately printed, 1964), pp. 12–13. All officers of state societies down to 1938 are listed in Bryce Metcalf,

Original Members and Other Officers Eligible to the Society of the Cincinnati, 1783-1938 (Strasburg, Va.: Shenandoah Publishing House for the Connecticut Society, 1938), pp. 12-27.

49. Henry Jackson to Knox, June 8, 1783, Knox Papers.

50. *Excerpts of the Proceedings of the Society of the Cincinnati in the State of New Jersey* (N.p.: New Jersey Society, 1908), p. 18.

51. After the initial organization at Schuylerville, the Rhode Island Society seems not to have met until it gathered in Providence on December 17. Minute Book, 1783-1835, Rhode Island Society, Rhode Island Society Archives.

52. *Records of the Connecticut State Society of the Cincinnati 1783-1804* (Hartford: Connecticut Historical Society, 1916), unpaginated.

53. Henry Hobart Bellas, *A History of the Delaware State Society of the Cincinnati* (Wilmington: Historical Society of Delaware, 1895), pp. 9-13.

54. Steuben to John Sullivan, July 1783, *The Institution and Records of the New Hampshire Society of the Cincinnati* (Concord: Evans, 1893), p. 5. Smallwood referred to such a letter from Steuben in writing Washington, November 29, 1783, Hume, *Washington Correspondence*, p. 31. St. Clair answered such a letter, St. Clair to Steuben, September 3, 1783, Anderson House. Moultrie received a copy of the institution and an exhortation to organize in August; see *Providence Gazette*, July 10, 1784.

55. Francis Apthorp Foster, *Materials Relating to the History of the Society of the Cincinnati in the State of Georgia from 1783 to Its Dissolution* (Savannah: Georgia Society, 1934), p. 2.

56. *Establishment of the Society of the Cincinnati* (Charleston: Miller, 1783), p. 7. The copy at Anderson House may be unique.

57. Arthur St. Clair to Steuben, September 3, 1783, Anderson House; *Synopsis of the Records of the State Society of the Cincinnati of Pennsylvania*, p. 17.

58. Hume, *Virginia History*, pp. 64-66, 74.

59. Jethro Sumner to Heath, October 28, 1783, as quoted in Curtis Carroll Davis, *Revolution's Godchild: The Birth, Death, and Regeneration of the Society of the Cincinnati in North Carolina* (Chapel Hill: University of North Carolina Press for the North Carolina Society, 1976), p. 5; see also Charles Lukens Davis, *North Carolina Society of the Cincinnati* (Boston: North Carolina Society, 1907), pp. 51-54.

60. GW to Knox, September 23, 1783, Washington, *Writings*, XXVII, 162-65.

61. Knox's response of September 28, 1783, seems not to survive, but it is referred to in Washington's letter of October 16, 1783, which suggests that Shaw may have delivered it and conferred about society affairs. Ibid., XXVII, 194-96.

62. GW to Knox, October 16, 1783, ibid., XXVII, 194-96.

63. A form letter went to the senior officers of Maryland, Virginia, North Carolina, South Carolina, and Georgia, October 24, 1783, Hume, *Washington Correspondence*, pp. 24-25. Washington to Lachlan McIntosh, October 24, 1783, Hume, *Washington Correspondence*, pp. 25-26.

64. *Records of the New Hampshire Society*, p. 14.

65. Ibid., p. 15.

66. William Smallwood to GW, November 29, 1783, Hume, *Washington Correspondence*, pp. 31-32.

Chapter Three

A New and Strange Order of Men

ONLY IN THE FALL OF 1783 did the country realize that such a thing as the Society of the Cincinnati existed. James Madison first mentions the society on September 12,[1] and members of Congress who had not known of the society before probably found out at the Princeton commencement on September 24. Congress was then meeting at Princeton, and the entire Congress and General Washington were invited to sit on the commencement platform. In the audience that day was a British officer named Michaelis, the disguised agent of Sir Guy Carleton, commander of the troops who still held New York. Michaelis was quite aware of the society, reporting that "all the Cincinnati in the neighborhood assisted at this entertainment. The Cincinnati sat together en corps." The Princeton commencement is thus the first instance in which Cincinnati appear as a group outside a society meeting.

Michaelis expected that the Cincinnati were about to join Washington, Princeton's president John Witherspoon, and others in supplanting Congress.[2] That internal revolution was near was a sentiment shared by a few officers, for the states had not accepted the impost, leaving commutation still uncertain. Officers and men had been sent home unpaid. Lt. Col. Ebenezer Huntington, one of the organizers of the society at Newburgh, wrote his brother in August that newspapers portrayed the officers as "the Harpies and Locusts of the Country." The future of the country looked dark indeed: "God grant us Government, as states, free & independent, or give us a king, even tyranny is better than Anarchy." Huntington anticipated "a revolution, which will happen in Eighteen Months, unless government is supported."[3] Despite the bitterness, moderation prevailed once more.

In September of 1783 Michaelis was all but alone in seeing the

Cincinnati as a threat to the government. Few seemed to care about a fraternal military society, but the same could not be said of commutation. Outcry against it was severe in New England, especially in Connecticut, Huntington's home state. There, objections in summer had brought two representative meetings in Middletown in September, urging the Connecticut legislature to investigate Congress's power to grant commutation. Only in one instance was commutation linked with the Cincinnati in these late summer protests.

The town meeting in Killingworth, Connecticut, on August 21, 1783, saw the Society of the Cincinnati as one reason why commutation was not needed. The officers' claim to poverty was a hoax. Otherwise, how could they build a fund worth £200,000 "by their own account." Rather than press Congress and the states, they should lend the money to their impoverished country. What the society intended to do remained "a secret." The secretary of the meeting even credited the Cincinnati with putting commutation through Congress, and given that "specimen of their skill in the arts of intrigue," they bore careful watching.[4]

Few were so critical until Judge Aedanus Burke of South Carolina published his *Considerations on the Order or Society of the Cincinnati*. He took as the motto for his title page, "Blow ye the Trumpet of Zion," and as Jefferson said later of the pamphlet, "its effect corresponded with its epigraph."[5] *Considerations* first appeared in Charleston in October. By late spring it had been published in pamphlet form in Hartford, New York City, Newport, and Philadelphia and reprinted in full in at least two newspapers.[6] The attack Heath had feared had begun. The hobgoblins were there.

Burke indicted the society as a nascent nobility. The officers were real heroes, but their successors in one generation would retain the pretensions without the civic virtues, and America would find itself saddled with a hereditary nobility of 20,000 to 30,000 members. These patricians would see it their duty to govern the ignorant plebians. Thereafter their pretenses would only be magnified, and "such are the extravagancies which enter into the heart of man," that its members might soon try to trace their lineage to heaven.[7]

Such an incipient nobility doomed the American experiment in republican government at the outset. A nation divided into two orders, whether army and commonality or patrician and plebian, would never be a unified society. Taking a swipe at Steuben, who he thought had created the society, he noted that a peerage may promote unity among the "petty princes of Germany," but in American it could only lead to disunity.[8]

Burke pointed to the history of Rome itself.[9] For centuries Rome was plagued by the struggle between patricians and plebians, yet the founders of Rome had not planned to create a nobility, an ominous fact since Burke judged the present Cincinnati were much better poised to establish a nobility than were those early Romans. Public outcry was the proper remedy, and Burke urged state legislatures to adopt "spirited Resolutions" against the society.[10]

Burke's own thinking had probably undergone considerable change during the Revolution. Born in Ireland in 1743, he had migrated to Virginia where he was studying law in 1769. Hereditary distinctions had their fascination before the war, for he spent considerable time investigating the family arms and knew all the details of ordering armorial bookplates. When the struggle came, he accepted a commission in the Second South Carolina Continental Regiment, but he resigned in February 1778 to become a judge on the state's supreme court. Three months later, he rejoiced from the bench that the new government was eliminating "unnatural distinctions between nobleman and commons."[11]

Burke recorded that one evening in August 1783 at the Corner Club in Charleston, General Moultrie was describing the new society he was to organize in South Carolina. Burke was horrified and within five minutes, or so he recalled, he had determined to spend what spare time he could opposing the order. Burke had a reason for remembering his first reactions. Critics later accused him of opposing the society because he was not eligible: he had not served three years and his application for honorary membership was rejected. Not true, Burke said. The man who published that was a "liar."[12]

Soon after the appearance of Burke's pamphlet, the Middletown, Connecticut, convention met for a third time, organizing a permanent committee to communicate with critics of commutation throughout the nation. The convention also recommended Burke's *Considerations* to the reading public. Henceforth, complaints against commutation would be joined to criticism of the Cincinnati, unless commutation was forgotten as the Cincinnati alone took the brunt of ever expanding attacks.

The *Independent Chronicle* of Boston, for example, became a major force against the society. Reprinting Burke's pamphlet in late January 1784, it invited its readers to submit their views, and the society received an almost weekly critique from March through May. One correspondent, worrying that the Cincinnati aimed at a "complete and perpetual Personal distinction" between its members and the "Plebeans," urged legislators, governors, and magistrates to take action. Another predicted that the society unchecked would overthrow the republic. Soon state legislatures would find 10 percent of their members were Cincinnati, after which the society would begin making inroads on Congress. "Then you may bid a lasting adieu to republican principles." The national government would become one of a governor general, a council, and a house of representatives, vaguely equivalent to king, lords, and commons. Soon formal titles would be added to "support the dignity of government." Another writer concluded the society was nothing but the "brat of despotism."[13]

When the *Chronicle* reported on April 29 that French officers had donated 60,000 livres (over $10,000) to the society, suspicion could only grow about the potential foreign influence to which Burke and others had pointed.[14]

Politicians began to share these suspicions. Samuel Osgood, a member of Congress from Massachusetts, worried in February that the Cincinnati were gaining strength in state legislatures and Congress. Three or four were already in Philadelphia, representing the "unprincipled and subtle intriguers of America" with their eyes on the national treasury.[15] That same month the Massachusetts legislature began a formal inquiry, and in March the legislature condemned the society. In trying to promote "certain important, publick and national purposes" the Cincinnati were usurping power already delegated to the state legislatures and Congress. In short, the society aimed at committing that great sin in political theory; it wanted to be an "*Imperium in Imperio*," a final authority in a context in which another final authority was already established. There were doubts about the society's military mentality and about the influence of foreign members who were attached to the principles of monarchal government. In sum, the society was leading toward hereditary nobility "contrary to the spirit of free government, and expressly inhibited by an article of the confederation of the United States." As such it was a threat to the "peace, liberty and safety of the United States in general, and this Commonwealth in particular." Such firm condemnation brought no legislation, as the legislators waited to see what the general meeting in May would produce.[16]

Newspapers reported that Rhode Island was determined to "disenfranchise" members and render them incapable of holding office, but the legislature voted no such prohibition. A writer to the *New Hampshire Gazette* in June 1784 offered a hint of what probably happened. To counter the Cincinnati, he argued, "associations" should be established in all states, "according to the example of the intelligent and virtuous state of Rhode Island." If he knew his facts, there was an anti-Cincinnati association in Rhode Island which advocated legislation never adopted.[17]

In Connecticut the Middletown convention assembled again in March, now equally critical of the society and commutation. Delegates worried that "a new and strange order of men had arisen under the eye of Congress," thinking themselves "the only saviours of the republic" and assuming "badges of peerage." If the people wanted a hereditary nobility, voting for candidates backing commutation was the technique to follow.[18]

Such protest was not confined to New England. In Virginia the society became an election issue in some districts that spring. Edmund Randolph wrote Jefferson in April that seven "military candidates" for the House of Delegates had been elected. Col. Samuel Hopkins, however, had been rejected because of the wide circulation of Burke's pamphlet and the rumor that he was a delegate to the May meeting of the society, which he was.[19] Farther south, Governor Benjamin Guerard of South Carolina had assailed the society before the legislature in February. Patriotism, charity, and piety, he thought, were only the "ostensible" purposes of the Cincinnati. Their real motives were a "thirst for dignities, gewgaws, and bawbles" and a desire to become a "power coeval with that of Legislation." Guerard suggested no legislation, but he warned that if the society was countenanced in its present form, it would be a dangerous precedent.[20]

Congress said nothing directly, but two measures took indirect aim at the Cincinnati. In late summer 1783 Washington had received a letter from Warsaw offering to make thirty-six of the senior officers Knights of the Order of Divine Providence. For a substantial initiation fee, the generals would have a star and badge to brighten their uniforms and wind up looking not unlike Steuben. Ever cautious, Washington asked the advice of Congress before replying. A congressional committee was appointed to look into the matter of the "Polish Order" as it was called. There is no evidence that anyone in Newburgh or Philadelphia discovered that the order was a fundamentally German association, in some ways rather like the Cincinnati. It was a self-created brotherhood of European nobility formed to gather a fund to support themselves in impoverished old age. That Congress knew none of this made little difference. An oral committee report in September was not followed by a written recommendation until January, when Congress voted that Washington might thank his Polish correspondent, but "Congress cannot, consistently with the principles of the Confederation, accept of their obliging proposal." Jefferson recalled that the vote was really an implied censure of the Cincinnati. (Thus it was probably no accident that Boston's *Independent Chronicle* printed the resolution about the Divine Providence just after a diatribe against the society.)[21]

A second measure indirectly aimed at the Cincinnati concerned western lands. In proposals for establishing new states published in April, Congress provided "that their respective governments shall be "Republican Forms, and shall admit no Person to be a Citizen who holds any hereditary Title." Membership in the Cincinnati in Jefferson's judgment was such a title.[22]

Reaction to the Cincinnati may have had an unexpected impact at Harvard. In 1783, to encourage achievement, the corporation voted to establish orders of merit among the undergraduates. Students who did best on voluntary examinations would wear gold medals on all public occasions, but the plan was never carried out, President Quincy later speculated, because it was regarded as "inconsistent with republican equality."[23]

American diplomats in Europe were almost uniformly critical of the society. John Jay, for example, wrote Elbridge Gerry in February, "Some of our best Friends think the order of Cincinnatus will eventually divide us into two mighty factions." John Adams confessed to Lafayette that he thought the society "the first step taken to deface the beauty of our temple of liberty," and to Gerry he wrote that it was "the deepest piece of cunning yet attempted."[24]

More whimsical was Benjamin Franklin, then minister to France. His daughter had sent him a copy of Burke's pamphlet, and he replied saying that a ribbon might have been acceptable, but a hereditary society was an "absurdity." After all, a father was only half responsible for his son, one quarter for his grandson, and in nine generations "our present Chevalier of the Order of Cincinnatus's share in the then existing knight will be but a five hundred twelfth part," so small that no citizen would willingly hazard the envy of his countrymen. After the practice of the Chinese mandarins, the Cincinnati should give their badges not to their sons but to their parents, and by extension to their ancestors for ten generations. Turning serious, Franklin concluded "I hope, therefore, that the Order will drop this part of their project, and content themselves, as the Knights of the Garter, Bath, Thistle, St. Louis, and other Orders of Europe do, with a life enjoyment of their little badge and riband, and let the distinction die with those who have merited it."[25]

Objections from whatever quarter surely came as a surprise to some members. In September of 1783, for example, the Georgia society had sent Governor Lyman Hall an address on hearing of a formal treaty of peace. The national outcry had not yet begun, and the society claimed it would "be a means of harmonizing the different classes of the community, and in some degree, contribute to the welfare and dignity of this extended empire." Its mix of generals and ensigns was a great unifying force. Governor Hall agreed that the society would support union and government, and its charitable efforts were worthy of the "approbation of all good men."[26] In Delaware, Burke's pamphlet could only excite the society to fix its republican principles more firmly, as the members reported in their first circular letter to other state societies.[27]

Quick to reply to Burke was "An Obscure Individual," probably Col. Stephen Moylan of the Pennsylvania society. His *Observations on a late Pamphlet entitled Considerations upon the Society or Order of the Cincinnati* appeared in Philadelphia in early December 1783. If the people were so sensitive to distinctions of rank, as Burke claimed, why did he need to chastise the public for its inattention to the Cincinnati? And, Moylan continued, was Congress as insensitive as the public, or should one conclude, rather, that Congress perceived no threat? If a hierarchy already existed in America, how would the Cincinnati make things any different? Moylan denied that absolute equality was possible in any system, for even republics conferred distinctions, but the Cincinnati was no cause for concern. There were no ulterior purposes, the society had no power, and it was completely controlled by civil law. As for the eagle, it was "not like the coronets and garters of modern ambition, but analogous to the wreath of parsley or of the olive branch which decorated the foreheads of ancient heroes."[28]

Not all newspaper correspondents were hostile. A writer to the *Connecticut Courant* in April thought it ridiculous to suppose that every subaltern by giving up a month's pay for a charitable fund became thereby a peer of the realm. The decision on the Order of Divine Providence proved that Congress would act should the Cincinnati aspire to nobility. And the *Boston Evening Post* in March reprinted the flattering account of Cincinnatus from L. M. Stretch's *Beauties of History,* the same book Knox had advertised in 1773. For Stretch, Cincinnatus was the very model of "disinterestedness."[29] Not all champions of the Cincinnati were members. Neither John Trumbull, the poet, nor Noah Webster was a member, but in the *Connecticut Courant* they defended commutation and did their best to discredit Aedanus Burke. Trumbull, for example, offered the doubly damning assertion that Burke wrote against the society because it refused to admit him on the grounds he was a tory. In other states, too, the argument would appear that opponents of commutation and the society were tories trying to weaken government and create anarchy.[30]

Washington was well aware that the growing controversy would involve his own reputation. The general's relation to the society was still vague in the public eye, and even a politician so well informed as Edmund Randolph would write Jefferson as late as April commenting, "How far General W. patronizes the association, is, as yet, an impenetrable secret." That uncertainty may have stemmed from Washington's adoption of circumspection as a policy. For instance, in writing state societies that the May meeting would be in Philadelphia, he suggested that delegates be so informed "by letter, rather than by a public Notification."[31]

Despite continuing faith in themselves, the Cincinnati were on the defense by midwinter. Knox and Steuben twitted each other genially over who had started the society, but it was no jest when the Massachusetts society met on February 16 and, in Knox's words, "it was thought prudent not to make any honorary members at present."[32]

Washington now began to exert a guiding hand in planning the meeting for May. He wanted it large and impressive, with all states represented by their most important members, as he wrote General St. Clair, "not only for the purpose of bare representation then, but that the Abilities of the Society of the Cincinnati may be convened at that time." To bring Nathanael Greene there he invoked the duty of patriotism: "If then private interest or convenience will hold the first characters from the Meeting, what may be the consequence? 'tis easier, and perhaps better to be conceived than told."[33]

The seriousness with which delegates were selected demonstrates that these men were not just going off to enjoy the fellowship of old times. The society was meant to accomplish something, and the example of New Hampshire is instructive. At a special meeting on April 2, Lt. Col. Henry Dearborn was chosen as the New Hampshire society's representative, and the members pooled $163 to pay for his trip. The contributions, which varied from General Sullivan's $40 to the $8 pledged by lieutenants, were technically loans later repaid from society funds, but it is revealing that the hard-pressed members were willing to inconvenience themselves further to make sure Dearborn went to the general meeting.[34]

In addition to urging delegates to attend, Washington was busy gathering opinions. On April 8 he asked Jefferson's advice,[35] and Jefferson urged him to dissociate himself from the organization completely. He doubted that the purpose of fellowship would be well met by annual meetings (such groups tend to generate acrimonious debates), but even more serious was the political implication the group carried for the new nation. The principal author of the Declaration of Independence summarized objections to the society, and though he wrote of "they" he seems to have shared every doubt. "They urged that it is against the confederation—against the letter of some of our constitution—against the spirit of all them—that the foundation on which all these are built is the natural equality of man, the denial of every preeminence but that annexed to legal office & particularly the denial of preeminence by birth." Jefferson worried further that the society clouded the distinction between civil and military, a prime component of his idea of free government.

What was the political future of the society? Jefferson thought that Congress left to itself would say nothing, but if forced it would recommend abolition. Apart from military men, "I have not found but one who is not opposed to the institution, & that with an anguish of mind, tho' covered under a guarded silence, which I have not seen produced by any circumstance before." He offered the further prediction that non-Cincinnati might well be preferred for most government appointments in the future.[36]

That same month General St. Clair reported from Philadelphia that there were "Strong Prejudices" against the society, but Washington's mail brought support as well as criticism. General Greene had not been much interested in the society when it began, but now he saw it as a prime prop of commutation. "Assuming honors hurt my delicacy; but persecution banishes the influence. . . . I am decided in my opinion not to abolish the order from the prevailing clamours against it. If this is done away the whole tide of abuse will run against commutation."[37]

From Thomas Paine, author of *Common Sense,* came not only an endorsement but a commemorative poem, now lost. Despite doubt "whether every part of the institution is perfectly consistent with a republic," he concluded that "it is material to the future freedom of the Country, that the example of the late Army retiring to private Life on the principles of Cincinnatus, should be commemorated." One poem that does survive also praised the society, so much so as perhaps to give Washington pause. Maj. Winthrop Sargent of Massachusetts had sent it in February, just as his sister had written it.

> HAIL CINCINNATI! GUARD OF UNION HAIL!
> O'er thy fair dawning may no Ill prevail;
> First Fruit of Peace—by conq'ring Heroes form'd—
> Heroes by Friendship, as by Valour Warm'd.

It was a long poem, but the Cincinnati were the prime guardians of the republic all the way through. What was not clear was how long a republic might last:

> A future Empire too I see Arise!
> PRINCES & MONARCHS good & great & Wise,

> Whose Care shall be to guard the public Weal:—
> Who—for the people's Wrongs shall keenly feel,
> PROTECTORS of the Rights of human kind.

The subsequent reference to "The rural Blessings of a Patriot King" may have made Washington glad he had the one manuscript copy, for the poem offered just those sentiments critics were sure the society harbored.[38]

Jefferson later recalled that Washington had not only written, but stopped to see him in Annapolis on his way to Philadelphia. As they talked over the correspondence which Washington had collected, the general made up his mind: "No! not a fibre of it must be retained—no half-way reformation will suffice. If the thing be bad, it must be totally abolished." Washington headed toward Philadelphia, hoping to abolish the Society of the Cincinnati, but he was soon to realize the distinction between hope and political possibility.[39]

Even critics were aware that the general meeting, or "Grand Convention," as some called it, was about to meet, but the Cincinnati were not issuing press bulletins. The *New Jersey Gazette,* for example, reported Washington's arrival in Philadelphia on May 1, but said nothing of why he had come.[40] As the meeting opened, one delegate moved that the sessions be public, a proposal quickly voted down. More in keeping with the spirit of the meeting was Maj. Winthrop Sargent of Massachusetts, who kept a coded journal. Easily deciphered, it provides a revealing picture of what went on.[41]

The sessions opened on May 4 with Washington presiding, Knox as secretary, and forty-five delegates from twelve states present. Only Rhode Island and France were not represented, and not until the twentieth century would so many states appear again at a national meeting.

Washington and Knox resigned their pro tem offices on May 5, but Washington was prevailed upon to remain as president until the proceedings closed. After a ceremonial reading of the institution, the meeting went into a committee of the whole. Washington spoke directly to the subjects on his mind, and from that point on he was anything but an impartial presiding officer.

Opposition to the society had grown "violent and formidable" in Virginia, and he asked for reports on other states.[42] Col. David Humphreys of Connecticut reported "a very general disapprobation of the People." General Knox of Massachusetts followed in the same vein, though he added that some were in favor of the society if it would alter its institution. Washington's ally and confidant thus introduced the major theme of the meeting—amending the institution.

Col. William S. Smith reported "no opposition" in New York. Dr. James Tilton of Delaware said there was opposition, but only from "the class of people denominated Tories." Col. Walton White added that "almost all the various classes" in South Carolina were opposed to the institution as it stood. Maj. Alexander Cuthbert, however, said that opinions in Georgia were "the very opposite" of those in South Carolina. Capt. Jonathan Dayton did not know the general sentiments in New Jersey, but that made little difference, for the New Jersey society was determined to "preserve and support its dignity." Governor John Dickinson reported Pennsylvanians objected strongly to the "hereditary part," and Col. Henry Dearborn rounded out the survey with the opinion that New Hampshire was "very generally in opposition to the Institution on its present Establishment."[43]

Having heard precisely what he expected, Washington took the floor once more to warn of the "disagreeable consequences" unless seven basic changes were made in the institution.

1. "Strike out every word, sentence, and clause which has a political tendency."
2. "Discontinue the hereditary part in all its connections *absolutely*, without any substitution which can be construed into concealment."
3. "Admit no more honorary Members into the Society."
4. "Reject subscriptions, or donations from every person who is not a Citizen of the United States."
5. Place the funds of each state society under the control of its legislature.
6. Let the French society decide upon the admission of all foreigners, except those who had commissions in particular state lines.
7. Abolish the general meetings.[44]

In support of abolition of general meetings, Washington virtually quoted Jefferson's letter of April 16, pointing out that debates in large meetings would loosen the bonds of friendship which the society had been formed to preserve.

Washington had hoped for abolition of the whole society when he left Jefferson, yet when Winthrop Sargent heard him he seemed to argue that the society must continue because of the "very distinguished Foreigners in this Institution." Washington probably nursed hopes that the delegates might disagree and themselves come to urge complete abolition. As he recounted events later, that at least was the strategy he seemed to be following.

As to the badge, Washington held that if the society explained why they wanted to keep it, any explanation would provoke as much criticism as the hereditary principle itself. At least the society should abolish the hereditary principle and thus demonstrate the badge was "a feather we cannot consent to pluck from *ourselves,* tho' we have taken it from our descendants."[45] In pressing all these points, as at Newburgh, Washington put his full prestige on the line, and his intent was not lost on Winthrop Sargent. If the society could not be reconciled to the nation, then the former commander "was determined at all events to withdraw his name from amongst us."[46]

The general went back to his informants and correspondents to make further points. "In confidence," Sargent wrote, Washington mentioned what Jefferson had told him, though he did not mention Jefferson by name: Unless the institution were changed to conform to Congress's sense of "republican principles," the society might expect "discouragement and even prosecution from them and the States severally."[47] Washington then produced Lafayette's letter of March 9, even though the marquis had ended, "Let the foregoing be confidential." Sargent summarized the letter as "objecting to the hereditary part of the Institution, as repugnant to a republican system, and very exceptionable."[48]

Washington's presentation met with anything but acclamation, for immediately the delegates from New Jersey and New York rose to oppose the abolition of the hereditary provisions, and on that note the first full day of the general meetings ended.

The next day Knox took the floor, producing a letter from Chastellux, which to Sargent "seemed opposed to the hereditary part" of the institution. Then Washington made another "very long speech," filled with "much warmth and agitation." The hereditary provisions were "particularly obnoxious to the people." Again he offered the society a choice: either drop the hereditary provisions or he would resign from the society. And once more the New York delegation spoke in favor of hereditary succession.

Washington, nonetheless, had convinced the delegates that changes were necessary, and a committee of one delegate from each state undertook a revision of the institution. On Saturday, May 8, the committee presented its draft. The hereditary principle was gone, but one's share in the charitable funds could be transferred by deed or gift. Should any member die without having made such a transfer, that state society might "elect a fit person in his place." The general meetings were continued as were "frequent communications" between state societies but only about the "benevolent purposes," not politics. Discussions began on Monday, May 10, and before substantial support for the new draft could develop, Washington, as Sargent noted, "expressly declared against it." Transfer of membership would seem a ruse to cover up what was still a hereditary institution. The general minced no words, for Sargent recorded "he warmly and in plain languages or by implication seemed desirous to expunge all the essentials with which the Society was endowed by those from whom it had its origins." New revisions were mandated from a committee of five: Knox, Governor Dickinson, General Otho H. Williams of Maryland, Col. Henry Lee of Virginia, and Col. William S. Smith. Washington could count on Knox and Lee to follow his own lead, and he knew that Dickinson shared many of his own political doubts about the society.[49]

But then things changed rapidly with the report, that day, of Major L'Enfant who brought news that the king of France had permitted his officers to wear the eagle and that the French had accepted their memberships eagerly. Abolition would be an insult to America's allies in victory. Dazzling to the American eye was the envelope of new gold eagles, fresh from Paris. Reports differ on when the eagles appeared and when they were distributed, but by the tenth the insignia was a tangible object, a possession, a personal decoration, not just a design or a concept criticized by some obscure South Carolina judge.

There was also a splendid present for Washington, an eagle set in diamonds, inscribed "D——d in the name of the french saillors to

His Excellency the General Washington." The first word, now chipped, was probably "Donated." It was customary in the eighteenth century to have badges of orders set in diamonds for use on festal occasions, and the practice of official award of an order "in diamonds" came somewhat later. Admiral d'Estaing had sent the diamond eagle on February 26 "in the name of all the French Navy," and Washington seems to have received it on May 11, the day after L'Enfant's report. On May 15 he wrote that he was "inexpressibly honored by that most respectable Body of men," the French navy.[50]

When the committee to modify the institution further reported on May 12, all traces of the hereditary part were gone, as were honorary members unless they were approved by the government of the state involved. General meetings were retained, but held only every three years to "regulate the distribution of surplus funds." State meetings were to be held annually, only to deal with the "benevolent purposes of the Society." To instill public confidence in the Cincinnati, each society was to lend its funds to the state "by permission of the legislature," spending only the interest for charitable purposes. When these nonhereditary societies began to die out, the state legislatures would dispose of the funds in ways "most correspondent with the original design of the Institution." The officers of the French army *and* navy were included explicitly, but with the stipulation that only generals and colonels, admirals and naval captains ranking as colonels could be admitted.

Subsequent debate dropped the requirement that honorary members be approved by the state legislatures, but demanded that each society ask its state legislature for a charter, thus obtaining a legal umbrella under which to operate. The final version of the amended institution also provided that "no donations shall be received, but from citizens of the United States." The general society would therefore decline the 60,000 livres pledged by the French. During the debates one vote did not amend the proposal but answered the question Virginians had raised during organization. The delegates agreed that officers of state units, as opposed to those with Continental commissions, who had "served in time and manner proposed" were eligible for membership. What that decision meant was to be debated a century later.

Amendments finished, all the state delegations voted for the rewritten institution except New York, which stood divided. Colonel Smith, on the committee of five, voted for it, but Maj. James Fairlie was against it. A new committee of three, Governor Dickinson, Colonel Smith, and Lt. Col. David Humphreys prepared a circular letter to explain what had been done.[51]

The circular letter spoke more to the critics than the members of the society. The original institution had been drawn up "in a hasty manner" as the army was disbanding. But the reforms now made should have "removed every possible objection." The innocent desire to perpetuate friendships "to the remotest ages" seemed "incompatible with the genius and spirit of the confederation" and the society relinquished the hereditary principle willingly. The Cincinnati had only sought to support the government and the union, but when their efforts were deemed "officious and improper interference," then all "interference with political subjects" was foresworn.[52]

Putting the funds of the societies in the hands of state legislatures would show the society's integrity, and state legislatures would acquire power over the membership rules, honorary and otherwise, through the charters they would grant. The badges were retained, "not as ostentatious marks of discrimination, but as pledges of our friendship, and emblems, whose appearance will never permit us to deviate from the paths of virtue." The badge was retained too because it was held "in the highest estimation by such of our allies as have become entitled to them." The letter ended with a strong exhortation for each state to accept the new institution as amended, but what was not clear was how many state societies had to accept the amended institution before it became effective. As a result, the question remained undecided for the next sixteen years.

With the institution amended, the meeting had all but finished its work. There was, however, one other discussion which did not find its way into the official minutes but which was communicated to the state societies and noted in Sargent's account—the question of wearing the badge. If the Cincinnati followed European models in designing the eagle, they did not follow continental precedents in wearing it. The statutes of the Order of the Bath, for example, provided that each member should "constantly wear the Badge, Cognizance, or Ensign, of this Order." That rule was honored, for

Sir William Morgan had his gold badge rudely snatched from him on a London street.[53] Sargent summarized the discussion in Philadelphia.

> It appeared fully to be the sense of the meeting that it [the badge] should not be ostentatious and in common; and only on days of convention to commemorate the Institution, or when we were to attend the funeral of some deceased Member. Though no vote was called or taken (as it was thought improper to do so), yet this was understood to be a general sentiment, and meant for the government of every Member of the Cincinnati while residing in this country. In France, it is supposed that a different practice would prevail, and as the Bald Eagle is there held in high estimation, that it will generally worn by Americans on their travels through that country:—at least, by all those who may be desirous of this distinction.[54]

Yet another item was discussed before the meeting adjourned, and it found its way into neither the official minutes nor Sargent's coded account. But in the Connecticut records, after the memorandum about the eagle, there is a further note from the Philadelphia session: "Also—That Applications should be made & signed by the Officers concerned in each State Meeting praying Congress to make speedy reply to their petition for a Grant of Western Lands, & c." The society as a whole had just renounced political activities, but that did not preclude organizing pressure for land grants.[55]

The election of officers was unanimous only in the choice of Washington as president general. Each state had one vote, and for vice president general nine favored General Gates, who was not present, while two supported General Greene, who was not present either despite Washington's repeated urging. For secretary general Knox won with the support of six states, while Greene had three, and Generals McDougall and Otho H. Williams each one. Williams in turn was just barely elected assistant secretary general with the support of six states. Col. Jonathan Trumbull had carried five. McDougall was chosen treasurer general.[56]

Their work done, the delegates headed home on May 18, leaving it to the country to judge the good faith of their measures. Newspapers soon carried the full text of the amended institution, the circular letter, and a letter to the French which the meeting also prepared.[57]

As one might expect, the immediate reaction was mixed. Some

found the amended institution reassuring. "Americanus" wrote to the *Massachusetts Centinel* that the amendments had cleared the air. "When their real intentions are known ... we not only acquiesce in their principles, but most fervently wish them success."[58]

If some were satisfied, others still retained their doubts. A correspondent of the *New Hampshire Gazette* still saw the Cincinnati leading to a "hereditary peerage." He urged all states to form associations on the model of "the intelligent and virtuous state of Rhode Island" to prevent the election of members of the society to any office whatever.[59]

Washington stopped at Annapolis to see Jefferson again as he headed south to Virginia, and the two sat late into the night as Washington recounted what had happened. Once more he affirmed that he had gone to Philadelphia in hopes of having the entire society abolished. As the debate proceeded Washington had concluded that in two or three days, the members would come round to abolishing the society. Thus his objections to the first set of reforms were perhaps delaying tactics to carry his argument further. But the appearance of L'Enfant and his badges had changed everything. Enthusiasm was rekindled, and the best the general could do was to achieve a modification of the institution. A year and a half later Washington's memories were still sharp. He wrote Hamilton. "Had it not been for the predicament we stood in with respect to the foreign Officers and the charitable part of the Institution I should, on that occasion, as far as my voice would have endeavored to convince the narrow minded part of our Country men that the Amor Patri(ae) was much stronger in our breasts than theirs— ... by abolishing the Society at once."[60]

Within the society opinions of the amended institution were mixed from the first. Major Fairlie, the New Yorker who had voted against the proposals in May, wrote Washington's aide-de-camp, Lt. Col. Benjamin Walker, in dismay about his colleagues. "What ever General Washington dictated, was done; every one esteems him as the *sine qua non* of the society." In Fairlie's view a "rage for popularity" had turned the earliest advocates of the society into compromising "trimmers." Well aware of the effect of L'Enfant's arrival and the commitment of the French to the society, Walker replied, "Our allies alone have saved the society."[61]

It was one thing to have a general meeting adopt a new institution under the personal and persistent influence of the former commander in chief. It was quite another thing for officers who still had little prospect that commutation would actually be paid to consent to those modifications. The first tests would come in July as the state societies voted on the amended institution at their annual meetings.

Notes

1. Elnathan Haskell to James Madison, September 12, 1783, Madison, *Papers*, VII, 311. The institution and other news of the society appeared in these papers: *Independent Gazetteer* (Philadelphia), September 20, 1783; *New York Gazette*, September 29, 1783; *Massachusetts Spy* (Worcester), October 16, 1783; *Vermont Gazette* (Bennington), October 16, 1783; *Freeman's Journal* (Philadelphia), November 5, 1783; *Connecticut Gazette* (New London), January 16, 1784; *Independent Chronicle* (Boston), February 12, 1784.

2. Michaelis, as quoted in Varnum Lansing Collins, *President Witherspoon* (Princeton: Princeton University Press, 1925), II, 133-35. The Princeton commencement took place September 24, 1783, two days after the New Jersey Cincinnati had met at Princeton. There had been 45 Cincinnati present for the meeting and many probably stayed for commencement. *Excerpts of the Proceedings* (New Jersey), pp. 18-19.

3. Ebenezer Huntington to Andrew Huntington, August 12, 1783, *Letters written by Ebenezer Huntington during the American Revolution* (New York: Heartman, 1914), p. 106.

4. *Connecticut Courant*, September 2, 1783.

5. Jefferson, Answer by Mr. Jefferson to Questions Addressed to him by Monsieur de Meusnier, *Writings of Thomas Jefferson, Memorial Edition* (Washington: Jefferson Memorial Association, 1903), XVII, 84.

6. Aedanus Burke, *Considerations on the Society or Order of Cincinnati* (Charleston: Timothy, 1783). The Boston *Independent Chronicle* ran the pamphlet on January 29 and February 5, 1784, while the *Connecticut Gazette* ran it in segments on March 26, April 2, 16, and 23, 1784. The pamphlet's Philadelphia printing was first advertised in *Freeman's Journal* on November 12, 1783.

7. Burke, *Considerations*, pp. 12, 16, 17.

8. Ibid., p. 11.

9. Burke gives no clue that he had read the accounts of Cincinnatus in Livy or Dionysius Halicarnassus, for had he done so he would have been even more suspicious of "Cincinnati." Cincinnatus had been poor when called from his plow, but he was not always that way. Earlier his family had possessed a "fortune inferior to none." His son Caeso Quinctius was an angry young patrician who delighted in antagonizing plebians who soon found, or invented, groups to put Caeso on trial for his life. They fabricated the charge that he had beaten a plebian to death for amusement. Before a verdict was rendered, Caeso might be free on bail, if ten men shared in guaranteeing a large bond. Caeso soon fled, but honor demanded that Cincinnatus repay the bonds of the ten. Selling all that he had, Cincinnatus moved into a hovel, where with his wife Racilla and a few slaves he tilled the soil himself, a victim essentially of plebian persecution, or at least prosecution. As dictator,

Cincinnatus dealt with the plebians more evenhandedly than they had expected. Livy, *Histories,* III, 19.

10. Burke, *Considerations,* p. 32.

11. *Dictionary of American Biography,* III, 280.

12. The accusation that Burke first solicited membership in the society is to be found from "A Connecticut Tory" in the *Connecticut Courant,* January 20, 1784. Burke's denial, published in the *South Carolina Gazette,* May 15, 1784, was reprinted in the *Providence Gazette,* July 10, 1784.

13. *Independent Chronicle,* January 29, February 5, March 18, April 22, April 29, 1784.

14. Ibid., April 29, 1784.

15. Samuel Osgood to Stephen Higginson, February 2, 1784, Burnett, *Letters,* VII, 434-35.

16. *Independent Chronicle,* March 25, 1784. General opposition to the society is well surveyed in Wallace Evan Davies, "The Society of the Cincinnati in New England, 1783-1800," *William and Mary Quarterly,* 3d ser. 5 (1948), 1-15.

17. *New Hampshire Gazette,* June 19, 1784. Other references to Rhode Island are in the *Independent Chronicle,* which suggested that Rhode Island would act to disenfranchise the society. *Freeman's Journal,* April 28, 1784; *Pennsylvania Packet,* April 29, 1784.

18. *Connecticut Journal,* April 7, 1784.

19. Edmund Randolph to Jefferson, April 24, 1784, Jefferson, *Papers,* VII, 116.

20. *Independent Chronicle,* April 8, 1784, quoting the *South Carolina Gazette,* February 19, 1784.

21. Minor Myers, Jr., "The 'Polish Order' of 1783 Identified," *Miscellany of Honours* of the Orders and Medals Research Society (London), no. 3, 1981, pp. 11-19; Jefferson, Observations on an article for the *Encyclopédie Methodique,* July 22, 1786, Jefferson, *Papers,* X, 50; *Independent Chronicle,* April 1, 1784.

22. *Providence Gazette,* April 10, 1784.

23. Josiah Quincy, *The History of Harvard University* (Cambridge: Owen, 1840), II, 276.

24. John Jay to Elbridge Gerry, February 19, 1784, *John Jay: The Winning of the Peace,* ed. Richard B. Morris (New York: Harper and Row, 1980) II, 694-95; John Adams to Lafayette, March 28, 1784, Adams to Elbridge Gerry, April 25, 1784, as quoted in Davis, "Society of the Cincinnati in New England," pp. 11, 17.

25. Benjamin Franklin to Sarah Bache, January 26, 1784, *Complete Works of Benjamin Franklin,* ed. John Bigelow (New York: Putnam, 1888), VIII, 440-43.

26. Lachlan McIntosh to Lyman Hall, September 4, 1783, Hall to McIntosh, September 2 (*sic*), 1784, Foster, *Materials Relating to the Cincinnati in Georgia,* pp. 5-7.

27. Bellas, *History of the Delaware State Society,* pp. 10-11.

28. [Stephen Moylan], *Observations on a late Pamphlet entitled Considerations upon the Society or Order of the Cincinnati* (Philadelphia: Bell, 1783), p. 21. Moylan's pamphlet was reprinted twice in Hartford in 1784.

29. *Connecticut Courant,* April 13, 1784, reprinted in *New Jersey Gazette,* May

3, 1784. *Boston Evening Post*, March 22, 1784; Stretch, *Beauties of History*, pp. 204–11.

30. *Connecticut Courant*, January 13, and 20, 1784; Louie M. Miner, *Our Rude Forefathers: American Political Verse, 1783–1788* (Cedar Rapids: Torch, 1937), pp. 91–92.

31. Edmund Randolph to Jefferson, April 24, 1784, Jefferson, *Papers*, VII, 116–17; GW to Jedediah Huntington, December 28, 1783, Hume, *Washington Correspondence*, pp. 42–43; see also Washington, *Writings*, XXVII, 286–87. GW to Knox, February 20, 1784, ibid., XXVII, 339–41.

32. Knox to GW, February 21, 1784, Hume, *Washington Correspondence*, pp. 95–96.

33. GW to Arthur St. Clair, February 22, 1784, Washington, *Writings*, XXVII, 343; GW to Nathanael Greene, March 20, 1784, and to Knox, March 20, 1784, ibid; XXVII, 366–67.

34. *Records of the New Hampshire Society*, pp. 18–20.

35. GW to Jefferson, April 8, 1784, Washington, *Writings*, XXVII, 388–89.

36. Jefferson to GW April 16, 1784, Jefferson, *Papers*, VII, 105–08.

37. Arthur St. Clair to Washington, April 20, 1784, Hume, *Washington Correspondence*, pp. 139–40; Nathanael Greene to GW, April 22, 1784, ibid., pp. 141–42.

38. Thomas Paine to GW, April 28, 1784, ibid., p. 145; Winthrop Sargent to GW February 20, 1784, and the poem by Sargent's Sister, ibid., pp. 83–91. Lt. Col. Benjamin Walker of New York, however, wrote that he had heard no objections to the society there or in New Jersey. He only knew of objections in New England, where he believed they had subsided. Walker to GW, April 6, 1784, ibid., p. 129.

39. Jefferson to Martin van Buren, June 29, 1824, Jefferson, *Works* (Ford ed.), XII, 366–68. Jefferson remembered William S. Smith and the younger officers generally as leading the resistance to reform.

40. *New Jersey Gazette*, May 17, 1784.

41. Winthrop Sargent, "A Journal of the general meeting of the Cincinnati, in 1784;" *Memoirs of the Historical Society of Pennsylvania*, 6 (1858). The original manuscript is in Anderson House. Gen. William Moultrie also kept a less detailed account, New-York Historical Society. The official minutes of the meeting are to be found in *Proceedings*, I, 5–22.

42. Sargent, "Journal," p. 79.

43. Ibid., pp. 80–81.

44. Washington, Extract from the Letter Books, May 4, 1784, Hume, *Washington Correspondence*, pp. 152–54.

45. Extract from the Letter Books, May 4, 1784, ibid., pp. 152–54.

46. Sargent, "Journal," p. 82.

47. Ibid., 82–83.

48. Lafayette to Washington, March 9, 1784, Hume, *Washington Correspondence*, pp. 110–11. For a somewhat different version of the letter, see *The Letters of Lafayette to Washington, 1777–1799*, ed Louis Gottschalk (Philadelphia: American Philosophical Society, 1976), pp. 278–81. Sargent, "Journal," p. 83.

49. Sargent, "Journal," pp. 84, 89, 91, 93, 97.

50. None of the accounts report the appearance of L'Enfant, but several later documents say that things changed immediately with his appearance, and the accounts of the meeting do show a rapid change in tone. L'Enfant had arrived in New York City on April 29, 1784. L'Enfant to GW, April 29, 1784, L'Enfant Papers. His report on the state of the society is addressed to Washington and the delegates and dated May 10, 1784. It is endorsed "read 10th May" and thus was read to the general meeting the day it was written. L'Enfant Papers. On May 10 the eagles appeared, though they may not have been distributed until May 17. See Edgar Erskine Hume, *General George Washington's Eagle of the Society of the Cincinnati* (N.p.: The Numismatist, 1933), p. 9. Cf. *Proceedings,* I, 21.

David Humphreys, a delegate to the 1784 meeting, had no hesitation in writing in 1787, however, "Major L'Enfant did not arrive & bring the Eagles during the session of the General Meeting, but some time before the Convention." David Humphreys to GW, May 28, 1787, Hume, *Washington Correspondence,* pp. 309-10. On the diamond eagle, see Hume, *Washington's Eagle,* pp. 9-11. D'Estaing to GW, February 26, 1784, Hume, *Washington Correspondence,* p. 100; GW to d'Estaing, May 15, 1784, ibid., p. 179.

51. *Proceedings,* I, 12-16.

52. The circular letter may be found ibid., pp. 16-19.

53. *Statutes of the Most Honourable Order of the Bath* (London: N.p., 1772), p. 29; James Charles Risk, *The History of the Order of the Bath and Its Insignia* (London: Spink, 1972), pp. 18-19.

54. Sargent, "Journal," pp. 114-15.

55 *Papers of the Connecticut State Society of the Cincinnati, 1783-1807* (Hartford: Connecticut Historical Society, 1916). This volume is unpaginated, but the entry on the badge falls on the next to the last page of a small pamphlet of notes entitled "Extracts from the Minutes of the Proceedings of the General Meeting of the Cincinnati holden at Philadelphia. May 1784."

56. Ibid., last page.

57. *Massachusetts Centinel,* June 2 and 5, 1784; *Connecticut Journal,* June 2 and 16, 1784; *Independent Chronicle,* June 3 and 10, 1784; *Providence Gazette,* June 5, 1784; *New Hampshire Gazette,* June 12, 1784; *Vermont Gazette,* June 21, 1784.

58. *Massachusetts Centinel,* June 5, 1784.

59. *New Hampshire Gazette,* June 19, 1784.

60. GW to Hamilton, December 11, 1785, Hamilton, *Papers,* III, 639.

61. James Fairlie to Benjamin Walker, Fairlie to Steuben, Walker to Fairlie, as quoted in Frederick Kapp, *Life of Frederick William von Steuben* (New York: Mason, 1859), pp. 567-68.

Chapter Four

Facing the Threat of Anarchy

THE CINCINNATI HAD RETREATED in the face of public outcry in 1784, quieting most critics, but by no means all. In the next two years, however, the society moved with ever increasing boldness. It expanded its membership and built its organization at the local and state levels, and developing traditions gave the members a sense of pride, reinforced by the eagles, diplomas, and porcelains decorated with the eagle design. By the fall of 1786, when many came to see the Articles of Confederation as a plan for anarchy rather than government, the society's organization was well consolidated, and there had been a marked retreat from the concessions of the amended institution.

The annual meetings in July 1784 had discussed the amended institution, and at month's end Massachusetts, Rhode Island, Pennsylvania, Maryland, North Carolina, South Carolina, and probably Georgia had approved the changes. In October, Virginia raised the count to eight.[1]

The amendments and their spreading approval seemed to quiet critics. Knox reported late in July that opposition to the Cincinnati in Massachusetts was "dead," a judgment in which Benjamin Lincoln concurred. Greene wrote from Charleston with much the same conclusion and a confession. He had not realized how extensive opposition to the society had been, and he admitted to Washington, "I am happy you did not listen to my advice." The amendments, however, had been able to "silence all the jealousies on the subject." Knox did his part to defend the new changes when Gen. Samuel Holden Parsons sent a letter of dissent. Keeping the original institution, Knox wrote, would have been to "hazard the peace of the country," while the changes served to "annihilate all terrors."[2] Washington's optimism was more guarded. As he wrote General St.

Clair in August 1785, until state societies had conformed to all provisions of the amended institution, "the jealousies of the people are rather asleep than removed on this occasion."[3]

Determined critics were not asleep. Immediately after the amended institution had been published, the *New Hampshire Gazette* urged the public to condemn the amendments as well as the original. A son would still possess his father's badge, and the society would still become a "hereditary peerage." In the North Carolina legislature in November a bill was introduced rendering Cincinnati "incapable of having a seat in either House of the General Assembly of this State." The proposal, quickly tabled, shows that criticism was by no means limited to those New Englanders more widely reported.

Writing from Europe in April 1785, John Adams was well aware of the amendments yet still distrustful of a group readily capable of becoming an aristocracy that would overwhelm the republic. His fellow Massachusetts politicians Elbridge Gerry, Samuel Adams, and Stephen Higginson carried on a regular correspondence on the dangers of the society in 1784 and 1785.[4] Gerry was a most persistent critic, but by the spring of 1785 he was convinced that the Cincinnati and the aristocratic movement associated with them had been held in check by proper republican vigilance. He and his allies in Congress had beaten back proposals for a national standing army, and a commission had been created to oversee federal finance (and Robert Morris) should the impost pass.[5] For Gerry, however, these victories were but temporary. In his judgment the aristocrats took up the offensive again in the summer of 1785, when a new wave of criticism of the society began.

In July 1785 the Massachusetts legislature called for a convention to revise the Articles of Confederation. Massachusetts delegates were instructed to present the resolutions to Congress, but in an extraordinary move they declined to do so. Elbridge Gerry, Samuel Holten, and Rufus King explained themselves to Governor Bowdoin.[6] They doubted Congress had the power to call such a convention, but even if it did, the timing was wrong. Each of the states had formed its government on "republican principles," but should changes be undertaken now, the results might be different. Republican governments had been established only by defeating the forces of aristocracy, but presently, the three held, the Cincinnati showed "the same fatal tendency." A call for a convention would bring forth, presumably from the Cincinnati, "an Exertion of the Friends of an Aristocracy, to send Members who would promote a Change of Government." Should the Cincinnati prevail, they hinted, there would emerge "an Aristocracy, which would require a Standing Army, and a numerous Train of pensioners and placemen to prop and support its exalted Administration." In sum, the Cincinnati were organized "Enemies to a Free Government" for whom a constitutional convention would be an ideal opportunity. Governor Bowdoin reported the opinion to the Massachusetts legislature which thereupon rescinded its call for a convention.

There is no evidence to suggest any plan on the part of the society to take over a convention or even to issue a formal call for such a convention. Yet there was a lingering suspicion that this single, national society of men with a common background and fiscal interest *might* move in such a direction and *might* dominate any convention that could be called.

That fall Congress offered a mild rebuke to the society. French officers often wrote Washington seeking membership, but in June 1785 a Frenchman named Barre addressed the secretary for foreign affairs, who sent the letter on to Congress. Barre claimed that "at the time of his last voyage to America he had reason to expect the Cross of Cincinnati and a grade in the American marine." Congress agreed on October 6 that Barre had no claim to a naval appointment. As to the eagle, "The Cross of the Cincinnati Congress have not a power to grant. The application to them for it arose, without doubt, from a mistaken opinion that the Society of the Cincinnati was an Order of Knighthood similar to those Orders instituted by the Sovereigns of Europe."[7]

Now abroad as minister to France, Thomas Jefferson remained ever vigilant for any reference to the society which might imply any legal status as a national decoration. Congress had voted medals for several heroes of the Revolution, and Jefferson was commissioned to have them produced by the master craftsmen of Paris. In making plans he was assisted by his aide, Lt. Col. David Humphreys, Washington's former aide-de-camp and a member of the Connecticut society. The medal voted Gates raised problems, for the designer, never having seen Gates, was given an engraving of him wearing the eagle. Was it not anachronistic to show the Cincinnati on a general presumably as he appeared in 1777, the designer asked. Jefferson agreed and wrote Humphreys. It *was* anachronistic, but there was a more important reason for omitting the badge: "Congress have studiously avoided giving to the public their sense of this institution. Should medals be prepared to be presented from them to certain officers and bearing on them the insignia of the order, as the presenting them would involve an approbation of the institution, a previous question would be forced on them, whether they would present these medals? I am of the opinion it would be very disagreeable to them to be placed under the necessity of making this declaration."[8] No eagle appeared on Gates's medal.

Jefferson found another opportunity in the following year to make a more public, though anonymous, statement about the society. Jean Nicholas de Meunier asked Jefferson for comments on an article on the United States for the forthcoming *Encyclopédie Méthodique*. Jefferson provided an account of the society, outlining events through the Philadelphia meeting of 1784. The society retained the badge because they wanted the French to wear it, but in the United States no member "is seen to offend the public eye with the display of this badge." Jefferson went on to observe that the society posed a continuing threat to the subordination of the military to civil authority, because the meetings maintained the sharp distinction between civil and military. Worrying that the charitable funds might transform the former officer into the "lazy lounger," he hoped that the society would abolish the charitable funds as it had hereditary succession.[9]

While these critics watched intently, the society continued to grow. The institution provided that those eligible had six months to join after the army disbanded, and by the July meetings in 1784 the thirteen state societies had probably enrolled at least three quarters of the 2,160 revolutionary officers who would join. But other officers would continue to be admitted during the next decade. The institution had provided that men could be enrolled after the six months' period in "extraordinary cases," and most societies gave that clause liberal interpretation. All thirteen state societies were active organizations, but only three states established the district societies envisaged by the founders. New York had two districts, one meeting in New York City, the other in Albany. Meetings at Albany had ceased by 1791. Georgia had at least one district society centered in

Augusta, and Virginia had three district societies. Though established in 1783, it is not clear that the Virginia district societies were active.[10]

State societies from the first were concerned with nurturing their charitable funds. The contributions of one month's pay had built substantial funds which reached, for example, nominal balances of $7,980 in Connecticut in 1785 and over $12,675 in Virginia in 1786. Since these funds were based on commutation certificates issued by Paymaster General John Pierce, Jr., Cincinnati were naturally concerned with the funding of those certificates for individual and collective reasons. Some states took over the obligation themselves, but others made no effort to fund what they regarded as national obligations. Generally Pierce's certificates were bringing 10 to 15 percent of their face value in hard cash, cash many veterans were happy to have. Buyers of these discounted certificates were increasingly speculators who anticipated that they would one day be funded at face value. Some of the principal speculators were members of the society, and a few of the state societies even joined in the buying. In 1785 the Pennsylvania society ordered their treasurer to buy "funded certificates of the state, in order to increase the stock of the society." In November 1786 the Virginia society likewise ordered the treasurer to put any specie into military certificates.[11]

By 1785 critics were already beginning to argue against funding the certificates, holding that the original patriot holders had sold them to speculators whom the taxpayers should feel no obligation to reward. The point was much debated, even though such speculations were only in their infancy.[12]

If the state societies were concerned with nurturing their charitable funds, they devoted equal and careful attention to planning their annual meetings. In the first three years each society developed its own traditions and rituals for the annual fourth of July celebration, but none was so colorful as the New York ceremony first conducted in 1786. Based on the ceremonies of European orders, it was the product of the fertile baroque imagination of Steuben.[13] The central focus of the investiture ceremony was the "Chair of State," the seat from which the baron officiated as president. With a light blue seat with white fringe, the chair of state sat on an elevated dais made of two semicircular steps with white fronts and light blue tops. Completing the setting was a flag of the society designed by the baron, a small square table with blue and white satin covering, and two white cushions with blue fringe, one to hold the badges, the other the diplomas.

The regalia prepared, the ceremony began with a formal procession. First came the two masters of ceremonies for the day, then the members, the secretary, the vice-president, and finally the president. As the president entered, the trumpeters and kettle drummers in the balcony "gave a flourish until the President had taken his seat." The master of ceremonies introduced the new members, who were seated opposite the president, while Alexander Hamilton delivered an oration. Then Steuben read the institution and assured the new members that the objects of the association were friendship and charity. A master of ceremonies brought the first new member before the chair of state, and Steuben asked him whether he would obey the rules of the society. After an affirmative answer the candidate was led to the small table, whereupon the standard bearer delivered the flag into the candidate's left hand. In this inconvenient position, he then signed the institution with his right hand. The president took one of the eagles and attached it to the new member's button hole saying, or rather intoning, "Receive this mark as a recompense for your merit; and in remembrance of our glorious independence." At that moment the drums and trumpets gave a flourish. The president then presented a diploma with an exhortation to follow the model of Cincinnatus, and once more there was a flourish. Each new member was so inducted, and then all processed out of the hall to continue their celebration of the fourth.

That same day in New York Nathaniel Gorham, president of Congress, held an official public levee at his house from 12 to 3. Congressmen, diplomats, and heads of the departments were all there, but Congress was outdone by the Cincinnati's celebration. Rufus King, delegate from Massachusetts, described it as having a "splendor, exceeding anything within the practice of government." King wrote Elbridge Gerry, the old foe of the society, that he was disgusted when "The Chapter of these Knights" sent a delegation of four to bring anniversary greetings to the official levee. "I was witness to the degradation of Government in seeing them recd."[14]

Members soon acquired material reminders of the association and its esprit de corps. Many officers bought the French badges L'Enfant had brought back from Paris, but Pennsylvanians and Georgians also patronized the work of Philadelphia goldsmith Jeremiah Andrews. The Pennsylvania society likewise had its own membership certificate engraved, and they issued a small booklet outlining the two year history of their society.[15] In addition to the eagle, several hundred members acquired diplomas produced from the plate engraved in Paris according to L'Enfant's design. Later critics thought that design somewhat ungallant: an eagle and an armored Cincinnatus, holding the banner of the society and a sword, appeared to be driving a cowering lion and an unarmed, lightly clothed Britannia into the sea.[16] Gallant or not, the certificate was a graphic reminder of one's service, signed by Knox and Washington himself.

Relatively few, however, had the Cincinnati porcelains which first appeared in 1785. Knights of the Garter or Bath had ordered Chinese armorial porcelains ornamented with the insignia of their orders, and it was not unnatural for Americans to think of china decorated with the Cincinnati. In 1784 Maj. Samuel Shaw, Knox's aide-de-camp, had gone as a supercargo on the *Empress of China,* the first American ship to enter the China trade. He carried with him L'Enfant's design for the badge, and with some difficulty he had Chinese artists prepare the china which the *Pallas* brought to Baltimore in 1785 where it was advertised in August. Among the buyers of that shipment were Lt. Col. Henry Lee and General Washington.[17]

As the 1780s went on, the society became an increasingly conservative organization, retreating from the liberalism of 1784. The use of military titles at meetings and the fate of the amended institution both illustrate this general trend. In 1784, except for "General Knox" and "General Washington," the minutes of the Philadelphia meeting recorded the presence of citizens, not soldiers. Thus Brig. Gen. Jedediah Huntington became "Mr. Huntington." Pennsylvania made such usage a rule in 1785, and Virginia adopted an identical rule a year later.[18] But at the general meeting of 1787, the "misters" were gone and the military titles were back in full array. Virginia never resumed the titles, but Pennsylvania did, and most states never gave them up at all. The Cincinnati remained a military society during the lives of the original members.

Equally revealing was the progressive fate of the amended institution. In 1784 Maryland was probably the most enthusiastic of the eight states offering their immediate approval. Marylanders voted "to conform in every respect to the spirit and intention of the amendments." But Pennsylvania adopted the amended institution with decided reluctance, holding that "the ground of the society has been too much narrowed." Without further changes, the society would within a few years reach "its final period." Pennsylvania had therefore proposed additional amendments, giving state societies the right to fill vacancies caused by death, resignation, or expulsion. Also proposed was the extension of charitable aid to "distressed descendants of members."[19] It was precisely such reintroduction of the hereditary principle that Washington had blocked at the general meeting in May.

If Pennsylvania was reluctant in 1784, other state societies were resistant. Connecticut tabled a motion to approve the amended institution, New York declined to take any action, and New Hampshire voted a firm no. New Hampshire officers would see the society abolished altogether before they accepted a modification of the original institution. They saw the mandate to put funds in the hands of state legislatures as little short of a violation of property rights, endangering their charitable funds. Because of government's failure, the men had little else to offer their families: "We could only present them with scars instead of cash and ruined Constitutions in lieu of the spoils of War." As to the badge, New Hampshire men asked "if wearing the emblems of our Order establishes a Rank of Nobility in America contrary to the Confederation we can see no reason why the Badge worn by the free-masons does not as effectually do it."[20] As to the abolition of the circular letters, they wondered why all other societies and individuals should enjoy the privilege of communicating whatever they chose without "molestation." New Hampshire stood firm, opposed.

July 1785 had seen no more states ratify the amended institution. Connecticut and New Jersey both discussed it but took no position. Pennsylvania again urged that states have the option of filling vacancies. Col. Jonathan Trumbull of Connecticut had suggested readoption of the old institution, but in 1786 Adam Boyd responded that there were still objections to the society in North Carolina. Adherence to the amended institution would end them, but readopting the old institution, Boyd suggested, "would cost most of the friends" who were not members.[21]

July 1786 brought a definite turn away from the earlier amendments. Once more Connecticut postponed action, New Hampshire appointed a committee to propose new modifications, and New Jersey voted to explore ways of installing successor members. Most eloquent of the societies was New York, for whom Alexander Hamilton, James Duane, and William Duer produced a circular letter. New York too hoped that societies which had approved the amended institution would concur in the "absolute necessity" of further revisions. New York was particularly reluctant to give up the society's claim to promote the union of the states. How could it be criminal that a "class of citizens" so conspicuous in the Revolution would work to support the union "by all means consistent with the law?" New York urged each state to give delegates to the next general meeting power to change the "original Constitution" as might be expedient. Massachusetts, which had approved the amended institution at the first possible moment, now voted to reconsider.[22]

The reasons for this growing conservatism are not hard to see. Economic conditions throughout the nation were chaotic, and Congress was demonstrably unable to bring about improvements. Of particular interest to the former officers, of course, was the continuing problem of funding the commutation certificates. By the summer of 1786 every state but New York had approved the impost amendment of 1783, which would fund commutation. When New York finally passed it, a national revenue system could begin, yet it became increasingly apparent that summer that the New York legislature and Governor Clinton, a member of the New York society, were taking an independent path. When the legislature approved the impost on May 4 it did so with the restrictive stipulation that the duties were to be collected by agents of New York. Such duties were already the basic source of the state's income, and sacrificing them to the confederation meant finding a new revenue basis for the state.

Toasts at the New York meeting in July about national interests being sacrificed for local concerns were surely veiled references to the state's unwillingness to cooperate with the impost. Congress considered New York's response, and in August voted to admonish the legislature to fall into line. Governor Clinton, however, refused to call a special session, and thus things stood at an impasse for the rest of the year. That commutation might be blocked again was certainly one reason for the increasing boldness of the Cincinnati during 1786.

Toasts at other July 4 meetings were equally concerned with the political state of the union. Delaware had led the way in 1785: "May Congress be vested with full and efficient powers to complete the happiness of America." In 1786 Massachusetts offered "May the enemies of public faith, public honor, and public justice hold no place in the Councils of America" and "Perpetuity to the Federal Union, and perpetual infamy to the man who would dissolve it." Equally committed were the New York Cincinnati: "May the powers of Congress be adequate to preserve the General Union." And North Carolinians in a similar vein drank to "May a close union of the States guard the temple they have erected to liberty!"[23]

By fall there was little reason for political optimism, especially in New England. Rhode Island sought to solve its financial problems by printing paper money and demanding that it be taken at face value. Massachusetts, which stood for sound money and payment in specie (a rare commodity), found that debtor prisons were filling up as eastern merchants pressed western merchants and farmers long accustomed to dealing more in credit than cash. No one went to jail unless ordered by a court, and by September western farmers began saving their property by preventing courts from meeting, a pattern that would culminate in Shays's rebellion. In New Hampshire armed men had surrounded the state legislature on September 20, demanding an issue of paper money and the remission of taxes. The president of New Hampshire, General John Sullivan, also president of the New Hampshire Cincinnati, used eloquence to disperse the mob and the militia to pursue them once disbanded. To many of the Cincinnati, anarchy seemed closer than ever.

In this atmosphere the Cincinnati of New England ignored any statements in the amended institution rejecting political involvement. For the next six months, they stood firmly for law and order, and perhaps more. Not surprisingly, the amended institution received still another battering, a pattern which suggests that national order and hereditary succession were issues moderately joined in the minds of some members.

Twenty-eight of the Rhode Island Cincinnati gathered in Providence on October 9 as Gen. James Mitchell Varnum presided over what was a conservative meeting throughout. Since not all states had approved the new institution and since no other state, so they thought, was following it, they voted "that the Order shall remain on its original plan with such limitations on its Succession and such other alterations as may appear necessary." The members were convinced that the internal "disturbances" and "depradations of the Savages upon their frontiers" were the product of "joint exertions of daring emissaries and disaffected Citizens." As will be seen, references to savages were euphemisms for protestors in Massachusetts. Jealousies between the states were likewise on the verge of endangering liberties and subverting the "National Compact." They concluded that "the Virtue, the firmness, and the Activity of every Class of People are necessary to meet the impending Evils."[24] For the Rhode Island Cincinnati that meant a mutual pledge of defense against "foreign Invasions and Internal Enemies," a pledge with an unexplained qualification—the Cincinnati would render services "consistently with those great Principles which first inspired our general Order." A committee of the society's officers was authorized to forward those goals when the whole society could not meet.

Events in Massachusetts were more dramatic. The protests that had prevented courts from meeting showed no signs of stopping. Since the protesters were active in counties near the 7,000 muskets and 1,300 barrels of powder in the national arsenal in Springfield, Secretary of War Henry Knox followed events with special interest. He made at least two trips to Massachusetts in September and October, ostensibly to supervise security of the arsenal, but also to take the measure of the insurgents.

By October 3 Knox saw his former companions in arms as his ultimate resource should other defenses of the arsenal fail. To Jeremiah Wadsworth, vice president of the Connecticut society, he wrote, "I shall depend on the noble and ind[ependent] spirit of the late continental officers to step forward." He wrote to Samuel Holden Parsons, president of the society, in much the same vein. To Wadsworth he stressed that his potential reliance on the Continental officers was to remain "entre nous."[25]

Knox was in Boston on October 11 when the Massachusetts Cincinnati met, just two days after the Rhode Island meeting. The meeting began by choosing a committee of seven to prepare public resolutions and an address to the state legislature. In view of the events that followed, its members, in addition to Knox himself, are worth noting: General Lincoln was president of the society, William Eustis was a confidant of Gates during the Newburgh days, and John Brooks had brought Washington news of the Newburgh plot. William Hull would gain prominence, and infamy, in the War of 1812, Henry Jackson was a confidant of Knox, and Capt. Joseph Crocker was a member of the standing committee, as were all except Knox.[26]

Their resolutions soon found their way into the newspapers. If anyone had complaints, the "*yet* unpaid army" certainly did, but no relief was to be expected from "tumults & from riots." Some officers and men might be "deluded" by "abandoned men" or led into disorder, but the Cincinnati implored them to resist. Despite renunciation of political activity, the society pledged to aid in "the preservation of the constitution" and in insuring that "public faith & private credit are made the sacred objects of government." The address to the state legislature asked for at least current interest on the notes it had given the soldiers. The committee took pains to point out that not all officers had sold their notes to speculators, a question much debated in the next decade. The petition said, in effect, do not forget the army in making concessions to insurgents.

New Hampshire held no meetings in October, and the Connecticut meeting of September 12 had been notably unpolitical, at least in what went into the official records.

Knox moved quickly when he returned to New York. Governor Bowdoin was unsure that he could rely on Massachusetts state militia to maintain order and thought national troops would be better. Knox and Steuben had been advocating a national standing army since 1783, but it had been a moot advocacy, for the government could not fund what many delegates would resist on principle. With the threat in Massachusetts, Knox brought Congress a secret request for an army of 2,040 to serve three years. Stationed in New England, its announced purpose would be to fight Indians, but he left no doubt in congressional minds that its real purpose was maintenance of order in Massachusetts. Congress accepted the plan on October 19 and 20, requisitioning $530,000 from the states to support the force.

Knox wrote Washington on October 23. The Indians had given "indisputable evidence of their hostile intentions," yet he as much as confessed that the army would not really be directed against Indians. It would, however, "tend to strengthen the principles of government, if necessary, as well as to defend the frontiers. I mention the idea of strengthening government as confidential."[27]

Most of that important letter of the twenty third was not about the army but about the deteriorating political condition of the nation. The thirteen states had been "perpetually operating against each other and against the federal head ever since the peace." Even the states individually lacked the power to preserve internal order, and the insurgents in Massachusetts were doing more than closing the county courts. Unless conditions were checked, "we shall have a formidable rebellion against reason, the principle of all government, and against the very name of liberty." Massachusetts politics, it seemed, had come down to the struggle of the principled and propertied against the insurgents, whose creed was "that the property of the United States has been protected from the confiscation of Britain by the joint exertions of all, and therefore ought to be the common property of all." Knox guessed that they amounted to "twelve to fifteen thousand desparate and unprincipled men" throughout New England.

What was to be done? Knox mused that Americans imagined they were a mild nation, "not as other nations, requiring brutal force to support the laws." That had proved an illusion, for "we are men,—actual men, possessing all the turbulent passions belonging to that animal, and that we must have a government proper and adequate for him." "The men of property and the men of station and principle" in Massachusetts, a group which surely included the Cincinnati, were determined to act. Yet his letter provided no clue as to what the principled and propertied wanted to do.

Steuben realized that the new army was not meant for Indians. He had followed events in Massachusetts closely, unsure on which side he stood. After all, as he would remind Congress again and again, he had been made many promises, but his claims for payment had gone unheeded. He wrote his former aide William North a letter full of classical musings on the incipient anarchy within the republic, yet by October 27 he had written an exposé of Knox's plan and on November 1 it appeared in the *New York Daily Advertiser* over the pseudonym "Bellisarius."[28] Did America need an army in

New England to fight Indians? No. War with a foreign power was out of the question. What therefore was the purpose of a New England army? Since Massachusetts was home to 92,000 militia, Steuben asked further why "Continental troops" might be needed, unless to support "an abominable oligarchy."[29]

Rufus King, a member of Congress from Massachusetts, soon figured out who Bellisarius was. Writing to Elbridge Gerry, King reported that "these opinions are his hourly conversation."[30] As Bellisarius, Steuben had undercut the standing army he and Knox had hoped to establish. Was the baron a man of deep egalitarian conviction? Nothing in his ruffles-and-flourished installation ceremony had suggested such sentiments, and he had never backed away from his title nor the society when Aedanus Burke attacked. Since the pseudonym was so easily detected and Steuben made no secret of his authorship, the article was perhaps more a ruse than an exposé. Steuben wrote a potentially far more important piece on November 2, when he asked his old commander Prince Henry of Prussia to assume an American crown.

That offer was one of the secrets of the fall of 1786 that would not emerge until published in what seemed rash, unfounded accusations in 1799. Similar stories emerged in 1825, again under highly political circumstances. Frederick Kapp's biography of Steuben included the story that someone had speculated Henry might be a good candidate for an American crown. Steuben responded, seemingly in jest, that he would never come to America. Purportedly, he continued, "I wrote to him a good while ago what kind of fellows you are; he would not have the patience to stay three days among you." The story had the aura of apocrypha about it until 1911, when Richard Krauel reported the discovery of a draft of Henry's answer in the Charlottenburg archives. The following account is based largely on that draft.[31]

The prince's answer, probably written in early 1787, said that Steuben's letter of November 2 transmitted a surprising letter from one of the baron's friends. Oral tradition, recorded by Rufus King in 1824, attributes that letter to the president of Congress, Nathaniel Gorham. Writing that the government was not a success and that he was exploring the possibility of adopting the British model of constitutional monarchy, Gorham had seemingly asked Prince

Henry whether he would accept an American crown. Either Steuben or Gorham suggested that a code be established to carry on correspondence about the matter.

Whether the prince wrote to Gorham is unknown. He wrote Steuben that he agreed the English model was most perfect, but that he was too old to take up new projects and that he would do nothing to change the government of the United States. He declined to establish a code, but far from rebuffing the proposal completely, he suggested that he would be in Paris in the fall where Steuben might arrange for a friend to see him.

To what degree was the society as an organization involved in the Prince Henry scheme? I have found no documented proof of any involvement at all, but several coincidences are worth noting.

Monarchal ideas in the army went back to at least May 1782 when Col. Lewis Nicola of the Corps of Invalids wrote Washington with the suggestion that the general become king. Washington responded with such a stern letter of rebuke that Nicola wrote no less than three letters of apology.[32] Several years later William Gordon, who somehow knew of the incident, asked if he might report it in his history. Washington urged silence, but commented that he had been pressed to assume a crown on *more* than one occasion.[33]

Likewise, shortly after Steuben's letter went to Prince Henry, something was afoot among the New England Cincinnati. It was long claimed by opponents that the Cincinnati were working for a change in government, and there is a baffling entry dated November 26, 1786, in the Rhode Island society's treasurer's accounts: "To cash paid Doctr. Hickok & my own Expenses 4 days at Boston as a Committee to meet the New England Society upon Confidental Business as per bill. 2.19.10."[34] The two Rhode Islanders involved were the treasurer, Col. Jeremiah Olney, and Dr. Enos Hitchcock, a Harvard graduate of 1767 who had served as a chaplain.[35] Hitchcock kept careful diaries which show that the two were in Boston from November 21 to November 24. The meeting in question took place on November 22, but the topic under discussion was seemingly so explosive that Hitchcock, even in his own private diaries, noted on that day only "Held conference with & c."[36] What was up?

Any answer is speculation, but two topics were possible: the growing disorders in Massachusetts and the possibility of calling Prince Henry to an American throne.

Perhaps both topics were discussed. Hitchcock later sent nominations for officers of the Massachusetts regiment being raised, and in later years Colonel Hull of the Massachusetts society purportedly had the papers about the offer to Prince Henry.

Though the Cincinnati as an organization has no demonstrable connection with the call to Prince Henry, every man originally identified with the scheme, save for Nathaniel Gorham, was a member of the society. The channel by which the story passed to the public is particularly interesting. Two men independently recorded the story as they heard it from President James Monroe, a member of the Virginia society. Monroe in turn had heard it from that master conspirator John Armstrong, the author of the Newburgh Addresses, and Armstrong probably heard it directly from Steuben with whom he shared quarters in New York City in the winter of 1788–89. Armstrong had further reported that the correspondence about the matter was in the hands of William Hull, who with Knox had served on the Massachusetts society's committee to draft resolutions in October 1786.[37]

The possibility that Washington knew of the offer makes the letter he wrote to Madison on March 31, 1787, all the more interesting. Those who favored monarchy, he wrote, had not "consulted the public mind" or they lived in areas where the "levelling principles in which they were bred" had been eradicated. Having said that monarchy was contrary to the American psyche, Washington then went on to make an astounding observation. "I am also clear, that even admitting the utility; nay the necessity of the form, yet that period is not yet arrived for adopting the change without shaking the Peace of this country to its foundation." That is, Washington's objections were to the timing, not the *idea* of monarchy. The time for monarchy had simply "not yet arrived."[38]

Thus in the fall of 1786 the Cincinnati braced themselves and Knox moved immediately to start raising the troops authorized by Congress. By the end of October, Col. Henry Jackson, Knox's old friend from the Massachusetts line, had been named commander of the Massachusetts regiment. In an era when formality governed letter writing, Jackson was the only one of Knox's correspondents to write him as "Dear Harry."[39] Jackson, of course, served on the committee of Massachusetts Cincinnati who wrote the resolutions adopted in October.

At least one other Cincinnatus had been eager for command of the Massachusetts regiment, and when he did not get it Jackson confided to Knox that John Brooks was "damn'd mad."[40] Jackson made the initial selection for the regiment's officers, and all who ranked as captains or above were Cincinnati. William Hull had been a lieutenant colonel in the Revolution, but with some persuasion he had agreed to serve as major. Jonathan Haskell was another major, as was William North, Steuben's aide-de-camp whom Knox had sent to Boston more or less as his agent. North sent back regular reports. William Eustis, who with Hull had been on the resolutions committee, was regimental surgeon. From Providence, the Reverend Enos Hitchcock, one of the Rhode Island Cincinnati who attended the secret Boston meeting on November 22, sent a list of nominees for ensigns, but too late, for the appointments had already been made.[41]

David Humphreys wrote Knox from New Haven suggesting in a "private" letter that Congress promote all the old Continental lieutenant colonels to brigadier generals and all the former majors to lieutenant colonels.[42] Such promotions would do more than gratify egos. They would insure that reliable Continental officers would have superiority of rank over the colonels of militia regiments which might be raised in a crisis. These promotions would thus "give a certain weight to federal affairs." Nothing came of the suggestion, but it is revealing that Humphreys too thought reliance on the Continental officer corps a political necessity.

Funding for the new regiments failed to materialize, and Daniel Shays proved more effective in organizing his forces than Henry Jackson. In January 1787 Governor Bowdoin issued a call for 4,400 men to put down the rebellion growing in the west. As David P. Szatmary discovered in his recent book on Shays's Rebellion, every member of the Cincinnati committee on resolutions of the previous October was prominent in either leading troops or recruiting them.[43]

Overall command of this new force was given to Benjamin Lincoln, Continental major general, former secretary of war, and president of the Massachusetts Cincinnati. Immediately upon his appointment, Lincoln began raising money among Boston merchants, and in six days he had pledges amounting to £6,000. By the end of the month the army was ready to head west.

Lincoln's force was not quite the uniformly Cincinnati organization Jackson's regiment would have been. Among the regimental commanders Rufus Putnam and David Cobb were members, but Jonathan Titcomb was not. Other Cincinnati who played important roles in the force which ultimately routed Shays were Benjamin Tupper, Moses Ashley, and William Shepard, the latter a major general of the Massachusetts militia. Gen. John Paterson commanded the Berkshire County militia, while William Eustis acted as surgeon, and other Cincinnati served in less prominent roles. With the force in the field, Shays and his men were routed and the insurgents crushed.

One might think it was only to be expected that the former officers of the Revolution would lead the suppression of Shays's Rebellion. Yet they were far from the only military talent in the state. As Steuben pointed out, the militia of Massachusetts numbered over 90,000, from major generals to privates. Colonel Titcomb, for example, had not served in the Continental army. The prominence of the Cincinnati in suppressing the rebellion therefore shows that Knox was right in his initial assumption that he could rely on the former Continental officers to support firm government. He was equally correct in assuming further that they would be effective as well as reliable.

The vigor of the Cincinnati in putting down Shays's Rebellion has often been noted, but what is sometimes ignored is that Daniel Shays himself had been eligible for the society but had not joined. Two prominent leaders of the rebellion *were* in fact members. Luke Day, a Revolutionary captain, was, in the estimation of some, more important than Shays in organizing insurgents. His brother Lt. Elijah Day was likewise a member. Both were expelled from the Massachusetts society in July 1787.[44]

Seventeen Hundred Eighty Seven began a year of uncertainty. Few knew that the offer of a crown had been made to a European prince, but the implications of Shays's Rebellion were discussed throughout the colonies. Would the Articles of Confederation lead only to anarchy? Would America frame a new government? Many had the impression that the Cincinnati had been the principal agents for maintaining order in Massachusetts, a cause for hope for some, a cause for fear for others. Knox had no doubt that the Cincinnati had staved off anarchy, and he would hint broadly that what the society had done for the state, it could do for the nation.

Notes

1. For a review of the action of each state society on the amended institution in 1784 and subsequent years, see Hume, "Early Opposition to the Cincinnati," pp. 618-21.

2. Knox to GW, July 26, 1784, Hume, *Washington Correspondence,* p. 201; Lincoln to GW, July 15, 1784, ibid., p. 201; Greene to GW, August 29, 1784, ibid., p. 205.

3. GW to Arthur St. Clair, August 31, 1785, Washington, *Writings,* XXVIII, 239-40.

4. *New Hampshire Gazette,* June 19, 1784, the article was reprinted in *Boston Evening Post,* June 28, 1784. John Butler introduced his bill in the North Carolina legislature November 2, 1784, *The State Records of North Carolina,* ed. Walter Crane (Goldsboro: Nash, 1901), XIX, 743. John Adams to Elbridge Gerry, April 25, 1785, quoted extensively in autograph catalogue no. 153 of Paul C. Richards, September 1981, item 210. The Gerry-Samuel Adams-Higginson correspondence may be found in part in Samuel Osgood to Gerry, April 4, 1784, Burnett, *Letters,* VII, 483; Samuel Adams to Gerry(?), April 19, 1784, Anderson House; Samuel Adams to Gerry, April 23, 1784, Adams, *Writings,* IV, 298; Gerry to S. Adams, May 7, 1784, Burnett, *Letters,* VII, 516; Gerry to Stephen Higginson, May 13, 1784, Burnett, *Letters,* VII, 522-24; Gerry to S. Adams, May 14, 1784, Burnett, *Letters,* VII, 526; Gerry to John Adams, April 25, 1785, quoted in George Athan Billias, *Elbridge Gerry: Founding Father and Republican Statesman* (New York: McGraw-Hill, 1976), p. 119.

5. For an excellent, well-documented discussion of Gerry's activities, see Billias, *Elbridge Gerry,* chap. 8.

6. Massachusetts Delegates to the Governor of Massachusetts, September 3, 1785, Burnett, *Letters,* VIII, 206-10.

7. Charles Thompson prepared a draft report on September 13, 1785, which was adopted by Congress on October 6, *JCC,* XXIX, 700-701.

8. Jefferson to David Humphreys, December 4, 1785, Jefferson, *Papers,* IX, 77; David Humphreys to Jefferson, undated (c. December 12, 1785), ibid., IX, 96; on the medals see ibid., XVI, 53-79.

9. Jefferson's observations for Demeunier are to be found ibid., X, 49-52. Jefferson reported to Washington later that Demeunier's first draft was a "mere Philippic" against the society, and in revising his text Jefferson was put in the paradoxical position of being a moderate defender of what the society was all about. Jefferson to GW, November 14, 1786, ibid., pp. 531-35.

10. David Franks, *The New-York Directory* (1786) (New York: Doggett, 1851), pp. 73-74, Foster, *Materials Relating to the Cincinnati in Georgia,* p. 21, quoting the *Georgia Gazette,* February 15, 1787; Hume, *Virginia History,* p. 68.

11. *Proceedings of the Pennsylvania Society of the Cincinnati* (Philadelphia: Steele, 1785), p. 86; Hume, *Virginia Documents,* pp. 28-29.

12. Ferguson, *Power of the Purse*, p. 229, referring to debates in Pennsylvania. In October 1786 the Massachusetts society informed the state legislature that rumors the debt was all in the hands of speculators were untrue. Storey, *Minutes of all meetings*, October 11, 1786, p. 27.

13. *Extracts from the Proceedings of the New-York State Society of the Cincinnati convened on The 4th of July, 1786.* (New York: N.p., 1786), pp. 3-10.

14. Rufus King to Elbridge Gerry, July 4, 1786, *The Life and Correspondence of Rufus King*, ed. Charles R. King (New York: Putnam, 1895), I, 186.

15. L'Enfant's badges continued to be the main supply of the society for many years. His bill to Francastel, the Paris jeweler, continued to be one of the society's principal problems. He had failed to pay for the badges he brought back eagerly, and despite sincere efforts he fared poorly collecting amounts due in America. Lafayette finally satisfied Francastel, and in 1787 the meeting of the general society ordered that the marquis be sent $894 to cover his expenses. *Proceedings*, I, 34. That meeting established a system for levying proportional expenses for each state to share in the cost of L'Enfant's project. See also Francastel to Lafayette, January 15, 1786; Lafayette to GW, February 11, 1786, L'Enfant Papers.

16. For a comprehensive review of the L'Enfant diploma and those of the state societies, see Edgar Erskine Hume, *The Diplomas of the Society of the Cincinnati* (New York: American Historical Society, 1935).

17. The most recent surveys of this important china are John Quentin Feller, "China Trade Porcelain Decorated with the Emblem of the Society of the Cincinnati," *Antiques*, 118 (October 1980), 760-68; Eleanor Lee Templeman, "The Lee Service of Cincinnati Porcelain," ibid., pp. 758-59.

18. *Proceedings of the Pennsylvania Society*, p. 71; Hume, *Virginia Documents*, pp. 17-20.

19. Meeting of July 5, 1784, *Proceedings of the Pennsylvania Society*, pp. 67, 68.

20. *Records of the New Hampshire Society*, pp. 29, 27-28.

21. Adam Boyd to Jonathan Trumbull, March 3, 1786, as quoted in Davis, *Revolution's Godchild*, p. 41.

22. The Connecticut meeting on July 4 was small and questions of delegates to the general meeting were postponed until September 12, when they were chosen. On that day the Connecticut Society formally postponed further action on amended institution. *Records of the Connecticut State Society*, *Records of the New Hampshire Society*, p. 30, *Excerpts of the Proceedings* (New Jersey), pp. 172-73; John Schuyler, *Institution of the Society of the Cincinnati* (New York: New York State Society of the Cincinnati, 1886), p. 91; Storey, *Minutes of all meetings*, p. 22.

23. Bellas, *History of the Delaware State Society*, p. 16; Drake, *Memorials*, p. 48; Schuyler, *Institution*, p. 90.

24. Minutes, Rhode Island Society, October 9, 1786, Rhode Island Society Archives.

25. See Knox to Jeremiah Wadsworth and to Samuel Holden Parsons, both October 3, 1786, Knox Papers.

26. For the record of the meeting, see Storey, *Minutes of all meetings*, pp. 23-28.

27. Knox to GW, October 23, 1786, in Drake, *Memorials*, pp. 176-77.

28. Palmer, *Steuben*, pp. 336–39.

29. *New York Daily Advertiser*, November 1, 1786, quoted in Palmer, *Steuben*, pp. 339–40.

30. King, as quoted in Palmer, *Steuben*, p. 341.

31. Philadelphia *Aurora*, March 2, 1799; Kapp, *Steuben*, p. 584., Richard Krauel, "Prince Henry of Prussia and the Regency of the United States, 1786," *American Historical Review*, 17(1911), 44–51. The documents surrounding the Prince Henry episode are well reviewed in Louise Burnham Dunbar, *A Study of "Monarchical" Tendencies in the United States from 1776 to 1801* (Urbana: University of Illinois, 1922), pp. 58–70.

32. GW to Nicola, May 22, 1782, Washington, *Writings*, XXIV, 272–73; for Nicola's three letters of apology to Washington, May 23, 24, and 28, 1782, see Dunbar, *Monarchical Tendencies*, pp. 129–34; Dunbar provides a review of the Nicola proposal, pp. 40–46.

33. GW to William Gordon, Washington, *Writings*, XXX, 168–70. One of those other instances may well have been James Mitchell Varnum's letter from Providence: "The Citizens at large are totally destitute of that Love of Equality which is absolutely requisite to support a democratic Republick: Avarice, Jealousy, & Luxury controul their Feelings, & consequently, absolute Monarchy, or a military State, can alone rescue them from all the Horrors of Subjugation." Varnum to GW, June 23, 1782, quoted in Dunbar, *Monarchical Tendencies*, pp. 47–48.

34. Treasurer's Accounts, November 25, 1786, Rhode Island Society Archives.

35. For a biography of Hitchcock see Shipton, *Biographical Sketches of Those Who Attended Harvard College*, XVI, 475–84.

36. Enos Hitchcock, Diary for 1786, November 21–25, 1786, Enos Hitchcock Papers, Rhode Island Historical Society.

37. Joseph Gardiner Swift, superintendent of West Point, heard the story from President Monroe in 1817 and recorded it in his *Memoirs*, published 25 years after his death. *Memoirs* (Worcester: Blanchard, 1890), p. 164. Rufus King heard the same story on May 10, 1824, from a Colonel Miller who also heard the story from Monroe. *Life and Correspondence of Rufus King*, VI, 643–44. See Dunbar, *Monarchical Tendencies*, pp. 60–61.

38. GW to James Madison, March 31, 1787, Washington, *Writings*, XXIX, 188–92.

39. See for example Henry Jackson to Knox, June 8, 1783, Knox Papers.

40. Jackson to Knox, November 12, 1786, Knox Papers.

41. Jackson to Hitchcock, November 19, 1786, Hitchcock Papers.

42. David Humphreys to Knox, November 10, 1786, Knox Papers.

43. David P. Szatmary, *Shays' Rebellion: The Making of an Agrarian Insurrection* (Amherst: University of Massachusetts Press, 1980), pp. 86–87.

44. The question of the Day brothers was discussed on July 4 and 5 by the meeting of the Massachusetts society and on July 13, 1787, by the standing committee. *Massachusetts Society of the Cincinnati: Minutes of All Meetings of the Society up to and Including the Meeting of October 1, 1825* (Boston: Privately printed, 1964), pp. 40, 42, 45.

Chapter Five
The Cincinnati and the Politics of a New Constitution

IT WOULD BE A MISTAKE to suggest that the new federal Constitution emerged because of pressure from the Cincinnati, even though at least one member made that claim. John Doughty was a member of the New York society serving with the army at Fort Pitt when he wrote Knox in July 1788, sharing his exuberance about the new government. The Cincinnati, he said, should be credited with the achievement, for they were "more generally advocates for good government than perhaps any other class of individuals."[1]

It would be equally erroneous, however, to assume that the Cincinnati were not a factor in bringing about the new government. Though their circular letters in 1786 and 1787 are notably unpolitical, the public reports of meetings put the Cincinnati squarely behind the movement for a stronger centralized government. The renewal of old fellowship at meetings and the continuing network of influence between old comrades at arms now in new positions of authority made the members of the society natural conduits of influence in the constitutional transformation.

Historians point to surviving evidence to document influence, but there was at times among the Cincinnati a notable propensity to avoid committing ideas to paper. The secret meeting of New England Cincinnati in November 1786 was covered up save for one expense chit, and in the spring of 1787 Knox writes that he has many things to tell Washington when he sees him. In the meantime nothing is put on paper. Other members correspond in a similar vein, and at the constitutional convention Hamilton was probably up to more than presenting an alternate to the Virginia plan. The Cincinnati knew they were under scrutiny, and if anything, their influence was probably stronger than can be proved directly from surviving documents, and that is just the way they wanted it.

There is another, more passive, but perhaps more potent influence which the society had during these critical years. Nonmembers speculated on what the society *might* do if changes were not made. The society was the only national, secular organization in the country and its members needed no further testimony of their ability to lead forceful action. Thus a French chargé reported to Paris that the Cincinnati *might* act if they did not like the results of the constitutional convention, Elbridge Gerry argued for an electoral college as a way of checking the *potential* influence of the society, and a Nova Scotia clergyman thought the Cincinnati *could* be the means of establishing a strong monarchy. Potential reactions of the Cincinnati were thus a constant factor nonmembers might consider in shaping their own suggestions on national policy.

If 1786 had seemed a year of incipient anarchy, 1787 was just the opposite. Shay's Rebellion was crushed, and a new constitution was written. Seventeen-hundred eighty-eight brought migration to land in the West and 1789 saw a new federal government with new federal jobs. Seventeen-hundred ninety offered funding for commutation certificates. From the Cincinnati's point of view, the fruits of the Revolution were finally at hand.

While the nation watched developments in Massachusetts, the Annapolis Convention opened on September 11, 1786, to discuss the Articles of Confederation. Three of its twelve members were Cincinnati: Alexander Hamilton and John Dickinson and Edmund Randolph, the last two honorary members. Before they disbanded they urged the states to send "commissioners" to Philadelphia on the second Monday in May to "consider the situation of the United States." The second Monday would be May 14.[2]

Spring was also the stated time for the next general meeting of the Cincinnati. By October 31, 1786 Washington had made up his mind that he would decline reelection as president general. In a circular letter he explained that he had been reluctant to accept the post in 1784, but "I prevailed upon myself to accept the appointment" only to avoid an unintended "deriliction of the Society" or a "disapprobation of the principles on which it was then established." Those principles were the provisions of the amended institution, principles which had now quieted critics, leaving him free to retire.[3]

To coordinate the society's meeting with the constitutional convention, Washington set the Cincinnati meetings for the first Monday in May, the seventh. His letters reveal that he had not kept touch with the society, for he had little idea who was president of several state societies. He guessed Clinton in New York (it was Steuben), he was right on Elias Dayton in New Jersey, but he was not sure, and to Benjamin Lincoln he wrote, "I have seen, I think, your name as President." Again he was right, but the uncertainty is revealing.[4]

Gates now had reason to think that he would be the next president general, for Washington alerted him of his decision in order that Gates as vice president general would preside in May.[5] Accordingly, when the Virginia society met, General Weedon was once more elected president in place of Gates, who anticipated a promotion.

By February 1787 Washington had already been named a delegate from Virginia to the constitutional convention, but he was uncertain whether to accept the appointment. To attend the federal convention and not the Cincinnati meetings would be "disrespectful" to the Cincinnati, and he asked Knox's advice, adding, "My first wish is to do for the best, and to act with propriety."[6]

Knox's solution was simple—Washington should attend both meetings. Cincinnatus could not yet go back to his plow, especially given events in Massachusetts.

> That the Society was formed with pure motives you well know— In the only instance in which it has had the least political operation, the effects have been truly noble. I mean in Massachusetts where the officers are still unpaid and extremely depressed in their private circumstances, but notwithstanding which the moment the government was in danger they unanimously pledged themselves for its Support—While the few wretched officers who were against the government were not of the Cincinnati. The clamor and prejudice which existed against it, are no more—The men who have been most against it Say, that the Society is the only bar to lawless ambition and dreadful anarchy to which the imbecility of government, renders us so liable, and the same men express their apprehensions of your resignation.[7]

Knox was saying, none too subtly, that the society could be the means of bringing order to the entire nation. Washington's leadership would be critical in carrying out that role, and Knox hoped to have a "private conversation" to persuade him of the necessity of continuing as president general. He also hinted a substantial personal interest in attending both meetings: "Should you attend the convention and not meet the Cincinnati, that would sorely wound your sincere friends and please those that dare not avow themselves your enemies." Gates was probably the implied leader of the latter group, as well as the likely choice for next president general.

By April 2 Washington had decided, with greatest reluctance, to attend both meetings.⁸

While Washington and Knox debated, critics of the Cincinnati remained watchful. Mercy Otis Warren had written John Adams in January that it was not easy to say where the political ship would land. There were two extremes in American politics: those who abhorred all authority and those who saw "the Necessity of drawing the Reigns of power much too taught [sic] for Republicanism, if not for a Wise & limited Monarchy." The Cincinnati were clearly leaders of the second group. "Some think the Cincinnati who are waiting for a favorable wind to Waft them on to the [*words uncertain*] of Nobility are manifestly elated by the present prospects. Others are flattering themselves that an Aristocratic power is fast forming. With many of the younger Class particularly the students at Law and the youth of fortune & pleasure are crying out for Monarchy & a standing army to support it."⁹ That spring James Warren wrote John Adams that the "Barefaced and Arrogant System of the Cincinnati Association is not yet fully matured, but it is rapidly progressing." John Quincy Adams likewise wrote his father that the society was "daily acquiring strength." The Cincinnati he thought would become "a body dangerous, if not fatal to the Constitution."¹⁰ A Philadelphia printing of Mirabeau's attack on the Cincinnati was further proof that controversy over the society was far from dead.

Jefferson still had hopes of seeing the society abolished. He wrote Washington from France that he had met no one "learned or unlearned" who did not think the society destructive of republican government.

> Every writing which has come out since my arrival here, in which it [the society] is mentioned considers it, even now as reformed, as the germ whose development is one day to destroy the fabric we have reared. I did not apprehend this while I had American ideas only. But I confess that what I have seen in Europe has brought

me over to that opinion: and that tho' the day may be at some distance, beyond the reach of our lives perhaps, yet it will certainly come, when, a single fibre left of this institution, will produce an hereditary aristocracy which will change the form of our governments from the best to the worst in the world. To know the mass of evil which flows from this fatal source, a person must be in France, must see the finest soil, the finest climate, the most compact state, the most benevolent character of people, and every earthly advantage combined, insufficient to prevent this scourge from rendering existence a curse to 24 out of 25 parts of the inhabitants of this country.[11]

Jefferson thought the southern societies particularly likely to contemplate establishing an aristocracy on the European model.

The paragraph quoted is long, but Washington copied that and more and sent it on to Knox to be laid before the society in May.[12] One senses again an unstated dilemma in Washington's thinking. He may have thought abolition of the society would be politically wise, yet he was equally concerned about the implications of offending his former colleagues, American or French. Somehow a middle ground had to be maintained, and thus Washington hoped the meeting in May would not address the status of the amended institution. Had it been adopted or not? At best the answer was ambiguous. To insist on its adoption would throw the society into "warmth and divisions." But, Washington had asked Knox in early April, if the amended institution were rejected, "in what light would my signature appear on contrary recommendations?" With great concern for his own public reputation, Washington therefore decided that he would attend part of the Cincinnati meetings, but someone else would preside.[13]

On April 27 Washington made it appear that circumstances had made still another decision for him. He had not been well, his arm was in a sling, his brother had just died; and now that his mother and his sister both seemed to be dying, he would be forced to make a 100-mile trip that would exhaust him further. He was not sure that the constitutional convention would ever assemble, and he canceled all plans to go to Philadelphia.[14]

Thus with no prospect that Washington would be present, the general meetings of the Cincinnati opened in Philadelphia on May 7. Several delegates were supposed to attend both the society meetings and the constitutional convention. In the end, however, only David Brearly and Jonathan Dayton of New Jersey, Alexander Hamilton of New York, and Thomas Mifflin of Pennsylvania participated in both. Two members accredited to both arrived in Philadelphia only after the Cincinnati meetings had adjourned, Charles Cotesworth Pinckney of South Carolina and Nicholas Gilman of New Hampshire. Almost paradoxically there was a Rhode Island delegation at the Cincinnati meetings, but the state sent no representatives to the constitutional convention.

The reform of 1784 was dead. A long debate on the institution resulted only in agreement that each state society should select delegates to attend a special general meeting in 1788 "to agree upon and finally establish all such alterations as may be necessary." It was obvious that the amended institution was not the final word. (The few delegates who appeared in 1788 could not muster a quorum.)[15]

South Carolina delegate George Turner reported general sentiments on May 12. "We are apparently, all hot for a Renewal of the old Institution, with some few additions and trifling alterations. The Society must live—and will, if we conduct it with *Firmness, Policy,* and *Prudence*. A Revolution is not, perhaps, far off. The Cincinnati in that case, must *si defendo*, become active and important." News had reached Philadelphia that Washington would attend the constitutional convention and that he would meet with the Cincinnati. Turner did not rejoice, for he thought Washington's influence far too moderating. "General Washington will be among us in few Hours more—But, entre nous, I could almost wish for the Absence of the Illustrious Chief,—whose extreme Prudence & Circumspection (having himself much Fame to lose) may cool our laudable and necessary Ebullition with a few Drops, if not a Torrent, of Cold Water—Let us never lose sight of the rational Liberties of the People; But let us remember That energetic Government is essential to their Security."[16]

Washington's support remained vital to the society, and if Turner lamented his moderation, others urged moderation if only to please the general. When Alexander Hamilton reported at the New York society meeting on July 5, he said that there had been reluctance to undertake radical changes, lest Washington refuse to serve again as president general.[17]

Washington had, of course, declined reelection, but many refused to accept his decision, and much of the out-of-session talk at the

Philadelphia meeting must have been devoted to resolving the question. Gates saw himself as Washington's logical successor, yet wrote Washington, "I cannot think of being even for a day, placed at the Head of The Institution; For unless You [sic] Excellency continues there The Dignity of the Order Will be Diminished."[18] This disclaimer had all the earmarks of *nolo episcopari*. Others could not think of Gates as president either, even for a day. In March, David Humphreys wrote from New Haven that the Cincinnati would reelect Washington regardless of his wishes. Knox probably encouraged Washington to attend the meetings as a way of checking Gates, and Arthur Lee wrote from New York that "it is the intention of the meeting of the Cincinnati to re-elect you as their President, notwithstanding your letter. They think you are so plegd to them, by some of your letters that you cannot refuse the Presidency."[19]

Washington arrived in Philadelphia on Sunday, May 13, but he took no part in the Cincinnati meetings, save for dining with the delegates on the evening of the fifteenth.[20] What conversations transpired are unknown, but after some negotiations Knox prevailed. Washington would serve as president general again. Thus he was elected on May 18, as was Knox for another term as secretary general. But Gates, who probably awaited news of his election as president general, was now dropped as vice president general, and General Mifflin, who had presided at the meetings, was named instead. General Otho Williams was at his own request relieved of the assistant secretary general's duties, and none other than Major Turner was elected in his place. McDougall continued as treasurer general.

In 1789 Washington outlined the conditions under which he had agreed to continue as president, conditions nowhere described in the minutes of the meeting. Washington referred to the general meeting planned for 1790, "at which meeting it is not expected I shall attend because it was agreed at the last Genl. Meeting that I should be leased of the duty of the President which were to be executed by the Vice President now Governor Mifflin."[21] For the rest of his life Washington continued to carry on a vast correspondence about the society, particularly with the French, and he signed membership certificates on a regular basis. But never again did he preside over or even attend one of the general meetings.

Given the publicity that followed the general meetings of 1784, the papers were curiously quiet about the meetings of 1787. Washington's decision not to stand for another term as president general was reported in April and May, shortly before the meetings opened.[22] But after the sessions ended, only the new officers were reported to the public and few papers even listed them. Why? Delegate Edward Carrington offered an explanation to the president of the Virginia society. The meeting had "avoided publication of any part of these proceedings except the election of Officers—publications answer no useful purpose to the Order, and are often the Means of bringing into Public speculation things that are not matured and of course liable to misconstruction." In a word, on the eve of the Constitutional Convention, the Cincinnati staged a news blackout.[23]

There were 21 Cincinnati among the 55 delegates who assembled for the constitutional convention.[24] In addition to those already mentioned, the following were members: from New York, John Lansing and Robert Yates (honorary); from New Jersey, William Livingston (honorary); from Pennsylvania, Robert Morris (honorary), and from Delaware, John Dickinson (honorary member of Pennsylvania). Maryland sent Daniel of St. Thomas Jenifer, while Virginia sent four Cincinnati, James McClurg, Nathaniel Pendleton, Governor Edmund Randolph (honorary), and General Washington. From North Carolina came Alexander Martin, plus honorary members William R. Davie, William Blount, and Richard Dobbs Spaight. Abraham Baldwin and William Pierce represented Georgia. The New York delegation was made up entirely of Cincinnati, and four out of seven Virginia representatives were members, as were four out of five North Carolina delegates. Connecticut and Massachusetts, on the other hand, sent no Cincinnati to Philadelphia. William Jackson of the Pennsylvania society was secretary to the convention. Members of the society therefore made up 38 percent of the convention's delegates in a nation in which the roughly 2,300 members were but seven-tenths of one percent of the national population.

As the constitutional convention opened, the Cincinnati were a national organization exerting a strong implicit, if not explicit, force for a vigorous national government. The French chargé in New York had no doubt that the Cincinnati were "interested in the establishment of solid government." He reported to Paris in June that the Cincinnati hoped for a new central government led by Washington "with all the prerogatives of a crowned head." The society would wait to see what the convention did, but if convinced it would accomplish little, they would try to establish a new government by force, an effort Otto thought sure to fail, for the society was too weak and unpopular. British dispatches make no mention of the Cincinnati, but, in September, Whitehall too assumed that Americans would ask for a prince. Lord Dorchester, governor of Quebec, was urged to use whatever influence he might "to discourage the strengthening their alliance with the house of Bourbon, which must naturally follow were a sovereign to be chosen from any branch of that family."[25] Such monarchal speculations were not limited to diplomats. In June the *New Hampshire Gazette* published a report emerging from Nova Scotia that three members of Congress had been deputed to go to Washington with a secret proposal to make him dictator for six years. Washington, of course, declined. The rumor cannot be confirmed from other sources, but had Washington himself followed the model of the Roman Cincinnatus, who did serve as dictator, it is not unlikely that many individual Cincinnati and possibly many state societies would have rallied to his side.[26]

Only once did the society arise as a topic during the debates at the constitutional convention. On July 25 the delegates discussed the means of choosing a national executive. Some favored election by the national legislature, others by popular election, and still others by what came to be called the electoral college. The society's old foe, Elbridge Gerry, was a firm advocate of the electoral college, and Madison's summary of his speech explains why.

> A popular election in this case is radically vicious. The ignorance of the people would put it in the power of some one set of men dispersed throughout the Union & acting in Concert to delude them into any appointment. He observed that such a Society existed in the Order of the Cincinnati. They are respectable, United, and influencial. They will in fact elect the chief Magistrate in every instance, if the election be referred to the people. His respect for the characters composing this Society could not blind him to the danger & impropriety of throwing such a power into their hands.[27]

It would be a mistake to say that the electoral college was created as a check on the Cincinnati, but in the influential judgment of Elbridge Gerry, that certainly was one of its merits.

Studying what the Cincinnati delegates to the convention said, it soon becomes evident that there was no Cincinnati line they argued as a group. Alexander Martin, John Lansing, and Jonathan Dayton all argued for the states as the basis of any national government, not a nationalist position at all. Martin, Lansing, and Yates all left in midsummer, convinced that the convention had exceed its authority.

Generally, however, the Cincinnati delegates did support a stronger national government, but from a variety of perspectives. Edmund Randolph, who presented the Virginia plan, urged stronger national government with authority centered in a legislature based on the population of the states. Randolph favored a plural executive, worrying about the accumulation of power in the hands of one individual. John Dickinson came to support a two-house legislature, one representing the states equally, the other proportioned to population, but with only moderate power in the hands of an executive. A national standing army had been a favorite project of Knox's for years, and Dayton and Charles Cotesworth Pinckney argued strongly for such an army. But Edmund Randolph opposed it. Livingston, Dayton, Randolph, and Pinckney, however, all agreed that the national government should have the power to supervise the state militias.

Alexander Hamilton argued a position very close to that expressed by some of his fellow Cincinnati, and nearly identical to that reported by French and British sources. On June 19 he made a long presentation of his own ideal constitution. Despite the Revolution, the British model remained for him the standard of the world. Order, power, and stability were fundamental requisites for successful government. A single chief executive would serve for life, subject, however, to impeachment. Hamilton was quick to point out that "the term monarchy cannot apply." A senate would serve during life or good behavior, and another legislative chamber would be chosen by popular election every three years. The executive would be commander in chief and the national government would be supreme over the states.[28]

McClurg was one of the few delegates who supported a life term for the executive. He was equally concerned that the executive have force adequate to compel obedience. Robert Morris agreed with Hamilton on life terms for senators. Livingston held that the national government should assume the debt of the states. Hamilton had argued for representation based on population rather than an equality of states. Pierce supported him but went further, arguing that state distinctions could well be abolished. Brearly wanted a government based on an equality of the states, but he was willing to have state borders redrawn to make thirteen equal states. In short, a few Cincinnati did form a small but generally ineffective nucleus for the ideas Hamilton advanced.[29]

Hamilton's position becomes more interesting in view of other events. There is no evidence that Hamilton knew Steuben had written to Prince Henry of Prussia. Prince Henry's response in April had expressed no interest in any American scheme, but nonetheless he invited Steuben to send a representative to see him in Paris that fall. Hamilton's plan would have created a throne that Henry might have occupied. The quiet controversy that arose in February 1804 also makes Hamilton's general position more fascinating. That month Hamilton learned that a former law clerk was spreading the story that about the time of the constitutional convention, Hamilton's law office had been responsible for copying a proposal to call the duke of York, also known as the bishop of Osnaburgh, to an American throne. The original proposal, it was claimed, came in a letter from John Adams to someone in Boston conveying a British plan to give the United States the Canadas, Nova Scotia, and all other American territory if they would accept one of the sons of George III as king. Hamilton denied that such a letter had come from his office, but Governor George Clinton remembered it distinctly.[30]

Nothing in the several letters written in 1804 mentions the Cincinnati, nor is there a hint of such a proposal in any society records I have seen. Yet David Humphreys was a member, and he had written Hamilton on September 1, 1787, while the constitutional convention was still in session, about the enthusiasm he found for the duke of York in Connecticut. He also wrote of a Nova Scotia clergyman who suggested that the Cincinnati might be instrumental in bringing about a reunion with Great Britain. Over a year later, Lord Dorchester reported to London that Hamilton had proposed monarchy at the convention, with the crown to go to a foreign prince.

Supported by "some of the ablest members of the convention," the plan nonetheless failed.[30]

It would be quite erroneous to say that the Cincinnati stood for monarchy in 1787, yet surely some individual members would have been a nucleus of support for such a change. Hamilton, Benjamin Tupper, John Armstrong, Steuben, and probably William Hull all supported monarchy in the late 1780s.

When the constitutional convention finished its work in September, fourteen Cincinnati delegates signed the new document, as did William Jackson, secretary of the convention. Edmund Randolph refused to sign. Lansing, Yates, and Martin had gone home earlier, displeased with the direction the convention had taken. William Pierce had left in July in an unsuccessful attempt to save his business, while McClurg had felt useless and left also in July. Davie supported the new plan, but slipped away quietly in August.[32] With the convention's work complete, the nation faced the larger question of ratification.

What emerged from the constitutional convention was a proposal for a strong presidency. Some critics would fear it as a plan for an uncrowned monarchy, while others saw it as a transitional phase to monarchy. Monarchy was the system under which the Continental officers, like their fellow countrymen, had grown up. For some, strong executive leadership still seemed a natural form of government, even though it at first had seemed contrary to the underlying principles of the Revolution. In the early phases of the struggle, the Revolution turned against the notion of strong executive leadership because of the political sins laid at the feet of George III. The New Hampshire Constitution of January 1776, for example, established only a legislature, with powers normally committed to an executive branch vested in one or both houses of the legislature. Many states that weakened executive power in the 1770s saw the need for strengthening it in the 1780s. Even republics needed leaders. To many the experience of the states was a lesson for the nation, and many of the Cincinnati wrote of the need for strong, unified leadership of the nation as a whole.

The likelihood that Washington would lead the nation as he had led the army was appealing to the Cincinnati, yet there is no evidence that the state societies or the general society undertook organized political activity on behalf of the new Constitution.

Circular letters between the state societies in 1787 and 1788 were concerned primarily with the amended institution. Nonetheless, state societies often published lists of toasts offered at their meetings, and these publicly proclaimed sentiments put the Cincinnati firmly in the Federalist camp. The individual activities of prominent members only reinforced that image.

Convinced that a new government was on the way, the Cincinnati, or at least some of them, had already begun to proceed with a new confidence. Chancellor Robert R. Livingston, an honorary member, delivered a Fourth of July oration before the New York Cincinnati in which he attacked any who thought governing a task which could be performed by those of "the meanest capacity." Ability and education were rendered suspect in the eyes of those who lacked them, and the Cincinnati were calmly assured that they should consider themselves properly in the governing class. Any doubts Knox may have shown about the badge in 1784 were gone that July. One evening Dr. Mannasseh Cutler dined with Knox and forty other men in New York, and "every gentleman at the table was of the 'Cincinnati' except myself, and wore the proper badges."[33]

Each state called a special convention to consider the new Constitution, and Cincinnati who were delegates to those conventions usually stood firmly behind the new plan.[34] In no case, however, do Cincinnati delegates seem to have acted as a unified group. Individual members often corresponded about the Constitution, but they made no reference to the society as a pro-Federalist apparatus.

Delaware was the first to approve the new Constitution, casting a unanimous vote on December 7, 1787. By the end of January 1788 Pennsylvania, New Jersey, Georgia, and Connecticut had approved as well. Invariably, Cincinnati delegates supported the proposal. In Georgia, for example, four out of twenty-six delegates were Cincinnati, while in New Jersey there were seven out of thirty-eight. All Cincinnati delegates voted for ratification. When Samuel Holden Parsons dispatched the news that Connecticut had approved, Knox responded that "the business now draws to a crisis."[35] If Massachusetts approved by a comfortable margin, then all would go well, but if Massachusetts rejected the constitution, Knox foresaw real difficulty. When the vote came in Boston on February 6, the new government was accepted by the uncomfortably close vote of 187 to

168. All eight members of the society who had been delegates, among them William Heath, Benjamin Lincoln, and John Brooks, sided with the Constitution.

Four more states voted in favor of the Constitution later that spring and early summer. In New Hampshire and Maryland the Cincinnati delegates were solidly Federalist, but in South Carolina and Virginia they split. As at the convention in Philadelphia, delegates voted the interest of their state or region more than that of the society. In the South Carolina convention, the Cincinnati delegates divided eleven to two in favor of the Constitution. Gen. Charles Cotesworth Pinckney, who had been a delegate to the constitutional convention in Philadelphia, led the debate on behalf of the new plan.

It has been assumed that the people of Virginia were generally against the new Constitution, but that it passed the convention 89 to 79 because of the large contingent of former officers among the delegates.[36] During the debates, Col. Henry Lee invoked the brotherhood of military service: "The people of America, sir, are one people. I love the people of the North, not because they have adopted the Constitution, but because I fought with them as countrymen, and because I consider them as such."[37] Federalists had run as many officers as they could in the election of delegates, and 46 (52%) of the 89 Federalist delegates who voted for the Constitution were former officers. Yet of the 79 who voted against the document, a surprising 35 (44%) had served as officers. Former *Continental* officers were more likely to support the Constitution (46 for, 35 against) than were those with state commissions (24 for, 23 against). Virginia was one of the states where comparatively few of the eligible officers joined the Cincinnati, and only 20 members were delegates. It does not fit the stereotype of the society to find that 9 Cincinnati voted for ratification, but 11 voted against it. The military may have put the Constitution over in Virginia, but the Cincinnati delegates did not.

Virginia's ratification put ten states behind the new system, one more than the minimum needed, and when the Cincinnati met that July they rejoiced. The Massachusetts society drank to "speedy and effective operation to the new Constitution." Delaware Cincinnati toasted both "the new constitution" and "the ten States that have adopted the new Constitution," and then they finished with "may our utmost hopes and wishes be exceeded in the blessings of the new Constitution." Rhode Island had rejected the Constitution in a popular referendum in February, and when the Georgia Cincinnati offered their toasts, one was "May our Sister-State, Rhode Island, be convinced of her error without the necessity of coercion," a sentiment which could be read both as a hope and a threat.[38]

The next critical vote came in New York, where Alexander Hamilton collaborated on the newspaper articles later collected as the *Federalist Papers* and where Robert Yates, an honorary member, was likewise penman to the Antifederalists with his "Letters of Brutus." The voters probably counted Yates far more successful, for they returned a slate of delegates largely opposed to the Constitution. In New York too Cincinnati delegates split—indeed, they guided both sides. Hamilton led the Federalist cause, while Governor George Clinton, the opposition. By the time the New York convention was ready to vote in late July, ten states had already ratified the Constitution, making the future of that document a given. When Hamilton and the Federalists threatened that New York City would secede from the state if the convention voted no, Clinton acquiesced and permitted ratification. The Constitution won by the narrow margin of 30 to 27, with six Cincinnati voting for ratification and two against. Clinton, as presiding officer, did not vote.[39]

Only six of the delegates to the North Carolina convention, which assembled in July seem to have been Cincinnati, and when the vote came the Constitution lost (84 to 184) and the Cincinnati split. Richard Dobbs Spaight and William R. Davie, both honorary members and both delegates to the constitutional convention at Philadelphia, stood for it, but four fellow Cincinnati were opposed. After the inauguration of Washington another convention assembled in November 1789, with probably ten of the delegates Cincinnati. The Constitution was now ratified, 194 to 77, and again the nine Cincinnati in the final tally divided, five for, four against. Once more Richard Dobbs Spaight was the principal leader of the Federalist side.[40]

North Carolina's ratification left Rhode Island the only holdout. In February 1788 the state legislature had rejected a proposal to call a state constitutional convention, but it did authorize a popular referendum on the Constitution which resulted in 237 votes for it, 2,708 against. By June 1789 the legislature had defeated five more motions to call a ratifying convention.

The Rhode Island Cincinnati had taken a public stand for the new Constitution in 1788 when the July 4 celebration in Providence was turned into a major festival on "Federal Plain."[41] The day began with an oration by Enos Hitchcock, one of those who had attended the secret Boston meeting of Cincinnati in November 1786. He emphasized the new Constitution rather than "the imbecility of the confederation," curiously the same phrase Knox had used as early as 1783. Hitchcock avowed that the new government would provide "every enjoyment which can be derived from human institutions."[42]

Then Hitchcock, his fellow Cincinnati, and the crowd (some 5,000 to 6,000 people) went to an outdoor dinner. The thousand-foot table was covered with a canopy, and thus the light rain did not dampen the party or the thirteen toasts accompanied by the discharge of thirteen cannon. After the public celebration the Cincinnati went off to Daggett's Tavern for a few more toasts, duly reported in the newspapers, including "The Order of the Cincinnati throughout the World" and "The Nine Pillars of the Federal Edifice."[43] No one could doubt where the Rhode Island Cincinnati stood politically.

In the fall of 1789 they sent Washington an address of congratulation which included hopes that "the mistaken zeal which has lately prevailed in this state will give way to more enlightened policy."[44] In addition to rejecting the Constitution, there was no better example of "mistaken zeal" than the paper money which the legislature had authorized in 1786. Continental officers had learned to fear the depreciation of paper money, and the Rhode Island Cincinnati tacitly agreed they would not take the new state issue at par, even though the law demanded it.

In April 1789 Providence Cincinnati, hearing that Lt. Joseph Arnold had demanded to pay a debt in paper money, protested to their president. "We conceive such conduct inconsistent with the character of a member of the Society of the Cincinnati." Arnold was accordingly warned, but replied that he had tried to pay his debt without the tender of paper money, only to be refused. He stood firm in now claiming what the law allowed and promised to explain himself at the July meeting, as he already had in the newspapers.⁴⁵ The president in turn reminded him of the opinion held by Cincinnati "not only in this state but throughout the United States, respecting the operation of the Law, which Legitimates the discharge of a *Bona fide* specie debt with the nominal sum of the present Bills of the State of Rhode Island."⁴⁶

When the Cincinnati met on July 4 they judged Arnold had "forfeited all claim to those principles of honor and justice which are the basis of the Institution, and thereby rendering himself no longer deserving of the friendship and confidence of that class of his fellow citizens," they expelled him.⁴⁷

The toasts later that day were in part political as usual. The members drank to "Liberty without anarchy," a phrase that well sums up the continuing attitude of the Cincinnati throughout the period, and they drank to "The Confederated States," a reminder that Rhode Island was not one of them. In January 1790 the legislature finally authorized a convention in March. Discussions carried over to May when the Constitution won by the narrow margin of 34 to 32, with all four Cincinnati delegates voting for the government already operating.⁴⁸

Once the Constitution was adopted by the minimum number of states, Washington seemed the inevitable choice for president, and needless to say the Cincinnati supported the choice with enthusiasm, despite any misgivings Washington may have had about the society. As the Delaware society put it in a toast in July 1788, "Farmer Washington, may he, like a second Cincinnatus, be called from the plough to rule a great people."⁴⁹

The Cincinnati had additional cause to celebrate in 1788, beyond the adoption of the Constitution. The Ohio Company had become reality.

From 1777 on there had been pressure to give the officers and men generous land grants when the conflict was over, and in early April 1783 Ebenezer Huntington, Rufus Putnam, and Timothy Pickering developed a plan that would have made Ohio a semimilitary state, settled by officers and men.⁵⁰ Land grants proportioned to rank would fulfill congressional commitments, and thus a private was to have 100 acres, an ensign, 150, a colonel, 500, and a major general, 1,100. To induce settlers to migrate, the government would provide funds for moving, tools and farm implements, livestock, and arms to protect the new settlement. And some who settled on their land within a year might receive bonus grants of land even bigger than the original allotments. Except for enlisted men, those extra land grants went to the same group eligible for the Cincinnati—those officers who served to the end of the war or those who had served three years.[51] Pickering, who was the primary exponent of the plan, foresaw a constitution for the new state written by the "associators," or settlers. He did, however, offer one specific provision: "The total exclusion of slavery from the State to form an essential and irrevocable part of the Constitution."

The plan developed in April seems to have been the basis of the petition to Congress signed by 288 officers on June 16. Once more there was the assumption that the western lands were "suitable to form a distinct Governor (or Colony of the United States) in time to be admitted one of the confederated States of America." Two hundred forty-three, or 86 percent, of the men who signed that petition were or would become members of the Cincinnati.[52]

Conflicting state and federal claims to western lands, and perhaps the controversy over the Cincinnati, prevented Congress from acting, but the states began issuing land grants to former soldiers. There was heavy settlement of families from Virginia, Maryland, and North Carolina in Kentucky, and what is now Tennessee also provided ample land grants for North Carolina men. In 1784 there was strong pressure in Tennessee for status as a separate state. Residents began taking matters into their own hands, drawing up constitutions and electing John Sevier, an honorary member of the Georgia and North Carolina societies, as governor of the State of Franklin. The new state collapsed when North Carolina officials came to terms with the settlers. After Congress organized the "Territory South of the River Ohio" in 1790, William Blount, an honorary member of the North Carolina society, was named first governor. Sevier became governor when Tennessee was admitted to the union in 1796.

The larger states were able to offer land grants within their own borders. General Steuben spent much of his time promoting settlement on the lands granted him in New York. He also had tracts in Pennsylvania and Virginia. Appropriately this Cincinnatus lived near what is now Rome, New York, and he named a stream on his property Cincinnati Creek.[53] (His horse was named Cincinnatus too.)

The Pennsylvania Cincinnati had accepted the new institution that renounced political activities, but that did not prevent them from doing a first-class lobbying job in 1785. A bill was before the legislature that would grant lands to officers and soldiers of the Revolution. The Pennsylvania society urged that William Irvine, then the society's treasurer, be appointed commissioner of the grants should the act pass, for he was "a gentleman well acquainted with the land appropriated for that purpose." The letter was addressed to John Dickinson, an honorary member who was himself a member of the standing committee. Irvine was appointed.[54]

While land grants were forthcoming in other states, Rufus Putnam had not given up on his Ohio project. In January 1786 he and Benjamin Tupper had published a prospectus for an Ohio Company, and of the eleven who gathered to organize in Boston on March 1, only two were not members of the Cincinnati. They decided to raise a million dollars in Continental paper to pay for the 1,500,000 acres of land they hoped to buy and develop. The organizers then spent the following months trying to collect funds and strike a bargain with Congress. They also lobbied for a constitution for the territory, and thus the Ordinance of 1787 was passed.

Lobbying efforts were originally in the hands of Samuel Holden Parsons, who had not been a success. In June 1787 the Reverend Dr. Manasseh Cutler, one of the few non-Cincinnati involved in the project, took over, and he soon found that the prospect of a secret deal all but guaranteed success. Col. William Duer, an honorary member of the New York society, was secretary of the United States Board of the Treasury. Duer would use his influence on behalf of the Ohio Company in exchange for certain considerations. Rather than the million and a half acres at a dollar each which the Ohio Company had sought, they should ask for five million acres at sixty-six cents each. Cutler should seek all the river land between the Scioto River and the eastern boundary of the intended Ohio Company lands. The Ohio Company would get the land it wanted, but Duer, Cutler, and others would have rights to 3,500,000 acres for their own promotional scheme. Cutler agreed, and on October

27, 1787, when Cutler and Maj. Winthrop Sargent took title to the Ohio Company lands, they also purchased options on the other parcel.

Interest in the Ohio Company was considerable among the Cincinnati, both in terms of investment and settlement. The society organization was a natural channel for sales, and among the papers of the Pennsylvania society there is still a blank printed sales slip for shares in the company. The first group of settlers left Danvers, Massachusetts, in early December 1787, followed by a second contingent, which left Hartford on New Year's Day. The parties met in Pennsylvania, and forty-eight settlers arrived at the mouth of the Muskingum River in Ohio on April 7. Of that first group only six were members of the society, but those six numbered most of the group's leaders. In the mid-nineteenth century Samuel Hildreth published a collection of thirty-nine short biographies of prominent Ohio pioneers, sixteen of them Cincinnati.[55] No less than twenty members of the Massachusetts society made their way to Ohio Company lands, and on a per capita basis Marietta, Ohio, may have been the heaviest concentration of Cincinnati in the United States. When the marquis de Lezay-Marnezia visited Marietta in the 1790s, he was quite aware of the Cincinnati as a presence.[56]

The Cincinnati gave the tone to the new settlement. The town itself was named Marietta, in honor of the Queen of France. Suspecting Indian attack, the settlers built a large fort, which they called Campus Martius, named for the field on which the troops of the Roman Republic had assembled. Another visitor there found that the Cincinnati on the frontier had not lost the art of celebrating the fourth of July. Josiah Harmar of the Pennsylvania society was host. James Mitchell Varnum of the Rhode Island society delivered an oration, and there was a cannon salute of fourteen guns. Although it rained twice during the outdoor dinner, the traditional thirteen toasts were offered, number seven to "General Washington and the Society of the Cincinnati."[57]

In addition to the Ohio Company, there were four other Ohio settlement schemes in which Cincinnati were involved.

The options to 3,500,000 acres which Cutler and Sargent had received had been transferred to the Scioto Company, whose company stock was divided into thirty shares. William Duer, the secretary of the Board of the Treasury who had engineered the deal, owned thirteen shares himself, a fact not made public for obvious reasons. Cutler and Sargent owned another thirteen shares, and the remaining four were to be sold in Europe. Cutler and Sargent transferred part of their interests to their old associates Rufus Putnam, Benjamin Tupper, Samuel Holden Parsons, and Royal Flint. Only Flint was not a member of the society. Duer also offered investments to others, and Steuben was delighted at the prospect of making a quick $30,000 in two years.[58]

The basic plan of the Scioto Company was to sell Ohio land to the French. They sent abroad as their agent Joel Barlow, the poet member of the Connecticut and Massachusetts societies. From the beginning, the plan was flawed, for Barlow was put in the position of selling land to which the company had only options. Cutler had written one promotional pamphlet, and when Barlow acquired an English associate, they produced another, making Ohio sound like a veritable Eden, free of taxes, military obligations, lions, and tigers.[59]

After the fall of the Bastille, Barlow and the Compagnie de Scioto were able to sell deeds readily. Barlow assumed that the proceeds of the deeds would enable the company to buy the rights the deeds conferred, but his new associate embezzled the funds, and soon the Scioto Company tottered and failed along with Duer's other projects. Despite the number of Cincinnati involved in establishing the Scioto Company, the American organizers did not exploit Cincinnati connections to promote the scheme through the French nobility.

The company, however, was more than a disastrous speculation. Five hundred French settlers sailed for the United States in 1790, and by October they had arrived on the Ohio River. A city for the French was laid out by Maj. John Burnham of the Massachusetts society and given the fitting name it bears to this day, Gallipolis.

Many of the French settlers traveled under terms that made them more or less indentured servants to the company, but the colony also contained a number of royalist émigrés including the marquis de Lezay-Marnezia, the marquis d'Hebecourt, the Comte Marlatic, and the comte de Barth, none of them Cincinnati. There were also doctors, lawyers, a Catholic priest, carvers and gilders to the court, and coach and peruke makers, all sure to feel out of place in rural Ohio. Nonetheless their culture followed them, for they had musical instruments and converted a blockhouse into a ballroom and filled their gardens with artichokes and almond trees.⁶⁰

The land between the Miami and Little Miami rivers was known as the Symmes Purchase, and here New Jersey officers and soldiers could have land grants. There were many settlers from Kentucky as well after development began in 1788. The principal town was first named Losantiville, but in 1790 Gen. Arthur St. Clair, territorial governor as well as president of the Pennsylvania society, changed the name to Cincinnati in honor of the society. David Zeigler, also of the Pennsylvania society, was the first mayor.

Settlement of the Virginia Military District, located between the lands of the Symmes Purchase and the Scioto Company, had begun in 1787. Col. Richard Clough Anderson of the Virginia Cincinnati was in charge of the distribution of Virginia bounty lands in Kentucky, and when tracts there were all assigned, he began making assignments in Ohio. Congress hesitated, but in 1790 opened the district and confirmed the assignments Anderson had made. Land was available to holders of certificates, whether they were the original soldiers or speculators who had bought those certificates at a great discount.

To the north, the Western Reserve did not see extensive settlement until July 4, 1796, when Moses Cleveland of the Connecticut Cincinnati led a band of settlers there. There were six toasts that day, but none of them to the Cincinnati.⁶¹ Unlike the Ohio Company, on which it was modeled, the Connecticut Land Company had relatively few Cincinnati involved. Benjamin Tallmadge of the Connecticut society was, however, one of its investors, and the town of Tallmadge, Ohio, remains a lasting reminder of this interest. It goes without saying that the names of prominent Revolutionary leaders, most of them Cincinnati, were given to counties and towns throughout the western expansion.

Cincinnati were prominent in the administration of the Ohio country. Gen. Arthur St. Clair was territorial governor as well as commander of the army detachments stationed there. Winthrop Sargent was secretary, and Samuel Holden Parsons and James Mitchell Varnum were judges. John Armstrong, author of the Newburgh Addresses, had also been named a judge but declined the appointment.⁶²

During the ratification debates, settlement in Ohio seemed a useful alternative to some Cincinnati should the Constitution fail. Knox, for example, wrote Samuel Holden Parsons in January 1788 that the forthcoming vote in Massachusetts would be critical for the whole nation. If the Constitution won there, all would be well, but "otherwise we must all I believe become inhabitants of the Ohio."[63] A few Cincinnati held the thirteen states already too large for a single nation, and it seemed inevitable that the western settlements would not become new states in a union, once established, but new nations.[64] However, if there was any continuing sentiment to see Ohio as the quasi-military colony envisaged early in the decade, it soon evaporated. The state proceeded unwaveringly under the federal system and joined the union as the seventeenth state in 1803.

The visionary nature of one scheme cannot be denied, and had it become reality it might have attracted some Cincinnati. Spain had worried that American independence would pose problems with the inevitable western expansion of the new nation into Spanish territory. The Spanish minister, Don Diego Guardoqui, and the governor of New Orleans were both instructed in September 1787 and again in November 1788 to do what they could to alienate settlers in the West from the United States government. They were to offer rich support for new colonies of Americans who might settle on Spanish territory and give allegiance to the Spanish crown. At least one Cincinnatus was ready with a plan for such a colony.

In 1788 Steuben, his fiscal condition bleak, presented a scheme to plant a colony of 4,200 farmers, artisans, and soldiers in Louisiana. For his efforts the baron and his associates would receive 200,000 acres, and other settlers would each get 230 acres. The Spanish government was to provide an additional bounty of $100 for farmers, craftsmen, and soldiers.

Settlers were to come only from the United States or "other foreign countries," with Spanish subjects excluded. Steuben expected some fellow Germans to come over in royal vessels provided by the king of Spain. Military protection of Spanish territories was the object of the colony, and the baron promised to organize a corps of 800 men in four battalions. He would be general and have the right to name other officers, all of whom would have Spanish royal commissions.[65] Nothing came of Steuben's plan, but Col. George Morgan and Lt. Col. James Wilkinson at about the same time offered the Spanish plans which were carried out. Though both men were eligible, neither joined the Cincinnati.[66]

Wilkinson's propensities for western intrigue came to the fore again in 1805 and 1806 with the dark intrigues of Aaron Burr, who had joined the New York society only in 1803. At least two Cincinnati, Israel Smith of New York and Jonathan Dayton of New Jersey, were involved in Burr's plans, but the society in no sense was a recruiting ground for adventurers.

Cincinnati were far more likely to continue military careers, not by western adventures, but by joining the expanding federal army. Lt. Cols. Jacob Kingsbury of the Connecticut society and Constant Freeman of Massachusetts and South Carolina were among the officers of the army which brought Burr's conspiracy to an end.

With few exceptions, the principal officers of the post-Revolutionary army were Cincinnati. Maj. John Doughty of the New York society was chief of artillery from 1789 to 1791 and for a time commander of the entire government force, and Cincinnati led the principal campaigns against the Indians. Brig. Gen. Josiah Harmar of Pennsylvania was general in chief of the army when he was defeated on the Miami River in Ohio, October 1790. Maj. Gen. St. Clair, governor of the Northwest Territory, general in chief, as well as president of the Pennsylvania Cincinnati, fared no better at Maumee on November 4, 1791, a battle in which many Cincinnati died. Among those who fell were Patrick Phelon of the Massachusetts society, John Reed and William Piatt of New Jersey, Richard Butler and Edward Spear of Pennsylvania, and Robert Kirkwood of Delaware. Winthrop Sargent was wounded.

In August 1794, however, Maj. Gen. Anthony Wayne, who had succeeded to the post of general in chief, was victorious at Fallen Timbers. His Treaty of Greenville the following year established peace with the Indians, and settlements in the West increased still further. Thomas Posey of the Virginia society, who held an appointment as brigadier general during that critical period, later went on to become governor of the Indiana Territory from 1813 to 1816.

Cincinnati were no less evident in naval commands. Of the six captains appointed in 1794, John Barry, Samuel Nicholson, Silas Talbot, Richard Dale, and James Sever were already members of the society. The sixth, Thomas Truxton, was elected an honorary member of New York in 1800. Unlike the army, the roster of junior naval officers did not include Cincinnati.

As the nation began life under the new Constitution, there were still those who had doubts about the Cincinnati. In Massachusetts during July of 1788 a writer to the *Boston Gazette* charged "a Distinct class of men" was becoming a "separate government." Members of the society were seeking charters under the specious label of a charitable society, yet a foreigner would blush to be considered a member of a "charitable society." "Every *real patriot* of *America* will view the *Cincinnati* as an actual assumption of Nobility—a daring invasion of the rights of *equality*." The "Grand Convention" in Philadelphia had been a farce, for the critic pointed out that the society could resume its old rules and he knew that some of the states had rejected the amended institution. The object of the Cincinnati, he warned, was still to engraft nobility to the Constitution.[67] It was an accusation which would hover over the society, and the Federalists, for another decade.

Notes

1. John Doughty to Knox, July 5, 1788, as quoted in North Callahan, *Henry Knox, George Washington's General* (New York: Rinehart, 1958) p. 270.

2. The Proceedings of the Annapolis meeting may be found in *Documents Illustrative of the Union*, pp. 39-43.

3. Circular Letter, George Washington to the State Societies, October 31, 1786, Hume, *Washington Correspondence,* pp. 264-66. Hume reprinted the copy sent to Gates, which included a special postscript to him.

4. GW to George Clinton, November 15, 1786, and to Elias Dayton, November 6, 1786, ibid., both p. 267; GW to Benjamin Lincoln, November 7, 1786, ibid., p. 269.

5. The comment is the postscript of the copy of the circular letter sent to Gates. See note 3.

6. GW to Knox, February 3, 1787, Washington, *Writings,* XXIX, 151-53.

7. Knox to Washington, March 19, 1787, Hume, *Washington Correspondence,* pp 296-97.

8. GW to Knox, April 2, 1787, Washington, *Writings,* XXIX, 193-95.

9. Mercy Otis Warren to John Adams, January 4, 1787, Adams Papers, Massachusetts Historical Society.

10. James Warren to John Adams, May 18, 1787, *Warren-Adams Letters,* Massachusetts Historical Society, *Collections* (Boston: Massachusetts Historical Society, 1925), II, 291. John Quincy Adams to John Adams, June 30, 1787, John Quincy Adams, *Writings,* I, 32-33. On objections to the society generally, see Wallace Evan Davies, "The Society of the Cincinnati in New England," pp. 1-25.

11. Jefferson to GW, November 14, 1786, Jefferson, *Papers,* X, 534.

12. GW to Knox, second letter of April 27, 1787, Washington, *Writings,* XXIX, 208-10.

13. GW to Knox, April 2, 1787, ibid., XXIX, 193-94.

14. GW to Knox, April 27, 1787, Anderson House.

15. *Proceedings,* I, 30, 30-31, 38-41.

16. George Turner to Samuel Blachley Webb, May 12, 1787, *Correspondence & Journals of Samuel Blachley Webb,* ed. Worthington C. Ford (New York: N.P., 1894), III, 78-79.

17. Schuyler, *Institution,* p. 95.

18. Gates to GW, January 19, 1787, Hume, *Washington Correspondence,* p. 287.

19. David Humphreys to GW, March 24, 1787, and April 9, 1787, ibid., pp. 297, 301-2; Arthur Lee to Washington, May 13, 1787, ibid., p. 307.

20. See Washington, *Writings,* XXIX, 213n.

21. GW to chevalier d'Annemours, February 20, 1789, ibid., XXX, 210-11; GW to de Grasse, August 18, 1788, ibid., XXX, 53-54.

22. Washington's letter declining reelection appeared in the *Boston Gazette,* May 14, 1787, and the *Carlisle Gazette,* May 23, 1787. The arrival of delegates for the Cincinnati meetings was reported in the *New Hampshire Gazette,* May 26, 1787. The *Boston Gazette,* June 4, 1787, listed the officers elected.

23. Edward Carrington to George Weedon, June 18, 1787, Hume, *Virginia Documents,* pp. 170-71.

24. Despite his many other writings of extraordinary value, Edgar Erskine Hume's article "The Role of the Society of the Cincinnati in the Birth of the Constitution of the United States," *Pennsylvania History,* 5 (1938), 101-7, is more confusing than helpful. Hume counts 27 Cincinnati at the Constitutional Convention as framers. Not even in a very broad sense was he right, for William Jackson was not a delegate at all, but secretary to the convention. Nathaniel Pendleton of the Virginia society had been named a delegate from Georgia, but did not attend, yet Hume counts him. Contrary to Hume's listing, the John Blair in the New Jersey society was not the same John Blair who was a delegate from Virginia. James McHenry of Maryland never joined the society, though he was eligible and, curiously, his son was admitted as a successor in 1816. A greater fault is that Hume counted as Cincinnati those who were admitted to the society at any point in their lives. Thus Hume's count, one would think as of 1787, includes Rufus King, who was not admitted an honorary member until 1822! Franklin and James Wilson were elected in 1789, Gouverneur Morris in 1803, and Pierce Butler in 1817. These men cannot be considered Cincinnati in any sense in 1787. Hume also missed three honorary members from North Carolina who *were* delegates, Davie, Blount, and Spaight. See Davis, *Revolution's Godchild* pp. 21-22.

25. Monsieur Otto to comte de Montmorin, New York, June 10, 1787, Farrand, *Records of the Federal Convention,* III, 43-44, Lord Sydney to Lord Dorchester, September 14, 1787, ibid., pp. 80-81.

26. *New Hampshire Gazette,* June 9, 1787. The story carried the dateline, "Halifax, Nova Scotia, May 10," and was reported by a "gentleman" who had come from New York. In a similar vein the *Independent Chronicle,* June 7, 1787,

p. 278; Livingston, p. 580; Pierce, p. 303; Brearly, pp. 181, 761.

30. Pierre van Cortlandt, Jr., who had been Hamilton's law clerk from 1784 to 1786, was spreading the story about the duke of York. He claimed too that Governor Clinton might still have a copy of the proposal. See "Nathaniel Pendleton's Memorandum on a Conversation between Alexander Hamilton and Ebenezer Purdy," February 25, 1804, Hamilton, *Papers,* XXVI, 196-99. Van Cortlandt explained that in the spring or summer of 1787 he found Joseph Strong (Hamilton's clerk from 1786 to 1789) copying the letter in question. Van Cortlandt was alarmed when he learned what Hamilton had proposed in the convention and he felt guilty at not having made the letter public, but he held back out of personal loyalty to his former mentor. Van Cortlandt to unnamed correspondent, February 27, 1804, ibid., pp. 198-99. Hamilton in 1804 labeled the story a "slander." Pendleton Memorandum, ibid., p. 197. Hamilton demanded to know whether Clinton still had a copy of the letter. He persisted in his requests, claiming a desire to clear his name. Clinton, who remembered substantially the same details van Cortlandt reported, was convinced Hamilton was simply trying to learn how much evidence survived and whether Clinton's copy was in Nathan Strong's handwriting. Hamilton to Clinton, February 27, 1804; Clinton to Hamilton, February 29, 1804; Hamilton to Clinton, March 2, 1804; Clinton to Hamilton, March 6, 1804; Clinton to Pierre Van Cortlandt, Jr., March 7, 1804; Hamilton to Clinton, March 7, 1804; Hamilton to Clinton, March 9, 1804, ibid., pp. 199-200, 202-3, 208-12.

I have not found a trace of the proposal in any records of the society, and Col. William Malcolm, who delivered a copy of the letter to Governor Clinton, was never a member of the society.

31. David Humphreys to Hamilton, September 1, 1787, ibid., IV, 240-42; Lord Sydney to Lord Dorchester, October 14, 1788, Farrand, *Records of the Federal Convention,* III, 354.

32. Clinton Rossiter, *1787: The Grand Convention* (New York: Macmillan, 1966), p. 211.

33. R. R. Livingston, "Draft of an Oration to the Society of the Cincinnati, given July 4, 1787," as quoted in Alfred F. Young, *The Democratic Republicans of New York: The Origins, 1763-1797* (Chapel Hill: University of North Carolina Press, 1967), p. 81; entry for July 19, 1787, Cutler and Cutler, *Manasseh Cutler,* I, 294.

34. In the absence of good biographical studies of members of many state societies, the figures, especially for the South, must be considered somewhat tentative. Identifications have been made on the basis of name (often perilous with repeated names in large, prominent families) and on other bases. Data on members of the state ratifying conventions may be found in Forrest McDonald, *We the People: Economic Origins of the Constitution* (Chicago: University of Chicago Press, 1958).

35. Knox to Samuel Holden Parsons, January 13, 1788, Knox Papers.

36. McDonald, *We the People,* pp. 261-63; Hugh Blair Grigsby, *The History of the Virginia Federal Convention of 1788* (Richmond: Virginia Historical Society, 1890), I, 160n.

37. As quoted in McDonald, *We the People,* p. 262.

38. Drake, *Memorials,* p. 51; Bellas, *History of the Delaware State Society,* pp. 19, 20; *Georgia Gazette,* September 4, 1788, as quoted in Foster, *Materials Relating to the Cincinnati in Georgia,* p. 23.

39. McDonald, *We the People,* pp. 286–88.

40. Delegates to the North Carolina convention are listed in *The State Records of North Carolina,* ed. Walter Clark (Goldsboro: Nash, 1907), XXII, 1–6. Their backgrounds, where they can be determined, have been analyzed carefully by William C. Pool, "An Economic Interpretation of the Ratification of the Federal Constitution in North Carolina," *North Carolina Historical Review,* 27 (1950), 119.

41. *Providence Gazette,* July 5, 1788.

42. Enos Hitchcock, *An Oration delivered July 4, 1788 at the Request of the Inhabitants of the Town of Providence* (Providence: Wheeler, [1788]), pp. 13, 14–15.

43. *Providence Gazette,* July 5, 1788.

44. Minutes of the Rhode Island Society, September 3, 1789, Rhode Island Society Archives.

45. Petition of Samuel Thayer and fourteen other members to Isaac Senter, April 27, 1789; Isaac Senter to the Cincinnati in Providence, May 5, 1789; Joseph Arnold to Senter, May 5, 1789, Rhode Island Society Archives.

46. Senter to Arnold, May 9, 1789, Rhode Island Society Archives.

47. Minutes of the Rhode Island Society, July 4, 1789, Rhode Island Society Archives. The resolution of expulsion was to be published in the *Newport Herald* and the *Providence Gazette.* Other state societies were likewise informed of the expulsion, as was normal in such cases. In the same period colleges too circulated names of students expelled to make sure punishment on one campus did not lead to welcome admission on another.

48. *Providence Gazette,* July 11, 1789. A complete list of the delegates for and against the constitution is to be found in *Providence Gazette,* June 5, 1790.

49. Bellas, *History of the Delaware Society,* p. 20.

50. Timothy Pickering, "Propositions for Settling a New State by Such Officers and Soldiers of the Federal Army as Shall Associate for That Purpose," Cutler and Cutler, *Manasseh Cutler,* I, 156–59.

51. Ibid., pp. 158–59.

52. "To His Excellent, the President and Honorable Delegates of the United States of America, in Congress Assembled," Petition on June 16, 1783. See also the letter of transmittal, Rufus Putnam to GW, June 16, 1783, ibid., pp. 159–72.

53. Palmer, *Steuben,* pp. 347n., 372.

54. *Proceedings of the Pennsylvania Society,* pp. 76, 80.

55. Cutler and Cutler, *Manasseh Cutler,* I, 178–95, provides basic organizational documents of the Ohio Company, while 203–319 offers a fascinating, detailed account of his lobbying efforts in July 1787. The list of first settlers at Marietta can be found in Joseph Barker, *Recollections of the First Settlement of Ohio,* ed. George Jordan Blazier (Marietta: Marietta College, 1958), pp. 5–6n. S. P. Hildreth, *Biographical and Historical Memoirs of the Early Pioneer Settlers of Ohio* (Cincinnati: Derby, 1852).

56. Claude François Adrien, marquis de Lezay-Marnezia, *Lettres écrites des rives de l'Ohio* (Fort Pitt [Paris]: Praullt, 1801), p. 2.

57. John May, *Journals and Letters of Col. John May* (Cincinnati: Clarke, 1873), pp. 77–79.

58. Palmer, *Steuben*, p. 369.

59. Their *Prospectus pour l'establishement sur les rivières d'Ohio et de Scioto en Amérique* is summarized in Theodore Thomas Belote, *The Scioto Speculation and the French Settlement at Gallipolis* (Cincinnati: University of Cincinnati, 1907), pp. 29-33; see also Henry Howe, *Historical Collections of Ohio* (Cincinnati: Krehbeil, 1907), I, 669.

60. Belote, *Scioto Speculation*, pp. 45-60; Howe, *Historical Collections*, I, 670-77; Beverley W. Bond, Jr., *The Foundations of Ohio* (Columbus: Ohio State Archaeological and Historical Society, 1941), p. 304.

61. Bond, *Foundations of Ohio*, p. 363.

62. Gates agreed when Armstrong resigned his appointment, and Armstrong in turn responded, "I think with you it was right & that a little in society is much more desirable than a great deal in a desert," Armstrong to Gates, as quoted in Skeen, *John Armstrong, Jr.*, p. 27.

63. Knox to Parsons, January 13, 1788, Knox Papers. In a similar vein William Constable, who would become an honorary member of the New York society in 1796, wrote a correspondent that if a civil war broke out "I mean to go to the Ohio." Constable to Henry Jarvis, February 10, 1788, as quoted in John D. Rolands Platt, "Jeremiah Wadsworth: Federalist Entrepreneur," Ph.D. diss., Columbia University, 1955, p. 191n.

64. George Turner to Winthrop Sargent, May 25, 1786, Sargent Papers, Massachusetts Historical Society: "We cannot reasonably expect they will ever become (or at the most continue) a part of the present confederation;—which is already too extensive, perhaps, to endure."

65. The proposal is quoted in Kapp, *Steuben*, pp. 586-88. See also Palmer, *Steuben*, pp. 355-59.

66. On Morgan's colony see Max Savelle, "The Founding of New Madrid," *Mississippi Valley Historical Review*, 19 (1939), 30-56.

67. *Boston Gazette*, May 26, 1788.

Chapter Six

The Original Members

GIVEN THE NATIONAL CONTROVERSY that erupted over the Cincinnati, one might well ask what kind of man would join the society? What were the members' backgrounds, education, professions, achievements, and interests? This chapter attempts to portray the characteristics of the typical and untypical members of the society.

By the 1790s the society was well established, though the general officers never really knew how well established. Despite repeated requests few societies reported the number of their members. Only New Jersey (1791) and Massachusetts (1801) printed rosters, and Knox probably never had a good idea how many Cincinnati there really were. Though names of officers of the state societies were usually published in local newspapers after July 4 meetings, the news often failed to reach the general officers. The best modern count puts the number of original members at 2,403. As 243 men were included in the French society, the Cincinnati in the United States stood at about 2,160.[1] Who were those men?

Generalizations are limited by the work that has been done on the original members. Biographical sketches of Massachusetts members have been published on four occasions (1873, 1890, 1931, 1964), making it the best-documented society. Similar studies are now being prepared for the Pennsylvania members. John Schuyler produced sketches of each member from New York, but his research was often limited to the military record alone, a comment that applies in part to published studies of Delaware and New Jersey members.[2] Asa Bird Gardiner wrote sketches of original members in Rhode Island, but never finished preparing the manuscript for publication.

On the average, at least in Massachusetts, the Cincinnati were younger men. The 213 members for whom ages in 1783 can be determined had an average age of just under 32. Generally, one assumes that generals were older than lieutenants, and usually they were. Col. Gamaliel Bradford was fifty-two in 1783, making him the oldest Massachusetts Cincinnatus, and Ens. Charles Jackson was sixteen. Yet Maj. Gen. Henry Knox, despite the mature look of the Peale portrait, was only thirty-three. Brig. Gen. John Paterson was forty.

Usually the members of the state societies were natives of that state, but migration and immigration changed that pattern to a degree. Many New England Cincinnati went to South Carolina or Georgia, and Louis Baury de Bellerive had not been eligible for the French society, for he had served as a major, but the Massachusetts society accepted him in 1789 after he became a resident of the state. His son in turn succeeded him in 1813. Steuben became a citizen of the United States on July 4, 1786, and thus was a full member, and president, of the New York society.

All officer ranks were well represented, but among those eligible, field officers were slightly more likely to join than captains or lieutenants. In New Jersey, for example, 92 percent of the eligible majors joined, but only 32 percent of the captains and 44 percent of the lieutenants. In terms of numbers, however, captains (24) and lieutenants (21) outnumbered the majors (11). Most generals, especially those who remained in the army to the close of the war, joined the society, but there were notable exceptions. Maj. Gen. Israel Putnam of Connecticut never joined, nor did Brig. Gen. John Stark of New Hampshire. Brig. Gen. John De Haas of Pennsylvania, who had left the army in 1779, never joined, but Brig. Gen. John Sullivan, who had resigned that same year, did.

Most members were army men. Navy and marine officers were welcomed, and many of them joined, but the society remained, as it began, fundamentally an army organization, and few of the naval officers became leaders of the Cincinnati.

The roster depended on the rules of admission, which varied from state to state and which varied too as states made exceptions. Virginia admitted Col. Theodoric Bland in 1785 even though he had served as a Continental officer less than half a year. Massachusetts took Capt. Samuel Newman, by special vote allowing service in the state artillery to "supply the place" of the missing year of Continental service.³ Connecticut modified its rules to require three "campaigns" rather than three years' service, and Connecticut too admitted Col. John Trumbull, who had resigned in February 1777 in a dispute over the date of his commission and precedence in rank. Trumbull had heard about the society in June 1783 and wrote Knox, well aware he had served only two years: "I flatter myself that the principle on which I quitted the Army, & which tho' at that early day little acted upon, is now acknowledged to be the Basis of Military Character[,] will be considered a full justification of my retirement."⁴ Trumbull was not the only officer who resigned over seniority or promotion, but he is the only one I have found who made the principle the basis of a successful claim to admission.

Were state troops eligible? The Virginia meeting of October 1783 held they were not, much to the chagrin of state officers. In April 1784 on behalf of such officers, Lt. Col. John Allison wrote Washington, saying of some regiments, "We composed a part of the American Army as well as those that had Continental Commissions."⁵ His letter was read at the general meeting in May 1784, and the delegates agreed that "such officers of the State troops as have served three years can be admitted as members." That decision was interpreted to mean state troops in Continental service, thus embracing units from Virginia, Rhode Island, and New Jersey. The society also accepted officers from the state navies of Virginia and Rhode Island.⁶

A mixture of motives brought individuals into the society. The Cincinnati offered a political voice to a disgruntled army and provided security through its charitable funds. Continuation of fellowship was another appealing feature. General Heath, who did explain his motives, feared that posterity would doubt his eligibility if he did not join, and Timothy Pickering claimed he had joined only because he thought all officers would. Family patterns explain some cases, as fathers and sons or brothers joined the society together as they had the army. From Newton, Massachusetts, came the Jackson family: Colonel Michael of the Eighth Massachusetts and his sons Captain Simon, Lieutenants Michael and Ebenezer, and Ensigns Charles and Amasa. All joined.

Whether a man joined probably depended too on local attitudes. Enthusiasm for the society varied from state to state, even among those qualified for membership (see table 1). Delaware had the

Table 1: Eligible officers who joined the Society of the Cincinnati

State	Total eligible officers	Number of Cincinnati	Percentage who joined
New Hampshire	201	30	15
Massachusetts	731	341	47
Rhode Island	137	72	53
Connecticut	595	251	42
New York	427	203	48
New Jersey	251	101	40
Pennsylvania	545	293	54
Delaware	57	38	67
Maryland	333	184	55
Virginia	1,417	292	21
North Carolina	331	66	20
South Carolina	212	96	45
Georgia	107	43	40
France	413	237	57
No state association		23	
Total	5,795	2,403	

smallest state line, with only fifty-seven officers eligible, but 38 (67%) of them joined, making them the most enthusiastic in enlisting under the society's banner. On the other hand, only 15 percent of the eligible New Hampshire officers joined, but, as has been seen, they were fiercely attached to the original institution. And only 20 percent of those eligible in North Carolina joined. In both states there was considerable feeling against the Cincinnati, but geography rather than philosophical doubt is the usual explanation of the small percentage (21%) of Virginians who joined. For those who settled in Kentucky, what is now West Virginia, or even the western part of Virginia proper, attendance at Richmond meetings was nearly impossible.

First to offer sociological generalizations about the Cincinnati was Mercy Otis Warren, who published her history of the Revolution in 1805. Her comments are all the more interesting because her son James was a member of the Massachusetts society. For this ardent Jeffersonian, the Cincinnati was the creation of Americans who were fascinated with "the fantastic fopperies of foreign nations." "Towards the end of the war, many gentlemen had indulged the most expensive modes of life, without resources sufficient to support pernicious habits, which they adopted from a wild fondness for novel ideas of ranks, titles, and privileged orders, little short of men of princely education, birth, and expectations. They probably might think that some badge of hereditary nobility might give consequence to certain characters and families." She saw the society as part of a historical pattern often seen in other countries. It was a "young aristocracy, that may start up from a sudden acquisition of wealth, where it had never before been tasted." These nouveaux riches disgusted patriots their senior in both respects. "The eagle and ribbon dangled at the button-hole of every youth who had for three years borne an office in the army, and taught him to look down with proud contempt on the patriot grown grey in the service of his country."[7]

In modern terms, she saw the Cincinnati as aggressively, upwardly mobile. For many, particularly in the North, that generalization was accurate.

The army was a classic means of social mobility in the eighteenth century. No less a character than George Washington had sought a military career in the 1750s as a means of personal advancement. Revolutionary service offered a chance for officer status, but not often quick promotion. Few experienced the meteoric rise of a Peter Johnston of the Virginia society. He was a student at Hampden-Sydney in 1779 when he became a cornet of light dragoons. In the Continental army he was promoted to lieutenant in 1780, captain in 1782, and in 1783 he was named brigadier general of Virginia militia, at the age of twenty.

The critical factor for most men in determining the rank at which they left the war was the rank at which they entered, and in most cases that was a reflection of previous military interests (as with Washington, Heath, and Knox) or of social or economic status or political commitment. It was common enough for a man to enter the army as an enlisted man and be promoted to lieutenant or perhaps captain, but only one member of the Massachusetts society had been promoted from ensign to lieutenant colonel, and only four who had entered the service as captains were advanced to colonel. Many officers spent the entire war in the grade in which they had entered, and if they were promoted at all, it was only by one or two ranks.

But officer rank conferred a permanent status and title, and Lt. Benjamin Pierce of the Massachusetts society was henceforth "Lt. Pierce" in daily life, until militia rank transformed him to "General

Pierce." Travelers remarked about the profusion of militia titles among Americans, but Cincinnati tended to continue using the Continental rank with which they had ended the war, often ignoring more grandiose militia rank. Aquila Giles of New York was a major at war's end, but he had become a major general of New York militia during the War of 1812. Some New York society records do refer to him as "Major General Giles," but the official notice in 1822 summoned members to the funeral of "Major Aquila Giles." It was as though Revolutionary rank was a title from a moment of historic glory, never to be altered by subsequent, less significant developments.[8]

Despite Mercy Otis Warren's comment, many Cincinnati remained in humble roles in small towns. In the Massachusetts society, for example, Oliver Brown and William Greenleaf were innkeepers. Ezra Newhall ran a stable, Sylvanus Smith was a carpenter, and Park Holland, Oliver Rice, and John Stafford were surveyors. Five members were teachers, over a dozen were local merchants, and several dozen were farmers.

Other members, however, *were* early prototypes of the American success story. Lt. Benjamin Pierce himself is a notable example. His father died young and the boy became a hand on his uncle's farm before the war, but he went on to become governor of New Hampshire. His son Franklin, a successor member, became president of the United States.

Undeniably many Cincinnati made great advances in their social and financial positions. One need look no further than Knox himself, the Boston bookseller become major general and secretary of war, the Boston lad who became proprietor of a vast estate and mansion in Maine. Hamilton too came from an obscure background to become secretary of the Treasury, son-in-law of a prominent New York family, and financial architect to the entire nation. McDougall's biographer refers to his subject's "compulsive need to achieve social recognition" and the Revolution transformed a rough sea captain on the outskirts of society into a major general and distinguished banker. The list could be expanded almost indefinitely.[9]

What role did the Cincinnati play in this mobility? The army experience, the context of creating a new political and financial structure for a new nation, and the social connections developed during the war were all more important factors than the society itself. Yet the society nurtured that old-boy network, in fact renewed it every Fourth of July. One can find letter after letter between former officers who were members of the society. Samuel Shaw left his job at the War Office in early 1786. Winthrop Sargent was looking for a post, and George Turner urged him to apply, but Constant Freeman thought Shaw's old job would not be filled. Sargent would have a better chance applying for a consulate in Europe. The salaries would be generous. As for Turner, he had written of his own plans to leave Philadelphia for Georgia where an initial investment of 1,000 guineas would buy a plantation which in three years would yield an equal amount annually. The Cincinnati as a society is not mentioned in this correspondence, yet the bond of active membership cements the relationships over the years.[10]

Many of the more successful Cincinnati were college graduates. Colleges, like the military, were a prime means of social mobility, and in either setting a young man made connections that offered a lifetime of usefulness. Those who were college graduates, or even college dropouts, *and* members of the Cincinnati are prominent among the Revolutionary officers who reached a prominence unknown to their fathers.

An estimate of the number of college men in each society appears in table 2. In the North about 10 percent of the Cincinnati had gone to college, except for Connecticut, where 20 percent were college

Table 2: College men in the society by state

State	Original members	Members who attended college	Percentage of college men
New Hampshire	30	2	7
Massachusetts	341	31	9
Rhode Island	75	10	13
Connecticut	251	54	20
New York	203	18	18
New Jersey	101	10	10
Pennsylvania	293	6+	2
Delaware	38	3	8
Maryland	184	4+	2
Virginia	292	21+	7
North Carolina	65	0?	0?
South Carolina	96	4+	4
Georgia	43	2+	5

men. It may be no accident that Connecticut was the only society to elect college presidents honorary members. For the South, the picture is different, and less clear. William and Mary alumni records are imperfect and the pattern of giving many members of a family the same name makes even a tentative count speculative, but I suspect that William and Mary alumni may account for nearly 10 percent of the Virginia society. In South Carolina and Virginia, families of wealth often sent their children to English universities or the Inns of Court in London. Thus Charles Cotesworth and Thomas Pinckney went to Oxford and the Middle Temple.

By actual count Yale produced the greatest number of collegiate Cincinnati. Princeton's twenty-six Cincinnati are perhaps more significant statistically than Harvard's thirty-five and perhaps even Yale's fifty-nine, for Princeton was a younger and smaller institution. Its president, John Witherspoon, was more a political activist than his prewar counterparts at Harvard or Yale. Table 3 reports alumni Cincinnati for all the pre-Revolutionary colleges. Figures for William and Mary and probably Pennsylvania are undoubtedly higher than the present data. King's was notably tory in its administration and alumni, but nonetheless managed to produce Alexander Hamilton. Rhode Island and Queen's were both relatively new and still small when the war began, but still contributed their share. Maj. John Stagg, one of the Queen's alumni, later became Knox's assistant at the War Department. Hampden-Sydney and Washington College (then called Liberty Hall) were both in their infancy as the war began, but Dartmouth was not. Even so, I have not found one Dartmouth alumnus among the Cincinnati.

Table 3: Society members by college attended

Institution	Members of the Cincinnati
Yale	59
Harvard	35
Princeton	26
William and Mary	10+
Philadelphia (Univ. Penn.)	7+
King's (Columbia)	5
Rhode Island (Brown)	4
Queen's (Rutgers)	3
Hampden-Sydney	2
Washington (Washington and Lee)	1?
Dartmouth	0

Mercy Otis Warren's comments were notably sharp, probably because the Massachusetts society included few sons of great families of wealth and power. They were in fact largely new men. The same comment might be made about Pennsylvania. E. Digby Baltzell has produced penetrating studies of the elites of Philadelphia, and his list of twenty-two Philadelphia families prominent before the end of the eighteenth century includes only two Cincinnati: Thomas McKean, elected an honorary member in 1783, and Charles Biddle, chosen an honorary member in 1789. Clifford Lewis has concluded that the typical Pennsylvania Cincinnatus came not from prominent Anglican or Quaker families, but from more recent Scots-Irish stock who were again the new men of the state.[11]

Mercy Otis Warren's generalization is wrong for some states, however, where several members came from the top ranks of wealth and social prominence. To name but a few examples, the South Carolina society included Charles Cotesworth and Thomas Pinckney, Isaac Huger, and John Middleton. In Virginia, Henry Lee, Benjamin Harrison, and Washington himself came from families of distinction. The New York society included several scions of the state's most prominent families. Two van Rensselaers (Jeremiah and Nicholas) were members. Philip van Cortlandt, colonel of the Second New York regiment, was son of Pierre van Cortlandt, the lord of the manor who was made an honorary member in 1784. The Livingstons were represented by Henry Beekman Livingston, brother of Chancellor Robert R. Livingston, who was made an honorary member in 1786. Henry Brockholst Livingston came from another line in the family, and his father, Governor William Livingston, was an honorary member of the New Jersey society. Lt. William Walton Morris was the son of Lewis Morris, signer of the Declaration of Independence, third lord of the manor, and an honorary member elected in 1784. Gouverneur Morris, half brother of Lewis Morris, became an honorary member in 1803.

Whether they saw themselves as a nascent or established aristocracy, there was a quality of grandeur—their critics thought pomposity—about many Cincinnati. Henry Jackson, Knox's old friend, wrote that he heard the general was living in his new mansion "in the style of an Eastern Nabob." McDougall sometimes referred to General Heath as the "Duke of Roxbury," and in a similar vein a recent biographer of Horatio Gates thought it fit to call his subject in retirement "The Knight of Traveller's Rest."[12] These may seem chance comments, but they point out a recurring pattern amongst biographies.

A propensity to elegance and luxury were only to be expected in their era among families of wealth. Knox's mansion, built in 1794, was rumored to have cost $50,000, but $15,000 seems more accurate. Its nineteen rooms were the height of architectural splendor, and Knox invited some five-hundred guests to the housewarming. Placed deliberately so that it faced France, Knox's mansion later welcomed the duc de la Rochefoucauld-Liancourt, Louis Phillipe, the future king of France, and probably the prince de Talleyrand, whose younger brother was a member of the French society. These guests presumably stayed in the "Gold Room" with its gold brocade and Aubusson rug.[13]

Knox was by no means alone in such stylish living. Steuben rented a country house near New York which he called the Louvre, and to the despair of his friends, he tried to live there on a scale in keeping with its name. By 1788 it was given up for rented quarters in New York City, where Major North kept a watchful eye on his accounts. When John Armstrong moved in for the season of 1788 and 1789, North knew the budget would not hold up. In New London, Connecticut, Jedediah Huntington, scion of a prominent Connecticut family and a founder of the society, built a mansion that echoed the architecture of Washington's Mount Vernon. In Baltimore, John Eager Howard built Belvidere between 1786 and 1794, and Samuel Smith built Montebello in 1799. All were examples of the most fashionable architecture. Elegance and luxury were part of the American dream in its earliest form, for many held that America might be a republic where virtue and a certain degree of elegance could coexist. Even opponents of the Cincinnati showed the same propensities to high style. Elbridge Gerry's credentials as a critic of the society were faultless, yet in 1786 after he married the daughter of a wealthy New York merchant, the couple foresook the fishery smells of Marblehead for the house in Cambridge formerly owned by Lieutenant Governor Thomas Oliver.[14] There they were surrounded by the same elegance which Knox himself sought.

Those who lived the grand life supported themselves from their incomes in agriculture, law (Charles Cotesworth Pinckney made some $20,000 a year in legal fees), business, or speculation—the latter a specialty with many Cincinnati. Not a few found additional security by marrying well, with Knox and Hamilton prime examples. After the war Henry Brockholst Livingston engaged in land speculations but told his father not to worry as long as he did not marry a poor wife. Father was much displeased when he seemed to do just that, but in the end his wife was heir to a sizable estate.[15]

In 1784 a Connecticut critic of the society worried that Cincinnati families might follow an "aristocratical policy" of intermarriages, and in Massachusetts at least there was a moderate propensity for Cincinnati offspring to marry each other. Two of Heath's five children married Cincinnati children, General Lincoln's daughter Elizabeth married Maj. Hodijah Baylies, himself a member, and the daughter of Rufus Putnam married Benjamin Tupper, Jr.

Marriage between a member of the society and the daughter of one of its strongest critics was sure to demand adjustments. Abigail Amelia Adams, daughter of the American minister to Great Britain, married Lt. Col. William Stephens Smith in 1786, and the Cincinnati assumed a new aspect in the Adams household. Two years later the senior Abigail Adams wrote her daughter of talks with Knox: "Genral Knox will tell you, when you see him, how completely I am initiated into the order of Cincinnatus, without any vote of the Society."[16]

If the Cincinnati were socially mobile, they were equally mobile in geographic terms. Only 19 percent of the Massachusetts Cincinnati lived after the war in the town where they had resided before the conflict, and when the New Jersey society published its roster of 102 members in 1791, 20 were no longer in the state. Six had gone to New York, 4 to the "Western Country," 2 each to Maryland, Virginia, and Pennsylvania, and one to Kentucky and one to Georgia. Two were serving in the Western Army.[17] As will be seen, the allure of western lands brought heavy migration of Cincinnati to upper New York, western Pennsylvania, Kentucky, Ohio, and Tennessee. There were also a significant number of northern Cincinnati who thought, as had Constant Freeman, that fortune awaited them in South Carolina or Georgia.

Maj. Lewis Morris IV, son of the last lord of the manor of Morrisania and a Princeton graduate of 1774, brings together several themes of this chapter. While serving in the South he met

Nancy Elliott, who reportedly already had a fortune worth at least £25,000 sterling, an extraordinary sum. After they were married, Morris divided his time between New York and South Carolina where he joined the Cincinnati.[18]

Cincinnati gained prominence in almost all fields, with the rather interesting exception of the clergy. Save for Connecticut, comparatively few of the Revolutionary chaplains became members of the society. I shall give a few examples of original members in several fields, though the lists could be expanded almost indefinitely.

In the law the Cincinnati were often dominant forces of state bench and bar. Hamilton was a principal figure among New York lawyers, just as Charles Cotesworth Pinckney was in Charleston. Henry Brockholst Livingston was a justice of the United States Supreme Court, while David Brearly and William Sandford Pennington, both of New Jersey, were federal district judges. Return Jonathan Meigs (Connecticut) and James Mitchell Varnum (Rhode Island) were judges in the Northwest Territory, and Joseph Anderson (Delaware) was territorial judge for the area south of the Ohio River. Edward Roche of Delaware, on the other hand, spent a quiet career as a local justice of the peace.

In state politics Cincinnati played varying roles. Many served in state legislatures or municipal elective offices, but the states varied considerably in their willingness to elect Cincinnati governors. The society itself was not an election issue, but where opposition to the society had been strong, voters seemed to remain wary of members. From 1783 to 1825 only one of the eleven men who were governor of New Hampshire was a member—John Sullivan. Connecticut chose nine governors during those years and elected only one member, Jonathan Trumbull, and Rhode Islanders waited until the War of 1812 to elect William Jones governor, again the only member out of nine incumbents. South Carolina, home state of Aedanus Burke, chosen sixteen governors before 1825, and among them only William Moultrie and Thomas Pinckney were members. Massachusetts, home state of the Adams family and Elbridge Gerry, also waited until the nineteenth century before entrusting the office to two Cincinnati. Both John Brooks and William Eustis had been involved in the drama at Newburgh in 1783. Paradoxically, Delaware, where officers were most eager in enrolling in the society, chose few Cincinnati governors. Three of twenty governors were

Cincinnati, among them David Haslet, first successor member to serve as a governor.

Other states chose members of the society with great regularity. Six of ten governors of New Jersey were Cincinnati, serving almost continuously from 1783 to 1815. The record in New York is not quite so continuous, but four out of seven were members. Morgan Lewis went on to become president general of the society, and De Witt Clinton was another successor member who held a governorship.

The other states elected governors intermittently, with the percentages of member governors ranging from 22 percent in Virginia to 43 percent in Pennsylvania.

A year-by-year analysis of Cincinnati governors shows that just after the Revolution members usually presided in six to seven state houses each year. Between 1789 and 1793 the figure slips to an average of five, but from 1793 to 1802 Cincinnati preside in at least six states each year. After 1808 Cincinnati generally account for only two to three governorships in a year. As will be seen, even though the society was in large measure a determined Federalist organization before 1800, a great number of later Cincinnati governors were Jeffersonian Republicans.

Those who had acted as regimental surgeons were more likely to join the society than the former chaplains. Twenty-one members of the Massachusetts society were doctors, and most continued in practice after the war, reaching perhaps more distinction in other fields than in medical scholarship or research. John Hart, for example, served five terms in the Massachusetts senate, and Francis Le Baron Goodwin became judge of the state supreme court. Eustis and Brooks were governors, and Brooks served as President of the Massachusetts Medical Society as well. James Tilton, president of the Delaware society, was a medical scholar of prominence, publishing *Economical Observations on Military Hospitals* (1813) as well as papers on rabies and agriculture.

Cincinnati were pioneers in commerce and industry. In large measure the China trade was opened by Cincinnati. Samuel Shaw of the Massachusetts society was supercargo on the *Empress of China*, the first American ship to enter the direct China trade. The captain of the ship was John Green of the New York society, Robert Johnston of New York was surgeon, and Andrew Caldwell of the

Pennsylvania society was surgeon's mate. Thomas Randall of Massachusetts was another supercargo, and Robert Morris, an honorary member in Pennsylvania, was half owner of the ship.[9] In later years three former naval officers were active in the China trade, John Barry and Richard Dale of the Pennsylvania society and Thomas Truxton, honorary member of New York.

In terms of marine innovation, David Bushnell of the Connecticut society was inventor of the submarine, though its first ventures were not a success. More successful on the water, at least for a while, was Aaron Ogden of New Jersey. He and fellow Cincinnatus Jonathan Dayton began a ferry service from New Jersey to New York City. Ogden later bought exclusive rights to a steamboat run from Chancellor Robert R. Livingston, honorary member of New York, and the New Jersey legislature confirmed the monopoly while Ogden was governor. The stormy end of that venture is part of chapter 9. Ogden was also an investor in the Associates of New Jersey, who founded Jersey City.

David Humphreys of the Connecticut society, in addition to his literary and diplomatic endeavors, opened mills to produce paper, wool, and cotton, and Isaac Craig of the Pennsylvania society was a pioneer in two senses when he opened a glassworks near Pittsburgh in 1798.

Cincinnati were prominent as bankers. Alexander McDougall was first president of the Bank of New York, which began in 1784 when the New York Cincinnati opened account No. 1. He was followed as president by Jeremiah Wadsworth of the Connecticut Society who served but a year, but Matthew Clarkson of the New York society ran the bank from 1804 to 1825.

Jedediah Huntington, one of the founders of the society, was a banker among other things. He was sheriff of New London County and judge of Probate in Norwich at the time he was chosen treasurer. He resigned from the bench upon election, but continued as sheriff. When Washington named him collector of the Port of New London, there was a public uproar about holding three posts simultaneously. He went on to add to his tasks the presidency of the Union Bank in New London, chartered in 1792. In nearby Norwich his half brother Ebenezer was president of the Bank of Norwich which opened in 1796.

As will be seen in Chapter 8, several members of the society were vigorous speculators. Richard Platt, Aaron Ogden's classmate at Princeton and a member of the New York society, often joined with William Duer, an honorary member of the New York society, in pursuit of a wide variety of speculations. On the whole, land deals had great appeal to the Cincinnati.

Artists were few among the Cincinnati, but two made a major contribution to developing the national iconography. John Trumbull of the Connecticut society produced a series of canvases illustrating the major moments of the Revolution, from the *Battle of Bunker Hill* to the *Surrender of Cornwallis* and the *Resignation of Washington*. In the Capitol of Washington, D.C., his paintings have provided millions of Americans with what is probably the standard image of Revolutionary scenes, and engraved versions spread his work even more widely. Trumbull also did a series of portraits of Revolutionary officers, plus many canvases of Washington.

James Peale of the Maryland society did his part too in developing the Washington iconography. Washington sat for him in 1787 and again in 1795, sittings which were the basis of many copies he and other members of the family produced. Peale also illustrated major scenes of the Revolution, most notably *Sir Peter Parker's Naval Attack on Fort Moultrie* (c. 1782) and *The Generals at Yorktown* (1785).

After the war some members continued their trades as craftsmen, often of high distinction. Pieces of furniture by Benjamin Frothingham of Massachusetts are counted among the classics of American decorative arts. Less well known as a cabinetmaker was Lebbeus Loomis, a member of a prominent cabinetmaking family in Connecticut who migrated to New York. Among his works was a coffin for his fellow member Aquila Giles.[20] Enos Reeves of Pennsylvania became an accomplished Charleston silversmith.

Cincinnati made a variety of contributions to literature. Joel Barlow, a Yale graduate of 1778 had served as a chaplain in the army, but later became a lawyer and journalist. In 1787 he produced his long poem *The Vision of Columbus,* an epic review of the broad sweep of history and the hope America held for the world. It was dedicated, with permission, to King Louis XVI, and subscribers to the original edition included 17 generals, 33 colonels, 17 majors, and 52 captains. With this aid from his fellow Cincinnati, Barlow made over $1,500 on the first edition. Barlow later went to Paris as agent for the Scioto Company, became filled with fervor for the French Revolution, and served as American consul in Algiers from 1795 to 1797. Later he followed John Armstrong as American minister to France.

David Humphreys, Washington's aide de camp and a Yale graduate of 1771, was associated with Barlow in writing the *Anarchiad,* a poetic satire of politics under the Confederation. It attacked the anarchistic tendencies in American society and Aedanus Burke and the comte de Mirabeau for their criticism of the society. Humphreys produced a notable body of nationalistic poetry (*A Poem on the Happiness of America,* 1786, *A Poem on Industry,* 1794), as well as a much reprinted life of Israel Putnam which he sent to the Connecticut society in manuscript form in 1788. Like Barlow, Humphreys was also a diplomat, serving in both Portugal and Spain.

Other Cincinnati published a variety of works. Simeon de Witt published the *Elements of Perspective* in 1813; Steuben's military manual remained in print for years; and Lewis Nicola translated several foreign military works for publication. Many members published orations, sermons, and political pamphlets, but Enos Hitchcock of the Rhode Island society was a novelist of sorts. His *Memoirs of the Bloomsgrove Family* (1790) was really a treatise on education in the form of a novel.

William Jackson of Philadelphia, who was secretary general for twenty-nine years, was by training a lawyer, but in 1804 he became editor of the *Philadelphia Political and Commercial Register,* a strongly Federalist publication which taught the deference due the upper levels of the social hierarchy.

Cincinnati were active members of the associations, academies, and historical societies that sprang up across the nation. Lewis Nicola was a member of the American Philosophical Society and editor of the *American Magazine, or General Repository.* John Trumbull was president of the American Academy of Fine Arts from 1816 to 1825, and James Monroe of Virginia was vice president of the Richmond Society for Promoting Agriculture when it was established in 1810.

Cincinnati were prominent on the boards of colleges. Joseph Bloomfield was a major figure on Princeton's board, as was Simeon de Witt on the Regents of the University of the State of New York.

Matthew Clarkson spent forty-one years on the New York Board of Regents, even longer than the thirty years he was a governor of the New York Hospital. In Marietta in 1801 Rufus Putnam became a trustee of the new Ohio University, and many more such examples of public service could be listed.

Abraham Baldwin was a prominent member connected with education whose career illustrates the social mobility possible for an individual with both army and college connections in addition to individual genius. He was the second son of a Connecticut blacksmith, but like his brothers he went to Yale, Class of 1772. A chaplain in the Revolution, he declined the professorship in divinity at Yale to study law. With the advice of General Nathanael Greene he moved to Georgia, where he joined the Georgia society. Almost immediately he was elected to the legislature, and in 1784 he proposed establishing the University of Georgia. When it was chartered in 1785, he became first president of the board of trustees, a post he relinquished in 1801 to become president of the university itself. Since he had been United States senator since 1799, he held the presidency only briefly. Earlier he had been a member of the constitutional convention of 1787, the role he regarded as his most important.

Early defenders of the Cincinnati argued that the society was no more harmful than the Masons, who were presumably no threat at all. In many instances the Cincinnati were the Masons. In Connecticut 40 percent of the Cincinnati were Freemasons, in Pennsylvania 36 percent. In many instances individuals joined the Masons after joining the society.[21] In both states distribution of Masonic membership was relatively even throughout the officer ranks, but again majors showed the highest propensity to join: 64 percent of Connecticut Cincinnati who had been majors were also Masons, 53 percent in Pennsylvania. It should be noted that Washington, Hamilton, Steuben, and Rufus Putnam were also Masons, as were dozens of other Cincinnati. Many, like Putnam, had joined the lodges which moved with the army during the war.

One Cincinnatus owed his life to Masonic rituals. Lt. Col. William Stacy was captured by a band of tories and Indians in 1778 and was about to be tortured at the stake. He made the Freemason's sign to the officer in command, who released him from torture but nonetheless held him prisoner.[22]

It is sometimes said that the last century in American history has been devoted to making the godlike Founding Fathers into humans with foibles, and there has been an equal assumption that history makes mortal leaders godlike in retrospect. To the twentieth century Jefferson seems a philosophical hero, while to his Federalist contemporaries he was something approaching the devil. Yet a salient aspect of Cincinnati orations was the praise members bestowed liberally on their fellow revolutionaries. They were conscious that they had been the means of a grand historical transformation, an event that would change European history as well as their own. Rhetorical praise for their compatriots knew few bounds, for the men had every confidence that they had been led by immortals and that history would give the whole army a superhuman stature. From their point of view, orations were filled with truth, not hyperbole.

The names of children document that admiration. Among the children of the original Cincinnati in Massachusetts, for example, might be found George Washington Cobb, George Washington Sargent, Horatio Gates Cook, Lafayette Perkins, William Augustus Steuben North, Frederick Augustus Sawyer, Henry Knox Hall, Rufus Putnam Stone, and Alexander Hamilton Gibbs. Henry Dearborn Pierce, brother of President Franklin Pierce, was born in 1812 when Dearborn had gained prominence in a second war.

It was not only the generals who were commemorated in names of sons. The father of Gamaliel Bradford Sawyer had not even served in the regiment Bradford commanded. Samuel Shaw Lillie was named for his father's colleague in Knox's artillery. Knox himself named a son Henry Jackson Knox after his old friend, colonel of the Fourth Massachusetts, and a regimental captain had likewise named his son Henry Jackson Hunt.

There was also a fashion, limited though persistent, of naming sons for Cincinnatus. Among children of Massachusetts members were Lucius Quintius Cincinnatus Bowles and L. Q. C. Nason. L. Q. C. Roberts, admitted to the New York society in 1861, was the son of an original member of the South Carolina society. Best known of the Cincinnatus namesakes was L. Q. C. Elmer (1793–1883), congressman, attorney general of New Jersey, and associate justice of the New Jersey Supreme Court. Fittingly, he was also president of the New Jersey Society from 1871 until his death. Perhaps the ultimate in patriotic names among the sons of the original members was David Washington Cincinnatus Olyphant of South Carolina. (Paradoxically, Cincinnatus Ashe, a captain of Marines had died during the war and never became a member. It may be worth noting that L. Q. C. Lamar, associate justice of the United States Supreme Court, was not the son of a member.)

In addition to the Revolutionary officers, who soon became known as legal or original members, the institution provided for honorary members, who could number no more than 25 percent of the number of legal members in a state society. The institution stipulated only that honorary members be men "eminent for their abilities and patriotism, whose views may be directed to the same laudable objects with those of the Cincinnati." Honorary members were admitted only for their own lives, without right of hereditary succession. (South Carolina, however, granted such a right in the mid-nineteenth century.)

The institution was mute on procedures for election, but honorary members were usually nominated by the former officers and elected at annual meetings. Somewhat surprising was Connecticut's establishment in 1784 of a committee to "receive Applications from any Gentlemen who may desire to become honorary members."[23]

States were uneven in their elections. Before 1800 Maryland chose only one honorary member, Governor William Paca, elected in 1783. New Hampshire, Massachusetts, Delaware, and South Carolina chose none. But by 1800 New York had chosen twenty-five and Pennsylvania eighteen.

Governors, senators, chief justices, and prominent political leaders were natural candidates, and New York added a few leaders of state troops who did not qualify as honorary members. In a few cases clergymen were chosen, as was John M. Mason in 1805 after delivering an oration on the death of Hamilton before the New York society the previous year.

Several honorary members clearly shared the same "laudable objects" as the former officers. Robert Morris, who had pressed for the impost to fund commutation and the national debt, was an obvious choice, and he was elected to Pennsylvania in 1783. Gouverneur Morris was an equally obvious choice, but he was omitted until New York elected him in 1803. New York speculator and financier William Duer was elected by the New York society in 1784, and Pennsylvania added three other speculators in Continental paper: William Bingham, David Lenox, and Blair McClenaghan. Charles Biddle, also elected in Pennsylvania, was a Federalist politician of considerable means, and neither Biddle nor Bingham made any effort to disguise a sense of elitism. Bingham's elegant country house became the symbolic focus of a very real attack by a Republican mob in 1795.

Generally, honorary members did not contribute to the charitable funds, nor were they eligible to share in benefits. However, in Pennsylvania Chief Justice Thomas McKean made a voluntary contribution of $117.89, while speculators Robert Morris and William Bingham offered the largest individual contributions in the state societies, $600 and $800, respectively.[24] That speculators should contribute so heavily to a group organized in part to promote the funding of securities is interesting to say the least.

Steuben may have tried to use honorary memberships to bring old opponents into the fold. In the Steuben papers there is an address delivered to the New York society on March 11, 1789. At the bottom is a note, in French, probably passed to Hamilton during the meeting. It translates: "Alexander Hamilton, how can we bring John Jay into our society? Is there not some way to receive high constables (*connetables*) as members?"[25] Jay never joined, but an even more unlikely man did. Benjamin Franklin had ridiculed the society in 1784 and helped Mirabeau with his pamphlet, but in 1789 he accepted honorary membership in the Pennsylvania society. That year the Pennsylvanians also elected James Wilson, another architect of the new Constitution which had just gone into effect.

There are surprises among those not elected honorary members. John Adams was an old foe, but in 1798 he and the Cincinnati had many flattering comments for each other during the Quasi War with France. He was never elected. John Witherspoon, president of Princeton, labored hard for independence, but he was never chosen, nor were college presidents generally in the 1790s when the colleges were as firmly Federalist as the Cincinnati. Only two presidents were elected, both from Yale.

Connecticut elected Ezra Stiles in July 1784, and in a year of clamor about the society, the president of Yale was anything but a critic. Accepting his election, he wrote: "This Fraternity will figure beyond any that was ever instituted in any part of the World, and it will build its Perpetuity and Universality of Estimation upon an

Achievement, which will be as immortal, or shall I rather say as durable as the World itself. All nations must be told of the Sovereignty of America; all nations must resound Praises & Glory of Gen. Washingtons Army; all Nations will honor the Society of the Cincinnati."[26] Given that restraint, one has little doubt of the direction Stiles urged on his students when they debated the following question at the September commencement that year: "Is the Society of the Cincinnati dangerous to the United States?" Stiles became an active member who attended many state meetings and went to the general meetings in 1787. In 1795 Timothy Dwight followed Stiles as president of Yale and as an honorary member of the Cincinnati society. He was a reliable Federalist, and when the Connecticut society disbanded in 1804, it lodged the residue of its funds in the politically safe hands of Timothy Dwight's Yale rather than the treasury of the state.

The status of honorary members was unclear in the institution. Were they fully members? Could they hold office? L'Enfant had taken pains to create a visible distinction between the two categories of membership. "Legal members" wore the eagle in the third buttonhole of the uniform, while honorary members wore the badge at the neck.

Records show that honorary members were often as active as legal members. Jonathan Dickinson was a delegate to the general meeting of 1784, where he played a major role in amending the institution. Thomas McKean was vice president of the Pennsylvania society from 1785 to 1798, and David Lenox was president from 1807 to 1828. Elias Boudinot of New Jersey was elected a delegate to general meetings on twelve occasions. Thus in the chapters that follow honorary members are treated as full members in terms of their mutuality of interests with the legal members. Honorary and legal members were just as likely to be on opposite sides of the constitutional debates of 1788 and 1789 and about equally likely to become Jeffersonian Republicans when Cincinnati began moving out of the Federalist fold. Attendance records of both groups at annual meetings were about the same too.

From the first, critics and some members, like Timothy Pickering, were dubious about the society's self-proclaimed role as defender of the nation's liberty. The Cincinnati never claimed an exclusive right to that role, but as will be evident, they did see it as their special mission. The exchange of letters between Generals Greene and McDougall in 1780 had set the tone, still reflected in memorials adopted in 1818. While civilian leaders were paid and living in baroque luxury in Philadelphia, the army officers were unpaid, sacrificing their lives, health, and fortunes in the camps. The Cincinnati had little doubt that they had played the principal role in making the United States a free and independent nation. Having done that, they were not about to see themselves forgotten or see independence transformed into anarchy. They were prepared to insist on the latter point much more than the former.

July 4 orations before the Cincinnati for the next forty years would view the Revolution as an achievement that imposed a duty on themselves and the rest of the nation to live up to the opportunity history had offered mankind. References to "mankind," "the world," and "history" abound in these orations, not as rhetorical flourishes but as the heartfelt perception of the real importance of their achievements.

As creators of independence and as children of the eighteenth-century Enlightenment, the Cincinnati never doubted that they knew what the nation was all about. For the Enlightenment, faction was the antithesis of the general good. Despite Hamilton's coauthorship of the *Federalist Papers* with its theory of checks and balances and countervailing forces between self-interested groups, Cincinnati orators generally saw one true and historic national interest.

Representative of the sentiments of many members, and orations, was the address Elias Boudinot delivered before the New Jersey society in 1793, the tenth anniversary of the peace and of the society. He reviewed the sacrifice of the officers during the war and reminded them that the society grew out of a rejection of the Newburgh conspiracy: "The victorious bands unite together, they despise the infamous idea, they refuse to listen to the Siren's song, they form the social tie, they cast in the remaining fragment of their scanty pay."

He then reminded his fellow members of their enduring obligation. "May the rights of men and the purity of a free, energetic, and independent government, be continually cherished and promoted by every Son of Cincinnatus!" The Cincinnati had helped create a society in which "the meanest citizen of America educates his beloved child with the well-founded hope, that if he should become equal to the task, he may rationally aspire to the command of our armies . . . or even to the filling of the presidential chair." Vigilance was the price of maintenance for such a free government, for "mistaken and wicked men (who cannot live but in troubled waters) are often laboring with indefatigable zeal . . . to sour the minds and derange the best formed systems." The Cincinnati should always therefore "keep the pure and unadulterated principles of our Constitution always in view," watching elected officials with great care lest some sour mind create a faction contrary to the general good.

Boudinot offered an extended, cosmic view of what the future might hold, concluding, "Who knows but the country for which we have fought and bled may hereafter become a theatre of greater events than yet have been known to mankind." It was a vision many Cincinnati shared.[27]

Who were the Cincinnati? The answer is available in visual form in the portrait of Benjamin Tallmadge and his son. Schooled in the Enlightenment view of history and men, a Yale graduate of 1773, Tallmadge had served with distinction as major in the Second Continental Dragoons. Subsequently he was a staff officer at Washington's headquarters. After the war he was a merchant, importer, investor in Ohio lands, and a Federalist member of Congress from 1801 to 1817. He bought an imposing house in Litchfield, Connecticut, and he served as president of the Connecticut Cincinnati. Ralph Earl painted him in 1790 in civilian dress, for in the words of the institution "the glory of soldiers cannot be completed without acting well the part of citizens." His look is one of pride in the past and confidence in the future. And with him in this prosperous setting, both scholarly and mercantile, was his son William, who he had every reason to think would succeed him in the Cincinnati and in the enjoyment of the growing blessings of a new free government in a transformed world.

Notes

1. Metcalf, *Original Members*, p. 360. A roster of original members is also to be found in William Sturgis Thomas, *Members of the Society of the Cincinnati* (New York: Wright, 1929).

2. Drake, *Memorials;* Bugbee, *Memorials;* Frank Smith, *Memorials of the Massachusetts Society of the Cincinnati* (Boston: Privately printed, 1931); Bradford Adams Whittemore, *Memorials of the Massachusetts Society of the Cincinnati*

(Boston: Society of the Cincinnati of Massachusetts, 1964); Schuyler, *Institution; The Society of the Cincinnati in the State of New Jersey* (Trenton: Murray, 1898); Irving C. Hanners, *The Society of the Cincinnati in the State of New Jersey* (Bethlehem, Pa.: Times Publishing, 1949); *Two Hundred Years of the Society of the Cincinnati in the State of New Jersey* (Washington, D.C.: Society of the Cincinnati in the State of New Jersey, 1981), a work which includes considerable information about the background of members; Bellas, *History of the Delaware State Society*.

3. July 4, 1788. *Massachusetts Minutes*, p. 66.

4. John Trumbull to Knox, June 20, 1783, Knox Papers.

5. John Allison to GW, April 26, 1784, Anderson House: *Proceedings*, I, 12.

6. See for example *Circular Letter of the Society of the Cincinnati in the State of Rhode Island and Providence Plantations*, June 13, 1893 (Providence: Rhode Island Society, 1893), p. 15.

7. Warren, *History*, III, 290, 298, 286.

8. Schuyler, *Institution*, p. 215.

9. Champagne, *McDougall*, p. 205.

10. George Turner to Winthrop Sargent, February 19, 1786; Constant Freeman to Sargent, February 26, 1786; Turner to Sargent, June 17, 1786; Turner to Sargent, May 25, 1786. Winthrop Sargent Papers.

11. Clifford Lewis 3d to Minor Myers, Jr., personal communication.

12. Henry Jackson to Knox, as quoted in Callahan, *Knox*, p. 357; Drake, *Memorials*, p. 15; Samuel White Patterson, *Horatio Gates: Defender of American Liberties* (New York: Columbia University Press, 1941), chap. 17.

13. Callahan, *Knox*, 338-64.

14. Billias, *Elbridge Gerry*, pp. 147-49. See also Edgar de N. Mayhew and Minor Myers, Jr., *A Documentary History of American Interiors from the Colonial Era to 1915* (New York: Scribners, 1980), pp. 78-86.

15. Richard A. Harrison, *Princetonians: 1769-1775: A Biographical Dictionary* (Princeton: Princeton University Press, 1980), pp. 401-4.

16. *Connecticut Journal*, March 31, 1784; Abigail Adams to Abigail Adams Smith, November 11, 1788, as quoted in Katherine Metcalf Roof, *Colonel William Smith and Lady* (Boston: Houghton Mifflin, 1929), p. 205.

17. On the Massachusetts society see Howard E. Arbesman, "The Society of the Cincinnati," Senior Honors Thesis, Harvard University, 1965; copy at Anderson House. *A List of Names of the Members of the Cincinnati in the State of New Jersey, with the Rank they held in the Army, made in 1791*, broadside, 1791.

18. Harrison, *Princetonians*, pp. 416-19.

19. I owe these references to Clifford Lewis 3d.

20. Loomis's bill for the coffin, dated June 17, 1822, is the New York Society papers, Anderson House.

21. Carleton M. Atwater, "Connecticut Society of the Cincinnati: Original Members and their Masonic Connections," manuscript, 1966, Anderson House. Clifford Lewis 3d provided data on the Pennsylvania members.

22. Smith, *Memorials*, p. 434.

23. Minutes of July 7, 1784. *Records of the Connecticut State Society*.

24. List of Members and State of Funds, 1789, Pennsylvania Society Archives.

25. Steuben, Draft Address, March 11, 1789, Steuben Papers, New-York Historical Society.

26. Ezra Stiles to Samuel Holden Parsons, July 24, 1784, *Papers of the Connecticut State Society.*

27. Elias Boudinot, "Oration before the Society of the Cincinnati in the State of New Jersey," July 4, 1793, in J. J. Boudinot, ed., *The Life, Public Services, Addresses, and Letters of Elias Boudinot, LL.D.* (Boston: Houghton Mifflin, 1896), II, 370, 371-72, 373, 366, 378.

Maj. Gen. Henry Knox, after a painting by Gilbert Stuart. Knox was principal founder of the society. (Boston Museum of Fine Arts)

Baron Frederick Wilhelm von Steuben, *from a painting by Ralph Earl. Steuben was presiding officer at early organizational meetings of the society. He is shown here wearing the badge of the society together with the collar badge and star of the Order of Fidelty of Baden. (Yale University Art Gallery. Gift of Mrs. Paul Moore in memory of her nephew Howard Melville Hanna, Jr.)*

Verplanck House, Fishkill, N.Y., Steuben's headquarters, where institution of the society was adopted May 13, 1783. (Society Collection)

His Excellency George Washington, Lieutenant General, *engraving by David Edwin c. 1798. This engraving is one of the few in the eighteenth century to show Washington wearing the eagle. It was issued when he assumed command of the army. Many prominent Cincinnati held important commands. (Yale University Art Gallery. Mabel Brandy Garvan Collection. Photograph by Josepy Szaszfai)*

The diploma, or certificate of membership, of the society, designed by Maj. Pierre L'Enfant. (Society Collection)

The badge of the society, France, 1784. This badge was the gift of General Washington to Lt. Col. Tench Tilghman. (Society Collection)

The diamond eagle, gift of the French navy to Washington in 1784. It is now the badge of office of the president general. (Society Collection)

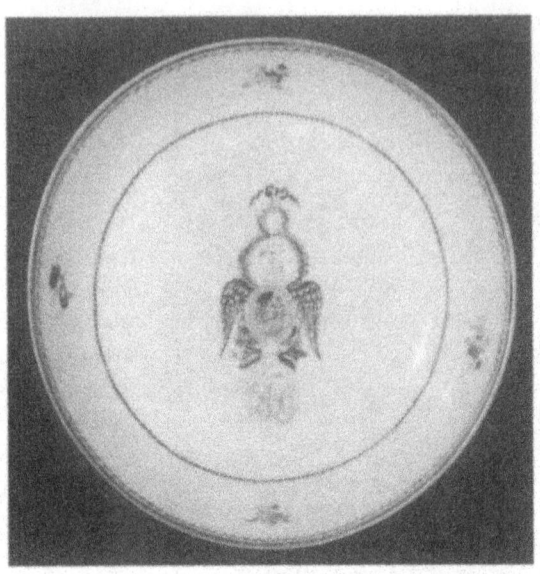

Chinese export porcelain decorated with the badge of the society. From a tea set owned by Maj. Gen. Benjamin Lincoln of Massachusetts. (Society Collection)

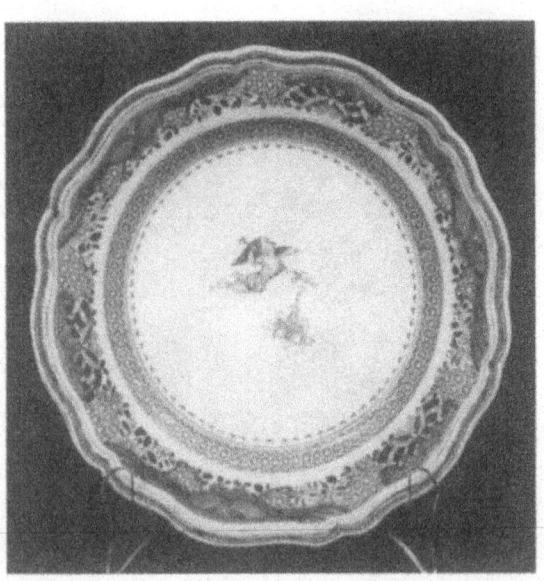

Chinese export porcelain decorated with the badge of the society. From a set owned by Washington. (Society Collection)

L'Enfant's design for the silver medal of the society. It was not struck in the eighteenth century. (Society Collection)

The marquis de Lafayette, prominent leader of the French society. He wears the eagle, the Order of Saint Louis, and the decoration voted the captors of the Bastille. (Society Collection)

Charles Hector, comte d'Estaing, president of the French society. (Society Collection)

The comte de Rochambeau. He wears the eagle of the society with the ribbon and star of the Order du Saint Esprit. (Society Collection)

Delegates to the 1884 Triennial Meeting at Princeton, N.J. (Society Collection)

Thomas Macdonough, U.S.N., hero of the war of 1812. Like other commanders who were made honorary members, he had himself painted wearing the eagle. (Society Collection)

Col. Morgan Lewis, president general of the society 1839–44. In this portrait by Richard Burlin he is wearing the Washington eagle. (Society Collection)

Hamilton Fish, president general, 1854–93. (Society Collection)

Asa Bird Gardiner, secretary general, 1884–1919. (Society Collection)

Banquet in Paris, 1926, to commemorate the reestablishment of the French society. (Society Collection)

Ambassador and Mrs. Larz Anderson. Mrs. Anderson gave their house to the society for its headquarters. (Society Collection)

President General Edgar Erskine Hume investing Winston S. Churchill as a hereditary member of the Society, Anderson House, 1952. (U.S. Army photograph)

President General Harry Ramsay presenting an eagle to Valery Giscard d'Estaing, president of the French Republic. Secretary General Stephen Caldwell Millet stands behind Mr. Hoyt. Treasurer General Reuben Grove Clark is at the left. Anderson House, 1965. (Associated Press)

Anderson House, 2118 Massachusetts Avenue N.W., Washington D.C., headquarters of the society. (Society Collection)

Five presidents general at the Williamsburg Triennial Meetings, 1980. Left to right: Frank Anderson Chisholm, Armistead Jones Maupin, Harry Ramsay Hoyt, John Taylor Gilman Nichols, and John Sanderson du Mont. (Photograph by Robert Livingston Acklen, Jr.)

Chapter Seven

The French Society

SELDOM DID THE SOCIETY meet without offering a toast to the king of France. Gratitude for the French alliance ran high, and American Cincinnati were flattered that the French saw membership as an honor. To at least one Frenchman, membership was more than an honor, it was a necessity. "Without the order of Cincinnatus there is no happiness for me."[1] So wrote the chevalier du Bouchet to General Gates in 1784. Bouchet was unquestionably the most eager of his countrymen, but the comment is revealing. For the Americans the society was a means of preserving friendships and funding commutation. To the French the society commemorated friendships, but the eagle was a decoration to be sought eagerly and worn with pride.

Most French regiments had left America by the time the society was formed, but from the first the French were considered members. Seven Frenchmen had been named in the institution itself, and there was the additional provision about the generals and colonels of Rochambeau's army that the society did itself "the honor to consider them members."

The French had come to America in three different groups. First were the soldiers of fortune, only a few of whom received the Continental commissions they sought. Second were men like Lafayette, de Kalb, and du Portail, nobles and regular officers of the French army who received Continental commissions and performed valiant service. Third, of course, were those officers who came after the formal alliance of 1778. The first group was rather systematically excluded from the Cincinnati, while the second and third were readily admitted. From the beginning, however, there was a distinction between those who had served under Continental commission and those who had served under the French flag.[2]

In September 1783 L'Enfant proposed to go to France to have the eagles, medals, and diplomas produced and to help organize the French society. As he put it to Knox, he wanted a commission as "chargé de affaires for the society." Even more important, he needed money to pay for the eagles which he assumed, when distributed among the French, would give the society international standing before the general meeting in May.[3] He got no special commission. Knox wrote that only a general meeting could authorize that, but he did have a certificate of membership and a general letter of introduction from Washington dated November 1, 1783. For money he had the $302 left over from the commutation funds, and he carried letters from Washington to the six French officers, other than La Luzerne, named in the institution. Washington wrote that the society had been founded to "perpetuate those friendships" formed during the war and "for other purposes mentioned in the institution."[4] With each letter went a copy of the institution and the promise of one of the first "orders" that L'Enfant was about to have made. Those French who had served under Continental commission were to pay the requisite month's pay, as Washington explained in a letter to Lafayette, which also went into L'Enfant's pouch.[5] Lafayette was fundamentally charged with recruiting these former Continental officers for the society.

Knox and L'Enfant, unfortunately, had entirely different understandings of the mission to France. Knox had done his best to correct Washington's and L'Enfant's assumption that L'Enfant would present gold eagles to all the French members. Giving them away would exceed the society's abilities and "be contrary to the practice in similar cases." The continental practice in conferring an order was to issue a certificate (thus L'Enfant's enthusiasm for the diploma) with a tinsel star. Apart from those named in the institution, it was Knox's intent that the French Cincinnati would be given a diploma and the silver medal. If they wanted eagles, Knox thought, they could buy them. That Knox was not more forceful on this point would prove costly and embarrassing.

L'Enfant was off on his own, a chargé d'affaires whether commissioned or not. By Christmas Day he could write from Paris that he had called on Rochambeau, d'Estaing, de Grasse, and Lafayette, all of whom he might have been expected to see. But he also took it upon himself to visit "such of the officers, residents in

Paris, as might from their services & rank be considered as fit for the Cincinnati." He was bouyant as he wrote back, "How highly honourable the French nation in general, think this distinguishing mark conferred by the American army."[6]

L'Enfant had arrived in France on December 8. The fundamental question facing those French officers whom he visited in the next few days was not whether the French would join but whether the court would *allow* them to join or allow the eagle to be worn. Except for the Order of the Golden Fleece, it was all but unknown for the king to allow foreign decorations at court.

On December 14 Rochambeau wrote the marquis de Ségur, the minister of war whose son had served in America. Rochambeau had the institution translated—"literally, yet in a manner to be intelligible to His Majesty"—and he wanted to know the king's pleasure in the matter. D'Estaing sent a similar inquiry to the marquis de Castries, minister of the marine and colonies, as did Lafayette to the comte de Vergennes, minister of foreign affairs and prime minister. Lafayette did not ask, he urged. "I beg of you, then Monsieur le Comte, to obtain the King's consent for those of us who are French and who are by the rules entitled to admission."[7]

News of the society spread quickly. At Strawberry Hill near London, Horace Walpole, indefatigable correspondent of the century, missed little. He heard about the society in late December, long before many Americans. Washington, he wrote the Reverend William Mason, had founded "a new military order" and sent it to Lafayette, sending Paris into an uproar. He told the same story to the countess of Upper Ossory: "As the *noblesse* spell only by ear, they took it for the order of St. Senatus. They had recourse to the calendar, and finding no such saint in heaven's almanac, they concluded it was a new canonization at Boston, and were enraged that Washington should encroach on the papacy as well as the diadem."[8]

In Paris things fell into place rapidly. After a discussion in the king's Council on December 18, the king not only approved but took the society under his personal direction. As head of state, he would be patron of the order, and he would give final assent in all claims for membership, just as he reviewed all candidates for the St. Louis. However, as the marquis de Castries explained to d'Estaing, Rochambeau and d'Estaing were to decide on the rules for the society, and the society itself could determine its size. The *Gazette de France* for December 23 carried the formal announcement together with the king's permission for his subjects to wear the eagle.

The marquis de Ségur saw the society as a means to "*preserve the names* of those who aided most actively in the establishment of independence and to *perpetuate the memory* of the alliance of France and the United States."[9] But the court saw the Cincinnati as a means to perpetuate, not just memorialize, the alliance with the new nation. It is also likely that the court thought the society might bring new fiscal stability, enabling the United States to begin paying the considerable debt it owed France.

Since the summer of 1783 the French had worried about the direction the new American government might take. Vergennes wrote La Luzerne in July that the United States continued to ask for larger loans but showed "unexampled obstinacy" in putting its finances in order. Vergennes was convinced that "we could not count on them if ever there should happen new distractions with England," and he lamented, "We are without the means of influencing the domestic arrangements of the United States."[10] The society therefore offered at least a subtle means for keeping Americans in the French orbit and closer to funding their debt. The context of international relations makes Lafayette's words to Washington on December 25 of special interest. "The Nation has been very much pleased with the attention our Society has paid to the alliance, and have found there is something very interesting in the brotherly affiliation."[11]

With royal permission at hand and L'Enfant in Paris, the first provisional meeting was held on January 7, 1784, at the Paris residence of Rochambeau, now 40 rue du Cherche-Midi. Twenty-four officers assembled, all approved by the king and all clearly included under the institution. There were two lieutenant generals (Rochambeau and Vioménil), eight maréchaux de camp (the equivalent of major general), two brigadier generals, ten colonels, and two mestres de camp commandants. Rochambeau read a letter from Washington, and those present thereupon made voluntary contributions according to their grade. Rochambeau pledged 6,000 livres, the colonels 1,000 each, and ultimately the pledges amounted to 60,000 livres, the equivalent of just under 11,000 silver dollars. This was money for the American society, not the French. Rochambeau wrote

Washington immediately that the purpose of the French society had been to "perpetuate that union which the alliance of His Majesty created between our two nations." He hoped that the subscription was "a sum worthy of this kingdom."[12]

January saw the creation of two divisions of the French society. Those who met at Rochambeau's hotel were those who had served in the French Auxiliary Army. Only those who ranked as colonels or higher were eligible. Later, men who had served in America as captains or lieutenants became eligible when they advanced to colonel. On the other hand, those who held Continental rather than French commissions were equally eligible regardless of rank. The Continental ensign was admitted to the French society, but the French major was not. D'Estaing and Rochambeau received claims of officers of the Auxiliary Army, while Lafayette became the principal judge of those with Continental commissions. Operating somewhat independently, the marquis de la Rouerie, who had commanded the Continental cavalry, admitted his officers to rights of membership without necessarily consulting Lafayette.[13]

The real day of organization for the French society was January 16, a busy time for Major L'Enfant. Soon after arriving in Paris he had commissioned the firm of Duval and Francastel to produce the order or eagle. Most would be taken to America, but some would be needed quickly for distribution to the French. Those for the French he later described as having been "made in a slight way."[14] They were substantially cheaper than those he brought back to the United States, but they were ready for distribution by January 16.

The sixteenth began with recognition of the French navy. There had been hard feelings among naval officers to whom the institution had made no reference. Were the captains excluded? Major L'Enfant had taken it upon himself to decide, as he reported to Washington, that they were "tacitly comprehended" and he handed out membership rights. He added, "How prejudicial such a forgetfulness would have been."[15]

L'Enfant therefore went first to the hotel of Admiral d'Estaing where he presented him "with the marks of the Association." He then gave the eagle to other naval officers, "as being directed by special command from the Society itself." That command, of course, was only what L'Enfant assumed the society would have said had it been asked.

That same morning officers with Continental commissions assembled at the hotel of Lafayette, and by the time L'Enfant arrived there were sixteen present, including the first successor member among the French, baron de Kalb, admitted in the place of his father, who had died in 1780.

Then the group at Lafayette's house proceeded to Rochambeau's hotel in the rue du Cherche-Midi, where the naval officers and army officers had gathered. With no small pride, L'Enfant reported he had "there invested with the order" the army officers of the French Auxiliary Army. Then followed an "elegant entertainment" which brought together all the elements of the Cincinnati in France.

The society was an instant success, and L'Enfant could write Steuben, "There are more wishes in France for the order of the Cincinnati than for that of St. Louis."[16] Many believed it was an official decoration of the new government, as the chevalier de Pontgibaud noted, "one of the first acts of the young Republic."[17]

The quest for membership soon focused on Washington, who for the next eight years carried on a vast correspondence concerning French claims, or demands.[18] Despite L'Enfant's efforts, the admirals were not satisfied their captains had been treated fairly. D'Estaing was "mortified" that the sea officers were not included on the same basis as the army colonels. And the comte de Barras, named in the institution itself, returned a conditional acceptance of membership: "I would not myself accept the decoration of the Society but that I look on it as certain that it will be very shortly in common with my ancient companions in arms." Just as the general meeting opened in May 1784, La Luzerne, a member as well as French minister to the United States delivered an official request that captains of ships (*capitanes de vaisseau*) be admitted just as the colonels of the army had been, and there were several "captains of frigates" who had been "equally useful in furthering the common cause."[19]

Lafayette too saw the omission of the captains as a mistake—"they will have much to do with American vessels, in preventing contraband trade, I suppose, or in receiving American ships into French harbours." It would be "impolitic not to put them in a good humour."[20]

The institution admitted the officers of Rochambeau's "Auxiliary Army," but what of the "Co-operating Army" under d'Estaing in

Rhode Island and Georgia? Washington was spared further concern when the French themselves decided both armies were equally entitled to admission.[21]

French admirals and generals became agents for their former subordinates, and Lafayette's private letter to Washington of March 9 carried comments on behalf of fifteen officers.[22] Some cases required clarification of rules. Others were pure politics, as in the case of Thomas Conway, who had been the focus of the Conway Cabal. His name had been suggested. Did he qualify? He served less than a year with a Continental commission, but after leaving America in 1778 he served with distinction in the French army. Lafayette had opposed any move to unseat Washington in 1778, and the marquis was convinced that Conway's candidacy was now being pressed to disgrace him. Like Washington, Lafayette was supremely conscious of his public image. "My popularity is great throughout the kingdom and this city—But amongst the great folks I have a large party against me, because they are jealous of my reputation— In a word, the pitt to one man is for me, and in the boxes there is a division." It was the men in the boxes who were holding secret meetings on Conway's membership, and Lafayette wrote, "To avoid the odium of having stifled Conway's claims, I have not discouraged a representation being made in his favor." As he put it, "The man is not worth troubling our heads about," and thus he was admitted an honorary member.

Lafayette hesitated in presenting candidates, for he held "the less members there will be in the Society, the more it is valued." Rochambeau, whose officers had been honored from the start, was dubious about admitting too many from the navy, but for different reasons. He wrote Washington that the king had allowed his officers to wear the eagle out of respect for the Americans and their general, but "if you admit all the demands that the officers of the navy make to you ... I fear that this extension may displease his majesty and I doubt he will accept." Rochambeau offered a reminder that the king approved all new members.

Lafayette, despite doubts about numbers, came out for the navy. The captains would not devalue the order, for they "are dispersed throughout the harbours" and "will not so much crowd as the land officers, because they very seldom come to the Capital."[23]

In addition to requests from commanders, Washington heard

directly from many officers seeking admission. Only one, however, came to the United States to present his case personally—the marquis du Bouchet, whose plight opened this chapter.

Bouchet had entered the artillery in 1767 at age fifteen and served continuously until 1777 when he came to the United States and was appointed a captain on the staff of General Gates. In December 1777 he went back to France for reasons of health, but he returned as an aide to Rochambeau in 1780 and stayed for the rest of the campaign. Did this French lieutenant colonel with a half-year of Continental service qualify? Lafayette, who warned Washington in advance, thought his case "groundless."[24]

The case sheds light on French military politics. Many believed that commanders supported subordinates at the expense of the subordinates of others. When it came to selecting members, Lafayette wrote, "Old Rochambeau wants to be as conspicuous as he can in that, as you know he does in every other affair."[25] Bouchet either believed such forces were working against him in France, or he was trying to invoke them in America when he sought Gates's help. Whether it was an offer or a metaphor is unclear, but he wrote Gates, "Two thousand guineas would not be so agreable, to me as this honorable reward for my services."[26]

If ancient politics were involved in Conway's case, the same issues were at work with Bouchet. He had served Gates and he was a relative of Conway, making him doubly dubious to some. Lafayette mentioned him in discussing Conway. "The whole family is a nest of rogues—du Bouchet excepted who is honest, but a fool." He continued, "Mr du Bouchet who, you know, is not a wit, has taken it in his head to go to America—Had I refused a letter it would have killed him, and out of pity I gave a private letter to you, wherein I observe that he is mad."[27]

Bouchet presented himself in Philadelphia at the general meeting, and he was a success. Indeed, it was his all but quixotic quest that made his case. He wrote Washington during the meeting that if he failed on his mission, which was no secret in France, he would "ruin Both my Carracter and all prospect, I may have of prefferment in the army." In sum, "Disappointment Would Be a Stain upon my honour, wich could never Be Blotted out."[28]

He left for France immediately after the general meeting voted to admit him. By mid-July he was back and sent a summary of his trip to Gates. "My expedition has been quick, they are amazed at it here. the fools can not conceive any one may cross the atlantick for a rubban, they only love Money and would not give a farthing for my red and light blue rubans, so much they have narrow and mercantile minds." But, he concluded, it was a question of honor, and "honour is the God of Frenchmen, and Glory their Sweet heart."[29]

When the French had met in January, they had hoped to be represented at the general meetings in May, but they were not sure whether France was to be considered one of the state societies. Accordingly, they left it to L'Enfant to ask Washington to name three delegates to represent France. Lafayette himself thought he might travel to Philadelphia for "the grand Cincinnati meeting," but business delayed his arrival in the United States until August 4.[30] The general meeting, however, was not a gathering of appointed delegates, and given the worry about foreign members, Washington was not likely to make exceptions. The marquis de La Rouerie, who was in Philadelphia, wrote that he and other French officers were ready to serve as delegates, if the assembly would admit them, but Washington delayed a response and then said that since the French were not yet fully organized no representatives could be admitted.[31]

The French were nonetheless a major focus of the meeting, as the delegates rejoiced that the French accepted membership, made provisions to admit the naval officers, but rejected the fund of 60,000 livres and forbade any future contributions from foreigners. The French society was henceforth the equal of the state societies in everything but name, for France could hardly be called a state. Washington said as much in writing Lafayette. Since "the Meeting of the Society in France, being now distinctly considered in all respects of the same authority as the State Meetings," the French would judge the claims of all French officers.[32]

In September, Rochambeau sent Washington a list of twenty-three officers duly admitted with the king's approval. But, just as Rochambeau had foretold when the naval officers were admitted, the king now ordered that there be no new admissions. The only reason offered by the marquis de Ségur who, as minister of war, reported the king's decision, was that the king thought it "not convenient that this association be perpetuated in this Kingdom." Rochambeau wrote that at least Washington would be saved some "troublesome" correspondence.[33]

On three subsequent occasions the king approved new admissions, but on April 17, 1785, the prohibition was renewed.[34] Why? In view of subsequent admissions, the growing number of Cincinnati cannot be the real cause. Two other reasons are plausible but mutually contradictory. Versailles might have responded to criticisms that the society was an aristocratic institution incompatible with the new American republic, but probably more weighty at court was the suspicion that the inherent republicanism of the Cincinnati was a threat to monarchy.

Liberal criticism of the society in France came to a head in September when the comte de Mirabeau became the French Aedanus Burke. Mirabeau, of course, would become a major figure in the French Revolution, but his career as a polemicist writing under his own name began with an attack on the Cincinnati. Earlier in 1784 the dissolute and impecunious count had sought a subject that would produce considerable royalties, and when Burke's pamphlet fell into his hands, he found his topic. At least one biographer suggests that his attack was spurred on by fraternal envy as well as philosophical conviction. His brother Boniface had served in America and just become a member of the society.[35]

By July, Mirabeau read a draft of his own pamphlet to Benjamin Franklin who approved and offered additional arguments against the society. The following month, in the midst of family legal battles, he fled to London where he finished the manuscript. The book appeared in French with a London imprint on September 20, 1784.

Considerations on the Order of Cincinnatus was an eclectic work. He borrowed from Burke's pamphlet and Franklin's letter to his daughter, and filled out the whole by reprinting a pamphlet by Richard Price and a letter from Turgot. Throughout he wrote of "us" and "our" constitution, as though he were an American. He turned to Roman history to prove that this nascent nobility would swallow the constitution and republican government along with it. "An order, which by its constitution, its extent, and its connections, must have the greatest influence in the state, will cabal, conspire, and destroy the government rather than relinquish its privileges; or, rather it will be itself the government." Like many critics, he focused on the badge, which would sprout "seeds of contagious vanity." In accepting the society, Americans were ignoring the most obvious lesson of their revolution: "Has not the American war convinced the world that an order of nobility is not necessary to our constitution?" Monarchies required nobility, but republics flourished on the principle of equality.[36]

Mirabeau counseled Americans to be content with nothing short of abolition of the society. Even with the amended institution, a century would leave descendants of the members "patricians" and all others "plebians."[37]

Doubts of liberals were matched by different doubts among conservatives. Was the society antithetical to monarchy? Mirabeau had described the Cincinnati as "a new order of citizens incompatible with our constitutions and our laws." If one assumed a French, rather than an American, orientation, one reached the same conclusion for different reasons. Of the eagles he had commented that France had permitted its officers "to accept these tokens of adoption into a republic, formed by the insurrection of discontented colonies."[38] With the hindsight of four decades the comte de Ségur, secretary of the French society, later wrote, "Such a novel decoration, and so republican, shining in the midst of the capital of a great monarchy, might well excite much reflection; but no person thought of it."[39] Ségur was wrong. The king of Sweden had great doubts about the society from the first, as will be seen, and following the July meeting, ministers at Versailles may have entertained similar suspicions.

Official organization of the French society had come, appropriately enough, on July 4, 1784. Lafayette had left for America by then, but when the French Cincinnati gathered at d'Estaing's residence, they saw the marquis as their logical president. A week later d'Estaing explained the choice. "The first rights to be president of the Society in France are without doubt to have been the most senior officer in America, to have the confidence of the President General, General Washington, to be his friend, his vicar; to be proposed by him, selected by Congress, named by the King, and received without criticism by the society. M. Le Marquis de la fayette brings together all these conditions."[40] He was to be president for life. There were to be two vice presidents, one from the navy, the other from the army. D'Estaing asked to represent the navy, and Rochambeau was chosen to represent the army. Original plans called for two secretaries. The "secretaire homme de lettres" was a post for life also, but the "secretaire militaire" was not and the comte de Ségur was selected for the latter post. No record of election of a literary secretary survives.

Of most interest to the court, perhaps, was the manner in which members dealt with the amended institution. They approved it, but with obvious reluctance, for they also asked that the hereditary principle be restored, even amplified. There had been a trend to structure European orders of merit in three to five grades, with the highest levels reserved for the great commanders. The French recognized that "it is impossible to have gradations in an American brotherhood," but they proposed some hereditary distinctions that might give similar "expression of these grades." For example, all male descendants of Lafayette should wear the eagle from the moment of their birth, while some of the children of Rochambeau and the eldest nephews of the Balli de Suffern might also wear the badge as an honor to the original officers.[41]

Some suggestions amounted to saying that the eagle would go to children, not just sons. Were the French prepared to admit women? Lest there be doubt, they declared that they were indeed: "Resolved that some French women (*Dames*) be proposed by Congress and receive an order of the King to wear the American eagle, because of service rendered by their husbands, or by their Fathers." They explained that the Order of Malta, also a military order, admitted women, yet somewhat defensively they added that the proposal was not "ridiculous or new." "The ladies of France had been the first attached to America; they had deified its defenders; they would be pleased to wear the badge, and governments have not yet drawn out all the effect which must be produced by the soft but so powerful influence of the most interesting portion of society."[42]

The French were determined to contribute to the support of the society, despite the determination of the general meeting. The treasurer was therefore to receive the month's pay from Continental officers, and the fund thus created would help any French or visiting American members who might need it. As the society explained, "France flatters herself as being also the homeland of an American."[43]

Leaders of the society were in touch with the court, for another proposal sought to smooth over a slight which the naive young nation had offered the French. A toast had been offered to the *former*

French minister to the United States at a Boston dinner, but alas none had been given for the current minister. The French thus proposed that all ministers who had served during the war be admitted. As they said, trifles (*les riens*) may have some influence on the greatest affairs.

In making this large list of proposals that July, it is not clear the French Cincinnati knew what was evident to Mirabeau—that the society was not an official order of the United States. The suggestion that Congress nominate members to the king indicates a great misreading of facts in New York.

The prohibition of new members—temporary as it happened—may have grown out of those July 4 resolutions, which included the rejection of hereditary succession and the selection of Lafayette. How well Lafayette's true opinions were known is unclear, for he was guarded in expressing himself. But d'Estaing's report was the last said of Lafayette as president. Invariably d'Estaing himself is listed as the only president the French society had before the Revolution. It is pure speculation on my part, but Lafayette must either have withdrawn after learning the results of the meeting, or he was ruled out after his opinions were known.

Lafayette had no desire to maintain hereditary succession. As early as March 8, 1784, he had written John Adams a stern letter, assuring him that the French had not created the society (Adams was reported to have called it a "French blessing") and that Lafayette had joined out of respect to his old comrades, despite his doubts about some aspects of the organization. He would gladly consent to destruction of the society should it become "unpopular" in the United States.[44]

He was more explicit about his doubts when he wrote Adams again in June. "My principles ever have been against heredity," he wrote. "Until heredity was given up, I forebore mentioning in Europe what sense I had expressed." He was even more blunt to Jeremiah Wadsworth in February 1786: "You ask my opinion respecting the Cincinnati. I wish it had not been thought of."[45]

When news of his sentiments spread, if it did, he would not have seemed the man to lead a group on record as favoring an expansion of the hereditary principle. He remained prominent in the French society, examining claims of Continental officers, but he himself was never an officer of the French society.

Honorary members were a regular part of the French society. In America honorary memberships were limited to men of considerable stature, and the French chose some of their honorary members in the same spirit, but the French also used the honorary membership in a much different way. Just as the St. Louis was awarded to those who had served twenty-five years *or* who had performed extraordinary feats, so the French gave honorary membership to a few men of great merit whose rank did not allow admission as regular members. Thus in August 1784 the French admitted the vicomte de Galbert, a lieutenant de vaisseau who had distinguished himself on numerous occasions.

The royal prohibitions of new members, issued in 1784 and 1785, were quickly forgotten, and the ministries of war and the navy were soon themselves providing documentation on behalf of candidates for the society. Rochambeau, d'Estaing, and Lafayette were again busy corresponding about officers newly proposed, and on January 11, 1788, Lafayette summoned a meeting of the Cincinnati in Paris to consider applications.[46] Those newly admitted were officers who had just been promoted to the requisite grade of colonel or capitaine de vaisseau. Since the French society had accepted the amended institution, hereditary admissions came to an end. Baron de Kalb had been admitted in 1784 before the changes were made, but in 1788 the comte de Grasse, son of the admiral who had died that year, made no headway with his own candidacy.[47] He was finally admitted to the South Carolina society in 1800.

After the war, most French members continued their careers in the army or navy. Others continued, or entered upon, diplomatic careers. The comte de Ségur was accredited to Russia, Prussia, and Rome, and, like Talleyrand, he flourished after the French Revolution despite changing political circumstances. La Luzerne became ambassador to Great Britain, while the chevalier Jean de Ternant was French minister to the United States from 1791 to 1793. Several Cincinnati were prominent in the colonial administration. Arthur, Comte Dillon was named governor of St. Christopher in 1782, before going on to succeed the vicomte d'Arrot as governor of Tobago in 1786. Comte Thomas Conway was governor general of the French establishment in the East Indies in 1787 and then became governor of French possessions beyond the Cape of Good Hope in 1789. The chevalier de Gimat served as governor of St. Lucia from

1789 to 1792, and Georges-Henry-Victor Collot governed Guadaloupe from 1792 until he was captured by the British. He was later sent on parole to the United States.

Two members of the society followed notable literary careers. The marquis de Chastellux gained fame for his volumes on travel and public policy and was elected to the French Academy. The comte de Saint Simon was one of the great writers on reform in the early nineteenth century and a principal founder of the French socialist tradition.

The comte de Bougainville was one of the prominent explorers of the century who had accomplished his important voyages before the American Revolution, while the comte de La Perouse undertook major voyages after the war.

With royal permission a few members of the society entered the service of other European nations. Eugene MacCarthy and the comte de La Prade served the Dutch, as did the chevalier de Segond, who went on to enter the Russian army in 1788. Also entering the Russian service that year was an officer who considered himself an American, John Paul Jones. As a rear admiral he took part in a campaign against the Turks. He was disappointed when he received the Russian Order of St. Anne, for others had been given the more prestigious Order of Saint George. Nonetheless, he asked Jefferson to intercede with Congress to give him permission to wear the decoration on his American uniform along with the eagle and the Merite Militaire.[48]

In the years after the war, the society provided a continuing bond between the United States and France. A good case in point was the visit to Boston of the *Leopard,* a French ship of seventy-four guns. The French Revolution was already in its first stages by September 1789 when the marquis de La Galissoniere, commander of the vessel and a member of the French society, invited the Massachusetts society to dine with him. Thirty-six members were rowed out to the ship where they found the vicomte de Ponteves-Gien, another member of the French society, a festive dinner, and toasts to "the President and Cincinnati in the United States" and "the President and Cincinnati in France." After the latter there was a cannon salute of thirteen guns. Equally splendid was the send-off. Seamen manned the yardarms and gave three cheers as the Cincinnati pulled away, and as the boats went on there was another cannon salute.[49]

If such treatment was meant to ingratiate, it was supremely successful. The Massachusetts society gave a return dinner for the French a few days later. No effort had been spared to decorate the Concert Hall, with a portrait of Washington at one end and a portrait of Louis XVI at the other. The orchestra box was a triumph of symbolism. The blue broadcloth edged in white that covered it was spangled with thirteen stars and thirteen fleurs-de-lis. The governor, state, and city officials were invited, but it was a Cincinnati party through and through. There were first toasts to Washington, Louis XVI, the vice president and Congress, the governor, and then "our President and all the Brethern of the Cincinnati." Another celebrated the harmony and friendship that had cemented the alliance of France and the United States.

Enthusiasm was still high a month later when Washington visited Boston. On October 27 the Cincinnati of Massachusetts and the French naval commanders who were members paid a formal call on the new president of the United States. The vicomte de Ponteves-Giens was commander of the squadron, the marquis de Traversay commanded the frigate *Active,* and Jean Baptiste Alexander, Durand de Braye commanded the *Sensible.* On the following day Washington took time to attend a reception aboard Ponteves-Gien's ship *Illustre.* In 1815, twenty six years later, ten officers who had been on the ship that day would go on record as saying that Washington had authorized all officers of the ship to wear the Cincinnati, a gesture to recognize the old alliance and to celebrate the new Constitution. Either the claim was dubious, or Washington had overindulged himself at a bibulous reception, for on no other occasion was he ever claimed to have marked an event by an effusive distribution of eagles. The general judgment was that the claim was dubious, and the officers were not admitted.[50]

Louis XVI had not been the only European monarch forced to make decisions about the Cincinnati. Gustavus III, king of Sweden, refused to allow his officers to wear it. As Rochambeau reported to Washington, the prohibition was "under the pretext that they were erstwhile republicans, and that he does not wish an order which recalls this."[51]

Only two Swedish officers had been considered members, the count von Stedingk and Count Axel von Fersen. Stedingk, who was already wearing the badge, was mortified by the king's rebuke. In

March 1784 he wrote his sovereign directly, saying that he had not bothered to ask permission to wear the eagle, for the society was not really an order but an organization of distinguished members who established a system of relief in a country founded on equality. In a comment which, considering its source, would have shaken Aedanus Burke to the core, Stedingk added, "Even if it one day became a title of nobility for the Americans, for the French and the Swedish it would never be anything but a mark that they had served in America with the agreement of their sovereign."[52]

Gustavus responded that as a subject and a member of the Order of the Sword, the count should have known it was forbidden to wear *any* such mark of honor without royal permission. Refusing to quibble about whether the Cincinnati was an order or a society, the king wrote that it was not in his interest to permit subjects to wear "a public mark of the success of a revolution against their legitimate sovereign." America, he recognized, was now an ally of Sweden, but the revolution which legalized independence made the eagle suspect.[53] Later, however, Gustavus seems to have relented and allowed Fersen to wear the badge while in French service. Stedingk and his descendants later wore it too.

The king of Poland was likewise critical. Thaddeus Kosciusko wore the eagle at a levee where it drew the attention of King Stanislaus Poniatowski, who studied the inscription *Omnia relinquit servare rempublicam*. He shook his head, suggesting that Poland's claim on Kosciusko should have been greater than that of some distant republic. "Methinks this inscription savours somewhat of fanaticism."[54] Kosciusko was ignored in retirement until 1788, until Princess Lubomirka interceded on his behalf. Within a year this Cincinnatus was the focal point of the Polish military effort against the Russians and Prussians.

Curiously, the monarchs of Prussia and Russia were not worried about the society. Frederick the Great recognized the eagle immediately when the comte de Ségur called on him in Potsdam, but for him it only symbolized the long absence of a French officer from the pleasures of Paris, living "without luxury, balls, perfumes and powder."[55]

One of the more romantic tales of the Cincinnati involves Maj. John Rose, as he was known to his brother officers, and the emperor of Russia. In reality he was Baron Gustavus H. de Rosenthal of

Livonia, a career officer who had killed a man and thus fled Russia as the American Revolution was beginning. He was commissioned a surgeon in the American forces in 1777, but later became an aide-de-camp to Gen. William Irvine. Only as he was about to sail back to Europe in 1783 did he reveal his identity. Once back, far from being thrown into prison on the old duelling charge, he was made grand marshal of Livonia. He continued to correspond with Irvine, and in 1805 he sent a report on the status of the Cincinnati at the imperial court. "The people have heard of my being a member of that order, will begin to think me a cheat if I do not wear it as a matter of great distinction agreeably to their notions—and moreover, the first man himself [Alexander I] has been asking me about it, and desires I should wear it." The baron said he had reached the age of fifty without the badge, but now asked Irvine to send him one, more to amuse the emperor than to gratify his own ego.[56]

Were Gustavus and Stanislaus justified in their suspicions about the Cincinnati? Were the Cincinnati naturally agents of republican thinking? Talleyrand said as much in his memoirs: "The young members of the French nobility who had enlisted in the cause of Independence devoted themselves afterward to the principles in defense of which they had shed their blood."[57]

Even though the French society consisted almost exclusively of nobles, members took a wide variety of political stances during the revolutionary struggles. Opposition to the Terror was near universal among the Cincinnati, but most seem to have supported the early phases of the French Revolution, with support dwindling as the Revolution became more and more radical. One of the first to emigrate was the vicomte de Mirabeau, the pamphleteer's brother, who left in 1790. Others adhered to the new government until the fall of the monarchy. Some maintained their enthusiasm even beyond.

On the whole the Revolution probably had the support of the greatest number of Cincinnati during its early constitutional stages. There is a curious continuity between the political centers of the Cincinnati in America and France. The French Cincinnati came to support a constitutional monarchy, the old royal family with liberal reforms tending toward the British parliamentary system. The American Cincinnati, on the other hand, were largely committed to the new Constitution of 1787 and were accused continually, and in most cases unjustly, of trying to transform it into a constitutional monarchy along British lines. Cincinnati on both sides of the Atlantic thus stood for a comparatively strong central government with balanced constitutional structures. They were all, in a sense, disciples of Montesquieu, the great French political philosopher whose grandson was a member of the French society.

Several French Cincinnati were prominent in liberal movements after 1783. Most notable of that group, Lafayette was committed to Anglo-American principles of liberty well before 1789. He worked against the legal restrictions imposed on Protestants, he was a leader of the antislavery movement, and he congratulated Washington on the new constitution in 1787, adding with respect to France, "I am heartily wishing for a Constitution, and a Bill of Rights."[58] In the Assembly of Notables in 1787 he proved himself the only notable willing to sign a request for the king to convoke the Estates General for the first time since 1615. He was convinced that America was a model worth the study of the French, and supporting his political liberalism was a domestic life far different from that of most nobles. He and his children often spoke English (a son was named George Washington Lafayette), he taught the children songs he had learned in America, and he had two Indians as servants.

The marquis de la Rouerie was a member of the assembly of the nobility in Britanny, and in April 1789 he convinced the nobles to vote for equal taxation for all. The Bailli de Suffern died for his liberal opinions in a duel following a political quarrel in 1788. And in the Estates General, it was the duc de Noailles who moved the abolition of the privileges of the nobility.

By my count, five members of the society served in the Assembly of Notables in 1787 and 1788, and no less than twenty-one were in the Estates General in 1789. Most were delegates of the nobility, but the marquis de Rostaing was a delegate to the third estate. Three Cincinnati sat for colonial possessions: the comte de Renaud de Villeverde, the marquis de Rouvray for Santo Domingo, and the vicomte de Galbert for Guadaloupe.

In 1790 Comte Alexandre de Lameth was president of the Constituent Assembly, to be followed by the duc de Noailles in February 1791 and Comte Charles de Lameth in June. The comte d'Estaing, president of the French society, supported the constitution of 1790, and when he heard that reactionaries were plotting to have the king flee, he warned the queen of the likely ill effects such a move would have.

Not only were Cincinnati leaders of the early phases of the Revolution, but the society itself became something of a political symbol. Consider the example of Camille Desmoulins on July 12, 1789. Word had just gone out that Necker had been dismissed, and Desmoulins raced to the garden of the Palais Royal, lept up on a table, and demanded that the astonished observers discuss the proper colors for a cockade. "What color shall it be? Shall it be green, the color of hope? Or shall it be blue, the color of the Cincinnati and of American independence?" Several responded, "Let it be green, the color of hope." But the color of hope was also the color of the duc d'Orléans, and the red and blue of Paris, to which Lafayette added the white of the ancien régime, thus won the day.[59]

The early phases of the Revolution soon produced their own ribbons of merit. In September 1789 the Paris Commune voted a gold medal for enlisted men who had taken part in the assault on the Bastille. It also went to staff officers of the Paris National Guard, and thus Lafayette acquired the third decoration, which appears with the eagle and the St. Louis in the portrait by J. Boze. Lafayette was responsible for the motto on the reverse, a quotation from Lucan's *Pharsalia:* "Could they be ignorant that arms are given them to defend themselves against slavery." Difficulties of earlier years must have been long past, for the medals were made by Francastel, the same jeweler who waited months to be paid for the eagles he had made for L'Enfant in 1784.[60]

Later the Constituent Assembly voted that the Vainqueurs de la Bastille, as they were now to be styled, would each receive a musket, saber, and uniform together with another medal and an engraved certificate of award.[61] At this stage, the Revolution was quite comfortable with rewards of merit.

Democratic feeling soon focused on the Cincinnati. In April 1790 the vicomte de Noailles wrote Washington to request that the Cincinnati be distributed throughout all officer ranks in France, just as it was in America. He noted that the St. Louis would now be "conferred throughout all ranks of the army," and hoped the Cincinnati might follow suit.[62]

Washington took no action on Noailles's request, but the Revolution soon turned against orders, decorations, and hereditary distinctions as vestiges of monarchal slavery. On June 19, 1790, the Assembly voted the abolition of all hereditary titles and armorial bearings. Henceforth, every French citizen could carry only "the true name of his famille." The abolition of nobility did not entail the suppression of orders, but as orders had traditionally been the province of the nobility, they were logically suspect. A year later the Assembly heard a report on orders of chivalry. Some members wanted to distinguish French orders from foreign ones, and amid a flurry of suggestions the clerk reduced the discussion to four propositions which were accepted.

First, all orders which supposed distinctions of birth were suppressed. Second, the Assembly reserved the right to decide whether there should be a single national decoration for merit, but in the meantime the military could continue to wear and receive the St. Louis and Merite Militaire. Third, no Frenchman could assume titles previously prohibited by referring to himself, for example, as a "former" count. Fourth, any Frenchman who joined a foreign order based on distinctions of birth forfeited his citizenship.[63]

For the moment, the Cincinnati was safe, for it was treated as a reward of merit like the St. Louis. The prohibition of 1785 was now forgotten, and on February 3, 1792, the king approved the admission of twenty-seven new members of the society.[64]

If some Cincinnati led the Revolution, others stood firmly with the royal family, resisting every encroachment on ancient prerogatives. In June 1791 the count von Fersen and comte de Damas d'Antigny assisted the king in his ill-fated attempt to escape, and when the end came for the monarchy on August 10, 1792, the baron de Vioménil was mortally wounded defending the royal family at the Tuilleries. The comte d'Hervilly also stood with the King that day.

The fateful tenth of August is usually seen as the end of the French society as an organization until it was formally revived in 1922. However, even though the society ceased to meet, the eagle would appear from time to time in a variety of scenes. On September 4, 1792, for example, a convoy of political prisoners from Orleans was massacred at Paris. Among them was Lamart de Noirman de La Neuville of the French society. Leading the procession after the massacre was one Fournier, a revolutionary fanatic from Martinique, and the historian Lamartine wrote "from the neck of his horse dangled a collar composed of Crosses of Saint-Louis, Eagles of

Cincinnatus, and other military decorations snatched from the breasts of victims."[65]

As the Revolution progressed, orders of any sort became suspect, and during a debate in the National Convention in October 1792, General Dumouriez took the cross of Saint Louis from his chest and, in the words of Gen. William Heath who was much impressed, "made an offering of it at the Shrine of Liberty." Dumouriez was not a member of the society, but when the event was reported in the American press, Heath wrote Knox in January 1793.

> If the *Cross of St. Louis,* long worn in France as an emblem of the distinguished merit of the wearer, is judged by this great man as improper to be worn in a Republick, how can I, a *citizen* of the *renowned American Republick* allow my name to stand affixed to an *institution,* or wear a *device* which is construed by many of our fellow-citizens the indication of an *order* and *distinction* in society. Animated by this example of the Gallic Citizen-General, I do hereby request that you will be pleased to *erase* my name from the *institution* of the Society of the Cincinnati, as I do from this moment for *myself,* renounce the institution.[66]

On November 18, 1793, the Convention all but suppressed the last vestiges of the society in France by decreeing that "all citizens decorated with the cross of Saint Louis or other decorations" who did not turn in their decorations within eight days would be considered suspect and arrested.[67] Nothing was said of the Cincinnati, but many an eagle surely went into the melting pot along with the badges of the St. Louis.

The Terror obviously did more than suppress insignia. Rochambeau and Lafayette, to name but two prominent Cincinnati, were imprisoned, while no fewer than eleven members perished on the guillotine. Philibert-Francois Rouxel de Blanchelande died in April 1793, the comte de Custine Sarreck in August, Baron Frederick de Kalb in November, and the comte de Kersaint and Armand Louis de Biron, formerly the duc de Lauzun and leader of Lauzun's Legion, in December. Six died in 1794. The comte de Gimoard in February, Jacques O'Moran in March, and his old chief, Comte Dillon, in April. The most notable loss of April was that of the president of the French society, the comte d'Estaing. The admiral had stood with Marie Antoinette, drawing suspicion on himself in the process. The marquis de Chastellet poisoned himself in April, rather than die on the guillotine, and the prince de Broglie was condemned in July.

By the time of the Terror, the Cincinnati were long gone from the leadership of the Revolution. Many emigrated, and several had joined the princes, the comte de Provence and the comte d'Artois, in their attempt to reestablish the monarchy.

As the Revolution progressed, French Cincinnati had joined the armies of other European powers, either with or without royal permission. In 1790 Catherine II had asked for naval officers, and the court sent the marquis de Traversay, who remained in Russian service until his death in 1831. From 1811 to 1819 this Cincinnatus was the Russian minister of the navy. The comte de Langeron, the duc de Montmorency-Laval, and the marquis de Vioménil all entered the Russian army. Vioménil served until 1810, when he became marshal general of Portugal. The baron de Vioménil, the duc de Castries, and the comte de Chastenet Puysegur had earlier served with Portuguese forces. Two brothers, the marquis and comte de Deux-Ponts entered the service of the king of Bavaria, and the marquis de Saint Simon joined the Spanish army.

These military emigrations brought the great anomaly of Cincinnati serving in the British army. There were three. Chastenet Puysegur had served with the British before going to Portugal. Eugene MacCarthy and Edward Stack both joined the counter-revolutionary army under the prince de Conde, and passed with their Irish Brigade into English service in 1794. MacCarthy served in Ireland and Jamaica until 1797, but Stack remained active until placed on half-pay in 1802. Nonetheless he was named brigadier general in 1803. After the Peace of Amiens he decided to visit France once more, only to be detained for the next eleven years after hostilities broke out unexpectedly. He received regular promotions and was a lieutenant general by the time he was freed. He was finally promoted general in 1830, three years before he died. One cannot imagine that he wore the eagle of the Cincinnati on the tunic of a British general.

Some Cincinnati émigrés saw America as an opportunity to recoup perquisites now gone at home. In September 1796 in London the comte de la Prade asked Rufus King, then American minister there, whether the United States had a pension for him as a member of the Cincinnati. He also inquired about land grants, military appointments, and passage to America.[68] King disappointed him on every ground.

Yet several officers did find their way into the American army, bringing strength especially to the artillery and engineer corps. Lt. Col. Anne-Louis Tousard emigrated to Philadelphia in 1793 and two years later was named major of the first Regiment, U.S. Artillery and Engineers. Later he became lieutenant colonel commandant of the Second Regiment and inspector of the new United States Military Academy. The chevalier de Rochefontaine, another political émigré, was named temporary engineer in 1794, overseeing New England fortifications. He was later named lieutenant colonel commandant of the First Regiment of engineers. Maj. Michel Gabriel Houdin in 1791 had become captain and deputy to the quartermaster general and in 1801 military storekeeper to the army. Capt. Joseph Leonard Poirey was named captain by brevet in 1790.

Emigration brought one French officer satisfaction denied at home. Capt. Denis-Nicholas Cottineau de Kerloguen had commanded a frigate during the Revolution, helped build Fort Hancock in North Carolina, and sailed with John Paul Jones, but he could not qualify for the French society.[69] He emigrated to Philadelphia and shortly thereafter moved to Azilum, a town on the Susquehanna River populated by many displaced French royalists. The Pennsylvania society admitted him an honorary member in 1795, and after he moved to Georgia he met regularly with the society there.

Royalists found other spots of refuge in the United States. The Castorland Company planned a settlement for French émigrés along the Black River Valley in upper New York State. Steuben was delighted, for he thought it would open his own lands nearby. One prominent Cincinnati family emigrated to the United States in 1794 and stayed on a farm near Albany until 1796. The marquis de La Tour du Pin was a member of the society himself as well as the son-in-law of Arthur, comte de Dillon, also a member. Gen. Philip Schuyler of the New York society helped the marquis, his wife, and son find their farm, and the *Memoirs* of the marquise record their life near Albany in fascinating detail.[70]

The Terror had suppressed orders and decorations, but Napoleon's attitude was far different, and in 1802 he proposed the creation of a national order of merit to recognize achievements, civil and military. Immediately some raised the question of the suitability of such symbols in a republic. Bonaparte's answer was ready: "I defy anyone to show me a republic, ancient or modern, in which there have not been distinctions. One calls these 'baubles.' But it is with such baubles that men are led."[71] Thus was born the Legion of Honor. Though established in 1802, it was not until the first consul had transformed himself into emperor that the first awards were made, on July 15, 1804. The five rayed badges, now called "stars," were then called "eagles," after the eagle design on the reverse.

Napoleon was right. Men would covet the badge and the distinction it brought. The baron de Closen Haydenbourg is an interesting example. In 1806 he wrote the grand chancellor of the Legion of Honor that he had given up his two previous decorations in the 1790s "out of respect for the new french laws."[72] He had been an honorary member of the Cincinnati as well as a chevalier of the Mérite Militaire, and he now asked for the Legion of Honor as a replacement. He had continued to serve in the army with honor, the chancellery agreed, and his name was enrolled.

Other members who had hidden their Cincinnati eagles, rather than turn them in, now brought them out. Vice Adm. Pleville-le-Pelley became a grand officer of the new Legion in 1804. He died the following year, but not before he had his portrait done wearing the plaque of the Legion and the eagle of the Cincinnati. At least thirty-three members of the Cincinnati received the Legion of Honor in its various grades during the Napoleonic era.

The hereditary principle had been the most controversial aspect of the Cincinnati, but that did not deter the French from adding a hereditary aspect to their official national order. In 1808 with the establishment of a new imperial nobility, all members of the Legion would bear the title *chevalier,* and under specific conditions that title became hereditary in the eldest male line, whether natural or adopted. If, at the death of the legionnaire, the eldest son had an annual income of 3,000 francs and secured letters patent from the arch-chancellor of the empire, he too became a chevalier. In 1810 the emperor modified the rule. Members of the Legion would still be chevaliers, but the title would descend to an eldest son only if the son were a legionnaire in his own right. After the title passed through three generations of legionnaires, it would then be hereditary for future generations regardless of personal achievement. Here the model was the St. Louis: when a third generation received the cross of the order that recipient and his descendants were thereafter noble. One should emphasize that though the title *chevalier* became hereditary, the right to wear the badge of the Legion did not.[73]

The Legion of Honor survived the Restoration of 1814 (with the judicious substitution of Henry IV for Napoleon on the badge) and so too did the hereditary principle. The third generation was now not just titled—it was noble as it had been under St. Louis. Louis XVIII kept the Legion but he was quick to restore the St. Louis and Mérite Militaire to their former status. Once more the eagle of the Cincinnati reappeared in the company of these prerevolutionary orders, especially since many of the old members once more returned to royal military service. Successors now sought membership too, even though there was no organization in France. The baron de Vioménil wrote President General Charles Cotesworth Pinckney that he hoped to be admitted, and the proper papers were prepared. In 1820 the baron de Bougainville was admitted after a correspondence between Secretary General William Jackson and the French minister to the United States. Two years later Major Jackson also authorized the admission of the marquis de Ponteves-Giens.[74] The king himself authorized Bougainville to wear the eagle, as he did the baron de Martineng de Gineste in 1822.

The society all but resumed its former status. When A. M. Perrot published his manual of orders of chivalry in 1820, he included the Cincinnati with a color plate of the eagle and the comment "This order is almost extinct, and the French officers who are still part of it today are the only ones who wear the decorations." Perrot was unaware of the few hereditary admissions. Since it was not the creation of a sovereign prince, late nineteenth-century manuals ignored it, but Nicholas Carlisle had included it in the guide he published in London in 1839.[75] An element of controversy even reappeared, for Mirabeau's pamphlet against the Cincinnati was reprinted in Paris in 1815. It was then more an attack on a renewed nobility rather than the society since it was given the title *Opinion du Comte de Mirabeau sur la noblesse ancienne et moderne.*[76]

Many new French societies and fraternities were issuing membership badges, and in April 1824 the king ruled that henceforth the court would recognize only orders and decorations conferred by sovereigns. In the following month the grand chancellor of the Legion of Honor spoke directly about the Cincinnati: "The American order of Cincinnatus begins to reappear. Many persons pretend that it is hereditary in their family. The King, by his decision of April 16, renews the prohibition pronounced the 7th of April 1785. However, some authorizations were allowed before the Ordonnance of last April 16: persons who were so authorized and who will document the authorizations or justify them, will be permitted to wear this Order. As for those authorizations granted before the 7th of April 1785, they must be renewed through the Grand Chancellor."[77]

Successors were thus generally deprived of the opportunity of membership, yet Charles X and Louis Philippe both seem to have approved descendants wearing the eagle. In similar fashion, the kings of Sweden gave their consent for subsequent descendants of the count von Stedingk to wear the badge.[78]

Though Theodore, comte de Lameth, the last original member of the French society lived until 1854, the organization was regarded by the 1830s as only a historical memory. In 1834 the Baron Girardot published a pamphlet entitled *L'Ordre americain de Cincinnatus en France*. Girardot was not a member, but he did a good job of searching out original sources. In 1858 he chanced to meet Hamilton Fish as the president general toured Europe, and Girardot was most surprised to find that the Cincinnati still existed at all.[79]

Perhaps inspired by Girardot's pamphlet, those entitled to hereditary membership made intermittent attempts to revive the French society during the reign of Louis Philippe, but any contingent plans were laid aside after the coup of Napoleon III in 1851.[80] As with many other original societies, it would be decades before efforts at revival succeeded.

Notes

1. Chevalier du Bouchet to Horatio Gates, February 17, 1784, Gates Papers.
2. Gardiner, *Order of the Cincinnati in France*, p. 44.
3. Pierre L'Enfant to Knox, September 27, 1783, L'Enfant Papers.
4. GW to chevalier de Gerard, October 29, 1783, Washington, *Writings*, XXVII, 210. Washington outlined his plans to write the French in his letter to Knox, October 12, 1783, ibid., XXVII, 194-96. Fundamentally the same letter which went to Gerard also went to de Grasse, d'Estaing, Barras, Destouches, and

Rochambeau, also on October 29, 1783. Ibid., p. 210n. For the letter to Rochambeau, see Hume, *Washington Correspondence,* p. 26.

5. Knox to L'Enfant, October 1, 1783, Anderson House. Membership Certificate for L'Enfant, signed by Washington, November 1, 1783, GW to L'Enfant, October 30, 1783, Hume, *Washington Correspondence,* pp. 30–31. Knox to GW, October 29, 1783, Anderson House.

6. L'Enfant to GW, December 25, 1783, Anderson House.

7. Rochambeau to the marquis de Ségur, December 14, 1783; Lafayette to Vergennes, December 16, 1783, Gardiner, *Order of the Cincinnati in France,* p. 9.

8. News of L'Enfant's landing did not appear in the *London Chronicle* until January 3, 1784. Horace Walpole to William Mason, December 30, 1783, *Horace Walpole's Correspondence with William Mason,* ed. W. S. Lewis, Grover Cronin, Jr., and Charles H. Bennett (New York: Yale University Press, 1955), II, 55. Horace Walpole to countess of Upper Ossory, December 30, 1783, *Horace Walpole's Correspondence with the Countess of Upper Ossory,* ed. W. S. Lewis and A. Dayle Wallace (New York: Yale University Press, 1965), II, 431.

In some ways Walpole's jest may be accurate as well as amusing. The comte de Ségur, secretary of the French society, recorded a similar incident in his memoirs. Ségur had been named commander of the Order of Saint Lazare and a chevalier of Saint Louis. He was wearing the badges of those orders together with his eagle when he encountered a colonel, "greatly distinguished by his birth . . . but whose education had been neglected."

"Why, my friend, you are rich in saints, for you have got three of them: Saint Louis, Saint Lazare, and Saint Cinnatus. But as to the last named, I cannot imagine where the deuce our American friends could have dug him up." The comment is all the more curious, for the colonel too was a member of the society. *Memoirs and Recollections of Count Segur* (London: Colburn, 1826), II, 36.

9. Marquis de Castries to d'Estaing, December 19, 1783; marquis de Ségur to Rochambeau, December 18, 1783, in Gardiner, *Order of the Cincinnati in France,* p. 10.

10. Vergennes to La Luzerne, July 21, 1783, in Bancroft, *History,* I, 324–25.

11. Lafayette to GW, December 25, 1783, Gardiner, *Order of the Cincinnati in France,* p. 13. Gottschalk, *Letters of Lafayette to Washington* gives a slightly different reading of the quotation without appreciable variation, p. 273.

12. Rochambeau to Washington, January 7, 1784, Hume, *Washington Correspondence,* p. 54; baron de Girardot, *L'Ordre américain de Cincinnatus en France* (Nantes: Mellinet, [1834]) provides the French text of the letter (p. 20) and the list of subscribers and the sums pledged (pp. 21–22).

13. See Gardiner, *Order of the Cincinnati in France,* p. 16n. La Rouerie was in the United States in 1783 and 1784, where he remained in government service after the war. He was much interested in the society and had a copy of the institution prepared for his own officers to sign. Marquis de La Rouerie to GW, July 30, 1783; La Rouerie to GW, May 10, 1784, Hume, *Washington Correspondence,* pp. 16, 167–69.

14. L'Enfant, Account submitted to the First General Meeting, May 1784, L'Enfant Papers.

15. L'Enfant to GW, April 29, 1784, Anderson House.

16. L'Enfant to Steuben, date unknown, as quoted in Steuben to GW, April 1784, Hume, *Washington Correspondence,* p. 150.

17. Charles Albert More, chevalier de Pontgibaud, *A French Volunteer of the War of Independence,* ed. Robert B. Douglas (Paris: Carrington, 1898), pp. 100-101.

18. Many of these letters are to be found in Hume, *Washington Correspondence.* Requests tapered off after the French Revolution, the last in the Hume collection being from M. de Flad, February 16, 1793, pp. 381-82.

19. D'Estaing to GW, December 25, 1783, Hume, *Washington Correspondence,* pp. 39-41; Barras to Washington, January 23, 1784, Gardiner, *Order of the Cincinnati in France,* pp. 17-18; La Luzerne to GW, May 6, 1784, Gardiner, *Order of the Cincinnati in France,* pp. 19-20.

20. Lafayette to GW, March 9, 1784, Hume, *Washington Correspondence,* p. 110. See also the other letter of March 9, p. 107.

21. Lafayette to GW, March 9, 1784, Hume, *Washington Correspondence,* p. 107. See also Gardiner, *Order of the Cincinnati in France,* p. 19.

22. Lafayette to GW, March 9, 1784, Gottschalk, *Letters of Lafayette to Washington,* pp. 278-81.

23. Rochambeau to GW, May 4, 1784, Hume, *Washington Correspondence,* pp. 151-52; Lafayette to GW, March 9, 1784, Gottschalk, *Letters of Lafayette to Washington,* p. 279.

24. Lafayette to GW, March 9, 1784, Gottschalk, *Letters of Lafayette to Washington,* p. 168.

25. Lafayette to GW, January 10, 1784, ibid., p. 274.

26. Bouchet to Gates, February 17, 1784, Gates Papers.

27. Lafayette to GW, March 9, 1784, Gottschalk, *Letters of Lafayette to Washington,* pp. 279-80.

28. Bouchet to GW, May 17, 1784, Hume, *Washington Correspondence,* p. 183.

29. Bouchet to Gates, July 16, 1784, Gates Papers.

30. L'Enfant to GW, April 29, 1784, L'Enfant Papers; Lafayette to GW, January 10, 1784, Gottschalk, *Letters of Lafayette to Washington,* p. 276.

31. La Rouerie to GW, May 10, 1784, Hume, *Washington Correspondence,* pp. 167-69. GW to La Rouerie, May 15, 1784, ibid., p. 181.

32. The intended French donation to the society had been reported publicly well before the general meeting. See the *Independent Chronicle,* April 29, 1784. GW to La Fayette, May 17, 1784, Hume, *Washington Correspondence,* p. 184.

33. Rochambeau to GW, September 9, 1784; marquis de Ségur to Rochambeau, August 28, 1784, Hume, *Washington Correspondence,* pp. 206-7.

34. The marquis de Ségur wrote to Rochambeau on August 28, 1784, reporting that the king had authorized admission of the latest list of names presented, but that there would be no more admissions. Hume, *Washington Correspondence,* p. 207. Yet the king gave special warrants to admit the baron de St. Simon on September 3 and the baron d'Angely on September 6. The marquis de Chastellet was admitted under a special warrant of November 9, 1784. Gardiner, *Order of the Cincinnati in France,* pp. 106-8. For the list of those admitted in August and September 1784, see Hume, *Washington Correspondence,* pp. 207-8. The marquis de Castries had

written a similar letter reporting the royal prohibition of new members on August 27, 1784. Baron Ludovic de Contenson, *La Société des Cincinnati de France* (Paris: Auguste Picard, 1934), p. 64.

35. Oliver J. G. Welch, *Mirabeau: A Study of a Democratic Monarchist* (London: Jonathan Cape, 1951), pp. 78, 124.

36. Honoré Gabriel Riqueti, comte de Mirabeau, *Considérations sur l'Ordre de Cincinnatus* (London: Johnson, 1784). Quotations here are from the English translation by Samuel Romilly authorized by Mirabeau: *Considerations on the Order of Cincinnatus* (Philadelphia: Seddon and Spotswood, 1786), pp. 24, 8, 9, 32.

37. Mirabeau, *Considerations,* pp. 4-5. Mirabeau was not alone in criticizing the society. For a summary of other liberal criticism, see Lewis Rosenthal, *America and France: The Influence of the United States on France in the Eighteenth Century* (New York: Holt, 1882), p. 96n.

38. Mirabeau, *Considerations,* pp. 12, iv.

39. Ségur, *Memoirs and Recollections,* II, 35-36.

40. Comte d'Estaing, "Idées Sur l'Association des Cincinnati, July 13, 1784," Anderson House. This eleven-page document was transmitted to the society in America but not considered until it was presented at the general meeting in Philadelphia, May 1787. None of the changes proposed were adopted.

41. The sixth and seventh propositions of the document.

42. The ninth proposition.

43. This proposal was the third: "La france doit se flatter d'être aussi la Patrie d'un Américain."

44. Lafayette to John Adams, March 8, 1784, Edgar Erskine Hume, *La Fayette and the Society of the Cincinnati* (Baltimore: Johns Hopkins University Press, 1934), pp. 23-26.

45. Lafayette to John Adams, June 25, 1784, Hume, *La Fayette and the Society,* pp. 30-31. Lafayette to Jeremiah Wadsworth, February 10, 1786, Connecticut State Library, Photostat in Anderson House.

46. Louis Gottschalk, *Lafayette between the American and the French Revolution (1783-1789),* (Chicago: University of Chicago Press, 1950), pp. 368-69.

47. Ibid., p. 369; Comte Auguste de Grasse to GW, March 11, 1788; GW to de Grasse, August 18, 1788, Hume, *Washington Correspondence,* pp. 324-26, 333-34.

48. Taylor, *Life and Correspondence of John Paul Jones,* pp. 425, 527. Jones was keenly sensitive to medals and decorations and what they symbolized for recognition of contributions of differing merit. See p. 445.

49. *Boston Centinel,* September 16, 1789, quoted in Drake, *Memorials,* pp. 54-56.

50. See the letter of baron de Nervo et al. to William Harris Crawford, February 26, 1815, in Gardiner, *Order of the Cincinnati in France,* p. 42. François Elzear, marquis de Ponteves-Giens, did, however, succeed his father, presumably on the authorization of Secretary General William Jackson. Contenson, *La Société des Cincinnati de France,* p. 246.

51. Rochambeau to Washington, June 16, 1784, Hume, *Washington Correspondence,* p. 199.

52. Baron Curt von Stedingk to Gustavus III, March 2, 1784, in Arvid Bergman, "Swedish Members of the Society of the Cincinnati," *New England Historical and Genealogical Register,* 109(April 1955), 82. Though Stedingk and Fersen were the only Swedish members, there were a significant number of Swedish officers serving in junior grades with French and American forces during the Revolution. Most were in the Navy. Adolph B. Benson, *Sweden and the American Revolution* (New York: Tuttle, Morehouse, and Taylor, 1926), pp. 9n, 167.

53. Gustavus III to baron von Stedingk, March 26, 1784, Bergman, "Swedish Members," pp. 82-83.

54. R. Nisbet Bain, *The Last King of Poland* (New York: Putnam, 1909), pp. 253-55. Kosciusko was but the best known of many Poles who served with American forces during the Revolution. As will be seen in chapter 11, there were those after World War I who thought there were enough eligible officers to have a Polish Society of the Cincinnati. Many served, however, as junior officers and were ineligible for the French society. Cornet Augustus Christian George Elmholm, a native of Norway who had served in the Prussian army before going to Poland in 1768, was an original member of the South Carolina Society. He later lived in Georgia. Capt. Frederick Paschke was a member of the Pennsylvania Society and called himself Polish, and Lieutenant Jervuturas or Jerzmanowski signed La Rouerie's copy of the institution. State societies in the United States were notably enthusiastic about the cause of Poland and offered many toasts to the land of Kosciusko and Pulaski in the 1790s: July 4, 1793 (Delaware), July 8, 1794 (Pennsylvania), July 9, 1794 (New Jersey), July 14, 1794 (Delaware), February 25, 1795 (Georgia), July 4, 1795 (Pennsylvania), July 6, 1796 (Massachusetts and Pennsylvania). See Edgar Erskine Hume, "Poland and the Society of the Cincinnati," *Polish American Review,* 1(1935), 11-31.

55. Ségur, *Memoirs and Recollections,* II, 104-5.

56. Baron George Pilar von Pilchau, "Journal of a Volunteer Expedition to Sandusky, from May 24 to June 13, 1782," *Pennsylvania Magazine of History and Biography,* 18 (1894), 129-37.

57. Talleyrand, as quoted in Gardiner, *Order of the Cincinnati in France,* p. 44.

58. Lafayette to GW, January 1, 1788, Gottschalk, *Letters of Lafayette to Washington,* p. 335.

59. See Edgar Erskine Hume, "Early Opposition to the Society of the Cincinnati," *Americana,* 30 (1936), 631.

60. *Trésor de Numismatique et de Glyptique: Médailles de la Révolution Française* (Paris: Bureau du Trésor de Numismatique et de Glyptique, 1836), p. 10; Charles Mendel, *La Légion d'Honneur et Les Décorations Françaises* (Paris: Charles Mendel, 1911), p. 49.

61. Mendel, *La Légion d'Honneur,* pp. 48-49.

62. Viscomte de Noailles to Washington, April 24, 1790, Hume, *Washington Correspondence,* pp. 367-68.

63. *Procès Verbal de L'Assemblée Nationale,* June 19, 1790, no. 324 (Paris: N.p, 1790), pp. 22-25.

64. These officers were admitted as honorary members. The king's approval of this group was his last official act connected with the society. Contenson, *La Société des Cincinnati de France,* p. 71. The names of that last group of officers admitted

are in Guy de Bessey, baron de Contenson, *L'Ordre Américain de Cincinnatus en France* (Paris: Plon-Nourrit, 1913), p. 82.

65. As quoted in Hume, "Early Opposition," p. 632.

66. Heath to Knox, January 18, 1793, as quoted in Bugbee, *Memorials,* pp. 239-40.

67. *Procès Verbal,* 28 Brumaire, Year 2 (November 18, 1793) (Paris: N.p., 1793), p. 310.

68. Rufus King to the comte de la Prade, September 18, 1796, *Life and Correspondence of Rufus King,* II, 88.

69. Denis-Nicholas Cottineau de Kerloguen to GW, September 4, 1788, Hume, *Washington Correspondence,* pp. 335-36; chevalier d'Annemours to GW, February 15, 1789, ibid., pp. 340-42. Kerloguen's name has been spelled also as Kerloguin.

70. Palmer, *Steuben,* pp. 394-97, 400-402. Henrietta-Lucy, marquise de La Tour du Pin, *Memoirs of Madame de La Tour du Pin,* ed. and tr. Felice Harcourt (New York: McCall, 1971). Pages 226-85 cover their stay in America. See also Alta M. Ralph, "The Chassanis or Castorland Settlement," New York State Historical Association *Quarterly Journal,* 10 (1929), 333-45.

71. Musée National de la Légion d'honneur et des Ordres de Chevalerie, *Napoléon et la Légion d'Honneur* (Paris: Société d'Entraide des Membres de la Légion d'honneur, 1968), unpaginated introduction. On the formation of the Légion d'honneur see Jules Renault, *La Légion d'Honneur et les Anciens Ordres Français* (Paris: Renault, 1924).

72. Baron de Closen Haydenbourg to comte de Lacépède, August 27, 1806, Anderson House. On members of the Cincinnati who became members of the Légion d'honneur, see Edgar Erskine Hume, "The Order of the Cincinnati in France and Original Members who were Legionnaires," *Légion d'Honneur,* 1(October 1930), 37-49.

73. Jean Daniel, *La Légion d'Honneur* (Paris: Bonne, 1948), pp. 44-46; see also Renault, *La Légion d'Honneur,* pp. 52 ff.

74. Contenson, *La Société des Cincinnati de France,* p. 79; Gardiner, *Order of the Cincinnati in France,* pp. 117-18.

75. A.-M. Perrot, *Collection Historique des Ordres de Chevalerie* (Paris: André, 1820), p. 111. Nicholas Carlisle, *A Concise Account of the Several Foreign Orders of Knighthood* (London: Hearne, 1839), p. 555.

76. Mirabeau, *Opinion du Comte de Mirabeau sur la Noblesse Ancienne et Moderne; Considérations sur l'Ordre de Cincinnatus* (Paris: Chaignieau, 1815). The favorable reference in the preface to a letter of Lazare N. M. Carnot dated in May suggests that this edition appeared during the Hundred Days when Carnot was minister of interior. He was proscribed after the second restoration of Louis XVIII.

77. As quoted in Contenson, *La Société des Cincinnati de France,* pp. 96-97.

78. On Swedish members in subsequent years see Bergman, "Swedish Members," pp. 79-84.

79. Hamilton Fish to Thomas McEuen, January 27, 1859, Anderson House. The pamphlet was presented to the society as the gift of Baron Girardot at the general meetings in 1860, *Proceedings,* I, 155.

80. Gardiner, *Order of the Cincinnati in France,* p. 80.

Chapter Eight

A New Government: Some Compensation for the Toils and Dangers

THE THREAT OF ANARCHY was past and a new government had been created with Washington at its head. For the Cincinnati it was a time of optimism and opportunity.

Appointments in the executive branch were the most obvious opportunities for the former officers, and Washington was quite aware that the new government would benefit the Cincinnati. Writing to John Sullivan, president of the New Hampshire society, he said, "The idea, that my former gallant Associates in the field are now about to receive, in a good national government, some compensation for the toils and dangers which they experienced in the course of a long and perilous war, is particularly consolatory to me."[1] And on September 25, 1789, Washington recommended to Hamilton thirty-five names for appointment. Of those fifteen were hereditary members and one was honorary.[2]

The Cincinnati were eager for appointments and pressed their cases. From Massachusetts came a letter from Benjamin Lincoln. Knox interceded on his behalf, but the best he could do for him was collector of the Port of Boston. Some members of the society persisted after an initial disappointment. Henry Jackson, merchant, treasurer of the Massachusetts Cincinnati, colonel of the regiment never quite organized in 1786, had missed out on the first round of federal patronage, but when the capital was moved from New York to Philadelphia he tried again, but in vain.[3]

The nomination of Benjamin Fishbourne of the Georgia society as naval officer in Savannah brought forth a procedure on appointments that survives, fundamentally, to this day. The Senate learned there were legal charges pending against Fishbourne and rejected the nomination in a closed session. Washington, who knew nothing of the charges, was distressed and renewed his confidence in Fishbourne's "irreproachable" conduct. He suggested that in the future the Senate ask the reasons behind the nomination before rejecting the candidate, a procedure that was adopted. Washington in turn nominated Lachlan McIntosh, former president of the Georgia society, for the post in Savannah.[4]

Nominations sent to the Senate made no reference to membership in the society, but the pattern did not go unnoticed. Senator William Maclay of Pennsylvania noted in his diary, "It really seems as if we were to go on making offices until all the Cincinnati are provided for."[5] Despite the pressure for posts and Maclay's remark, the number of Cincinnati in the executive branch was not so great as one might expect.

In the Treasury Department offices in 1794, only the secretary, Alexander Hamilton, was a member.[6] And only four of the thirteen commissioners of loans were members: John Cochran of New York, Stephen Moylan of Pennsylvania, James Tilton of Delaware, and Richard Wylly of Georgia. Similarly, only twenty-four of the sixty-seven collectors of ports were members, though Cincinnati did have the most important and lucrative posts. Benjamin Lincoln was at Boston, Jeremiah Olney at Providence, Jedediah Huntington at New London, John Lamb at New York, and George Bush at Wilmington. Gen. Otho H. Williams was collector for Baltimore, as Robert Denny was at Annapolis. John Habersham was collector for Savannah. Each state also had a federal "Officer of Excise," and, as with the loan commissioners, society members held four of the thirteen posts: John Chester in Connecticut, Nicholas Fish in New York, Edward Carrington in Virginia, and William Polk in North Carolina.

In the War Department, Knox presided as secretary, while Maj. John Stagg, Jr., of New York was his principal clerk. Accountant Joseph Howell had been John Pierce's assistant in issuing commutation certificates at the end of the war.

With Thomas Jefferson as secretary of state, it was a wonder that the society was as well represented there as it was. None of the clerks were members, but two of the four ministers abroad were, Thomas

Pinckney in Britain and David Humphreys in Portugal. Two of the consuls were members, John Parrish in Hamburg and Samuel Shaw in China.

Washington's second postmaster general, Timothy Pickering, was a member, as was the third, Joseph Habersham of the Georgia society. Edmund Randolph, the attorney general, was an honorary member of the Virginia society.

The federal judiciary was likewise under Washington's appointment, but there the Cincinnati were not well represented. Only one justice of the Supreme Court was a member, James Wilson, honorary in Pennsylvania. Among the federal judges John Sullivan of New Hampshire and Nathaniel Pendleton of Georgia were hereditary members, while William Paca in Maryland was an honorary member.

In Congress the Cincinnati were a prominent, but hardly a dominant force. Seventeen of the ninety-five men who served in the First Congress were members. The four in the Senate James Gunn, Ga., Benjamin Hawkins, N.C., William Grayson, Va., and James Monroe, Va. were all from the South; the Cincinnati in the house also came primarily from the South, though there were a few from the North: Abraham Baldwin, Ga., George Matthews, Ga., Thomas Tudor Tucker, S.C., John Baptista Ashe, N.C., Theodoric Bland, Va., Josiah Parker, Va., Thomas Hartley, Pa., John P. G. Muhlenberg, Pa., Elias Boudinot, hon. N.J., Jeremiah van Rensselaer, N.Y., Jonathan Trumbull, Conn., Jeremiah Wadsworth, Conn., and Nicholas Gilman, N.H.

If members were prominent in the new government, the eagle was not, and no one could accuse the society of trying to establish itself as an order of knighthood in a climate where titles and precedence were very much at issue. There was considerable debate over how a republic conducted itself, distinguishing between the propriety necessary to any civil government and the pomp of monarchy. Much discussed, for example, was the title of the president. Robert R. Livingston, an honorary member of the New York society, advised that "Supreme Magistrate and President of the United States" was to be preferred to "His Most Christian Majesty."[7] The Senate, with some dissenters, favored "His Highness, the President of the United States of America, and Protector of their Liberties," a title proposed by John Adams and Richard Henry Lee. But the House stood firm against such titles, and the simple "Mr. President" was the outcome.

How did a president address Congress? George III addressed parliament from a throne in the House of Lords, and Americans may have had such ceremonies in mind as they constructed the senate chamber with the president's chair elevated three feet from the floor, a canopy of crimson damask above. John Fenno's *Gazette of the United States* soon began listing those present at Martha Washington's receptions as "Lady Kitty Duer," "Lady Sterling," or "the Lady of his Excellency the Governor."[8] Though an Albany writer reminded Fenno that the Constitution forbade titles, most nonetheless seemed content to refer to the First Lady as "Lady Washington."

Receptions, or levees, as they were called, were stiffly formal. Colonel John Hoskins Stone of the Maryland society commented, "None were admitted... but those who had either a right by official station to be there, or were entitled to the privilege by established merit and character; and full dress was required of all."[9]

Did "full dress" require, or preclude, the eagle of the Cincinnati? At only one annual event did the eagle appear regularly at official functions, Washington's birthday. No less a witness than the British minister's wife provided an account of Washington wearing the diamond eagle. In 1797 she described the magnificent ball attended by about a thousand for the last such celebration while Washington was still president: "The President appeared in the American Uniform (blue and buff) with the Cross of Cincinnatus at his breast in diamonds, it is on this occasion only that the order is permitted to appear—you know, perhaps that the fellow soldiers of Washington had this order conferred upon them after the Revolution, the propriety of admitting any thing like hereditary honor which might be handed down to the Sons, was disputed in Congress, and was, at last, agreed that on the General's Birth day those who survived might show their cross, and to be remembered no more."[10]

Apart from Washington's birthday, no official formalities arose about the Cincinnati. When British General Clinton was given the Order of the Bath, he became thereafter Sir Henry Clinton, K.B., but no member adopted postnominal initials referring to the Cincinnati. Likewise, the eagle made virtually no impact on the official iconography of the new nation. It did not appear on the coins, as orders did in Europe, and though there was a similarity between the eagle and the Great Seal of the United States, the seal is a year older. Yet those who wanted to see the influence of the Cincinnati might well confuse the two. L'Enfant, who designed the badge, was also principal architect for the new federal building in New York City. He incorporated the Great Seal in the pediment, but one writer described "the great gold eagle of the Cincinnati ensconsed in its pendiment."[11]

If Washington rarely wore the eagle on official occasions, he was equally reluctant to wear it when sitting for a portrait. Only in the canvas the Edward Savage did for Harvard in 1789 does it appear, and when John Adams had that portrait copied, the eagle was omitted. Other members of the society, however, were eager to have themselves painted wearing the eagle, but, paradoxically, portraits by John Trumbull and James Peale, both members, were less likely to show the eagle than were portraits by Ralph Earl, a former tory. Sitting for Earl, Steuben typically showed no reluctance to wear all his decorations.

A prime task of the new government, once established, was funding the commutation and pay certificates, as well as the other Revolutionary debt. By 1790 many, perhaps most, of those certificates had passed from the men who had risked their lives to speculators who had paid as little as twelve cents on the dollar. Several Cincinnati were among the major speculators. In New York, Theodosius Fowler held $202,387 worth of certificates, and Philip Schuyler (Hamilton's father-in-law) held $67,000 in partnership with a nonmember. Richard Platt had more than $200,000 in certificates, and Andrew Craigie, Leonard Bleecker, and Daniel Parker were other major New York investors. So too was William Duer, an honorary member who was perhaps the greatest speculator of all. In Philadelphia Robert Morris, an honorary member who had a network of associates throughout the country (Craigie was one of them), held securities well into the six-figure range, Matthew McConnell had $87,272, and two other honorary members also had considerable holdings: Blair McClenachan ($74,434) and William Bingham ($293,360, held with a partner). Walter Stewart, who had played a part at Newburgh, held $48,000 in Continental paper.

Elias Boudinot, an honorary member in New Jersey, had a minimum of $36,737 and probably much more, and in Maryland Uriah Forrest held $100,000 together with a partner.[12]

The individual state societies were inevitably speculators too. The institution had provided that members direct the paymaster general to credit the society with certificates for one month's pay, and thus the society received roughly one sixtieth of the commutation that otherwise would have gone directly to the officers. The societies as a group then were interested parties in any legislation dealing with funding the federal debt, for the future of the debt was the future of their charitable funds.

Politicians felt no obligation to reward speculators. Expressing the sentiments of many, James Madison introduced a motion in the House of Representatives to discriminate in favor of the original holders of the notes. That is, those who had actually served would be compensated in some measure, even if they had sold their original certificates. As he wrote Edmund Pendleton, he thought there was "something radically wrong in suffering those who rendered a bona fide consideration to lose $7/8$ of their dues, and those who have no particular merit towards their Country, to gain 7 or 8 times as much as they advanced."[13]

The proposal had an inevitable appeal to its beneficiaries, and former officers in New York circulated a petition urging Congress to adopt discrimination. The Cincinnati there met on February 1, 1790, in a protracted meeting that led nonetheless to the unanimous condemnation of the principles behind their brother officers' petition. It was, they voted, contrary to their character "to seek any advantage to themselves which might be incompatible with the principles of an honorable policy." It fell to Maj. John Stagg, secretary of the society as well as clerk in the War Department, to announce the decision to the press.[14]

By 1790 the motives of any group of Cincinnati were sure to be mixed. They were men of high honor, and pursuit of an "honorable policy" was a real consideration. Some men still had their original certificates, while for others "honorable policy" was a speculator's dream.

Congress debated the issue in February. Some thought discrimination too complex and therefore impractical. The society's old foe, Aedanus Burke, then a member of Congress, argued against discrimination, saying many already had conspicuous marks of gratitude for their services, most notably their many appointments to civil offices. Despite Madison's response that "the debt due in gold and silver, is not payable in honor or appointments, nor in paper," his motion lost 36 to 13.[15]

The act that finally passed on August 4, 1790, called for holders or bearers of the earlier commutation certificates to exchange them for new certificates, or "stock," in the United States. Two thirds of the value would be given in 6 percent stock, while the other third would be in deferred stock, which would begin bearing 6 percent interest after ten years. Those with "idents" or certificates issued for interest payment on their commutation notes could trade them for a 3 percent stock.

The legislation was all that speculators, and some of the societies, could have wanted. Commutation certificates that had been trading at 12 cents on the dollar in 1783 had risen to 50 cents in 1789. By the summer of 1790 they were trading at 75 cents, and in February 1792 they reached $1.02.[16] The act provided that there be commissioners of loans in each state, but of those commissioners only two were Cincinnati: John Cochran of New York, where the post paid $1,500 a year, and Richard Wylly, treasurer of the Georgia society. The Georgia commissioner received but $700 a year.

Speculators continued to increase their holdings of government securities as best they could, trading the old paper for new government stock. In New York there was a network of Cincinnati which engaged in speculations in a variety of fields, of which stock was only one.

William Duer had been secretary of the treasury board under the Confederation and, for a short time, assistant secretary of the Treasury under Hamilton. He left government to engage in private speculation with fellow member Richard Platt. Together they were investing in Ohio lands through the Scioto Company, trying to establish a strong position in international banking, and taking control of vast tracts of land in Massachusetts, Maine, and Vermont. They also had contracts to supply the United States Army, and hoped to corner the market in the new 6 percent stock, while taking control of the Bank of New York at the same time. The bubble burst in early 1792 when the federal government brought charges against Duer over his treasury accounts. Duer was found insolvent and went to debtor's prison where he died in 1799. With the help of his fellow Cincinnatus Henry Brockholst Livingston, Platt spent the next eight years trying to avoid prison by having himself declared bankrupt. He succeeded.[17]

The crash of Duer and Platt that spring of 1792 led to a short but sharp depression in which many small speculators suffered devastating losses. During that period, the officers renewed their pleas for discrimination.

In New York City, Col. Ebenezer Stevens, a member of the Cincinnati, took the lead in organizing a meeting of former officers, whether members of the society or not. In large measure, that was a tacit criticism of the Cincinnati, who had refused to take a stand for discrimination two years earlier. The pressure group had exerted no pressure. Stevens called his meeting for July 4, forcing officers to choose between Stevens or the Cincinnati, which met at the same time. As will be seen, events at the Cincinnati meeting that day took an unfortunate turn, but those who met with Stevens began drawing up a memorial to Congress.

When distributed in September, the memorial reviewed the privations the officers had suffered and reminded Congress that many had sold their original certificates out of pressing fiscal necessity. They had not protested the new funding system of 1790 until it became clear that the resources of the new nation were quite adequate to discharge its debts. Now, in a phrase reminiscent of 1782, they protested, "Shadows have been given your Memorialists, whilst the Substance has been gleaned by a Set of Men whose comparative Merits it is not for us to draw." They proposed no specific plan of discrimination, but they demanded their due for "the debt now due the Army is the Price of their Blood."

Stevens's efforts did not cease with the preparation of the memorial, and the officers met again on September 3, when Governor Clinton himself joined the organizing committee and Joseph Brown was appointed "our Agent to solicit our Claim" before Congress. Though the New Yorkers had begun apart from the Cincinnati, they turned to the state societies in an effort to build national support for their proposal.[18]

Only the Georgians stood with them, and they had acted independently in July. The tone of the Georgia circular letter more or less suggests that the officers did not stage a coup in 1783 because they were promised payment, a promise now sadly neglected. At the end of the war "large arrears" were due the officers, and in a "noble proof of moderation" they had laid down their arms, "relying with an honest confidence on the faith of Congress, and the assurance of their General" that they would be paid "speedily" and with interest. "This unexampled instance of moderation" went unrewarded, for the old confederacy lacked sufficient powers to raise funds. The new constitution "was formed to establish Justice," but Congress spoke with a contradictory voice in claiming insufficient funds to pay off certificates, yet funding the foreign debt ($22,000,000) at the same time. Many officers had sold their certificates, but the Georgia society proposed that "consistently with fair principles of Equity and Justice" some "proportion" of the debt be paid to the original holders rather than their subsequent assignees.[19]

The movement spread outside the society, and by the end of 1792 Congress had petitions from officers and soldiers in New Hampshire, Massachusetts, New York, Pennsylvania, Delaware, and Maryland. When the subject was discussed on January 16, 1793, however, legislators were in no mood to introduce changes, and discrimination lost again by a vote of 10 to 43. Three Cincinnati Congressmen had voted for discrimination, four against.[20]

As the 1790s went on, state societies turned to a variety of investments for their charitable funds. Perhaps under the influence of Enos Hitchcock, who had a penchant for such things, the Rhode Island society tried its hand at lotteries. But neither their fifty tickets in the Congregational Lottery of 1795 nor the one ticket costing $50 in the Newport Long Wharf and Hotel Lottery paid off. Wisely, they put greater faith in government securities starting in 1792. In 1794, for example, they bought $200 of the deferred stock for 55 percent of face value, while the $300 of the 6 percent stock they bought that year cost them 90 percent of face. The Rhode Island society continued to buy government securities until 1810 when they ordered their holdings sold and the proceeds invested in the Exchange Bank of Providence or in some other Providence bank. Connecticut likewise kept its funds in government stock, reinvesting its income on a regular basis throughout the 1790s and early 1800s.[21]

The New Jersey society invested not in government stock but in the United States Bank. In 1791 the treasurer was instructed to "subscribe" all of the 6 percent funds toward bank stock. As the purchase of each share required some cash, he was instructed further to sell as much of the 3 percent or deferred stock as was necessary "to pay the specie proportion required." In the event all shares of the bank were sold by the time the treasurer applied, he was to "contract for shares with individuals who hold them and if necessary give a premium for the same." The Massachusetts society, on the other hand, was making its investments in Massachusetts State Notes, which in 1793 and 1794 it could buy for roughly 65 percent to 79 percent of face value.[22]

Fellowship continued a major purpose of the society, and the Fourth of July in almost every state brought the former officers together again to review the past and ponder the future. Typically members would gather in one place and march together, wearing the eagle, to a church for a public oration, usually by a member of the society but sometimes not. In Connecticut younger members of the Yale faculty were often invited, and in South Carolina Cincinnati alternated annually with members of the Revolution Society, another group for whom the memories of 1776 were dear.

The oration finished, members would process to a nearby inn or house to spend the rest of the day in celebration. Such meetings were public news, and papers reported widely on toasts offered and new officers elected. Perhaps sensing that the sentiments of the societies were political barometers, editors frequently offered news of societies in other states.

The Cincinnati celebrations were major events, sometimes the envy of those planning town celebrations. In 1791 Boston planned its official town oration for noon, in competition with William Eustis's before the Cincinnati; and inveterate diarist William Bentley noted that "There was a direct interference between this & the Town Oration." As party politics warmed in the 1790s, even the hour of an oration could assume political overtones. Col. Benjamin Walker of the New Jersey society complained that "our demagoges always fix their meetings at the hour of twelve in order to take in all the mechanics and labourers—over whom they alone have influence."[23]

The dinners that followed the orations were merry events indeed. In addition to the toasts there was often singing, led in the New York society for years by Alexander Hamilton. In 1804, just before his fatal duel and with Burr present, Hamilton sang once more, but without the spirit of previous years.[24] Just how spirited some of these dinners were should be evident from the bill for the Massachusetts dinner at Boston's Exchange Coffee House in 1809. Coffee was the last thing the members were drinking, for the account ran thus:

78 dinners	@ $1.50	$117
45 Bottles Madeira	1.25	56.25
20 Bottles Claret	1.25	25.
23 Bottles Porter	.50	11.50
14 Bottles Port	1.25	17.50
6 Bottles Cider	.25	1.50
3 Qts. Brandy	1...	3...
3 Qts. Rum	1...	3...
9 gls Lemonade	2...	18...
200 cigars	3...	6...
18 wine Glasses destroyed		4.50
2 Glass Jelly Stands		5...
Cash paid Hackman		2...
		270.25

Was Hackman an individual or an anonymous driver who took home a member or two unable to walk? The record is eloquently mute, but I calculate each member averaged well over a quart of wine or spirits.[25] The papers of many state societies could provide similar documents from July 4 celebrations.

Records show too that almost every state society began carrying out charitable functions in the 1790s. Widows, children, and members themselves benefited from the invested funds, now buoyed by the new issue of stock. Though planned in 1783, some states were slow to initiate charitable payments. When asked for help by an officer and a widow in 1796, the New Hampshire society put off a decision for a year. Compassionate members, however, pooled eight dollars for the officer, money refunded to the donors from the society treasury two years later.[26]

Funds went for the general support of the needy, but education was a major concern. Bylaws adopted by South Carolina in 1783 provided that the society was to take care "to have the male children instructed in the mathematics and such sciences as officers should be acquainted with, that if this country should be ever again unhappily plunged in war, they may be the more readily qualified to defend those Rights and Liberties, their fathers were instrumental in establishing." New Jersey likewise in 1795 awarded $50 to a widow and children, with special direction that the trustee "pay particular attention to the education of the eldest son."[27] In 1798 the society sent an officer in Kentucky $40 for the education of his children, and thereafter education was a regular use of New Jersey funds.

Not all members understood that the society's aid was for the needy. In 1805 the widow of a New York member applied for aid, only to be told that "the funds are exclusively reserved for the relief of *indigent* members, their widows and children." Simply being a widow did not count.[28]

And not all who perceived need turned to the society for support. Lt. Col. Peregrine Smith of the Maryland society started his own lottery to raise money. He had 3,827 tickets printed and sent some to Washington, who passed them out in the cabinet. Henry Knox was a winner, but his prize of 3,000 acres in Kentucky proved very difficult to collect.[29]

As the years went by the ranks of the society began to thin, and not unnaturally a protocol for mourning developed. In the New York society after the death of Washington, members were to "wear full mourning as for a Father" for six months. Whenever worn during that period, the ribbon of the badge was to be decorated with black crepe. Mourning for other members was not so elaborate, but a New York resolution of 1804 did provide that during mourning the ribbon of the eagle was to be covered with crepe and a crepe chevron was to be worn on the left arm, all for a month.[30]

All aspects of the society as an organization were thus in full operation, but the status of the amended institution continued ambiguous. Washington as president of the United States continued as president general of the Cincinnati. He corresponded about the society and continued to sign membership diplomas, but he took a neutral view of the amended institution, probably still convinced that its ambiguous status was a political asset. Pressing adoption might alienate the society, yet reviving the old institution would rekindle criticism, largely now subsided. In state meetings, however, the pressure for some form of hereditary succession was mounting.

South Carolina in 1787 had ordered its delegates to the general meeting to seek means to replace members lost through death, resignation, or expulsion. Pennsylvania rejected the amended institution in 1789. Georgia likewise withdrew support of the amended institution, and in 1790 Gen. Anthony Wayne, president of the Georgia society, cautioned delegates to the general meeting that abolition of the hereditary principle would prevent a perpetual succession of members, leaving the accumulated funds "ineffectual." Wayne hoped the "original Constitution" could be retained, but he was ready to distinguish between hereditary succession and primogeniture. He wanted the Georgia society to be able to choose the "worthiest," not necessarily the eldest, son.[31] Massachusetts and Maryland agreed. In 1791 the Massachusetts society voted that the Cincinnati should be perpetuated through election of members, "giving the prefferance to the nearest of kin" but not by "hereditary discent." The following year Maryland voted that its delegates should urge adherence to the original institution "as nearly as possible." Maryland asked that "some mode may be established for perpetuating the society instead of the right of Primogeniture."[32]

These carefully wrought motions were in vain, for the general meetings of the decade were able to accomplish nearly nothing. Those critics who in the 1780s had warned against the excessive activity of the society must have been amazed at the inaction that had overtaken the national organization. Though the national Constitution had changed, the spirit (and problems) of the Articles of Confederation lived on in the group that sometimes took credit for replacing them. Unanimous approval of all states still seemed necessary to change the institution or approve the amendments of 1784. When seven states appeared at the 1790 meetings, the delegates could only call a special meeting in 1791. When only nine states assembled, the 1791 session, following the spirit of the new Constitution, did propose that delegations from nine states might act for the whole society.[33]

In May 1793 only seven states were represented, five of them by a single individual, and only five states had approved the resolution allowing nine states to act for all, another disappointment. In 1796 there were five states and more exhortations to attendance, while 1799 saw only two states (New Jersey and Pennsylvania) represented. The delegates of 1799 nonetheless elected a fundamentally new roster of general officers. Washington remained as president general. Mifflin, who had been vice president general since 1787, was replaced by Alexander Hamilton, and for reasons which will be touched upon later, the great stalwart of the society, Henry Knox, was no longer to be secretary general. His place was taken by Maj. William Jackson, whose services were to prove no less loyal.[34]

Enthusiasm for France continued high among the Cincinnati, but doubts grew about the French government as the moderate constitutional monarchy gave way to the radical republicanism of 1792 and the terror of 1793. A shifting attitude was evident among the Cincinnati in 1793, most notably in the politics surrounding two July meetings.

Pennsylvania Cincinnati had been generous, and eclectic, with invitations in the national capital. Washington did not attend, but, mirabile dictu, Jefferson did, as did Knox and Hamilton. Mixed feelings about the French were evident as Citizen Genet was invited, as was the emigré vicomte de Noailles. When Genet heard that Noailles would attend, he refused, certainly much to the delight of members with growing doubts about the government of France.[35] In Connecticut, shortly after the July meeting, Benjamin Tallmadge complained about Ebenezer Huntington, the new president. He bore watching. "In drinking Toasts after Dinner, our P....t gave the *French Republic,* before the *Congress,* to my great mortification."[36] After 1793 Cincinnati began to keep a watchful eye on France.

Not all joined the Cincinnati and the Federalists in criticizing France. In many cities Democratic or Republican societies (both names were common) sprang up to praise the French and ridicule what they saw as monarchist or at least aristocratic trends in the new federal government. In the developing party politics of America, these societies were the natural allies of the Jeffersonians and Antifederalists. In the South at least, several Cincinnati joined these democratic societies, and Dr. James Tilton, president of the Delaware Cincinnati, was also president of the Patriotic Society of New Castle. But to Federalists, and probably most Cincinnati, these democratic societies were little better than the suspicious agents of anarchy, and members rejoiced when Washington attacked these "self-created" organizations in 1794 as promoting the "arts of delusion" to produce "symptoms of riot and violence."[37]

Jefferson resented such criticism. High irony, he thought, that those leading the denunciation of the self-created democratic societies were leaders of the self-created Cincinnati. The Cincinnati, he continued to hold, remained "lowering over our Constitution eternally, meeting together in all parts of the Union, periodically, with closed doors, accumulating a capital in their separate treasury, corresponding secretly & regularly."[38]

Even though the national organization of the society seemed almost moribund, state societies were proving, or were portentially, useful instruments of political influence. Accordingly, they were sometimes drawn into party struggles. New York provides the best example.

On July 4, 1792, while Ebenezer Stevens was holding his meeting to organize lobbying efforts on behalf of discrimination, political chaos broke out at the New York Cincinnati meeting. As elsewhere, the New York society had been a bastion of Federalism, but unlike the societies of other states, it included leaders of both parties. Governor George Clinton, head of the Republicans, had been vice president of the New York society from 1783 to 1785. Since 1786 the presidency had been in the hands of the firm Federalist Steuben, whose land ventures often kept him away from New York City in the summer. Thus in 1792 he was out of town when the Cincinnati gathered.

As usual, members assembled at Corre's hotel, and by noon the acting secretary had thirty-three names on his list, thirty New Yorkers and three visitors from other state societies. With a quorum present, balloting for officers began.

The election was reminiscent of the gubernatorial campaign of May with its charges of rampant fraud on both sides. There Federalist John Jay had more votes, but on technical grounds, a special board of canvassers had rejected votes from three counties, giving the election to Clinton. The Cincinnati met just three days after Clinton's inauguration for a sixth term, with Federalists calling for a resignation or a new election.

When the counting ended at the Cincinnati meeting, the secretary found that thirty members eligible to vote had submitted thirty-six ballots, ousting the baron and electing Clinton in his place. Naturally some debate followed, as did a motion for a new ballot. That too was debated, but Vice President Alexander Hamilton, a staunch Federalist once more facing an uncertain outcome with Clinton the seeming victor, refused even to put the question and bolted from the chair, leaving the meeting in complete disorder.

The members regrouped for dinner, and it was then that a

self-appointed committee decided to inform Governor Clinton of his election. Accordingly, the *New York Journal* of July 7 announced the choice of Clinton and two of his supporters. John Lamb was named vice president and James Miles Hughes, secretary.[39] In the July 21 *Journal* a "Member of the Society of the Cincinnati" reported that no one had really been elected at all. All had ended in unresolved confusion, and to this day the minute book of the New York society has a blank page where the record of the 1792 meeting should be.[40]

"Candidus," probably a Clintonian, made the most of the incident in the *Journal* of August 4. The question was not whether a baron or a governor should be president, but who should win the struggle between rich and poor, aristocrats and democrats, speculators and nonspeculators. Probably reporting talk he had heard after the fracas of July 4, Candidus continued, "The aristocrats finding the society no longer a first engine to promote their views, talk of dissolving it."[41]

Any thoughts of disbanding the society soon evaporated, but the society elections became an annual battle between parties. In 1793 the old order was restored—Clinton was out and Steuben reelected. A new resolution, undoubtedly aimed at Clintonians, required that out-of-state members be required to produce their certificates before being allowed to vote or participate in debate.

Steuben missed the meeting of 1794, when the Clintonians were once more able to name the governor president, but John Adams' son-in-law Williams Stephens Smith was chosen vice president. The following year brought another reverse with Clinton out and Federalist Smith assuming the chair. Named vice president was Nicholas Fish, another Federalist. Smith and Fish alternated in the presidency until 1806 when Federalist Richard Varick was elected. He held the office until his death in 1831.[42]

It was during the 1790s that Tammany Hall became a political power. It has sometimes been written that Tammany was founded to counteract the political influence of the Cincinnati. Such is not true. The New York Society of St. Tammany, or Columbian Order, named for the Indian Tamanend who aided the peaceful settlement of the colonies, appeared in New York as a purely social or fraternal organization in 1787, when it had many members in common with the Cincinnati. Initially there was considerable affection between the two societies. In 1790 John Pintard, president of Tammany, wrote Steuben and urged closer cooperation. "Established on national principles, the Columbian Order considers your society as brothers, with whom they desire to promote a mutual interchange of civilities." As the "junior establishment," Pintard continued, Tammany made the first advances.[43]

While enthusiasm for the French Revolution remained high among the Cincinnati, so did the mutual regard of both societies. In 1792 the New York Cincinnati offered a toast to "Thomas Paine, the magnanimous defender of the rights of man," as well as one to the French Revolution, and the Tammany meeting offered one to "the Cincinnati; and the memory of their brothers, who fell in the cause of liberty." The following year the Cincinnati drank to the Tammany Society.[44]

As the French Revolution, and New York politics, progressed, most Cincinnati adhered to the Federalist position, while Tammany fell into line with the Republicans, and by 1800 the Society of St. Tammany was a political machine on the way to becoming Tammany Hall.

In the politics of the 1790s the members of the society were once more associated with the cause of firm, steady government. In summer 1794 western Pennsylvania became the focal point of resistance to federal taxes on whiskey. Republican Governor Thomas Mifflin, still president of the Pennsylvania society, was reluctant to force the protesters into submission, but some Federalist Cincinnati were ready to take up the task. Washington called out the militia, and a force headed west led by the president himself, together with Generals Daniel Morgan, Henry Lee, and Alexander Hamilton (in uniform), all Cincinnati. Mifflin, once the militia was called out, assumed personal command of state forces, and the Whiskey Rebellion was crushed. Individual Cincinnati had rallied to the government's support once more as they had in 1786 and 1787, but as in the case of Shays's Rebellion, there were at least some members on the other side. One Cincinnati protester, Lt. James McFarlane of the Pennsylvania society, managed to get himself killed during the struggle.[45]

Republican writers aimed cutting remarks at the Cincinnati, with the society now more a symbol of Federalist attitudes, rather than the direct object of attack it had been in 1783. In Philadelphia the

Aurora led the ridicule. In February 1795 "an Officer" invited the Philadelphia militia "to march with the Cincinnati to congratulate the President that he is a year older." Such a birthday parade would be quite useful in "establishing *monarchical* fashions among us." In September there were criticisms that Washington was trying to use the Cincinnati and the army (dominated by many Cincinnati) to establish a monarchy, and in December another writer claimed that Washington really supported the hereditary principle in the society, contrary to any public professions.[46]

Though there were advocates of monarchy, they were fundamentally not of the Cincinnati and should Hamilton or Timothy Pickering have put forward a plan to establish a monarchy, the Cincinnati would not have rallied to it. The circumstances in 1787 had been far different. In 1795 the government was established, the stock funded, the charitable funds in use, and beyond the real purpose of fellowship, the goals in establishing the society had been met, or at least so it seemed for the time being.

There were pockets of opposition to the government within the society, especially on the subject of Jay's treaty. The Delaware meeting in July 1795 produced a volunteer toast (one not planned in advance) to "The *ten* patriotic senators who refused to ratify the British treaty." The vice president of the society then followed up with "John Jay, may he enjoy the benefits of a Purgatory."[47] These comments, which come from a state *society*, underscore the fact that Cincinnati in New York and elsewhere were beginning to stray into the opposition camp.

But despite these notable converts to the Jeffersonian persuasion, the society remained a Federalist organization. Rudolph and Margaret Pasler, twentieth-century students of the Federalist party in New Jersey, determined that only 2 of the 101 original members of the New Jersey society could be called Republicans, and those two were never leaders of the society. In the South the Charleston *City Gazette* charged in the 1790s that the society was basically an auxiliary arm of the Federalist party.[48]

As party differences sharpened in 1796, some Cincinnati were ready to see the society as an active political force, but in February Gen. William Irvine of Pennsylvania advised Federalist leader Edward Hand against any such efforts.[49] Leaders had lost some of that reluctance by 1798, the year of the XYZ affair and the Alien and Sedition Acts. Jeremiah Wadsworth worried that Republican members might take control of the Connecticut society in July. President Benjamin Tallmadge responded that he had not planned to attend, but now he vowed "I will endeavour to be at Hartford in season with all the firm federal Characters, I can collect." He had already seen to it that a dependable Federalist would deliver the annual oration.[50]

At those July meetings in 1798 several societies adopted strong political declarations as war with France seemed imminent. The New York society wrote to President Adams that America's rights were "at every hazard to be maintained." Invasion must be resisted, the government must never submit to "national degradation," and the constitution must be "defended against all foreign control or influence." The societies in Rhode Island, Pennsylvania, and South Carolina addressed Adams in a similar vein.[51]

As Congress moved to create a national army, Washington resumed his role as commander and prepared a list of potential generals and field officers. Of the sixty-two names he proposed, only three were not Cincinnati. For major generals he wanted, in order of seniority, Alexander Hamilton, Charles Cotesworth Pinckney, and Henry Knox. If one of them refused, he would add the name of Henry Lee, who would otherwise be a brigadier general. Other brigadier generals were John Brooks, William S. Smith, and John E. Howard. For adjutant general he offered three names, Smith, Edward Hand, and Jonathan Dayton. Edward Carrington would become quartermaster general and James Craik director of hospitals. Only four of that group had not been officers of their state societies. Nothing was said of Cincinnati membership in the nominations. That he chose three nonmembers of the society could suggest he was choosing talent rather than installing Cincinnati, but Washington must have thought equally that there was a high concentration of dependable talent within the society and perhaps precious little outside it.[52]

These nominations, accepted by Congress in July 1798, probably explain why Knox ceased to be secretary general. Knox had been a major general in the Revolution, commander of the entire army after Washington, and secretary of war. He was now to be ranked third after Hamilton, who had ended the war as a brevet colonel, and he resented it. Eight months of correspondence followed among Knox,

Washington, Hamilton, and Pinckney, gentlemanly but revealing Knox's keen sense of rejection. It was perhaps all the more cutting when in October 1798, "believing you are still the Secretary General of the Society of the Cincinnati," Washington sent him some papers. Whether he withdrew or was excluded is uncertain, but when the delegates met in May 1799 Knox was secretary general no longer. As in the army, Alexander Hamilton, the new vice president general, was triumphant.[53]

The Quasi War with France brought out the conservative streak in the society again, and three notable proposals came out of South Carolina in 1799. Several members asked whether the society still represented the alliance or "union" of France and the United States. Thinking it certainly did not, they proposed altering the ribbon from which the badge was suspended by eliminating the white border.[54] The South Carolina society itself voted to accept *all* male descendants of original members. So much for the abolition of hereditary succession. And South Carolinians moved to make the Cincinnati what would have become a national decoration, much like the St. Louis in France. They proposed that all officers who had served since the Revolution for six years be admitted members, and that all officers of the army and navy in the future who shall serve for six years, or be deranged after three years' service, might be eligible. As before, those "deranged" were those who Congress declared no longer needed. In each case candidates would have to be elected by state societies, but the Cincinnati would become an expanding body of influential leaders rather than the dwindling band of old men to which the amended institution had destined it.[55]

It was in 1798 that one New England Jeffersonian hoped to persuade fellow Republicans to copy the Cincinnati's organization. William Manning (1747–1814) was a farmer and tavern keeper in Billerica, Massachusetts, and he was an attentive reader of newspapers. During the war mania he had produced his "Key to Libberty," which the *Independent Chronicle* refused to publish. Other writers had traced the collapse of republics to licentiousness, corruption, or luxury. Not Manning. Republics collapsed through the "ungoverned dispositions & Combinations of the few, & the ignorance of the Many." No group or "combination" he thought was better at making its influence felt than the Cincinnati.

As he understood the society, it had originated when the officers thought they had too little influence in framing state constitutions and thus in securing their back pay. When complaints arose about the institution, they amended it and tried "to make the world believ" they were a harmless group. When the call for the constitutional convention of 1787 had gone out, "a hard tusel was made chiefly by this ordir to establish a monorcal government in ordir to have their president made king." That effort failed, but they succeeded in putting through "the funding system, by which those that labour for a living will have millions and millions of dollors to pay."

The Cincinnati was the leading association in a nation increasingly dominated by associations of the powerful. Physicians had their medical societies, merchants their chambers of commerce, and lawyers their bar meetings. Manning proposed that the many, the laborers, form their own association. Introducing his society, he wrote, "I have draughted a Constitution as nearly after the Constitution of Cincinaty as the circomstances will admit of." Any who were free males, 21 years of age, "who labour for a living" were eligible for his Labouring Society. The group's primary purpose would be to publish a cheap monthly magazine to keep Jeffersonian principles alive and guarantee that legislatures were filled with "true Republicans." To guarantee success, he proposed to follow the Cincinnati's model of organization on several levels. There would be local "class" meetings for all subscribers, town meetings, county meetings, state meetings, and "Continental meetings."[56]

Manning did not realize that despite the Federalist front of the society, an ever increasing number of Cincinnati began to appear among the ranks of Jeffersonians. Aaron Burr joined the Cincinnati in 1803 while serving as vice president of the United States. The staunchly Federalist Fifth Congress, which had produced the Alien and Sedition Acts, saw 162 men serve in it, 16 of them Cincinnati. But the Seventh Congress, swept in with the Jeffersonian revolution of 1800, saw an *increase* in the percentage of Cincinnati serving. Of the members of the Fifth Congress 9.8 percent had been Cincinnati, but the Seventh was 12.6 percent. Six senators were Cincinnati, 3 Federalists, and 3 Republicans, and of the 16 members who were representatives, at least 9 were Republicans and 5 were Federalists. After 1800 one could no longer assume that a member of the Society of the Cincinnati was a Federalist.

One Jeffersonian project the Cincinnati might applaud was the establishment of the United States Military Academy in 1802. Army disasters in the West had illustrated the need for better instruction in artillery and military engineering, and an act expanding the army in 1798 provided for such instruction. About the same time the chevalier de Tousard of the French society, who had emigrated to the United States, offered a plan for an academy. It drew the enthusiastic support of President Adams, but while Congress debated Adams left office, and it fell to Jefferson to implement the project. The new president saw it as an opportunity to create a center of scientific learning, and pushed ahead. The new secretary of war, Henry Dearborn of the Massachusetts society, ordered Tousard to West Point to begin instruction of twelve cadets. The first time those cadets paraded as a group was for the funeral of Capt. John Lillie of the Massachusetts society, then in command of the artillery at West Point. His son John, age ten, was admitted a member of the first West Point Class. Tousard left the service in 1802, and under Jefferson faculty appointments were men of science and mathematics rather than the officers of the former Revolutionary army, but children of the Cincinnati were regularly represented among the cadets from the first classes on.

The seven years between 1799 and 1806 mark the end of an era for the Cincinnati. As a national organization, the society was becoming, not dominant, but dormant.

The greatest change came with the death of Washington himself, an occasion of great mourning for the Cincinnati throughout the nation. Probably all the state societies held special services in memory of Washington, many of them with formal processions and orations, and members of the society were prominent in memorials held outside Cincinnati auspices. Before Congress, Henry Lee uttered the enduring description of Washington, "First in war, first in peace, and first in the hearts of his countrymen."[57]

Washington's role in the society cannot be underestimated. Though he took no active part in the original organization, he approved Knox's plans and agreed to serve as president, thus adding his prestige to Knox's idea. Likewise, he used his personal influence to see the state societies organized in the fall of 1783. In response to the public outcry of the winter of 1783–84, his leadership allowed the society to remain intact while accepting the amended institution. Probably no other individual could have persuaded the officers to accept the changes as he did. At several moments it was probably Washington's own personal influence which quieted what monarchist sentiment there surely was within the society, and he probably discouraged any ideas members might have had of using the organization as an instrument of constitutional change. Had Washington's sentiments been otherwise, the society could well have become the major force critics thought it would be. Washington was thus the perfect example of the modern Cincinnatus. Like the ancient Roman, he had served in arms and returned to civilian life as soon as possible, asking neither riches nor power. Washington's personal example was a powerful influence on his old comrades.

After 1787 Washington had taken little active part in Cincinnati affairs. He carried on an extensive correspondence and continued to sign certificates, but he was not to be seen at the general meetings. His role as titular head still brought pride to the members, who remained devoted to his leadership during the Revolution. It was Washington himself who probably saw to it that the status of the amended institution remained ambiguous, a condition offensive neither to members nor critics. By the time of his death, fears about the society had subsided. The society had allowed the generals of 1783 to quiet the army, and Washington in subsequent years was able to quiet both the society and the country, retaining the deep admiration of both.

Despite their continued veneration for their old commander, the Cincinnati cast aside the amended institution at the first possible opportunity. Delegates were still wearing mourning when a special general meeting opened in Philadelphia on May 5, 1800. Representatives from eight states decided that the silence of the state societies indicated their disapproval of the amended institution. Their conclusion was thus "that the institution of the Society of the Cincinnati remains as it was originally proposed and adopted by the officers of the American army."[58] The South Carolina resolutions of 1799 had been a harbinger of things to come, for the amended institution was dead, and hereditary succession was restored.

One sad duty of the 1800 general meeting was the election of a new president general, and vice president general Alexander Hamilton was the ready choice. If anyone thought of Knox, there is no record of it. Charles Cotesworth Pinckney became the vice president general. At Mrs. Washington's request, the diamond eagle which the French sailors had presented Washington was sent to Hamilton, whose own term was brief. Charles Cotesworth Pinckney was chosen to succeed Hamilton at the general meeting of 1805, when the faithful Knox was restored and made vice president. Mrs. Hamilton sent the diamond eagle to Pinckney, who suggested that this gift of the French continue to be the official badge of the president general, and so it has remained.

In October 1806 the society lost Henry Knox as well. He died in Maine at age fifty-six of complications from swallowing a chicken bone. Steuben had died in 1794, Washington was gone, Hamilton was gone, and now Knox. The society passed into hands different from those which had given it birth.

If the founding leaders had departed, so too had some of the state societies. The North Carolina society seems to have collapsed in the late 1790s. Its records have been lost, but there is not a hint of it after 1800. The Georgia society fades from the public eye after February 1800, though a report of officers elected in 1822 shows that some minimal organization still continued. The officers, however, were not bothering to collect their dividends from the United States stock.[59] The Delaware society dissolved itself at its July meeting in 1802, and funds were distributed to members in proportion to their original contributions. A few of them migrated to the Pennsylvania society.[60] Though the general society restored hereditary succession, the Virginia society kept to the amended institution and never accepted hereditary members. In the early 1800s it began to regard its ultimate extinction as inevitable.

The Connecticut society at least disappeared with a flare. Even though the amended institution was dropped, together with its mandate that each society seek a state charter, several states approached their legislatures for incorporation. The New York society, for example, tried for incorporation ten times between 1805 and 1825. Each application came to naught.

In 1803 the Connecticut society had named a committee to seek incorporation. The House looked on the bill with favor, but the Senate did not, even though the senators had been told that rejection meant the death of the society. So David Humphreys informed his compatriots in July 1804, "To acquiesce is our obligation."[61] Whereupon the Connecticut society voted to abolish itself and distribute its funds, with the remainder of the funds ($3,778) deposited in the treasury of Yale College. Members had anticipated the outcome before the meeting, and David Humphreys came prepared with a valedictory discourse. Washington's old aide concluded, "We may expect more justice from posterity, than from the present age." Washington himself had given Humphreys his eagle. Now he would keep it, but he would never wear it again.[62]

Notes

1. GW to John Sullivan, September 1, 1788, Washington, *Writings*, XXX, 38.

2. GW to Hamilton, September 25, 1789, ibid., XXX, 413.

3. On Lincoln, see Callahan, *Knox*, p. 277. Henry Jackson to Knox, December 26, 1790, April 20 and 24, 1791, Knox Papers.

4. GW to Benjamin Fishbourne, December 23, 1788, Washington, *Writings*, XXX, 170-71. GW to the Senate of the United States, August 6, 1789, ibid., XXX, 370-71; see Callahan, *Knox*, pp. 277 f.

5. William Maclay, *Journal of William Maclay*, ed. Edgar S. Maclay. (New York: Appleton, 1890), p. 320. See also pages 100 and 194, where the society is described as one of Hamilton's "machines."

6. My survey is based largely on *The United States Register for the Year 1794* (Philadelphia: Stewart and Cochran and McColloch, 1794), the first full published roster of the Federal bureaucracy. For a careful account of the early civil service based on extensive work in manuscript sources, see Carl E. Prince, *The Federalists and the Origins of the U.S. Civil Service* (New York: New York University Press, 1977). Prince is quite aware of the Cincinnati, but says little about the society itself as a group exerting influence. His statistics too suggest that the Cincinnati were probably not so prominent in the early bureaucracy as Senator Maclay believed. Some 2,435 individuals were appointed to federal office between 1789 and 1801. Of that number only 134 were former Continental officers, and of that group 74 (55%) were Cincinnati. In sum, Cincinnati accounted for but 2.2% of the civil servants under Federalist administrations. Prince, *Origins of the U.S. Civil Service*, pp. 270, 275-76.

7. R.R. Livingston to GW, May 2, 1789, quoted in Young, *Democratic Republicans of New York*, p. 155; James Madison to Thomas Jefferson, May 23, 1789, Madison, *Papers*, XII, 182-83. Fenno's *Gazette of the United States* suggested "Your Supremacy" or "Your Magistracy." Douglas Southall Freeman, *George Washington* (New York: Scribners, 1952), VI, 398.

8. *Gazette of the United States*, May 30, June 3, 1790; *Albany Register*, June 6, 1789, as quoted in Young, *Democratic Republicans of New York*, pp. 155-56.

9. Rufus Wilmot Griswold, *The Republican Court, or American Society in the Days of Washington* (New York: Appleton, 1856), p. 165n.

10. Henrietta Liston to James Jackson of Glasgow, February 24(?), 1797, in *William and Mary Quarterly*, 3d ser. II (1954), 608-9.

11. Callahan, *Knox*, p. 274, quoting an unnamed source, possibly the *New York Packet*.

12. See Ferguson, *Power of the Purse*, pp. 251-86; Young, *Democratic Republicans of New York*, pp. 170-71.

13. Madison to Edmund Pendleton, March 4, 1790, Madison, *Papers*, XIII, 85.

14. Schuyler, *Institution*, p. 96. The vote came at the meeting of February 1, 1790. Young, *Democratic Republicans of New York*, pp. 173-74.

15. Madison, *Papers*, XIII, 58. Thomas Lloyd, *The Congressional Register* (New York: Hodge Allen and Cambell, 1790), III, 451-54. Burke told Congress that Washington had been raised to the status of a "sovereign prince!" (p. 452). In South Carolina, he reported, the former officers dominated the government: "No other class of citizens stand any chance in competition with officers" (p. 453).

16. Ferguson, *Power of the Purse*, pp. 256-57, 327, 329.

17. On Platt see Harrison, *Princetonians*, 334-40.

18. Ebenezer Stevens, *To the Honorable Senate and House of Representatives of the United States of America . . . The Memorial of the Officers* broadside, 1792; George Clinton, Ebenezer Stevens, Marinus Willett, et al., *Gentlemen*, broadside, September 1792. Originals in Rhode Island Society Archives.

19. The Georgia Petition of July 6, 1792, Hume, *Virginia Documents*, pp. 217-19.

20. *History of Congress, Exhibiting a Classification of the Proceedings of the Senate and the House of Representatives* (Philadelphia: Lea and Blanchard, 1843), pp. 678-79. The House as a committee of the whole voted on January 16, 1793. Cincinnati voting for discrimination were John B. Ashe (N.C.), Abraham Baldwin (Ga.), and Thomas Hartley (Pa.). Those against discrimination included Nicholas Gilman (N.H.), John P. G. Muhlenberg (Pa.), and two major speculators Jeremiah Wadsworth (Ct.) and Elias Boudinot (honorary, N.J.).

21. Rhode Island Society, Treasurer's Records, Rhode Island Society Archives; Connecticut Society, Treasurer's Records, Beinecke Rare Book Library, Yale University.

22. *Excerpts of the Proceedings (New Jersey)*, pp. 95-96; Rudolph J. Pasler and Margaret C. Pasler, *The New Jersey Federalists* (Rutherford: Fairleigh Dickinson University Press, 1975), p. 60; *Massachusetts Minutes*, pp. 121-24.

23. William Bentley, *The Diary of William Bentley, D.D.* (Salem: Essex Institute, 1905), I, 271; Benjamin Walker to Joseph Webb, July 25, 1795, as quoted in Young, *Democratic Republicans of New York*, p. 449.

24. "What was Hamilton's 'Favorite Song?' " *William and Mary Quarterly*, 3d ser. 12 (1955), 298-307.

25. Storey, *Minutes of all meetings*, p. 344.

26. *Records of the New Hampshire Society*, pp. 37-39.

27. *Establishment of the Society of the Cincinnati (South Carolina)*, p. 7; *Excerpts of the Proceedings* (New Jersey), p. 150.

28. *The Institution of the Society of the Cincinnati . . . together with Some of the Proceedings of the General Society and of the New-York State Society* (New York: New York Society, 1851), p. 61.

29. Callahan, *Knox*, pp. 293, 302.

30. Meetings of December 21, 1799, and July 13, 1804. Schuyler, *Institution*, pp. 99, 101.

31. Hume, "Early Opposition to the Society of the Cincinnati," p. 621; Anthony Wayne to Georgia delegates to the general meeting, April 15, 1790, in Foster, *Materials Relating to the Cincinnati in Georgia*, pp. 25-27.

32. Storey, *Minutes of all meetings*, p. 95; *Register of the Society of the Cincinnati of Maryland* (1897), pp. 38-39, 45, 46-47.

33. *Proceedings*, I, 42-47 (the meeting of 1790), 48-52 (the meeting of 1791).

34. *Proceedings*, I, 53-54 (meeting of 1793), 55-58 (meeting of 1796), 59-60 (meeting of 1799).

35. List of Officers & others who dined at Oeller's, July 4, 1793, Archives, Pennsylvania Society; Howard Swigget, *The Extraordinary Mr. Morris* (Garden City: Doubleday, 1952), p. 265.

36. Benjamin Tallmadge to Jeremiah Wadsworth, August 8, 1793, as quoted in Charles S. Hall, *Benjamin Tallmadge* (New York: Columbia University Press, 1943), p. 165.

37. Bellas, *History of the Delaware State Society*, pp. 34-35; GW, Sixth Annual Address, November 19, 1794, Washington, *Writings*, XXXIV, 29; see also GW to John Jay, November 5, 1794, ibid., XXXIV, 17. On opposition to these societies generally, see Eugene Perry Link, *Democratic Republican Societies, 1790-1800* (New York: Columbia University Press, 1942), pp. 175-209.

38. Jefferson to Madison, December 28, 1794, Jefferson, *Works*, VIII, 156-59.

39. *New York Journal*, July 7, 1792.

40. *Ibid.*, July 21, 1794.

41. *Ibid.*, August 4, 1794. "Candidus" appeared again on August 18, 1792, when he implicitly criticized the decision of the New York Cincinnati not to support the drive for discrimination. A "junto" of Cincinnati, he wrote, had thrown their brother officers into poverty and distress.

42. On Varick and Fish as political figures, see David Hackett Fischer, *The Revolution of American Conservatism: The Federalist Party in the Era of Jeffersonian Democracy* (New York: Harper and Row, 1965), pp. 308, 301.

43. John Pintard to Steuben, May 13, 1790, New York Society Papers, Anderson House.

44. *New York Journal*, July 7, 1792 and July 6, 1793. Jerome Mushkat, *Tammany: The Evolution of a Political Machine, 1789-1865* (Syracuse: Syracuse University Press, 1971), pp. 11-26.

45. Leland Dewitt Baldwin, *Whisky Rebels: The Story of a Frontier Uprising* (Pittsburgh: University of Pittsburgh Press, 1939), pp. 116-20.

46. *Philadelphia General Advertiser*, February 21, 1795, reprinting the *Aurora; Aurora*, September 30, and December 1, 1795.

47. Bellas, *History of the Delaware State Society*, pp. 25-26.

48. Pasler and Pasler, *New Jersey Federalists*, p. 70 n. 56; Martin R. Zahniser, *Charles Cotesworth Pinckney: Founding Father* (Chapel Hill: University of North Carolina Press, 1967), pp. 265-66.

49. William Irvine to Edward Hand, February 21, 1796, Manuscripts and Archives, Sterling Memorial Library, Yale University.

50. Benjamin Tallmadge to Jeremiah Wadsworth, June 9, 1798, Joseph Trumbull Collection, Connecticut State Library. Photostat at Anderson House.

51. *Institution with Some Proceedings of the New York Society,* pp. 57-58. New York was not the only society to produce an address of support during the crisis of 1798. Many towns, societies, and colleges produced such documents, and a collection of them was published as *A Selection of the Patriotic Addresses to the President of the United States, together with the President's Answers* (Boston: Folsom, 1798). Included are addresses from the Rhode Island Cincinnati (pp. 119 f.) and the Pennsylvania society (pp. 231 f.). An address from the South Carolina society may be found in Adams, *Works,* IX, 222.

52. GW to Hamilton, July 14, 1798, Washington, *Writings,* XXXVI, 329-34.

53. Callahan, *Knox,* pp. 365-74; GW to Knox, October 23, 1798, Hume, *Washington Correspondence,* p. 392.

54. GW to J. F. Grimke, Thomas Pinckney, and Adam Gilchrist, October 20, 1798, Hume, *Washington Correspondence,* pp. 390-91. The text of the South Carolina resolution is found on p. 391.

55. For the South Carolina resolution on expanded membership, see Schuyler, *Institution,* pp. 98-99.

56. William Manning, "The Key of Libberty," *William and Mary Quarterly,* 3d sec. 13 (1956), 209-54.

57. *Eulogies and Orations on the Life and Death of General George Washington* (Boston: Blake and Manning and Loring, 1800), p. 17.

58. *Proceedings,* I, 65.

59. Davis, *Revolution's Godchild,* pp. 55, 252. The letters were advertised in the *Wilmington Gazette,* July 3 and 10, 1800. Foster, *Materials, Relating to the Cincinnati in Georgia* pp. 46-51, 52-54 (election of officers on March 2, 1822).

60. Bellas, *History of the Delaware State Society,* p. 32. The Massachusetts society was informed in 1812 of the dissolution of the Delaware society in 1802. Others claimed that the society lasted until 1804 or even as late as 1828 (pp. 32-33).

61. David Humphreys, *A Valedictory Discourse,* July 4, 1804 (Boston: Gilbert and Dean, 1804), pp. 5-6; Benjamin Tallmadge, *Memoir of Col. Benjamin Tallmadge* (New York: Holman, 1858), p. 56. A total of $15,212 of the society's funds was paid out to members, with the rest going to Yale. *Proceedings,* II, 104-5.

62. Humphreys, *Valedictory Discourse,* p. 36. For additional information on the Connecticut Society's efforts to obtain a charter, see "Proceedings for obtaining an Act of the Legislature for securing the Funds of the Cincinnati, in the State of Connecticut," David Humphreys, *The Miscellaneous Works of David Humphreys* (New York: Swords, 1804), pp. 373-79.

Chapter Nine

Frustration, Success, and Decline

IN ITS FIRST FIFTY YEARS the Society of the Cincinnati went from being a constitutional threat to an all but forgotten organization of revered veterans and their sons. There were elements of both images during the Jefferson presidency.

Mercy Otis Warren, who produced her history in 1805, saw the society as a danger, an organization "capable of becoming a preponderating weight in the political scale of their country."[1]

For others the society was already an object of little concern, even of jest. Hugh Henry Brackenridge, though a prominent Pennsylvania judge, is now remembered as a playwright and novelist. In *Modern Chivalry,* published in 1792, his hero, Captain Farrago, encountered a member of the Cincinnati wearing his eagle. Not everyone at the inn knew what to make of it, and Farrago's servant concluded that it meant the gentleman liked to dine on roast goose. When Farrago asked whether the Cincinnati produce anything but orations, the unnamed member got out his draft of a Fourth of July oration, a short parody of many the Cincinnati heard. He is calling to mind scenes from the Revolution: "What will it contribute to our immediate enjoyment to go over such scenes, unless the particular achievements of each officer can be enumerated, which decency forbids, and which indeed, cannot be done in the limits of one harangue. Leaving, therefore, ourselves, and these scenes, wholly out of the question, let us speak a little of those whom we left behind. But why need we speak; for all time will speak of them. The bards that shall live, will draw hence their choicest allusions." Farrago considers honorary members, but finds the concept difficult as "nature makes no honorary animals." Some, he thinks, contributed more to the Revolution than others, so perhaps the Cincinnati should hand out the eagle in silver, brass, tin, or pot metal according to merit. Some could wear it at the breast, others at the pocket. All said, Farrago (and Brackenridge) see nothing really wrong with the society, for "it is pleasing to indulge a whim."[2]

Charles William Janson, an English traveler during Jefferson's presidency, came to the same conclusion. The society amounted to "little more than a yearly meeting in the form and nature of a society, for the purpose of partaking of a good dinner and a social glass; over which they may be permitted, like Alexander, 'to fight all their battles o'er again, and thrice slay the slain.'" Basically the society was harmless. He made the point by quoting Brackenridge without citing him: "there would have been less tinsel, and more bullion, in the patriotism of retiring without a badge, as Cincinnatus did; but it is a thing that can do little harm, and it is pleasing to indulge a whim."[3]

Cincinnati generally, and especially Federalists, remained fiercely loyal to the memory of Washington, a man whose memory called for extraordinary commemoration. Congress had voted to erect an equestrian statue of Washington in 1783, but no action had been taken by January 1802, when the New York society took matters into its own hands. By December they had committed themselves to a bronze equestrian statue in New York City. A committee of five with Nicholas Fish as chairman and John Stagg, Jr., as secretary would supervise the project, planned for "the square called the park." The society assumed that the requisite $30,000 could be raised by canvassing every house in New York, door to door, and they hoped to find an American artist to do the work.[4] By early 1803 the committee began hearing about John Eckstein, or Johann Eckstein, as he is usually known.[5] He had been a historical painter and sculptor at the Prussian court before coming to the United States in 1794, and once in Philadelphia he had specialized in painting and modeling in clay and wax.

Summoned to New York, Eckstein was ready with plans and an estimate for a statue of Washington "in an antic roman military dress, riding on horseback." The Cincinnatus of his time was thus to be portrayed as an ancient Roman, fourteen and a half feet high from head to hoof. Eckstein calculated he would need 53,000 pounds of bronze at a cost of $24,910. His compensation for three year's work, "my recompense as an artist," and other costs brought the estimate to a whopping $64,800.20.[6] Pledges of $12,350 looked paltry by comparison, and debate on the estimates did not take long. On February 27 Nicholas Fish complimented Eckstein on his "work of genius" but concluded "the Plan (herewith returned) cannot be adopted."[7]

Fish asked the aid of John Trumbull in London and Robert R. Livingston, then American minister to France, but cheaper artists were not forthcoming, and the funds were eventually returned to the donors—with interest.[8] Thus came to an end the plan of this early visionary monument in New York.

Eckstein continued to hope, and in 1810 the Pennsylvania society voted to undertake their own statue of Washington, possibly as a result of the failure of the New York project. That same year Eckstein helped found the Society of Artists, where in 1811 he exhibited a design for an equestrian statue of Washington. Whether that was the old design, which he hoped might attract the support of the Pennsylvania society, is unknown. Pennsylvania may well have considered Eckstein's other design for a standing figure of Washington, wearing a uniform with the eagle, and they surely weighed a plan by Frederic Lemot of Paris.[9] Not so easily discouraged, the Pennsylvania society stuck with the project for eighty-seven years.

In the Jefferson presidency, proposing a statue of Washington was both a pious gesture and a moderate political statement—an affirmation of faith in a great Federalist. Political issues were also subtly at work in the disposition of the funds of the Virginia society. Having abolished the hereditary provision, the Virginia society voted tentatively in December 1802 that its funds would someday go to Washington College, the forebear of Washington and Lee University. A final decision would be made the following year. There followed a predictable scrambling for the cash, as Washington College and Hampden-Sydney both made concerted efforts,[10] and by December 1803 the question for some had become not which college to support but whether to support any. Many members opposed any disbursement of money, arguing that the society was founded for specific purposes, and education was not one of them. Several suggested returning the money to the individual members, and Richard Claiborne wrote from Washington that he needed the money more than any college.

Others were willing to consider other educational options. One member favored a school for the poor, Brig. Gen. Thomas Posey wrote from Kentucky that several Cincinnati hoped to help an academy there, and a Virginian designated his seventy-five dollars for Winchester Academy.[11]

When the vote came in December 1803 there were eighteen for Washington College, sixteen for Hampden-Sydney, and many opposed to any gift. The president concluded that "the sense of a majority of this Society cannot now be obtained," and the question remained open.[12]

No one had suggested that the funds be given to William and Mary, and one does not need to look long for reasons, for William and Mary was a notably Republican college. It was the only major campus that celebrated news of Jefferson's election, and it was the only campus where students had balked at wearing mourning for Washington. Students actually debated the question before voting to go along with the suggestion, except for six or seven who refused.[13]

The whole question still seemed open as late as 1817, when none other than Thomas Jefferson solicited the funds on behalf of his new University of Virginia. He had heard that the Cincinnati talked of starting a "school for the military arts of gunnery and fortification," and the University of Virginia would be happy to establish a professorship of just those subjects. He must have hesitated when he even offered to name the chair "the Cincinnati professorship." At least one member of the society supported Jefferson's proposal, but it met with no success, and by 1822 Washington College heard officially that it would receive the funds. There was a stipulation that the money be used for a professorship of military science and for an annual oration commemorating the society itself.[14] The college finally received the money in 1848.

In the early 1800s the general society was in decline. Charles Cotesworth Pinckney's presidency was not an auspicious one. He had begun with vigor, writing a firm letter to the state societies in August 1811. It had been "inconsiderate" for some state societies to dissolve themselves and distribute their funds, money which was no longer the property of individuals. Despite his urging, only four states appeared at the general meeting on September 7, 1812. Once more Pinckney exhorted the state societies to send delegates to another session on September 29, but only three states were represented then. It is easy to see why he probably became discouraged.[15]

The triennial meetings ceased after 1812, and there was a general period of dormancy at the national level, as Pinckney failed to provide the leadership other presidents would offer later. Two more state societies became dormant in the 1820s. The Virginia society held its last meeting at the state capitol in Richmond on May 14, 1824. The Virginians realized that their society had come to an end, but the men of New Hampshire did not. From 1810 to 1823 the New Hampshire society met regularly, though often the meeting consisted only of the faithful secretary Daniel Gookin and treasurer Michael McClary. By comparison, the meeting of 1806 was a crowd when eight members gathered. When Gookin and McClary met in 1823, they had no sense that it was their last meeting, and in 1842 Gookin's son pronounced the society extinct and sent the records to the New Hampshire Historical Society.[16]

Other state societies continued with vigor. Massachusetts, New York, New Jersey, Pennsylvania, Maryland, and South Carolina never faltered, and Rhode Island was still at least holding on. On two occasions the Cincinnati either rejected or ignored opportunities to establish new state societies that might have given the whole organization new life.

Marietta, Ohio, had a higher concentration of Cincinnati than probably any other town in the nation, and in 1804 Rufus Putnam and others there petitioned the Massachusetts society for their portion of the Massachusetts funds. They hoped to establish their own society in Ohio, and it would appear they had already taken steps to organize. A year later leaders of the Massachusetts society responded that the proposal was "novel" and "irregular." The society was intended "to form one Family of brethren to consist of *thirteen* Cantons and *no more,* forever," and if individuals could withdraw their funds at will the charitable funds would be imperiled. They assured their Marietta brethren of their "unabated friendship" and that their pledges still remained "a sacred deposit for their benefit in common with the other Members."[17] Thus came to an end an Ohio society.

Kentucky members raised the same question in 1808. The Virginia society made no response to their request, but Secretary General William Jackson promised to do whatever he could to aid their cause. He assured them that they were perfectly within the original institution in starting a new society, and he looked to

President General Pinckney to champion their cause at the general meeting in May, but nothing came of the proposal.[18]

The effect of the decisions on Ohio and Kentucky was to make it nearly impossible for many members to remain active participants, and as families began to lose interest, those eligible ignored their rights to hereditary succession. Aedanus Burke would have been astounded. One distinguished student of the Pennsylvania society suggests that membership was more likely to be maintained by those living near the cities in which the societies met and those families having need of the charitable funds. There were of course notable exceptions.[19]

Successor members came to be more and more prominent at the annual meetings. Each society defined its own rules for admission, but some problems were common to all. If the eldest son was not interested in the society but the second son was, could the elder waive his rights? New York decided no in 1813, and then yes in 1818. What about sons of officers who never joined? In 1816 New York rejected such an applicant, but in the following year the Maryland society elected John McHenry, son of the secretary of war under Washington and Adams. A most unusual question of succession came up in the Rhode Island society in 1819. William Jones, former governor of the state, had no son and wondered whether his son-in-law might succeed him. After some debate, the members agreed, but when Jones died the place went unfilled. Jones's grandson was admitted to the New York society in 1877.[20]

These younger men of course had not shared the Revolutionary experiences of the old officers, but generally all Cincinnati of whatever age met to celebrate the Fourth of July together. New Jersey provided an occasional exception. In 1803 young and old Federalists had held separate Fourth of July meetings, and in 1804 the New Jersey Cincinnati did the same. There was one dinner for the veterans, now called more and more "original members," and a separate meeting of the younger "successor members."[21]

Members young and old and their families now made regular use of the charitable funds in time of need. Individual claims were to be presented to the state societies to which an original member had contributed, and the certificates of membership which the individual state societies produced were more than ornaments. They were grants of access to the charitable funds. New York (1790), New

Jersey (1808), Maryland (c. 1810), and Massachusetts (c. 1812) all produced such diplomas, most following the original L'Enfant design.[22]

By the 1820s all trace of partisan activity was gone from society affairs, and the Cincinnati were now venerated rather than ridiculed. They were senior statesmen, founding fathers, not a threat to the Constitution. In 1823 the Corporation of the City of New York invited the New York Cincinnati to dine with them at City Hall on July 4. The Cincinnati declined. They explained that they had been formed to maintain the fellowship of the Revolution on its principal anniversary. But three years later they relented and dined with the corporation on the fourth.[23]

The War of 1812 found the old Cincinnati often unsympathetic at the outset and generally undistinguished at the end. Federalists were largely opposed to the war, and in Baltimore riots over an antiwar newspaper editor, Gen. Henry Lee was injured and James H. Lingan of the Maryland society was killed. De Witt Clinton, the Federalist antiwar candidate for president defeated that fall, became a successor member of the New York society the following summer. In New Jersey Aaron Ogden's antiwar sentiments made him governor.

Once more the Cincinnati rallied to the flag, but the magic which had won the Revolution failed for the many veteran commanders in 1812. William Hull surrendered Detroit in August and spent the rest of his life trying to clear his name. Major Generals Samuel Hopkins of the Virginia society and Henry Dearborn of the Massachusetts society were unable to persuade their militia to attack, and General Zebulon Pike was killed in a raid on York, the capital of Upper Canada. The following year with a small detachment of sailors and naval guns on land, Commodore Joshua Barney did his best to resist British advances on Washington. When the city fell, John Armstrong, author of the Newburgh Addresses, received the brunt of public criticism and was promptly forced out as secretary of war. James Monroe of the Virginia society replaced him, acting for the time being as secretary of both state and war.

There were victorious commanders in the War of 1812, and many of them quickly found their way into the ranks of the Cincinnati. The New York society used the honorary membership much like the Order of the Bath or the Legion of Honor, as a reward for distinguished military valour. In 1813 and 1815 New York elected a total of eleven honorary members, all naval commanders. In 1813 they selected Commodores William Bainbridge, Stephen Decatur, and Oliver Hazard Perry and Captains Jacob Jones and James Lawrence. Two years later they elected Commodore Thomas Macdonough and Captains Johnston Blakeley, Isaac Hull, and Lewis Warrington. The election of Lawrence is particularly noteworthy, for it was posthumous and I have found no other such bestowal of honorary membership. In 1813 Pennsylvania made Capt. James Biddle an honorary member, and they too elected Bainbridge. Pennsylvania also elected two generals that year, Winfield Scott and George Izard. New York filled out the rosters by adding generals Jacob Brown in 1818 and Andrew Jackson in 1819. Maryland elected Commodore Jesse Duncan Elliott in 1818, and Pennsylvania added Capt. Charles Stewart in 1816. When Macdonough and Perry had their portaits painted, they wore the eagle with their uniform as though it were the national decoration.

The 1820s brought a brief resurgence of enthusiasm for the society. Rhode Island, for example, commissioned a firm in Philadelphia to make a new group of eagles, a sure sign of enduring interest. There were two great stimuli bringing life to the organization, the visit of Lafayette and the renewed campaign for half pay for life. With the latter the society once more found a purpose beyond fellowship.[24]

Lafayette's tour from August 1824 to September 1825 provided the occasion for large reunions. In his travels he met with every extant state society, a claim few early presidents general could make. In August 1824 he met with the New York, Rhode Island, and Massachusetts societies, and in September the New York society gave him a birthday dinner and he dined with the New Jersey society. October took him to the Maryland society, and in the following month he attended two functions of the South Carolina society.[25] While in South Carolina he paused to allow Charles Fraser to paint a miniature of him wearing Washington's own eagle, which had been given to him at Mount Vernon by Mrs. Lawrence Lewis.[26] After a tour of the West, he attended a reception given by the Pennsylvania society in July.

As Lafayette traveled, his secretary, Auguste Levasseur, recorded his impressions of America, and memories of the birthday dinner in New York were vivid.

> About four in the afternoon we saw arriving a long line of old men marching two by two arm in arm for their mutual support, made necessary by the weight of years. They were preceded by a military band which made vain efforts to regulate the cadence of their steps. We descended to meet them. In the button-hole of General Lafayette was the decoration of the Order of Cincinnatus which had once been worn by Washington, and we marched with them to the hall where the dinner was laid. It was indeed a touching picture made by these ancient warriors, glorious survivors of the war of Independence, leading in their midst the companion of Washington and the adopted son of America. The crowds that lined the streets through which we passed evinced by their grave and silent attention, the respect which the cortege inspired.

In Europe, he had still heard attacks on the society as tending to destroy a republican government, but after that evening he saw nothing "destructive of equality" in the Cincinnati.[27]

Officers had never been satisfied fully with the pay settlements after the Revolution. The campaigns for discrimination in funding the Continental securities had gone nowhere in 1790 and 1792. The issue arose anew in Pittsburgh during the depression of 1808 when Stephen Bayard and Isaac Craig of the Pennsylvania society and Adamson Tannehill of the Maryland society sent a circular letter to the state societies. It was not discrimination that they sought. Rather, they wanted the government to "make good the original promise" and establish half pay for life.[28]

The campaign of 1808 was a predominately Cincinnati effort. Leaders sought support from nonmembers, but the basic strategy centered around the society with no effort made to create a national mass movement. The Pittsburgh men hoped each society would prepare a memorial to Congress. Philadelphia officers likewise urged the Fourth of July meetings in each state to pass resolutions calling for half pay, and David Lenox, president of the Pennsylvania society, would coordinate the effort. In May, Stephen Bayard wrote from Pittsburgh again, suggesting the formula destined to become the focus of twenty years of effort: Congress should pay each officer half pay from the year 1783, deducting therefrom the nominal sum paid as the five years' commutation. Bayard wanted petitions to Congress with signatures from "every old officer, who is now alive." He also wanted each state society to send "one of its members whose services may have been conspicuous and whose standing in life is respectable" to call on Congress, with his expenses to be funded by the state society.[29] That summer the Pennsylvania society sent out yet another mailing, urging each society to maximum activity.[30]

Virginia officers gathered at the capitol in Richmond on December 12 in what was not technically a Cincinnati meeting, even though fourteen of the twenty present were members. By a vote of 18 to 2 they supported the Pennsylvania effort and appointed Gen. Peter Johnston to "use his influence & exertions" for half pay. They urged the Virginia society to pay his expenses, and on December 31 the society paid him $100.[31]

On July 4, 1809, after embarking on the campaign for half pay, the Pennsylvania society voted $500 for a monument to the memory of Maj. Gen. Anthony Wayne. Though one member thought the sum too small ($2,000 would have been better), Bayard, Craig, Tannehill, and four other members wrote from Pittsburgh to demand reconsideration. The funds of the Cincinnati were not collected to build monuments but to help the needy. Perhaps more important, Bayard and the others wondered how they could press their case for need when the Cincinnati had assets adequate to squander $500 on a monument. In somewhat sarcastic tones they asked whether there would be monuments to all members, proportioned in expense "to the merit of each of the deceased?"[32]

Despite the protest, the Pennsylvania society went ahead with the campaign and the monument, later installed over Wayne's tomb at Radnor, Pennsylvania. In militant tones the members even refused contributions toward the project from outside the society. With $200 for expenses, Gen. Thomas Boude was named agent for the society "to promote the claims of the officers of the Revolutionary army."[33]

By 1810 it looked as though continuing pressure might bear fruit when a congressional committee supported the officers' cause. Their report might well have been written by the society itself, and the recommendation for action consisted of but thirteen words: "That the prayer of the petitioners is reasonable and ought to be granted." In July the Pennsylvania society was told that General Boude "had procured a favourable report to be made upon the petition of the officers." However, "owing to the pressure or interference of other business, the report was not taken up, nor any further proceedings had on the case."[34]

General meetings added no momentum to the campaign. All four attempts to hold such meetings in 1811 and 1812 drew minimal representation, and any hope for success lay with the state societies.[35] The year 1812, with its requirement for the funding of a new war, was hardly an auspicious time to seek pensions for the veterans of an old one. In 1816, however, after peace was restored, Congress for the first time increased the pensions paid to invalids under the legislation of 1792. Noncommissioned officers and privates would henceforth receive $8 a month rather than $5, and officers would receive a minimum of at least two to three dollars a month more than the half pay they had been receiving. It was probably this new congressional support that spurred the Cincinnati to renewed activity on their own behalf.[36]

In 1817 a new strategy emerged that mirrors the transformation of American politics. The society became convinced that mass support was necessary for political success. In June 1817 a committee of the Pennsylvania society sent a mailing to extant state societies. The packet included the congressional report of 1810, papers sent to President Madison and Congress the year before, a letter (presumably typical) from a veteran, an estimate of the cost of the legislation ($1,152,000), the address of the Pennsylvania society to the citizens of the state, and a proposed petition to Congress which state societies might circulate. They hoped to collect "a general signature in every district in the union," in what amounted to a media campaign.

The anonymous letter to a member of Congress about an anonymous major general (surely Rufus Putnam) would make good copy. It told of a sequestered spot on an Alleghany mountain, where a log cabin sheltered "the shriveled frame of one of the best and bravest warriors of the revolution." Here one found "the withered victim of *legislative* ingratitude and injustice, lingering out the remanent of an honorable and useful life in unmerited and unalleviated affliction." Putnam was living in Marietta, Ohio, and at his death in 1824 he was the last of the Continental major generals, save for Lafayette.[37]

By fall the New York and New Jersey societies had formed a joint committee which sent out its own packet of printed documents, adding letters from Washington and more blank petitions. Each society was urged to do its best to get "one old Officer" from each state to go to Washington to lobby in person by December 25. It may be revealing of inaction that the Rhode Island society still has three of the blank petitions in crisp, uncirculated condition.[38]

Congressional action in March 1818 must have been encouraging yet frustrating. In the first major change in pension policy since 1792, Congress adopted the Limited Service Pension Act, and pensions were no longer just for invalids. President Monroe (of the Virginia society) had recommended support for indigent survivors of the war in December 1817, confident there were relatively few, and Joseph Bloomfield of the New Jersey society introduced a bill providing pensions for all "in need of assistance" who had served nine months or to the end of the war. Noncommissioned officers and men would have $8 a month, officers, $20. No one had any idea how many might apply when Congress adopted the plan on March 18.[39]

The Cincinnati lost no time in continuing to press for half pay, and William Jackson, the faithful secretary general, took charge of the lobbying. The Pennsylvania society was especially committed to the cause, and at a special meeting on May 4, 1818, members voted that "it is a duty which the surviving Officers of the Revolutionary Army owe themselves & country to renew the application to Government for an equitable settlement of the half pay for life." The society then named Jackson "solicitor" to carry out that duty. If Congress refused to grant "an equitable settlement," then each surviving officer would be assessed to cover the solicitor's expenses. But should the mission be a success, then he would receive 4 percent of whatever Congress gave to each officer. Jackson wrote each state society, hoping for more resolutions and a barrage of letters to Congress. With great optimism, he speculated that "more than a million of the most respectable names" would sign the petition blanks he sent.[40]

Jackson's printed memorial to Congress reviewed the relevant legislation, and provided some interesting post-Revolutionary sociology. Pressure from officers senior in age and rank had forced the junior officers to accept commutation in 1783. Though New Englanders may have acquiesced, officers from Georgia, South

Carolina, North Carolina, and some corps of Virginia had no voice at all in the matter. In retrospect commutation was an "error of the most injurious nature to the Officers." Jackson explained the wrong in actuarial terms. In 1783 the average age of the officers was 35 years, which, according "to the most approved writers on annuities," would have meant the average commutation for each should have been ten years and six months of full pay, instead of five years. Younger officers, however, should have received twelve years of full pay.[41]

Jackson asked that Congress renew the half-pay promise, pay the balance due each officer with six percent interest, subtracting any sum received for commutation. Each would henceforth be paid at the half-pay rate. His proposal fared poorly in 1818, but some congressmen urged that the officers bring up the question at the following session. Pennsylvania officers met still again to offer new support in May 1819, and in 1820 the Pennsylvania society praised Jackson for his efforts, but success still eluded them.[42] It is easy to see why.

In 1818 Congress had assumed there were but few veterans "in need of assistance," but there was an immediate rush for pensions, and, in the judgment of many, fraud was rampant. The federal pension budget mushroomed from $104,900 in 1818 to $1,811,328 a year later—an increase of over 1,700 percent. Remedial legislation demanding proof of need reduced the cost by $400,000 by 1822, but the government was still supporting 12,331 soldiers, and Congress might be expected to look at any new proposals with great care.[43]

To the dismay of some, Lafayette's visit renewed interest in the quest for half pay. This time the circular letter emerged from a Boston meeting in April 1825, and there was a touch of sarcasm. The government had been exceedingly generous in welcoming Lafayette, and these officers only hoped for some of the same liberality.[44] Though the proposals were sent to the state societies, the organizers avoided an explicit association with the society, and they lowered their demand, or rather their request. They gave up, implicitly, the hope of half pay retroactive to 1783. All they asked was half pay for life for the few remaining veterans, for, as they noted lugubriously, "the grave has closed on the principal part of the officers who served in the war of American Independence."

Daniel Lyman, president of the Rhode Island society, thought it was "altogether unavailing to make any further effort." "Our days will soon be numbered," he continued, and at least there was the comfort of knowing the Cincinnati could pay for funerals of the indigent.[45]

The delegates seemed more interested in discussing lobbying efforts than in electing a new president general, when the death of Charles Cotesworth Pinckney necessitated a general meeting in November 1825, the first since 1812. Once more they petitioned Congress, now asking even less. They said nothing of renewed half pay for life, but merely hoped Congress would do them justice "to smooth the passage to the grave of the remaining few." There was also a direct appeal to President John Quincy Adams.[46]

Aaron Ogden, president of the New Jersey society, had led much of the discussion of the claims and was chosen vice president general for his efforts. The diamond eagle went to Maj. Gen. Thomas Pinckney, brother of the previous president general.

Back home from Philadelphia, the delegates began lobbying. For example, John Singer Dexter of Rhode Island sent Congressman Tristram Burges a packet of memorials and promised more. Burges wrote that the memorials would get his "zealous attention."[47]

In addition to the Cincinnati meeting in Philadelphia, there was a meeting of former officers in Baltimore which named four agents to lobby on behalf of their claims. In the event of failure the agents would receive nothing, not even their expenses. But in the event of success the agents would recove 5 percent of each claim, making it a gamble well worth the risk.[48]

Chief among the agents was Aaron Ogden, now vice president general. More than his devotion to the cause led him to undertake the task. As he admitted later, he needed the money. Every student of American constitutional law knows that *Gibbons v. Ogden* in 1824 ended the exclusive right that New York state had given Robert Fulton to navigate the Hudson. Ogden's exclusive license through Fulton collapsed, and as Ogden would write in 1828, "I had lost by a wicked prosecution my hard earned fortune." The chance to secure the Revolutionary claims offered, therefore, great personal interest.[49]

The effort gained a new momentum after President Adams ended his annual address in December 1827 by urging Congress to deal with "the debt, rather of justice than gratitude, to the surviving warriors of the Revolutionary war."[50] In May 1828 Congress voted, not half, but *full* pay for life to all surviving Continental officers who had been entitled to half pay. Enlisted men received the same award. The first payment would be large, for pay was made retroactive to March 3, 1826, and by the end of 1828 there were 850 officers receiving full pay.

The four lobbyists now found the beneficiaries reluctant to pay the commissions promised. New York officers agreed to pay Ogden 10 percent of the first payment rather than 5 percent of subsequent receipts, but many refused to pay anything. Some who had not been at the Baltimore meeting in 1825 denied any obligation to pay, while others said that Ogden's efforts had been useless, because such a just claim would have been funded anyway—to which Ogden could cite forty-five years of history to the contrary. Still others thought the commissions too high. In late spring 1829 Ogden and his fellow agents held their own meeting to explain their position, and whatever they received finally in commissions was far below their initial expectations.

With the final funding of full pay for life, part of the rationale binding the society since 1783 collapsed; and with the number of members and state societies on the decline, the general meetings soon entered another period of dormancy. After 1825 another general meeting was not held until the election of a new president general in 1829. Meetings were held in the 1830s, but they did little more than plan the next meeting, hitting an all-time low in 1838 when the general meeting consisted of three people: the president general, the secretary general, and one delegate from Pennsylvania. The three voted to give up even the pretext of "triennial" meetings—only when necessary would general meetings be called.[51]

Another state society slipped into oblivion on July 4, 1835, when the Rhode Island society held its last meeting. Activity was minimal in other states, and general officers had difficulty discovering the status of the constituent societies.[52] Membership in the entire society probably fell to not more than two-hundred fifty.

In the middle decades of the nineteenth century, the office of president general changed hands often, despite the unwritten rule that tenure was for life. Thomas Pinckney, elected in 1825, lived only until 1828. Pinckney had been governor, minister to Great Britain, congressman, and major general in the War of 1812, but his short presidency left no enduring mark on the society. Given his success as a lobbyist, Aaron Ogden, who was already vice president general, was a natural choice to succeed Pinckney. Having been governor and senator from New Jersey, he too was a public figure as well as the first industrial capitalist to become president general. His presidency was paradoxical, for the society as a whole declined, probably because of his success as a lobbyist. Ogden enjoyed society meetings, and, unlike many early presidents general, was a regular presence at general meetings.

At Ogden's death in 1839, the society once more chose a prominent officer as president general. Morgan Lewis had been both chief justice and governor of New York before serving as a major general in the War of 1812. Though he sat proudly for his portrait wearing the diamond eagle, the general meeting that elected him was the last held in his lifetime.

When Morgan Lewis died, the diamond eagle had been forwarded to Maj. William Popham, new president of the New York society. On November 23, 1844, four days before the general meeting began, Popham wrote a New York delegate that he had the badge, and he obviously believed that the office went with physical possession of the eagle. Younger men (he was ninety-three at the time) would not know the origins of the society, and "I have presumed as President General, for the time being" to offer a short account of the early years. Accordingly he sent along a copy of his address before the New York society, as well as a hint of his desire to have the eagle by right.[53]

After the delegates read his address, his election must have been guaranteed, for seldom had the society had so eloquent a defender of any age. Some had proposed abolishing the society. "Perish the thought! No! Never while I live, though I shall through the natural infirmities of old age be denied the power in appearing in it again, I will never consent to consign to eternal oblivion an Institution which received the sanction of Washington, and been consecrated by his own signature. . . . I consider it as the Alma Mater of the greatest and most resplendent empire that the world has ever seen."[54]

Popham was the first president general who owed his office to longevity and interest in the society rather than public prominence. He had spent his career as an official of the New York judicial system. He was the last of the presidents general who had served in the Revolution, and fittingly he had been at Newburgh for Washington's stirring address on March 15, 1783.

The venerable Popham would have been excused for following the do-nothing pattern of some of his predecessors, but that was not his plan. He moved right ahead with plans for a general gathering of state societies in New York on November 25, 1845, the anniversary of the British evacuation of the city. The general meeting of 1844 had approved the plan, but the states were unenthusiastic. South Carolina appointed a delegation, and New Jersey voted to attend as a body. But Maryland was uncertain whether any members could attend, and the secretary general despaired of knowing what other societies might be doing. In October, Popham, who was bedridden, was forced to cancel his plans, but an idea had taken root.[55] A Cincinnati meeting did not have to be in Philadelphia.

Charles S. Daveis of Massachusetts wrote that the Massachusetts society would "give their brethern a hearty New England welcome." Daveis, who later became vice president general, was a strong force for the mutual cooperation of all state societies. In a similar vein Joseph Warren Scott, treasurer general, wrote the secretary general that there was interest in reestablishing a Georgia society. Both men hinted that the society had been too much oriented toward Philadelphia and that national meetings were planned on a local schedule, making it almost impossible for delegates from distant societies to attend. Scott hoped that Massachusetts might send one of its surviving Revolutionary officers as a delegate to the general meeting in Philadelphia planned for 1848—"I shall look on him with reverence."[56] Original members were few by then, and with the death of Robert Burnet, Jr., of the New York society on November 29, 1854, they were gone.

Like Popham, Scott was a promoter of social interaction among the state societies, and he proposed that the New Jersey and Pennsylvania societies hold a joint meeting in Trenton on July 4, 1849. Pennsylvanians might have to meet early in Philadelphia to do their legal business, but then why not come to Trenton? He promised to arrange all to suit their convenience.[57] Popham's short presidency marked a turning point and the awakening of a new, purely social interest among the members.

Delegates gathered in Philadelphia to elect a new president

general in 1848, and for the first time a successor member would be chosen. For the first time too there was a real contest. Gen. Henry A. S. Dearborn, son of Col. Henry Dearborn, was a former collector of the Port of Boston, former congressman, and a brigadier general of Massachusetts militia. A graduate of William and Mary in 1803, his was an extraordinarily fertile mind. His published works included *Commerce of the Black Sea, History of Navigation, Internal Improvement and Commerce of the West, Sketch of the Life of the Apostle Eliot,* and a defense of his father. At his death he left other works in manuscript: eleven volumes of the life and correspondence of his father, an account of Bunker Hill, a life of Jesus, a life of Col. W. R. Lee, his father-in-law, a life of Commodore Bainbridge, and a treatise on Greek architecture. Later in the century the Cincinnati were to develop an interest in historic commemorations, something Dearborn had already mastered as a promoter of the Bunker Hill Monument. Curiously, he had never held any offices in the Massachusetts society or attended a single triennial meeting.

Dearborn was not present in Philadelphia, but New York's lieutenant governor Hamilton Fish was. The son of Nicholas Fish, a Columbia graduate who had entered the law, he too had been a congressman. It was Fish's first general meeting, but he seems to have made it his own. He must have been on his feet nearly the entire time, for he made or seconded, it would seem, at least half the resolutions. He was a man marked for office.

When the voting for president general came, as the secretary's minutes note, "there was no election."[58] A second ballot chose Dearborn as president general and Fish as vice president general. Death would claim Dearborn in 1851, two months after the general meetings in New York that year. But Hamilton Fish would remain an institution of the society for the next forty-five years.

When Fish became president general in 1854, he had moved from the governor's office in Albany to the United States Senate. He was a man used to the process of legislation, and the changes he wanted were soon adopted.

Notes

1. Warren, *History*, III, 292.

2. Hugh Henry Brackenridge, *Modern Chivalry* (New York: American Book Co., 1937), pp. 69–75.

3. Charles William Janson, *The Stranger in America* (London: Cundee, 1807), pp. 285, 294.

4. Minutes of December 15, 1802, HM 9568, Huntington Library.

5. Charles Willson Peale to John Stagg, Jr., January 16, 1803, HM 9573, Huntington Library.

6. Eckstein's estimate of costs, February 14, 1803, HM 9581, Huntington Library.

7. Nicholas Fish to Johann Eckstein, February 27, 1803, HM 9582, Huntington Library.

8. Minutes of Committee Meeting, March 1803, HM 9585, Huntington Library; George C. Groce and David H. Wallace, *The New-York Historical Society's Dictionary of Artists in America, 1564-1860* (New York: Yale, 1957), p. 205.

9. Note of Mr. Frederic Lemot, February 29, 1812, Pennsylvania Society Archives.

10. Alfred J. Morrison, *College of Hampden Sidney: Calendar of Minutes, 1776-1876* (Richmond: Hermitage, 1912), p. 56.

11. Richard Claiborne to Samuel Coleman, April 14, 1803; Philip Mallory to James Wood, December 7, 1803; Thomas Posey to J. Blackburn and G. A. Baxter, June 18, 1803; Alexander Balmain to James Wood, November 31, 1803; all in Hume, *Virginia Documents*, pp. 266-67, 273-74, 276, 262.

12. Ibid., p. 70.

13. J. Shelton Watson to David Watson, December 24, 1799, "Letters from William and Mary College, 1798-1801," *Virginia Magazine of History and Biography*, 29 (1921), 167-68.

14. Thomas Jefferson to Francis Brooke, November 7, 1817, Hume, *Virginia Documents*, pp. 258-59.

15. Zahniser, *Pinckney*, pp. 265-66; Charles Cotesworth Pinckney to the State Societies, August 9, 1811, New York Society Papers; *Proceedings*, I, 75-76.

16. Hume, *Virginia History*, pp. 132-33, *Records of the New Hampshire Society*, p. 17.

17. Massachusetts Society, Minutes of July 4, 1804, May 27 and July 5, 1805, Storey, *Minutes of all meetings*, pp. 192, 195, 196, 197.

18. Robert Breckenridge, Richard Clough Anderson, Abraham Hill, William Croghan, and G. Gray to General Society, April 14, 1808; draft of William Jackson to Breckenridge et al., undated, 1808, Anderson House.

19. Personal communication from Clifford Lewis 3d.

20. *Institution with Proceedings of the New York Society*, p. 62; Rhode Island, Meeting of July 5, 1819, Minutes of Rhode Island Society, Rhode Island Society Archives.

21. Pasler and Pasler, *New Jersey Federalists*, p. 134 n. 27, citing *The Federalist*, July 11, 1803 and July 9, 1804.

22. Hume, *The Diplomas of the Society of the Cincinnati; Proceedings of the Pennsylvania Society*, pp. 82-83.

23. Schuyler, *Institution*, pp. 105-6, 108.

24. Rhode Island Society, Treasurer's Records for 1821, Rhode Island Society

Archives. Possibly the same firm had approached the Massachusetts society, which also considered the new manufacture of eagles in 1820, but deferred any action. Meetings of July 4 and August 5, 1820, Storey, *Minutes of all meetings,* pp. 304, 305.

25. For the itinerary of Lafayette's visit, see J. Bennett Nolan, *Lafayette in America Day by Day* (Baltimore: Johns Hopkins University Press, 1934).

26. The miniature is illustrated in Hume, *Virginia History,* p. 140.

27. As quoted in Hume, *La Fayette and the Society of the Cincinnati,* p. 50.

28. Stephen Bayard, Isaac Craig, and Adam Tannehill, Pittsburgh, March 8, 1808, broadside, Rhode Island Society Archives.

29. Circular letter from Matthew McConnell, Abraham Claypoole, Robert Porter, April 30, 1808, Rhode Island Society Archives; circular letter from Stephen Bayard, Pittsburgh, May 20, 1808, broadside, Rhode Island Society Archives.

30. M. McConnell, R. Porter, A. Claypoole, *To the Honorable the Senate and House of Representatives,* Philadelphia, July 1808, broadside, Rhode Island Society Archives.

31. Virginia meeting of December 12, 1808, Hume, *Virginia Documents,* pp. 285-87, 460, 477.

32. David Zeigler to David Lenox, August 4, 1809; Stephen Bayard and six others to David Lenox, July 14, 1809, Pennsylvania Society Archives.

33. Pennsylvania, Meeting of July 4, 1810, Minutes, Pennsylvania Society Archives. Friends of Wayne had proposed to give "eighty or ninety dollars." Thomas Boude had served as a captain in the Revolution and was a Federalist congressman from Pennsylvania from 1801 to 1803. He was therefore well acquainted with Congress, its methods, and members. For a sketch of Boude see Fischer, *Revolution of American Conservatism,* p. 335. Though the Pennsylvania society voted to name an agent on July 4, 1809, Boude is not named as the agent in the records until January 15, 1810.

34. The committee's report was reprinted in a circular, no. 1, prepared by the New York and New Jersey societies in 1817. Rhode Island Society Archives. Pennsylvania, Meeting of July 4, 1810, Minutes, Pennsylvania Society Archives.

35. *Proceedings,* I, 71-74 (1811), 75-76 (1812).

36. Glasson, *History of Military Pension Legislation,* p. 33.

37. Circular letter from Thomas Robinson, Charles Biddle, John Markland, and William Jackson, Philadelphia, June 16, 1817, broadside, Rhode Island Society Archives. The Rhode Island society still has the six printed enclosures which came with the letter. The quotations about Putnam are from Anonymous to Member of Congress, Philadelphia, February 12, 1817, no. 4 of the enclosures.

38. Circular letter, Richard Platt to Presidents of State Societies, New York, November 8, 1817, broadside, Rhode Island Society Archives. This letter reported on the joint ventures of the New York and New Jersey societies and brought four enclosures with it, one of them the report of the congressional committee in 1810.

39. Glasson, *History of Military Pension Legislation,* pp. 33-36.

40. Pennsylvania, Meeting of May 4, 1818, Minutes of Pennsylvania Society, Pennsylvania Society Archives; circular letter of David Lenox to the State Societies, Philadelphia, May 1818, broadside, Rhode Island Society Archives; circular letter of William Jackson to State Societies, Philadelphia, June 30, 1818, Rhode Island Society Archives.

41. The memorial was, or became, the petition to be signed by the millions the society would approach. *To the Honorable the Senate, and the Honorable the House of Representatives,* broadside, 1818, Rhode Island Society Archives.

42. *At a Meeting of the Surviving Officers,* Philadelphia, May 31, 1819, broadside, Anderson House; Pennsylvania, Meeting of July 4, 1820, Minutes, Pennsylvania Society Archives.

43. Glasson, *History of Military Pension Legislation,* pp. 33–39.

44. Circular letter of Daniel Jackson, Francis Green, and Robert Williams to State Societies, Boston, April 1825, Rhode Island Society Archives.

45. Daniel Lyman to Robert Williams, May 21, 1825, Rhode Island Society Archives.

46. In summoning delegates to a general meeting, William Jackson wrote, "The contemplated application to Congress at the ensuing session on behalf of the surviving officers of the Revolutionary Army will form an essential object." Once more he was ready to raise his banner. William Jackson to President, Rhode Island Society, August 29, 1825, Rhode Island Society Archives. *Proceedings,* I, 79–80.

47. John Singer Dexter to Tristram Burges, November 22, 1825, Burges to Dexter, December 7, 1825, Rhode Island Society Archives.

48. Alden Bradford, editor of the Boston *Gazette* and son of Col. Gamaliel Bradford, was another of the agents. I have been unable to identify the other two.

49. *Copy of a Letter from Col. Aaron Ogden to Major James Fairlie,* Jersey City, July 27, 1829, circular, Private Collection. New York not only appointed Ogden their own agent but produced a seven-page printed memorial to support his efforts. Once more New Jersey and New York agreed to cooperate, and they urged that other state societies join with them. They hoped that Rhode Island at least might stage a convention to support the effort. Richard Platt, Leonard Bleeker, and Lebbeus Loomis to the President of the Society of the Cincinnati in the State of Rhode Island or in his Absence to One of the Senior Officers of the Revolutionary Army, December 10, 1825, Rhode Island Society Archives.

50. John Quincy Adams, Third Annual Message, December 4, 1827, *Messages and Papers of the Presidents* (1897), II, 392. See also Glasson, *History of Military Pension Legislation,* pp. 40 f.

51. *Proceedings,* I, 87.

52. Alexander William Johnston to State Societies, June 25, 1844; Johnston to William Jackson, June 25, 1844; Johnston to Edward Marcellin, July 3, 1844, Anderson House.

53. William Popham to George C. Thomas, November 23, 1844, Anderson House.

54. Popham's address is quoted in Schuyler, *Institution,* p. 117.

55. *Register of the Society of the Cincinnati of Maryland,* p. 57; *Excerpts of the Proceedings* (New Jersey), p. 214; William Popham to A. W. Johnston, October 15, 1845, A. W. Johnston to State Societies, October 15, 1845, Anderson House.

56. Charles S. Davis to A. W. Johnston, October 11, 1845; Charles S. Davis to A. W. Johnston, October 15, 1847; Joseph Warren Scott to Johnston, June 12, 1848, Anderson House.

57. Scott to A. W. Johnston, July 10, 1848, Anderson House.

58. *Proceedings,* I, 97.

Chapter Ten

Rebirth

IN THE SECOND HALF of the nineteenth century, the "nascent aristocracy" of the eighteenth century became the model for over a dozen new hereditary patriotic societies. Naturally, the Cincinnati grew as a result of this national enthusiasm, but the efforts of two individuals were largely responsible for guiding that growth, Hamilton Fish and Asa Bird Gardiner.

In choosing Fish for president general, the society reverted to an old standard yet established a new one. Like many predecessors, he was a man of public distinction. Yet like all his successors, he was also devoted to the welfare of the society. As vice president general, Fish had carried on an extensive correspondence concerned with the most intricate details of society business. The Maryland society had invited the general meeting of May 1854 to meet in Baltimore. By March, Fish knew of no arrangements and he began nudging the Marylanders. In April, less than a month before the meeting, he still did not know where the meetings would be held, and thus he chose the hotel—Barnum's—and reserved the parlor himself.[1] If other presidents were so concerned with detail, their correspondence does not survive to prove it.

Fish and others realized that if the society were to recover from the doldrums of the 1830s, more members were needed, and the general meeting of 1848 approached that subject directly. President General Dearborn proposed that the entire society follow the South Carolina plan of 1799, admission of all male descendants of original members.[2] The issue was committed to three men, Fish among them, with the charge of bringing in a recommendation in 1851. Having studied the rules of each state society, they concluded that inheritance of membership "by title of primogeniture, is wholly subordinate to the claim of worth and merit on the part of the applicant."[3] Thereupon they too recommended that the society adopt the South Carolina plan. They also urged admission of descendants of eligible officers who had never joined. Both recommendations were adopted unanimously in 1851 and sent to the six state societies for approval. When delegates met again in Baltimore in 1854, they learned that while New York and Pennsylvania had adopted the 1851 proposals immediately, Maryland had voted a strong no, effectively killing the changes.

The 1854 meeting in turn voted to accept descendants of officers who had not joined, but to leave each state the right to regulate its own admissions otherwise. Societies were moderately encouraged to accept descendants of original members of societies disbanded, and once more the recommendations needed the approval of all state societies before becoming effective.[4] Since all six states were represented in Baltimore and all delegates approved unanimously, they assumed that approval would come quickly. A special meeting in Charleston in February 1855 would bring final approval to the Rule of 1854, as it would come to be called. But too few societies appeared in Charleston, and another special meeting in Trenton in 1856 brought news that Pennsylvania, which had immediately approved the changes in 1854, had now voted no.

Senate business kept Fish away from the Trenton meeting, but one sees his hand at work, for the Rule of 1854 was not to be stopped. If the requirement of unanimous approval stood in its way, then the requirement should be changed, and that is in essence what happened. Since all states had been represented in 1854 and since they concluded that the minority should not control the whole, the Trenton delegates simply declared unanimous approval unnecessary and the Rule of 1854 operative. Even the Pennsylvanians voted unanimously for that interpretation.[5]

Since 1854 each state society has set its own admission standards. Pennsylvania still does not recognize the Rule of 1854 and admits only descendants of original members. The general meetings of the 1850s never took a stand on Dearborn's South Carolina proposal, but the South Carolina society has continued to follow that rule, which was adopted also by New Jersey in 1981 and Delaware in 1982. Somewhat similar was the rule Fish's own New York society adopted in 1857, whereby multiple descendants of an original member might be admitted, but for their lives only. Membership would continue to be hereditary in the line of primogeniture.

The Rule of 1854 opened the possibility of many new memberships, but there was no vast influx. New York admitted a large group in 1860 under their own Rule of 1857, but the Rule of 1854 made little difference, and by the late 1860s New York was accepting about one new member a year, approximately the same rate as in the 1830s. The pattern was roughly the same in South Carolina. Massachusetts had averaged two a year in the 1830s, and thirty-three new members were admitted in the 1860s, but only four entered under the Rule of 1854.

The institution dedicated the society to preserving the unity between the states, a unity much in doubt in 1860. The records of the Cincinnati show little sign of the great national debate or of any effort that could be seen as an attempt to preserve national unity without conflict between the North and the South. When the Civil War broke out, only the New York society seems to have contemplated action. The standing committee resolved that the members supporting the South were "unworthy successors to the heroes of the Revolution," and for over a month they weighed the desirability of raising a regiment of infantry themselves, before turning the plan down.[6] If the societies themselves did little, several members served as generals in the Union forces. The New York society had admitted Maj. Gen. George Webb Morrell and Brig. Gen. John Cochran in 1858, Brig. Gen. Alexander Stuart Webb in 1860; and the Pennsylvania society elected Maj. Gen. William B. Franklin in 1861.

Several generals would become hereditary members after the war: Thomas Leonidas Crittenden (Maryland), Edward Davis Townsend (Massachusetts), Henry Jackson Hunt (Massachusetts), Silas Casey (Massachusetts), David Hunter (New Jersey), Nicholas Longworth Anderson (Maryland), Edward B. Grubb (New Jersey), William Raymond Lee (Massachusetts), Horatio Rogers (Rhode Island), and Hazard Stevens (Rhode Island).

Union naval commanders included Rear Adm. Charles Henry Davis and Henry Knox's grandson, Rear Adm. Henry Knox Thatcher. Both were members of the Massachusetts society.

The South Carolina society produced two generals for the Confederacy, Gen. Albert Sidney Johnston, who had joined in 1846, and Brig. Gen. Thomas F. Drayton, admitted in 1848. Contrary to what one might expect, the Massachusetts society also provided a Confederate general, Mansfield Lovell, who had been admitted in 1854. As in the North, several generals found their way into the society after the war. South Carolina admitted Lieutenant Generals Wade Hampton and Richard Heron Anderson, Virginia elected

Maj. Gen. Henry Heth in 1893, and Brig. Gen. George Doherty Johnston joined North Carolina in 1902.

Reconciliation between Northern and Southern Cincinnati came quickly. The South Carolina society began meeting again in 1866, and a delegate would have attended the general meetings that year had not business prevented him. South Carolina did attend in 1869, and in 1872 John Simons of South Carolina was elected vice president general. Triennial meetings were held in Charleston in 1881, and in Newport in 1887 it was even possible to play "Dixie" after a toast to the South Carolina society. However, in the membership roster of the whole society printed in 1890, officers of the Union army were noted by rank, but there was no mention whatever of the service of Confederate leaders.

In the postwar years the Cincinnati served as a model for many other hereditary societies. Among the first was the Military Order of the Loyal Legion.[7] Unlike other officers' organizations that also appeared, the legion was hereditary, passing from eldest son to eldest son. There were funds to help indigent families and provisions for honorary members. Creators of the Loyal Legion encountered little of the criticism that had surrounded the creation of the Cincinnati, because hereditary associations were growing in number and style throughout the nation. By the end of the nineteenth century there were dozens of them, commemorating ancestors from all periods of America's history. All were a distant reflection of the Cincinnati, and high society rushed, or rather moved discreetly, to find spots in the "right" societies. The *Social Register* soon included abbreviations to show who belonged to what.[8]

There were several groups for descendants of Revolutionary soldiers, and the first of them was intended as an alternate to the Cincinnati. John Austin Stevens, grandson of Ebenezer Stevens and a New York merchant, hoped Cincinnati rules could be modified to include lines other than that of primogeniture. When Hamilton Fish assured him they could not, he organized the Sons of the Revolution in 1876. The Sons of the American Revolution followed in 1889. For women, the Daughters of the American Revolution was established in 1890, supplemented in 1891 by the National Society of the Daughters of the Revolution of 1776. Completing the group was the National Society of Children of the American Revolution, started in 1895 for descendants under age twenty-one.

Logically enough, 1894 saw the creation of the Daughters of the

Cincinnati founded by Mrs. James M. Lawton of New York, a descendent of Col. Richard Clough Anderson. John Schuyler, treasurer general of the Cincinnati, offered advice, the Reverend Alexander Hamilton agreed to be chaplain, and by 1897 there were fifty-seven members, all descendants of original members of the Cincinnati. Some in the society were anything but pleased with the appearance of the Daughters. The 1896 general meeting expressed its sympathy with the good purpose of all patriotic societies, but at the same time "courteously but firmly" conveyed its "decided unwillingness to have the name historically its own . . . attached to another organization."[9]

General interest in a revival of the Cincinnati had begun in the early 1870s when general officers received inquiries from descendants of original members in Rhode Island and Connecticut, and the general meeting of 1872 drew up guidelines for reviving disbanded societies.[10]

Revival succeeded first in Rhode Island, with a stimulus from outside the society. The original society disbanded in 1832, but stock worth $640 still remained in the name of the society, and the legislature was considering giving the money to the Rhode Island Historical Society. Twelve who thought themselves eligible gathered quickly for a meeting at the State House in Providence on December 12, 1877, and by April the money was saved, a charter confirmed, and officers elected, among them one of the greatest champions of the society in the nineteenth century, Asa Bird Gardiner.

Unlike all the others who revived the Rhode Island society, Gardiner entered under the Rule of 1854, representing a New Hampshire lieutenant. Seven years later he was secretary general, an office he held for the rest of his life. He had just finished New York University Law School when the Civil War broke out, and his gallantry in the Gettysburg campaign won him the Medal of Honor. He continued a career soldier, on active duty until he retired as lieutenant colonel in 1888. When the Rhode Island society was reorganized, Gardiner was professor of law at West Point, and Professor Gardiner, as he was invariably called then, had researched his subject with a scholar's fervor. He was a person of extraordinary force, ability, and conviction. After his death the *New York Times* wrote, "His essential genius was that of getting into and making trouble," and it took a polished historian to doubt any conclusion the lawyer-professor advanced. Few tried. His penchant for moving in and taking charge was evident from the first.[11]

After a dormancy of forty-two years, on its first day of reorganization the Rhode Island society had a set of bylaws more intricate than anything the eighteenth century had known. Gardiner's influence was evident throughout, especially on matters pertaining to the badge. On occasions of ceremony the eagle was worn by hereditary members on the left breast, by honorary members around the neck—the old eighteenth century rule. But in a state where no one had worn the eagle for almost half a century, Rhode Islanders now learned that on other occasions members could wear a ribbon in the lapel (officers a rosette, other members could wear the ribbon shaped into a "Stafford Knot"), and there were instructions on its position to the fraction of an inch. Gardiner was only beginning.

He threw himself into the life of the society, and many a member owed his claim to admission to Gardiner. As he said, modestly, "The familiarity of the Secretary General with the Revolutionary rolls and histories of State Lines, added to possession of a very unique and valuable library on those subjects have enabled many a present member of the Cincinnati to complete the record of his praepositus and be duly admitted."[12] Gardiner had a genius for finding records. Many had looked, in vain, for the papers of the Virginia society, and in the hot summer of 1875 Gardiner was visiting the Virginia State Library in another fruitless search. He stopped to say goodbye to the librarian, noticed an old candlebox in the corner of his office, and there were the missing records.

Having led the revival in Rhode Island, Gardiner presided over the reestablishment of all other American societies. That France was not revived in his lifetime was due to no lack of effort on his part. As the number of patriotic societies expanded, Gardiner was a veritable watchdog in sniffing out specious colleagues and self-proclaimed state societies. Under his guidance there was a legalistic sharpening of membership rules and a few embarrassments for those found not qualified.

From his perspective, Connecticut's revival got off to a very bad start. Eight men had appeared at a meeting called at the state capitol on July 4, 1888, declared the Connecticut society revived, chosen officers, and even elected honorary members. What galled the secretary general was their self-assurance that they were all rightfully members. Hearing they would meet again, he published a letter in the *Hartford Courant,* denying they were the Connecticut "Society" and pointing out one member who was not eligible for membership. Undeterred, the Connecticut men continued to meet, but Gardiner finally got the upper hand and could report cooperation by the triennial meeting of 1890. In 1896 Connecticut once more joined the ranks of the other state societies.

Virginia followed three years later, an amazing feat in view of Gardiner's comments of 1896. Gardiner thought it impossible to find an adequate number of qualified men in the state, given the migration of Virginians all over the union. Either Virginia would have to take "junior and collateral lines" or the Virginia society would have to organize in Kentucky. "But this cannot be done, because Kentucky is not one of the original thirteen states."[13]

By the triennial meetings of 1899 all the other dormant American societies were in the process of reestablishment. Under the rules adopted each member of these reorganized societies was to contribute $150 to the treasury, no small sum at the time.[14] The general meeting of 1902 approved the new organizations in New Hampshire, Delaware, and North Carolina. It also gave preliminary approval to a Georgia organization, a group given final approval in October of the same year. Once more there were thirteen societies on the North American continent.

These revivals had a predictable impact on the roster. With the new organizations and the Rule of 1854, the membership doubled between 1890, when there were 411 members, and 1908, when 840 were reported. That figure was still just over a third of the size of the society in the eighteenth century, but, curiously, two societies (New Hampshire and North Carolina) became larger in the twentieth century than they ever had been in the eighteenth.

Inevitably members asked the question, "What is the mission of the Cincinnati," and the Reverend Marinus Willet spoke to that point in New York at a Washington's Birthday dinner in 1874. He was one of the few who did. Willet said that social occasions were far from the real use which the society might perform, for "Divine Providence has arranged the development of this country, that we are enabled to exert a wider and more powerful influence in our land than any body of men of equal numbers." That was the sort of claim Jefferson had feared back in the 1780s, yet the four-part program Willet advised would have been near to Jefferson's heart.[15]

First, Willet was concerned with immigrants, many of whom were used to "arbitrary and despotic authority." The society should support education for them in the fundamental principles of the American system. Second, Cincinnati should promote policies to protect those politically weak. Far from urging an alliance with big business, Willet indicted the "despotism of soulless corporations, the combination of corrupt officials, and of men in positions of influence, trampling under foot all rights in their mad thirst for wealth." Particularly, he wanted legislation on child labor. Third, the society should promote the union of the states. That was an implicit indictment of Reconstruction policies, for Willet sympathized with the secretary of the South Carolina society, who lamented the "gloomy condition" there. Fourth, the Cincinnati must dirty their hands and get into politics. Condemning the "criminal neglect" on the part of the "conservative men" of the country, he urged them to "descend into the arena, great as may be their repugnance."[16]

Willet thus urged an active political role for the society. His statement was handsomely printed but hardly influential. Unlike other hereditary societies, the Cincinnati did not engage in the political education of immigrants, nor was the society active in lobbying for social legislation, nor is there any sign that members took up political action because of encouragement from the society. The mission the society did take up was historical commemoration. Under the direction of Asa Bird Gardiner, commemorations developed into a form of art.

The Yorktown celebrations of 1881 were but the first of many in which the society was invited to take part. Officers took pride in the attention they received there, for the Society of the Cincinnati was the only nongovernmental organization invited. Under Gardiner's influence an invitation turned into a status, and he reported to the general meetings in 1893 that by act of Congress, January 29, 1885, general officers of the Cincinnati ranked in precedence next behind governors of states and territories. Members who were not officers ranked just after the officers of the army and navy.

The society sent delegations to the dedication of the Washington Monument in 1885 and the celebrations marking the centennial of the Constitution (1887) and the inauguration of Washington (1889).

Then there was a stream of dedications of major statues and tombs: the Washington statue in Philadelphia in 1897, the statue of Rochambeau in Washington in 1902, L'Enfant's tomb in Washington in 1909, the statues of Kosciusko and Pulaski in 1910, of Columbus in 1912, and of John Barry in 1914. The society also took part in the centennial of the Star Spangled Banner in Washington in 1914.

The presence of the Cincinnati at these events usually meant the presence of Asa Bird Gardiner. At times even he seemed embarrassed by his prominence. When he reported on events surrounding the 1913 commemoration of Oliver Hazard Perry's victory on Lake Erie, he noted that the "Secretary General" made the principal address in Buffalo, while in Rhode Island's ceremonies the president of the Rhode Island society delivered the oration. It was the same gentleman speaking in each case.[17]

Gardiner was enthusiastic about events where he was asked to speak, sometimes critical about those where he was not. One of the latter was the reinterment of John Paul Jones, exhumed from an unmarked grave in Paris. Gardiner doubted they had the right body. An admiral would have been buried with his uniform with its military buttons and his sword. The body brought to Annapolis had been buried in a shroud.[18]

He was even more outspoken about one of the statues in Lafayette Park in Washington, D.C. It was probably Gardiner who made sure that the statues of Rochambeau and Lafayette appeared with the eagle, but the figure of Steuben escaped his influence. He called it "an atrocious piece of bronze work" which depicted the baron with "a baby face and crooked legs and a faulty uniform." Even worse, the base called him "von Steuben." Gardiner was right in pointing out that the baron had signed himself "de Steuben" after the Revolution. His eloquence was so powerful that one member at the 1911 meetings moved that the government replace the "monstrously abortive statue," but the question was committed to the standing committee where it died.[19]

Many of these commemorations were organized in whole or part by the state societies themselves. The Rhode Island and South Carolina societies, for example, joined with the Georgia Historical Society and the Georgia Sons of the Revolution in finding the remains of Gen. Nathanael Greene and having them transferred to the Greene Monument in Savannah.

Undoubtedly, the greatest project organized by a state society was the Washington Monument in Philadelphia, constructed and dedicated by the Pennsylvania society. Though the project had begun in 1810, it was eighty-seven years before it was finished. The society maintained its efforts to raise funds for the project more or less intermittently over the years. A separate citizen's fund for a statue had been established in 1824, and for decades there were squabbles concerning consolidation of the two funds. By the 1880s the two funds were joined, Rudolph Siemering of Berlin was commissioned to execute the $250,000 monument, and in 1897 the statue was in place in Fairmount Park. President William McKinley spoke at the dedication on May 15. Afterward there was a parade, including military units and a bicycle division. Said the *Philadelphia Times*, "The bicycle parade, too, has its significance and signifies the peace which Washington as a soldier and citizen most desired, as where bicycles are numerous there must be peace."[20]

In another project Gardiner and the Rhode Island society thought something needed to be done about the song "America." It was inappropriate to sing a song commemorating independence to the tune of "God Save the King." Thus the triennial meeting of 1902 authorized a national contest for an alternate tune, the prize a gold medal with a value of $500. Over five hundred entries were submitted, and in 1905 Arthur Edward Johnstone of New York City was announced as the winner. One wonders whether Gardiner knew he was a native of England. What did impress Gardiner was that his tune had not been written for the contest but long before in a spirit of "patriotic fervor." Said Gardiner, "This shows plainly that pieces of a patriotic nature cannot, in order to have any stability, be evolved by a mere mental process, but must result from patriotic inspiration to guide musical knowledge." The Rhode Island society adopted the tune immediately, as did one church in New York City and a few schools and congregations across the country. But Johnstone's tune was not slated to be another "La Marseillaise," despite the fervor which gave it birth.[21]

Following the tradition developed in 1851, when the society took the unheard of step of meeting in New York rather than Philadelphia, the triennial meetings moved around the country to the main cities in states with active societies. Delegates to the meetings, and the same men went time after time, thus came to know individual members of the host societies, and the state societies all but tried to outdo each other in entertaining the delegates lavishly. Each general meeting offered a program of excursions to historic sites and museums as well as sumptuous dinners with elaborately printed menus.

Hamilton Fish, who had become president general in 1854, continued in that office until his death in 1893, but poor health prevented his attendance at general meetings after 1884, the meeting which elected Gardiner secretary general. By the meeting of 1893 he had become the senior member in the entire society, having been admitted 59 years before. He had found the society an all but dormant organization and left it on the verge of complete revival.

Next to wear the diamond eagle was William Wayne, a descendant of Gen. Anthony Wayne. Elected in 1896, he had been president of the Pennsylvania society since 1887, and though he served four terms in the Pennsylvania legislature, he was a gentleman farmer devoted to the hereditary societies to which he belonged. (He was also president of the Pennsylvania Sons of the Revolution.) His death in 1901 made his presidency a short one. Winslow Warren, president of the Massachusetts society, followed next as president general. Ironically, he was a descendant of that peppery critic of the Cincinnati, Mercy Otis Warren. Elected in 1902, Warren remained president general for the next twenty-eight years. He was a prominent Boston lawyer and participant in reformist politics, but as the 1931 edition of the *Memorials of the Massachusetts Society of the Cincinnati* said, "Next to his family, this Society was his chief interest."[22]

The presidencies of Wayne and Warren completed the restoration of the society, and once more all fourteen societies flourished. Despite the dramatic growth, however, both administrations were fundamentally conservative. There were no great changes, and what had been done well before continued to be done well.

Warren had tried to do something new when he suggested a general meeting of all Cincinnati at Philadelphia in 1915 on the anniversary of the surrender at Yorktown. Warren made the proposal at the 1914 general meeting, and as usual Gardiner had done his homework. He informed the delegates that such general meetings had been contemplated when the original institution was drafted, but they were left out of the final version, hardly an endorsement from the founders. Nonetheless, Warren's suggestion drew unanimous approval, but that was the last ever heard of it.

As was evident, Gardiner was often in a position to exert more authority than the president general. He was never president general himself, but in the years when Hamilton Fish was not well, the triennial meetings were in Gardiner's hands. His long reports usually turned out to be the agenda for the rest of the meetings, and committees were appointed to deal with Gardiner's topics as they had been numbered in his report. In 1890, for example, the second committee found itself assigned to cover his topics 8, 9, 11, 16, 21, and 22.

Gardiner disliked unregulated variation in what was easily reduced to a rule. During the revivals many state societies developed their own variants of the eagle, but Gardiner led the struggle to have the society adopt a standard design for the entire society. One should add that under his influence the Rhode Island legislature in 1909 made it a punishable, *criminal* offense to wear the badge or rosette of the society without proper authority.[23]

But Gardiner did not always prevail. At the 1890 meetings he proposed that the general society as a matter of regular policy admit all presidents of both the United States and France as honorary members. Former president Cleveland had been admitted to the New York society, while President Harrison had been made a member of the Pennsylvania society. Gardiner proposed that former president Hayes be admitted by the general society, along with any future presidents. The meeting gave unanimous approval, but nothing more was heard of the plan.

If the general society was slow to admit presidents, the state societies were not. Washington and Monroe had been original members. Franklin Pierce had been the only successor member to serve as president, but Zachary Taylor could have been a hereditary member had the Virginia society not been dormant. He was, however, an honorary member of New York, elected in 1847. New York also elected James Buchanan in 1859 and U. S. Grant in 1884. All had died by the time Gardiner offered his resolution. Despite Gardiner's advocacy, Hayes was not elected by any of the states, but subsequent presidents were: McKinley by Pennsylvania in 1897, Theodore Roosevelt by New York in 1902, William Howard Taft by New Jersey in 1909, and Woodrow Wilson by Virginia, North Carolina, and South Carolina, all in 1913. Warren G. Harding was elected to the New Jersey society in 1921, but Coolidge was not made a member.

The selection of other honorary members had been intermittent during the nineteenth century. New York and Pennsylvania had used the eagle more or less as a military decoration during the War of 1812, and New York did so again during the Mexican War, honoring Stephen W. Kearney, William J. Worth, and Matthew C. Perry along with Zachary Taylor in 1847. Two more generals were admitted in 1849.

By comparison, honorary memberships for Civil War generals were comparatively scarce, given the number of general officers. Robert Anderson, Union commander of Fort Sumter, was admitted to the New York society in 1862. New York also elected General Meade in 1865, Admiral Farragut in 1866, General Sherman in 1879, and Gen. Winfield Scott Hancock in 1881. New Jersey elected Gershom Mott in 1867 and John M. Schofield in 1887. Adm. Charles H. Bell was added in 1871. Needless to say, Confederate leaders were entirely absent from such elections in the North, and the South Carolina society was not electing honorary members.

Support for the needy continued to be a regular part of the annual budget of many state societies, and while the number of beneficiaries held steady at around sixty a year, the average amount they received climbed from about $80 in 1911 to $120 a year in the late 1920s. Roughly half the beneficiaries were supported by the Massachusetts society. The Great Depression brought no substantial increase in the number of recipients, but the average payment in 1932 had risen to about $142 a year.[24]

Active members of the Cincinnati often joined other hereditary societies, groups Asa Bird Gardiner classified by their purpose. He explained his four categories at the triennial meeting of 1911. Some were "Historic Commemorative," like the Mayflower Society or the Society of Colonial Wars. A second group included the Masons and Odd Fellows; a third group was "wholly patriotic," like the Sons of the Revolution or the Descendants of the Signers of the Declaration of Independence. The fourth group, the "strictly Military societies," included the Cincinnati, the Military Society of the War of 1812, the Aztec Club, and the Loyal Legion.[25] (Gardiner was then president of the Military Society of the War of 1812.) Some Cincinnati disputed Gardiner's classification of the society as a military society, but Congress had been so persuaded for twenty years.

Like the Cincinnati, these many hereditary societies had distinctive badges, many modeled on European orders. They were normally worn at meetings, but with congressional approval on September 25, 1890, members of the armed forces might wear the badges of the military societies on a daily basis. Until 1898, the government issued no campaign medals or decorations, apart from the Medal of Honor, and the insignia of patriotic societies thus added color to an otherwise plain uniform. Only badges in the category Gardiner later described as military societies were authorized, but others were readily added to the group, and the cadet or new recruit of the 1890s might appear with sixteen different badges, if his heritage allowed it. Once the government began issuing its own medals, however, regulations required that the military wear either their official medals *or* the insignia of societies. The two were not to be mixed.[26]

In addition to the medals of other societies, European orders began to appear on the chests of Americans. Though a few Americans, like Richard MacSherry of the Maryland society, had received Spanish orders, the French Legion of Honor was the most common foreign order awarded to Americans. First given to United States citizens in 1855, by 1903 some 198 Americans then living had it, and by 1919 the number had risen to 1,750.[27] The first member of the society to receive the Legion of Honor was Brig. Gen. Thomas Lincoln Casey of Massachusetts in 1873, a career army engineer who had studied the torpedo defenses of Britain, Germany, France, and Austria. Generally, however, the Cincinnati were not prominent among the early recipients. Hamilton Fish never received the Legion of Honor, nor, despite his efforts to revive the French society, did Asa Bird Gardiner. By 1935, however, William S. Thomas, president of the New York society, could count some 46 living Cincinnati who had been decorated with France's order of merit. In 1922 W. Francklyn Paris had suggested an American Society of the French Legion of Honor modeled on the Cincinnati, an organization which began in 1924.[28]

Revival of the French society would wait until 1922, despite the persistent efforts of Asa Bird Gardiner. In 1881 the Rhode Island society urged Congress to provide funds for a French delegation to the centennial celebrations at Yorktown. Congress responded with an invitation and $20,000. Fourteen descendants of officers who had served with the French at Yorktown were part of the French delegation. And after they were entertained by the Cincinnati in Rhode Island, Massachusetts, and New York, discussions of reviving the French society were natural. Gardiner saw to it that the marquis de Rochambeau, the comte d'Ollone, and the marquis du Quesne were admitted to the Rhode Island society in 1882.

These three and others asked whether the French government would object to a revived society, and, receiving approval, they met on July 1, 1887, to form a temporary organization. Rochambeau was president, d'Ollone vice president, and the vicomte de Noailles secretary. The general meeting of 1887 offered hearty endorsement of the movement, yet the revival soon came to a halt because of the death of Rochambeau and d'Ollone and probably because of American opposition to Gardiner.

In 1887 Gen. John Cochran of the New York society had spoken in favor of the French revival. Seven years later he took a much different line, and in two brief pamphlets he leveled a blast at Gardiner. Previously, minutes of triennial meetings had been relatively simple, but now they were "obstructed with programmes, supplemented with necrological compilations, and injected with personal opinions." Under Gardiner the general society was usurping the rights of the "sovereign" state societies. Cochran accused the secretary general of historical error, and his greatest error, it seems, was assuming there had ever been a French society at all. Cochran summarized his own opinion in the phrase "no Society of the Cincinnati in France."[29] The founders had admitted the French out of fellowship and fraternity for their lives only, and there had been no intent to start a fourteenth society. If the amended institution tended to hint otherwise, one needed to remember that that institution had been rejected.

But Gardiner persisted, and the Rhode Island society continued to admit descendants of the French, five more of them by 1906. Rhode Island also admitted the count von Stedingk of Sweden. When another delegation, including descendants, came to the United States for the dedication of the Rochambeau statue in 1902, once more there were dinners given by the Rhode Island and New York societies, and the Rhode Island society elected Emile François Loubet, president of France, to honorary membership. He accepted most graciously. Gardiner followed in 1905 with his *Order of the Cincinnati in France,* which included biographies of the original members in France. Again that year the general meeting authorized revival of the French society, but despite these stimuli French interest lagged until the baron de Contenson worked some of Gardiner's materials into a series of articles later published as *L'Ordre Americain de Cincinnatus en France* (1913). The baron labored to revive the society, but 1914 was not an auspicious year for such efforts.

The Cincinnati met for their triennial meeting in North Carolina in May 1917, a month after the United States entered World War I, and Moorfield Storey of the Massachusetts society, a Boston lawyer, offered a resolution supporting the war effort. Adopted by acclamation, it read in part, "Remembering that it was the aid of France that made the United States a nation, we welcome the opportunity to repay the debt which was then incurred and to help a people whom we love and admire."[30] That same meeting elected Marshal Joseph Jacques Césaire Joffre an honorary member of the general society, the first such honorary member ever elected. Joffre was visiting the United States at the time, and the vote on May 10 was followed by presentation of the eagle to the marshal the next day at Washington's headquarters at Newburgh.

In France the baron de Contenson organized descendants of French officers of the Revolution to present flags and standards to the American Expeditionary Force. On behalf of thirteen such descendants the marquis de Dampierre, great-grand-nephew of Lafayette, made the formal presentation at the Invalides on July 4, 1917. Within hours Colonel Stanton, perhaps with that ceremony in mind, had uttered his famous line "Lafayette! We are here."

By the end of the war Contenson and the other descendants had developed a camaraderie of their own, and on the Fourth of July 1919 they organized, elected the duc de Broglie president, and took the name the "Alliance américaine."[31] It was a logical nucleus for a revived Society of the Cincinnati in France, and so it appeared to the triennial meeting of 1920.

When the delegates gathered in New Hampshire, the membership stood at 990. Five members had died during the war, one of them the baron de Bougainville of the Rhode Island society. William Warren and Asa Bird Gardiner had both died since the last triennial meeting. Gardiner had always seen the Cincinnati as a "military society," yet John C. Daves, assistant secretary general, reported that "owing to the exigencies of the war, the activities of the State Societies . . . were practically suspended."[32] Principle leaders of the Allies had, or would be, elected honorary members, among them Albert, king of the Belgians, elected by the New York society, and Gen. Peyton C. March, named by Virginia. Marshal Foch, like Joffre before him, was made an honorary member of the general society at the meetings in 1920, and in 1921 New York elected Gen. Robert Georges Nivelle of France. Marshal Pétain was chosen in 1931 by both the revived French society and Virginia, but General Pershing was not elected until 1932, when admitted by New Hampshire.

The triennial meeting named a committee to promote reestablishment of the French society, and by 1922 the leaders of the Alliance américaine had decided to transform the group into a branch of the Cincinnati. The 1923 triennial meetings gave unanimous approval to the proposal, pending final approval by the standing committee after formal organization in Paris. On July 4, 1925, the duc de Broglie was chosen president, the marquis de MacMahon and the comte d'Ollone vice presidents, and on December 31 the standing committee gave its final approval. The fourteen parts of the society were all functioning for the first time in 130 years, and the revival begun in the nineteenth century was now complete.

Notes

1. Hamilton Fish to A. W. Johnston, March 17, April 12 and 18, 1854, Anderson House.

2. H. A. S. Dearborn to Charles S. Daveis, November 29, 1848, quoted in *Proceedings*, I, 98.

3. Ibid., pp. 109, 115.

4. Ibid., pp. 128-30.

5. Ibid., pp. 139-40.

6. Schuyler, *Institution*, pp. 125-26. The motion to raise a regiment came out of the standing committee meeting of May 21, 1861, but was rejected at the July 4 meeting.

7. The Aztec Club of 1847 was also an officer's organization made up of officers of the Mexican War, but its organization was somewhat intermittent until after the Civil War. After the Mexican War it had met in St. Louis in 1852, but then not again until 1867. *The Hereditary Register of the United States of America* (Washington: United States Hereditary Register, 1974), p. 57. The Military Society, War of 1812, had been organized in 1826 and had admitted some hereditary members by the 1850s, but only in 1894 did new rules limit new lines of hereditary admissions to descendants of officers. Ibid., pp. 36-39. The General

Society of the War of 1812 had been formed in 1854, and only in 1894 did it become a hereditary organization. Ibid., pp. 42-43; Wallace Evan Davies, *Patriotism on Parade: The Story of Veterans' and Hereditary Organizations in America* (Cambridge: Harvard University Press, 1955), pp. 54-55. While technically older than the Loyal Legion, groups representing the men of 1812 and the Mexican War became hereditary societies much later.

8. Davies, *Patriotism on Parade* provides the best extended account of the rapid growth of these societies. Sketches of most are to be found in the *Hereditary Register*.

9. *Proceedings*, II, 156. The Daughters of the Cincinnati produced an extensive series of yearbooks or annual reports. The *Year Book, 1910-1911* (New York: Daughters of the Cincinnati, 1911) contains a history of the Daughters from 1894 to 1910, pp. 27-30. The book also has an interesting collection of portraits of Cincinnati, as does *Truths and Traditions of the Daughters of the Cincinnati* (New York: Knickerbocker Press, 1931).

10. *Proceedings*, I, 193. Interest in reviving the dormant state societies had appeared just before the Civil War, with the strong encouragement of Hamilton Fish. He carried on an extensive correspondence, trying to find the records of the dormant groups. While in Europe in 1858, he continued to make inquiries. He sought out details of the history of the French society, and wrote the secretary general that he knew the whereabouts of the Connecticut and New Hampshire records, but he had not yet found Rhode Island's archive. He heard that Virginia records still existed, and offered to pay $15 to $20 personally to have them copied when found. His project to produce a general history of the society fell a victim to the Civil War. Fish to Thomas McEuen, January 29, 1858, Anderson House.

11. *New York Times*, May 30, 1919, p. 8; Rhode Island, Meeting of December 12, 1877, Rhode Island Society Archives.

12. *Proceedings*, III, 26-27.

13. Ibid., II, 63.

14. Ibid., pp. 104-5. The Connecticut revival was a model for other states.

15. Marinus Willett, *The Mission of the Cincinnati: An Address Delivered before the New York State Society of the Cincinnati, February 23, 1874* (New York: New York Society, 1874), pp. 41-42.

16. Willet, *Mission of the Cincinnati*, pp. 28-29, 24, 38.

17. *Proceedings*, III, 56.

18. Ibid., pp. 55-56.

19. Ibid., pp. 18-19, 29.

20. For details of the ceremonies see *Ceremonies attending the Unveiling of the Washington Monument erected in Fairmount Park* (Philadelphia: Allen, Lane and Scott, 1897). *Philadelphia Times*, May 2, 1897, p. 2.

21. *Proceedings*, II, 235-36, 282-85.

22. Smith, *Memorials*, p. 487.

23. This statute was adopted by the Rhode Island legislature in 1900 and reaffirmed in 1909. Society of the Cincinnati, *Roll of the General Society, 1917* (N.p.: Society of the Cincinnati, 1917), p. 21.

24. Reports of the number of beneficiaries and the average payments made by each society were a regular part of the reports at the triennial meetings after 1890.

25. *Proceedings,* III, 24-27.

26. Robert E. Wylie, *Orders, Decorations and Insignia* (New York: Putnam's, 1920), pp. 11-12; William S. Thomas, *The Society of the Cincinnati, 1783-1935* (New York: Putnam's, 1935), pp. 57-58.

27. James Howard Gore, *Legionnaires: A Directory of Citizens of the United States on whom France has Conferred her National Order, The Legion of Honor* (Washington: N.p., 1903); W. Francklyn Paris, *Napoleon's Legion* (New York: Funk and Wagnalls, 1928), p. 158; Thomas, *Society of the Cincinnati,* pp. 172-75.

28. Paris, *Napoleon's Legion,* p. 157.

29. John Cochrane, *Letters (July 4, 1894, July 4, 1895) of Gen'l John Cochrane, President of the Cincinnati Society of the State of New York to the New York Cincinnati,* rev. and enl. ed. (Np., n.d.) pp. 89, 80, 7-28.

30. *Proceedings,* III, 101.

31. Contenson, *Société des Cincinnati de France,* pp. 107-9.

32. *Proceedings,* III, 124.

Chapter Eleven

Esto Perpetua

AS IT APPROACHES its two-hundredth year, the Society of the Cincinnati survives and flourishes. Contrary to the expectations of Jefferson, Aedanus Burke, and Mirabeau, it has proved no constitutional threat but became an organization devoted to principles Jefferson himself approved, the principles of the Revolution, the preservation of history, and the diffusion of historical knowledge.

Historic preservation and commemoration are principal tasks of many state societies. To mention but a few such activities, the Georgia society has recently placed a commemorative plaque at Fort McIntosh and cooperated in development of a Revolutionary Battle Park in Savannah. The New York and the New Jersey societies have both erected plaques at cemeteries where original members are buried, and the North Carolina society has marked the site of the James Hill House in Hillsborough, where the state society was founded. The Connecticut society donated a flagpole to the Nathan Hale homestead.

State societies have joined readily with other groups in advancing worthwhile projects. Through such mutual efforts the Georgia society helped erect a monument at the Old City Cemetery in Darien, Georgia, the Maryland Society supported the restoration of the Paca House in Annapolis, and the entire society supported the efforts of the Mount Gulian Society to rebuild and furnish the Verplanck House at Beacon, New York, Steuben's headquarters where the institution was adopted on May 13, 1783.

The past decade has seen a development rejected in the early nineteenth century, the emergence of Cincinnati "associations" in Texas, California, Florida, Kentucky, and the city of Cincinnati. These are not state societies, and all members belong also to one of the fourteen constituent societies, but they hold regular meetings and carry on much the same activities as the state societies. The Lone Star Association marked the grave of Lt. Robert Rankin, believed to be the original member buried farthest west, and the Cincinnati association installed a tablet explaining how the city got its name.

For many years several societies have awarded prizes for academic excellence. The New Hampshire society presents a history prize at Phillips Exeter, the Pennsylvania society offers an award to a cadet in the University of Pennsylvania R.O.T.C. program, and the South Carolina society gives a medal for excellence at the Citadel. The Virginia society presents four academic awards on a regular basis, to students at the Virginia Military Institute, Virginia Polytechnic Institute and State University, the United States Military Academy, and the United States Naval Academy.[1] Both Virginia and Pennsylvania make scholarship awards, and it is worth noting that the Virginia funds given to Washington and Lee University are still doing their work a century and a half later. The Cincinnati Professorship of Mathematics is the university's oldest endowed chair, and, in the words of the catalogue, "for qualified students who may request it, a course in fortification, gunnery and ballistics will be offered." History students compete each year for a Society of the Cincinnati Award, and the annual Phi Beta Kappa initiation is held, when possible, on April 12, the day the Virginia society first voted in 1802 to present its funds to the college. The New Jersey society has recently established a Cincinnati History Prize of $1,000 for the best work on United States history published each year.

State societies have remained active supporters of historical publications. North Carolina has supported several volumes, most recently Curtis Carroll Davis's *Revolution's Godchild*, a history of the North Carolina society. Rhode Island has aided publication of primary sources of the Revolution, and most recently has turned its attention to aiding publication of the papers of Gen. Nathanael Greene. Massachusetts in 1964 and New Jersey in 1981 published historical sketches of each member admitted since those societies were founded, and out of the French society in 1980 came *Armorial des Cincinnati de France*, a lavishly printed compendium of the genealogies of their current members. Pennsylvania is sponsoring research on its early members under the leadership of Clifford Lewis 3d.

Discovery and preservation of documents from the Revolutionary period have remained important functions. Most societies were careful to keep their own papers in good order, but Maryland was a leader in expanding its efforts. In 1841 the society asked members to gather Revolutionary documents with the hope that other groups would join the society in starting a historical society to preserve them, and when the Maryland Historical Society was founded three years later it chose as president John Spear Smith, also president of the Maryland Cincinnati.

The society as a whole had no regular publication until the *Bulletin of the Society of the Cincinnati* appeared in April 1943. The editors said that it would be issued "sporadically," and it disappeared with the sixth issue in 1948. More enduring has been *Cincinnati Fourteen*, a newsletter begun in the sixties to report on activities of the state societies. Also part of the general society's program is publication of the George Rogers Clark lecture series. Begun in 1975 by Samuel Eliot Morison, an honorary member of the Massachusetts society, the series has included subsequent presentations by J. H. Plumb, Edmund S. Morgan, Page Smith, and John W. Shy.[2]

There are three museums associated with the Cincinnati. At Exeter the New Hampshire society maintains the Ladd Gilman House, which it purchased in 1902. Built in 1721, the house was the home of an original member, Nicholas Gilman, who was a delegate to the constitutional convention of 1787. (The New Hampshire society possesses his draft copy of the constitution with marginal notes.) The building is furnished with period furniture and is open during the summer tourist season. Visitors may see a portrait of Washington wearing the eagle, attributed to Gilbert Stuart. The Pennsylvania society does not have a whole museum, but maintains a room in the Hill-Physick-Keith House in Philadelphia, a structure built in 1786. The Pennsylvania society has also furnished the Cincinnati Room in the rebuilt City Tavern.

The great pride of the entire society is Anderson House, its museum and headquarters in Washington, D.C. The society began looking for a headquarters in the 1920s. Its archives were in a New York safety deposit box, while the Daughters of the American Revolution, the Colonial Dames, and the Sons of the American Revolution all had headquarters in Washington. In New York the Sons of the Revolution had Fraunces Tavern. In 1929 the society debating buying 8 Jackson Place, facing Lafayette Square.[3] The owner, a member of the Virginia society, made the society a generous offer, but delegates to the general meeting were so widely split over the wisdom of buying the property that the offer was withdrawn.

Nine years later the society acquired the headquarters it needed as a gift, when Mrs. Larz Anderson presented the house she and her husband had built in 1905. Larz Anderson was the great-grandson of Richard Clough Anderson of the Virginia society. The family had gained considerable wealth by the time Larz Anderson was born in Paris in 1866, and after graduating from Harvard in 1888, he spent two years traveling before entering into a diplomatic career. He was stationed at the embassies in London and Rome before entering the army in the Spanish American War. In 1911 he was named minister to Belgium, where he served until made ambassador to Japan in 1912. He left the diplomatic service again with the coming of the Wilson administration in 1913.

He had been admitted to the Maryland society in 1894, while he was serving in Rome, and he remained an enthusiastic member of the society. Ambassador Anderson died in April 1937, and shortly thereafter his widow decided to present the house to the society. Isabel Anderson was an interesting figure in her own right. The author of forty-seven volumes of prose, drama, and poetry, she had honorary doctorates from George Washington University and Boston University, and the grateful Society of the Cincinnati voted her an Honorary Associate of the Society with the right of wearing her husband's eagle.[4]

Anderson House is an important District of Columbia site for four reasons. First, it is one of the few remaining palatial residences from the turn of the century. Designed by the Boston firm of Little and Brown, its estimated cost in 1905 was $800,000. Many of its rooms appear today as they did when the Andersons lived there, for Mrs. Anderson presented many of the furnishings as well as the house.

Second, Anderson House presents an ever growing museum collection devoted to the Revolution and the society. There are many eighteenth- and nineteenth-century portraits, a collection of badges and several examples of Chinese export porcelain decorated with the badge, and changing exhibits illustrating the variety of materials that have found their way into the society's collections. In spring

1982, for example, visitors could see a much corroded hatchethead unearthed at Washington's father's estate. It was exhibited at the Jamestown Exposition of 1907 as *the* hatchet of the cherry tree legend. The French society has made significant contributions to the collections. One notable gift was a set of military figurines by the French historian Marcel Baldet illustrating the French allies during the Revolution.

Third, the library is a facility of increasing national importance for scholarly research. With the help of several generous donors, John D. Kilbourne, director of the museum and library, and his predecessors have assembled a major collection of manuscripts and printed materials pertaining to the Revolutionary era. The archives of the general society and the papers of some state societies are also housed in the library.

Fourth, the house not only interests the general public, but its elegance often serves the nation when the State Department holds receptions there. Anderson House makes a contribution to the cultural life of Washington too with its regular series of concerts and lectures open to the public.

The expense of maintaining a museum of quality has, of course, mounted over the years. In 1944 the curator estimated that an annual budget of $12,000 was needed, and the society undertook a campaign to increase annual contributions to guarantee that amount. Even in the 1940s publicity emphasized the tax benefits of such contributions. By 1981 the general society's current budget had grown to $330,000. Although each of the state societies has its own funds, the general society is dependent on contributions from the state organizations and on its own endowments. Seeing real need in the future, the society's leaders launched a development campaign at the triennial meetings in 1980 to raise $1,000,000 for the endowment of Anderson House. Under the leadership of Armistead Jones Maupin, past president general and general chairman, the campaign reached its goal in just a little over a year.

Additional support will come from the million-dollar gift of the George Olmsted Foundation announced in 1981. Maj. Gen. George Olmstead is a member of the New York society and chairman and chief executive officer of International Bank.

Leadership of the society in the twentieth century began in the traditional pattern of the nineteenth, with the president general chosen for life, though he was nominally elected every three years. Winslow Warren was followed in 1932 by John Collins Daves of the North Carolina society. By training an engineer, Daves was employed much of his life in the City Commissioner's office of Baltimore. He was the first president general chosen from one of the societies that had been dormant in the nineteenth century, and the most notable achievement of his presidency was the gift of Anderson House in 1938.

As vice president general, Bryce Metcalf of the Connecticut society succeeded upon the death of Daves. He was an architect, and not only did he too come from a revived society, but he was also the first president general whose membership was based on the Rule of 1854. He lived in Washington where he paid close attention to society business at Anderson House, and he was one of three men responsible for codifying the roster of members since 1783. Francis Apthorp Foster, a Boston lawyer instrumental in reviving the Georgia society, began a card file still in daily use in Anderson House, and similar efforts were underway by Dr. William Sturgis Thomas of the New York society. In 1929 Thomas published a roster of all members, the first such publication in the society's history. Metcalf produced still another roster, carried down to 1938. The membership of the society had grown from 411 in 1890 to 1,080 in 1926, the first twentieth-century count to include all fourteen societies. By 1935 the number had reached 1,344, and by 1947 the total stood at 1,435.[5]

The general meeting at Charleston in 1950 marked a change in basic policy. No longer would election of general officers be for life, and it has since been presumed that a president general will serve but one three-year term. At those meetings Bryce Metcalf became president general emeritus, and the society named Isaac Pennypacker of Maryland as the new president general. Pennypacker was a brilliant trial lawyer from Philadelphia whose tenure as president general was short, for he died later that year, to be succeeded by one of the most astonishing characters the twentieth-century society has produced.

Edgar Erskine Hume joined the society in 1913, the same year he finished Johns Hopkins Medical School. He stayed in the Army Medical Corps after World War I, and, following Red Cross work in Serbia, returned to the United States for assignments in Massachusetts, Washington, D.C., and Georgia. In World War II, he served in Europe where he was promoted to brigadier general, and as senior officer in the area received the surrender of Naples. He was for a time chief of the Allied Military Government of the Fifth Army and was later made major general.

His energy was boundless. By 1948 he reported he had written about three hundred books and papers. Many were on the medical subjects one might expect—fighting typhus, sandfly fever, war and medicine, or even ornithologists in the Army Medical Corps. But he also wrote on military operations, the Vesuvius Eruption in 1944, a colonial Scottish Jacobite family, and the Society of the Cincinnati. Once he was named assistant secretary general in 1932, these publications came in a steady stream. To mention but a few, he wrote on Washington's diamond eagle, the Cincinnati and the Army Corps of Engineers, commorative medals of the society, Lafayette and the Cincinnati, the diplomas of the society, Steuben and the society, Poland and the Cincinnati, and Cincinnati who had appeared on postage stamps. There were also an edition of the Virginia records, a summary of these records, and *General Washington's Correspondence concerning the Society of the Cincinnati*, a volume given to all delegates at the general meeting of 1941. In an appendix to that collection he listed nine books and forty-six articles about the society. He had a penchant for counting things, and it is equally interesting to count his own honors as reported in the 1948 edition of *Who's Who in America:* twenty-one honorary doctorates and decorations from thirty-six nations, plus the Order of Malta.

He had been elected vice president general in 1941 and thus succeeded upon Pennypacker's death in 1950. Hume's tenure too was short, for he died in January 1952, just days after one of the society's most symbolic postwar events, the presentation of an eagle to Winston S. Churchill, a hereditary member of the Connecticut society.

It took the society a long time to make its peace with the British. Just after the Revolution, the bylaws of the South Carolina society prohibited members from wearing scarlet to meetings.[6] Reconciliation was evident in 1911 when Winslow Warren and Asa Bird Gardiner sent congratulations to King George V and Queen Mary upon their coronation. When it was explained that the greeting came from the descendants of Washington's army, the king himself sat down and wrote a reply ending, "I cordially reciprocate their hopes for the still further strengthening of the tie of friendship between the two English speaking peoples of the world."[7] In 1937 the New York society went further, electing the British ambassador to the United States, Sir Ronald Charles Lindsay, an honorary member.

In 1947 it was discovered that Winston Churchill was descended from a Connecticut officer of the Revolution, and the Connecticut society elected him a full hereditary member. He accepted, but he had never been invested with the eagle. The occasion of his visit to the United States in January 1952 provided that opportunity. Protocol demanded that major Washington officials be invited to the ceremony, and many of them came, including Vice President Barkley and Chief Justice Frederick M. Vinson, an honorary member of the Virginia society. But President Truman, another honorary member of the Virginia society, declined. As his aide Maj. Gen. Harry Vaughan wrote, "The President feels it is 'Winnie's' show and that there should be no detractions."[8]

It was a splendid evening. After President General Hume had invested him with the eagle, the descendant of the dukes of Marlborough and the great-great-grandson of Lt. Murray of Connecticut spoke: "History unfolds itself by strange and unpredictable path [sic]. We have little control over the future and none at all over the past and therefore, it seems to me that I may say that when the events took place which this society commemorates, I may say that I was on both sides then in a war between us and we."[9]

The roster of honorary members in the post war years included many prominent figures, among them King Gustavus Adolphus VI of Sweden (of the Virginia society), Generals Douglas MacArthur and Omar Bradley (both New York), Adm. William Halsey (New Jersey), and Gen. George C. Marshall (Virginia). Connecticut elected former president Herbert Hoover in 1949, while Franklin Roosevelt had been elected by New York at the outset of his presidency in 1934.

Less military and political was the honorary roster of the Massachusetts society, which included poet Robert Frost, historian Samuel Eliot Morison, Henry Knox Sherrill, presiding bishop of the Episcopal Church, James Phinney Baxter, president of Williams College, and Lewis Parry, principal of Phillips Exeter. Other old families were represented by banker Ralph Lowell, former secretary of the navy Charles Francis Adams, and Senator Leverett Saltonstall.

Honorary members were invited to join and might reasonably be expected to be men of consequence. Yet as a group the hereditary members continued to represent high levels of achievement. In 1945 one member found that 155 of the 1,193 hereditary members on the roster in 1938 were included in *Who's Who in America*.[10] While 12 percent of the society was included, the rate for the population generally was 2 thousandths of one percent.

There is little reason to think that a contemporary count would be much different. It would be a mistake, however, to think that even most members of the society are luminaries. As in the post-Revolutionary era, many live quietly, very much out of the public eye. For many, that fact is summarized by an incident that happened to James Orr Denby, former director of Anderson House. He was rushing to Anderson House and hailed a Washington cab.

"Please take me to the Anderson House, headquarters of the Society of the Cincinnati." Upon reflection, Denby mused the driver might not know where that was. "The address is 2118 Massachusetts Avenue. It is west of Dupont Circle, and the house is a grey building with a porte cochere just opposite the Cosmos Club."

To which the driver responded, "Sir, you do not have to go into so much detail. I know where the house is. I am a member of the Society."[11]

Since the presidency of Edgar Erskine Hume, the leadership of the society has passed to men of business and law able to provide the fiscal leadership a large organization and museum need. Col. John Fulton Reynolds Scott, the secretary general, served as president general from the death of Edgar Erskine Hume until the general meeting of 1953, when the delegates chose a lawyer, Richard Hooker Wilmer of the New Jersey society, a prominent member of the Washington bar. He in turn was succeeded by a member of the Virginia society, Col. Catesby ap Catesby Jones, a career army officer. It was during Jones's presidency that the triennial meetings were first held in France. Next chosen was Blanchard Randall of the Maryland society, a banker, merchant, and realtor before becoming Maryland's secretary of state.

Francis Hatch of the Massachusetts society became president general in 1962. A Boston advertising executive, he led in the creation of the society's French scholar program, in part to thank the French for their hospitality in 1959. Each year the society sponsors a visit by a French student during the summer. Next to wear the diamond eagle was Col. Charles Warren Lippitt of the Rhode Island Society and an associate of a real estate firm in New York City. During World War II, the Germans had destroyed a statue of Rochambeau at Vendôme, and he was determined to see it replaced. Through his efforts it was, in 1974, on the occasion of the second triennial meetings in France.

Next to serve as president general was a Georgian, Frank Anderson Chisholm, a Savannah stockbroker. During his presidency a generous bequest from Harold Leonard Stuart was used to transform part of Anderson House into the present research library. Armistead Jones Maupin of the North Carolina society was chosen next. He is another leader of the bar, having been president of the North Carolina Bar Association. He in turn was followed by Harry Ramsay Hoyt, a manufacturer who is a member of the Pennsylvania society. Next to wear the diamond eagle was John Taylor Gilman Nichols, the former chairman of the State Street Bank & Trust Company of Boston and a member of the New Hampshire society. John Sanderson du Mont, the current president general, is a manufacturer and a member of the New York society. Du Mont represented the society at the Yorktown celebrations in 1981, where he presented a bust of General Washington on behalf of the society. By Felix de Weldon, the bust becomes a permanent part of the Yorktown Park exhibits. Du Mont will also preside over the society's own bicentennial celebrations at Newburgh in May 1983.

As it has since the eighteenth century, eligibility for membership varies with the requirements of the individual state societies. South Carolina, New Jersey, and Delaware admit more than one individual to represent an eighteenth-century officer, but most states continue to follow the early standard that each Revolutionary officer should be represented by but one modern member at a time. In those states the line of primogeniture is still preferred, if it can be found, and each state society judges whether and how it may vary from that line in admissions. All state societies, save Pennsylvania, have accepted the Rule of 1854 whereby descendants of eligible officers who never joined in their own lives may be admitted.

Membership in the society has seen steady growth in the past thirty years. In 1950 the state societies, including France, reported a total of 1,679 members, in 1962 the figure was 2,000, and in 1968 it reached 2,404, one more than the estimated number of original members in the eighteenth century. The growth has continued, reaching 2,764 in 1980. Curiously, the bicentennial period did not bring forth an extraordinary increase in applications from families unrepresented for years. In 1974 there were 2,611 members, and in 1977 just 18 more. By comparison, the Washington Bicentennial of 1932 was a time of great growth. The membership increased by 113 between 1929 and mid-1932. When current successor and honorary members were added to the 1980 figure, the total membership reached 3,054 a record for any period of the society's history.

One of the original purposes of the society was to maintain friendships formed during the Revolution. Even the grandsons of the original members are long gone, but friendships have endured between families through generations, and social functions are a regular part of every society's activity. Some of the names are still the same after 200 years, and on the society roster today one finds Alexander van Cortlandt Hamilton, John Armstrong, Thomas Pinckney, Benjamin Lincoln, John Sullivan, and two Charles Cotesworth Pinckneys.

The state societies and the new associations now meet at least once a year. Most have given up July 4 as their official meeting, but the Connecticut society still assembles at the state capitol regularly on the fourth. Some societies move their meetings from place to place to explore their states, while others meet in their same traditional spots, as the French society does at the Jockey Club in Paris.

Orations and parades have largely disappeared, but as in the eighteenth century most gatherings include a business meeting followed by a dinner. Some of the state societies have become renowned for the fare expected. The Maryland society regularly offers diamondback terrapin soup, while an anticipated feature of Georgia meetings is the oyster roast. As in the nineteenth century, the triennial meetings still move from city to city, and planning for these events often begins nine years in advance.

The society still provides a bond of affection between the citizens of the United States and France, and on May 17, 1976, Anderson House was the scene of the investiture of Valéry Giscard d'Estaing, the president of the Republic of France. As part of the bicentennial celebration, the president was chosen an honorary member of the general society, an honor previously extended only to Joffre and Foch. In presenting the eagle, President General Harry Ramsay Hoyt said: "This is a glorious day for all America; one that will live long in the memory of countless Americans for, Mr. President, no greater honor can or will be rendered to our country's Bicentennial than by your distinguished state visit, representing the country without whose generosity of men and supplies there would in all probability be no Bicentennial to celebrate." President Giscard d'Estaing in turn responded: "You, the present members of the Society of the Cincinnati are the most staunch, steadfast and faithful friends of France in times of glory as in trial—through these words I wish to express the pride I feel in accepting this distinguished honor your Society is awarding today."[12] Later that evening President Giscard d'Estaing wore the eagle at a state dinner at the French Embassy.

The society gained its fourth honorary member of the general society on February 21, 1983, when President Ronald Reagan accepted an honorary membership. President General John Sanderson du Mont presided over the ceremony at Anderson House on Washington's official birthday.

The bicentennial period saw the selection of the first general officer from the French society, as the standing committee chose Gérard Le Saige, comte de La Villèsbrunne, as vice president general following the death of Henry Charles Cheeves, who had been elected in 1977. And during the bicentennial the eagle acquired once more an official status in France. Reviewing the historical record, the Grand Chancellery of the Legion of Honor offered no recognition of the society as an order but authorized French citizens eligible to wear it on the right lapel.

Jefferson, Burke, and Mirabeau were hasty in assuming that a hereditary society would ultimately swallow up the Constitution. The society over the years has been a generally conservative organization, standing for firm government, but it has been no constitutional threat. Critics were wrong in assuming that admission of French members would corrupt American manners and morals through the introduction of foreign, monarchical ideas. As events have happened, the bond between American and French Cincinnati has helped cement the alliance of two principal republics of the free world.

Its members have gained a prominence in American and French life in each generation, and the society has been a model for dozens of other patriotic and hereditary societies. The charitable functions, which were of vital importance in the early nineteenth century before government pension systems began, have tapered off in the twentieth century, but the fellowship of the society that Knox and Steuben had envisioned has shown no sign of abating, as friendships have passed from family to family over many generations. It has remained, in the institution's phrase, "one Society of Friends." In preparing the institution, Knox chose as one of the mottoes of the society *Esto perpetua,* Be thou perpetuated. As it approaches 200 years, the Society of the Cincinnati is quiet, dignified, constitutional, and it shows every sign of taking that motto to heart.

Notes

1. James M. Morgan, Jr., *The Jackson-Hope and The Society of the Cincinnati Medals of the Virginia Military Institute: Biographical Sketches of all Recipients, 1877-1977* (Verona, Va.: McClure, 1979).

2. Samuel Eliot Morison, *The Conservative American Revolution* (Washington: Society of the Cincinnati, 1976); J. H. Plumb, *New Light on the Tyrant George III* (Washington: Society of the Cincinnati, 1978); Edmund S. Morgan, *The Genius of George Washington* (Washington: Society of the Cincinnati, 1980).

3. *A Plea for a House for the Society of the Cincinnati in Washington, D.C.* (N.p., 1929).

4. The Triennial Meeting of 1938 voted her an "Honorary Associate of the Society," June 15, 1938. *Proceedings* (1938), pp. 35-36.

5. Membership reports are included as part of each issue of the *Proceedings.*

6. *Establishment of the Society of the Cincinnati* (South Carolina), p. 11.

7. *Proceedings,* III, 29, 35-36.

8. Harry H. Vaughan to Edgar Erskine Hume, January 10, 1952, Anderson House.

9. Winston S. Churchill, Typescript of Remarks, January 16, 1952, Anderson House.

10. John R. M. Taylor, untitled article, *Bulletin of the Society of the Cincinnati,* no. 4 (April 1945), p. 18.

11. James Orr Denby, *The Society of the Cincinnati and Its Museum* (Washington: Society of the Cincinnati, 1967), p. 9.

12. *Cincinnati Fourteen,* 13 (October 1976), 9.

Appendix

The Institution of the Society of the Cincinnati

CANTONMENT OF THE AMERICAN ARMY, ON HUDSON'S RIVER, 10TH MAY, 1783.

PROPOSALS for establishing a Society, upon principles therein mentioned, whose Members shall be officers of the American Army, having been communicated to the several regiments of the respective lines, they appointed an officer from each, who, in conjunction with the general officers, should take the same into consideration at their meeting this day, at which the Honorable MAJOR GENERAL BARON DE STEUBEN, the senior officer present, was pleased to preside.

The proposals being read, fully considered, paragraph by paragraph, and the amendments agreed to, MAJOR GENERAL KNOX, BRIGADIER GENERAL HAND, BRIGADIER GENERAL HUNTINGTON and CAPTAIN SHAW, were chosen to revise the same, and prepare a copy to be laid before this assembly at their next meeting, to be holden at MAJOR GENERAL BARON DE STEUBEN'S quarters, on Tuesday, the 13th instant.

Tuesday, 13th May, 1783.

The representatives of the American Army being assembled agreeably to adjournment, the plan for establishing a Society, whereof the officers of the American Army are to be Members, is accepted, and is as follows, viz.:

"It having pleased the Supreme Governor of the Universe, in the disposition of human affairs, to cause the separation of the colonies of North America from the domination of Great Britain, and, after a bloody conflict of eight years, to establish them free, independent and sovereign States, connected, by alliances founded on reciprocal advantage, with some of the great princes and powers of the earth.

"To perpetuate, therefore, as well the remembrance of this vast event, as the mutual friendships which have been formed under the pressure of common danger, and, in many instances, cemented by the blood of the parties, the officers of the American Army do hereby, in the most solemn manner, associate, constitute and combine themselves into one SOCIETY OF FRIENDS, to endure as long as they shall endure, or any of their eldest male posterity, and, in failure thereof, the collateral branches who may be judged worthy of becoming its supporters and Members.

"The officers of the American Army having generally been taken from the citizens of America, possess high veneration for the character of that illustrious Roman, Lucius Quintus Cincinnatus; and being resolved to follow his example, by returning to their citizenship, they think they may with propriety denominate themselves—

THE SOCIETY OF THE CINCINNATI

"The following principles shall be immutable and form the basis of the Society of the Cincinnati:

"AN INCESSANT ATTENTION TO PRESERVE INVIOLATE THOSE EXALTED RIGHTS AND LIBERTIES OF HUMAN NATURE, FOR WHICH THEY HAVE FOUGHT AND BLED, AND WITHOUT WHICH THE HIGH RANK OF A RATIONAL BEING IS A CURSE INSTEAD OF A BLESSING.

"AN UNALTERABLE DETERMINATION TO PROMOTE AND CHERISH, BETWEEN THE RESPECTIVE STATES, THAT UNION AND NATIONAL HONOR SO ESSENTIALLY NECESSARY TO THEIR HAPPINESS, AND THE FUTURE DIGNITY OF THE AMERICAN EMPIRE.

"TO RENDER PERMANENT THE CORDIAL AFFECTION SUBSISTING AMONG THE OFFICERS. THIS SPIRIT WILL DICTATE BROTHERLY KINDNESS IN ALL THINGS, AND PARTICULARLY, EXTEND TO THE MOST SUBSTANTIAL ACTS OF BENEFICENCE, ACCORDING TO THE ABILITY OF THE SOCIETY, TOWARDS THOSE OFFICERS AND THEIR FAMILIES, WHO UNFORTUNATELY MAY BE UNDER THE NECESSITY OF RECEIVING IT.

"The General Society will, for the sake of frequent communications, be divided into State Societies, and these again into such districts as shall be directed by the State Society.

"The Societies of the districts to meet as often as shall be agreed upon by the State Society, those of the State on the fourth day of July annually, or oftener, if they shall find it expedient, and the General Society on the first Monday in May, annually, so long as they shall deem it necessary, and afterwards, at least once in every three years.

"At each meeting, the principles of the Institution will be fully considered, and the best measures to promote them adopted.

"The State Societies will consist of all the members resident in each State respectively; and any member removing from one State to another, is to be considered, in all respects, as belonging to the Society of the State in which he shall actually reside.

"The State Societies to have a President, Vice-President, Secretary, Treasurer, and Assistant Treasurer, to be chosen annually, by a majority of votes, at the State meeting.

"Each State meeting shall write annually, or oftener, if necessary, a circular letter, to the State Societies, noting whatever they may think worthy of observation, respecting the good of the Society, or the general union of the States, and giving information of the officers chosen for the current year; copies of these letters shall be regularly transmitted to the Secretary-General of the Society, who will record them in a book to be assigned for that purpose.

"The State Society will regulate everything respecting itself and the Societies of its districts consistent with the general maxims of the Cincinnati, judge of the qualifications of the members who may be proposed, and expel any member who, by a conduct inconsistent with a gentleman and a man of honor, or by an opposition to the interests of the community in general, or the Society in particular, may render himself unworthy to continue a member.

"In order to form funds which may be respectable, and assist the unfortunate, each officer shall deliver to the Treasurer of the State Society one month's pay, which shall remain for ever to the use of the State Society; the interest only of which, if necessary, to be appropriated to the relief of the unfortunate.

"Donations may be made by persons not of the Society, and by members of the Society, for the express purpose of forming permanent funds for the use of the State Society, and the interests of these donations appropriated in the same manner as that of the month's pay.

"Moneys, at the pleasure of each member, may be subscribed in the Societies of the districts, or the State Societies, for the relief of the unfortunate members, or their widows and orphans, to be appropriated by the State Society only.

"The meeting of the General Society shall consist of its officers and a representation from each State Society, in number not exceeding five, whose expenses shall be borne by their respective State Societies.

"In the general meeting, the President, Vice-President, Secretary, Assistant Secretary, Treasurer, and Assistant Treasurer-Generals, shall be chosen, to serve until the next meeting.

"The circular letters which have been written by the respective State Societies to each other, and their particular laws, shall be read and considered, and all measures concerted which may conduce to the general intendment of the Society.

"It is probable that some persons may make donations to the General Society, for the purpose of establishing funds for the further comfort of the unfortuante, in which case, such donations must be placed in the hands of the Treasurer-General, the interests only of which to be disposed of, if necessary, by the general meeting.

"All the officers of the American army, as well as those who have resigned with honor, after three years' service in the capacity of officers, or who have been deranged by the resolution of Congress upon the several reforms of the army, as those who shall have continued to the end of the war, have the right to become parties to this institution; provided that they subscribe one month's pay, and sign their names to the general rules, in their respective State Societies, those who are present with the Army immediately; and others within six months after the Army shall be disbanded, extraordinary cases excepted; the rank, time of service, resolution of Congress by which any have been deranged, and place of residence must be added to each name—and as a testimony of affection to the memory and the off-spring of such officers as have died in the service, their eldest male branches shall have the same right of becoming members, as the children of the actual members of the Society.

"Those officers who are foreigners, not resident in any of the States, will have their names enrolled by the Secretary-General, and are to be considered as members in the Societies of any of the States in which they may happen to be.

"And as there are, and will at all times be, men in the respective States eminent for their abilities and patriotism, whose views may be directed to the same laudable objects with those of the Cincinnati, it shall be a rule to admit such characters, as Honorary Members of the Society, for their own lives only: Provided always, That the number of Honorary Members, in each State, does not exceed a ratio of one to four of the officers or their descendants.

"Each State Society shall obtain a list of its members, and at the first annual meeting, the State Secretary shall have engrossed, on parchment, two copies of the Institution of the Society, which every member present shall sign, and the Secretary shall endeavor to procure the signature of every absent member; one of those lists to be transmitted to the Secretary-General, to be kept in the archives of the Society, and the other to remain in the hands of the State Secretary. From the State lists, the Secretary-General must make out, at the first general meeting, a complete list of the whole Society, with a copy of which he will furnish each State Society.

"The Society shall have an Order, by which its members shall be known and distinguished, which shall be a medal of gold, of a proper size to receive the emblems, and suspended by a deep blue riband two inches wide, edged with white, descriptive of the union of France and America, viz.:

"The principal figure,

CINCINNATUS:

Three Senators presenting him with a sword and other military ensigns—on a field in the background, his wife standing at the door of their Cottage—near it.
A PLOUGH AND INSTRUMENTS OF HUSBANDRY.
Round the whole,
OMNIA RELINQUIT SERVARE REMPUBLICAM.
On the reverse,
Sun rising—a city with open gates, and vessels entering the port—Fame crowning CINCINNATUS with a wreath, inscribed
VIRTUTIS PRAEMIUM.
Below,
HANDS JOINED, SUPPORTING A HEART,
With the motto,
ESTO PERPETUA.
Round the whole,
SOCIETAS CINCINNATORUM INSTITUTA.
A. D. 1783."

The Society, deeply impressed with a sense of the generous assistance this country has received from France, and desirous of perpetuating the friendships which have been formed, and so happily subsisted, between the officers of the allied forces in the prosecution of the war, direct that the President-General transmit, as soon as may be, to each of the characters hereafter named, a medal containing the Order of the Society, viz.:

His Excellency the CHEVALIER DE LA LUZERNE, Minister Plenipotentiary,

His Excellency the SIEUR GERARD, late Minister Plenipotentiary,
Their Excellencies

> The COUNT D'ESTAING,
> The COUNT DE GRASSE,
> The COUNT DE BARRAS,
> The CHEVALIER DES TOUCHES,

Admirals and Commanders in the Navy,

His Excellency the COUNT DE ROCHAMBEAU, Commander in Chief,

And the Generals and Colonels of his army, and acquaint them, that the Society does itself the honor to consider them members.

Resolved, That a copy of the aforegoing Institution be given to the senior officer of each State line, and that the officers of the respective State lines sign their names to the same, in manner and form following, viz.:

"We the subscribers, officers of the American army, do hereby voluntarily become parties to the foregoing Institution, and do bind ourselves to observe, and be governed by, the principles therein contained. For the performance whereof we do solemnly pledge to each other our sacred honor.
"Done in the Cantonment, on Hudson's River, in the year 1783."

That the members of the Society, at the time of subscribing their names to the Institution do also assign a draft on the Paymaster-General, in the following terms (the regiments to do it regimentally, and the generals and other officers not belonging to regiments, each for himself, individually), viz.:

"*To* JOHN PIERCE, *Esquire, Pay-Master General to the Army of the United States:*

"*Sir:* Please to pay to _____ Treasurer for the _____ State association of the Cincinnati, or his order, one month's pay of our several grades respectively, and deduct the same from the balance which shall be found due to us on the final liquidation of our accounts; for which this shall be your warrant."

That the members of the several State Societies assemble as soon as may be, for the choice of their President and other officers; and that the Presidents correspond together, and appoint a meeting of the officers who may be chosen from each State, in order to pursue such further measures as may be judged necessary.

That the General officers, and the officers delegated to represent the several corps of the Army, subscribe to the Institution of the General Society, for themselves and their constituents, in the manner and form before prescribed.

That GENERAL HEATH, GENERAL BARON DE STEUBEN, and GENERAL KNOX, be a committee to wait on his Excellency the Commander-in-Chief, with a copy of the Institution, and request him to honor the Society by placing his name at the head of it.

That MAJOR GENERAL WILLIAM HEATH, second in command in this Army, be, and he hereby is, desired to transmit copies of the

Institution, with the proceedings thereon, to the commanding officer of the Southern Army, the senior officer in each State, from Pennsylvania to Georgia, inclusive, and to the commanding officer of the Rhode Island line, requesting them to communicate the same to the officers under their several commands, and to take such measures as may appear to them necessary for expediting the establishment of their State Societies, and sending a delegation to represent them in the first general meeting, to be holden on the first Monday in May, 1784.

The meeting then adjourned without day.

Index

Adams, Abigail Amelia, 130
Adams, Charles Francis, 253
Adams, John, 16, 53–54, 71, 94, 101, 139, 157, 179, 198
Adams, John Quincy, 94, 218
Adams, Samuel, 71
Albert, king of the Belgians, 242
Alexander, Jean Baptiste, 160
Alliance américain, 241–42
Allison, John, 122
Anderson, Joseph, 131
Anderson, Larz, 248
Anderson, Mrs. Larz, 248
Anderson, Nicholas Longworth, 228
Anderson, Richard Clough, 112, 248
Anderson, Richard Heron, 229
Anderson, Robert, 238
Anderson House, 247–49, 250, 253, 254, 255
Andrews, Jeremiah, 76
Annapolis Convention (1786), 92
Aristocracy, 71–72, 95, 115
Armorial des Cincinnati de France, 246
Armstrong, John, Jr., 11, 12, 13, 35–36, 38, 85, 102, 112, 129, 135, 211
Armstrong, John (current member), 255
Army: disbanding of, 15, 23, 24, 29–30, 36; and half-pay scheme, 2–3, 5, 6, 8, 213–18; national standing, 71, 81–82, 100, 195; New England, 81–83, 85–87; pay withheld from, 1–2, 3, 7, 23, 26, 81; pensions, 215–19; poor treatment of, 1–2; post-Revolutionary, 114; promotions, 86; representative political organization in, 8, 13; and social mobility, 124–25; and state funding, 4–5; threatened mutiny of, 10–11; three months pay granted to, 23
Army generals: aides of, 11; and pay, (cont.) 3–4
Army officers, resignation of, 2, 3, 5, 6
Arnold, Benedict, 5
Arnold, Joseph, 106–7
Arrot, vicomte d', 158
Articles of Confederation, 70, 71–72, 92; army's criticism of, 18; and institution, 25
Artists, members as, 134
Artois, comte d', 167
Ashe, Cincinnatus, 138
Ashe, John Baptista, 179
Ashley, Moses, 87
Associations, 245–46, 255

Badge(s), 54, 60, 61–62, 63, 73, 75, 76, 77, 103, 180–81, 231, 237; designs of, 33–34; and French society, 145, 146, 149, 154, 156; Knox's conception of, 16, 17, 19; versus medal, 19; of other hereditary societies, 239
Bainbridge, William, 212
Baldwin, Abraham, 98, 136, 179
Baltzell, E. Digby, 128
Barber, William, 12
Barkley, Alben W., 252
Barlow, Joel, 111, 134–35
Barney, Joshua, 211
Barras, comte de, 27, 150
Barre (a Frenchman), 72
Barry, John, 114, 133
Barth, comte de, 111
Bastille, Vainqueurs de la, 164
Baxter, James Phinney, 252
Bayard, Stephen, 213, 214
Baylies, Hodijah, 130
Beauties of History (Stretch), 55
Bell, Charles H., 238
Bellerive, Louis Baury de, 121

Bellisarius. *See* Steuben, Friedrich Wilhelm Augustus von
Bentley, William, 186
Bicentennial, U.S., 255–56
Biddle, Charles, 128, 138
Biddle, James, 212
Bingham, William, 139, 181
Biron, Armand Louis de, 166
Blakeley, Johnston, 212
Blanchelande, Philibert-François Rouxel de, 166
Bland, Theodoric, 121, 179
Bleecker, Leonard, 181
Bloomfield, Joseph, 135, 216
Blount, William, 98, 108
Boston Evening Post, 55
Bouchet, marquis du, 145, 152–53
Boude, Thomas, 214
Boudinot, Elias, 140, 141–42, 179, 181
Bougainville, baron de, 170, 242
Bougainville, comte de, 159
Bowdoin, Governor, 71, 72, 81, 86
Bowles, Lucius Quintius Cincinnatus, 137
Boyd, Adam, 77
Bradley, Omar, 252
Brackenridge, Hugh Henry, 205
Bradford, Gamaliel, 121
Brearly, David, 96, 101, 131
Britain, 251–52
British army, 167
Broglie, duc de, 241, 242
Broglie, prince de, 167
Brooks, John, 6, 7, 9, 10, 13, 14, 39, 81, 86, 104, 131, 132, 195
Brown, Jacob, 212
Brown, Joseph, 184
Brown, Oliver, 125
"Brutus," 10, 19, 105
Buchanan, James, 237
Bulletin of the Society of the Cincinnati, 247
Burges, Tristram, 218
Burke, Aedanus, 40, 49, 50, 51, 52, 54, 55, 83, 154, 182, 245, 256
Burnet, Robert, Jr., 221
Burr, Aaron, 113–14, 197
Bush, George, 178
Bushnell, David, 133
Butler, Richard, 114

Caldwell, Andrew, 132–33
"Candidus," 192
Carberry, Henry, 35, 37
Carleton, Guy, 11, 48
Carlisle, Nicholas, 170
Carrington, Edward, 98, 178, 195
Casey, Silas, 228
Casey, Thomas Lincoln, 239
Castorland Company, 168
Castries, duc de, 167
Castries, marquis de, 147
Cato, 18–19
Charitable funds, 17–18, 25–26, 43, 61, 62, 73, 74, 77, 187–88, 210–11, 238, 257; grants of access to, 210–11; honorary members' contributions to, 138; investments of, 185–86; nonmembers' contributions to, 27
Charles X, 171
Chastellex, marquis de, 166
Chastellux, chevalier de, 30, 60, 159
Charters, 62, 63
Chastenet Puysegur, comte de, 167
Cheeves, Henry Charles, 256
Chester, John, 178
China trade, 132–33
Chisholm, Frank Anderson, 254
Churchill, Winston S., as hereditary member, 251, 252
Cincinnati Fourteen, 247
Cincinnati, Ohio, 112
Cincinnatus, 18
Circular letters, 25, 63, 77, 78, 91, 92, 103, 217; proposal of, 18
Citizen Genet, 190
City Tavern, 247
Civil War, 228
Claiborne, Richard, 207
Clajon, William, 36
Clark, George Rogers, lecture series, 247
Clarkson, Matthew, 133, 136
Cleveland, Grover, 237
Cleveland, Moses, 112
Clinton, De Witt, 39, 78, 132, 184, 211
Clinton, George, 101, 105, 191, 192
Clinton, Henry, 180
Cobb, David, 87
Cobb, George Washington, 137

INDEX

Cochran, John, 178, 228, 240
Colleges: attended by members, 126–27; boards of, members on, 135–36; funds for, 207–8
Collot, Georges-Henry-Victor, 159
Commerce and industry, members in, 132–34
Commutation, 6, 9–10, 14–15, 23, 25, 43, 48, 49, 50–51, 52, 55, 65, 216–17
Commutation certificates, 74, 78–79, 92, 181–85
Conde, prince de, 167
Congress: criticism of society by, 72; opposition to society in, 52–53; December 1782 memorial to, 7–8; society's members in, 179
Connecticut, opposition to commutation in, 49, 50, 52
Connecticut Courant, 55
Connecticut Land Company, 112
Connecticut society, 122, 200–201, 231–32; and amended institution, 77, 78; organizing 39–40
Considerations on the Order of Cincinnatus (Mirabeau), 154–55, 170
Considerations on the Order or Society of the Cincinnati (Burke), 49, 50, 51, 52, 54
Constitution: ratification of, 103–7, 112–13; and society, 102, 103, 104, 107; titles forbidden by, 180
Constitutional convention, 72, 92, 93, 95, 98–102; number of Cincinnati as delegates, 98
Contenson, baron de, 241
Conway, Thomas, 151, 158
Cook, Horatio Gates, 137
Coolidge, Calvin, 238
Corps of Invalids, 5, 84
County societies: frequency of meetings of, 18; functions of, 18
Craftsmen, members as, 134
Craig, Isaac, 133, 213, 214
Craigie, Andrew, 181
Crane, John, 7
Credit arrangements, and charitable fund, 25–26
Creditors, organization of, 10
Crittenden, Thomas Leonidas, 228
Crocker, Joseph, 81

Crown, proposed American: and duke of York, 101; and Prince Henry of Prussia, 83–85; and Washington, 84, 99
Cummings, John Noble, 8
Cuthbert, Alexander, 59
Cutler, Mannasseh, 103, 109, 110

Dale, Richard, 114, 133
Damas d'Antigny, comte de, 165
Dampierre, marquis de, 241
Daniel of St. Thomas Jenifer, 98
Daughters of the American Revolution, 229
Daughters of the Cincinnati, 230
Daveis, Charles S., 221
Daves, John C., 242, 250
Davie, William R., 98, 105
Davis, Charles Henry, 228
Davis, Curtis Carroll, 246
Day, Elijah, 87
Day, Luke, 87
Dayton, Elias, 39, 93
Dayton, Jonathan, 59, 96, 100, 114, 133, 195
Dearborn, Henry, 56, 59, 198, 211
Dearborn, Henry A. S., 221–22, 226
Decatur, Stephen, 212
Decoration, 32–34; conversion of medal to, 27
De Haas, John, 121
Delaware society, 54, 232; dissolution of, 200; organizing, 40
Denby, James Orr, 253
Denny, Robert, 178
Desmoulins, Camille, 164
Destouches, Admiral, 27
Deux-Ponts, Comte, 167
Deux-Ponts, Marquis, 167
de Weldon, Felix, 254
de Witt, Simeon, 135
Dexter, John Singer, 218
Diamond eagle, 61–62, 180, 181, 199, 200, 220
Dickinson, John, 59, 61, 63, 92, 98, 100, 109
Dickinson, Jonathan, 140
Dillon, Comte, 166
Diplomas, 76, 211
Diplomats, and criticism of society, 53–54

Discrimination, in funding continental securities, 182–85, 213
District societies, 73–74
Doctors, members as, 132
Dorchester, Lord, 99, 101
Doughty, John, 91, 114
Drayton, Thomas F., 228
Duane, James, 78
Duer, William, 78, 109, 110, 111, 138; as speculator, 134, 181, 183
du Mont, John Sanderson, 254, 256
Dumouriez, General, 166
Dwight, Timothy, 140

Eckstein, Johann, 206, 207
Education: and awards for excellence, 246; charitable funds for, 187–88, 207–8, 233
Electoral college, 92, 99–100
Elliott, Jesse Duncan, 212
Elliott, Nancy, 131
Elmer, Lucius Quintius Cincinnatus, 137
Encyclopédie Méthodique, 73
Enlightenment, 141
Estaing, Charles Hector, comte d', 27, 62, 146, 147, 149, 150, 155, 157, 158, 163, 166
Estaing, Valéry Giscard d', 255–56
Eustis, William, 7, 8, 11–12, 17, 86, 87, 131, 132
Evans, Israel, 11
Executive branch, society's members in, 177–79

Fairlee, James, 62–63, 65
Farragut, David G., 238
Federalist Papers, 105, 141
Fenno, John, 180
Fersen, Count Axel von, 160, 161, 165
Fish, Hamilton, 222, 226, 227, 229, 236, 237
Fish, Nicholas, 12, 178, 192, 206, 207
Fishbourne, Benjamin, 177–78
Flint, Royal, 111
Foch, Ferdinand, 242
Foreign officers: as members, 26, 30; participation in society, 19

Forrest, Uriah, 182
Foster, Francis Apthorp, 250
Fournier (revolutionary fanatic), 165
Fowler, Theodosius, 181
France: criticism of society in, 154–55; criticisms of, 190; Quasi War with, 196
Franklin, Benjamin, 54, 154; as honorary member, 139; and order of Liberty, 17
Frederick the Great, 161
Freeman, Constant, 38, 114, 126
Freemasons, members as, 136
French settlers, 111
French leaders, medals sent to, 27
French Revolution, 162–67, 193
French scholar program, 254
French society, 42, 44, 61, 62, 65, 145–76; and amended institution, 156; and badges, 145, 146, 149, 154, 156; hereditary aspects of, 156, 157; honorary members of, 158; and king, 147, 153, 154, 158; and naval officers, 149, 150, 151, 153; number of members of, 120; officers of, 155–56, 256; qualifications for membership in, 149; revival of, 240, 241, 242; and U.S. alliance, 148, 149, 159–60, 196, 255–56; voluntary contributions to American society, 148, 153, 156; women in, 156
Frost, Robert, 252
Frothingham, Benjamin, 134

Galbert, vicomte de, 158, 163
Gardiner, Asa Bird, 120, 226, 230–31, 232, 233, 234, 236, 237, 238, 240, 241, 242, 251
Gates, Horatio, 5, 11, 12, 13, 35, 36, 37, 64, 72–73, 81, 93, 94, 97, 129, 152, 153; and birth of society, 17; on land grants, 34
General Washington's Correspondence concerning the Society of the Cincinnati, 251
Genet, Citizen, 190
George V, 251–52
George Olmsted Foundation, 249
George Rogers Clark lecture series, 247

INDEX

Georgia society, 54, 76, 200; organizing, 40
Gerry, Elbridge, 53, 54, 71, 75, 83, 92, 99, 100, 129
Gibbons v. *Ogden*, 218
Gibbs, Alexander Hamilton, 137
Giles, Aquila, 125, 134
Gilman, Nicholas, 96, 179, 247
Gimat, chevalier de, 158-59
Gimoard, comte de, 166
Girardot, Baron, 171
Goodwin, Francis Le Baron, 132
Gookin, Daniel, 209
Gordon, William, 15, 33, 84
Gorham, Nathaniel, 75, 83, 85
Gouvion, Jean Baptiste, 29, 30
Grant, U. S., 237
Grasse, Auguste, comte de, 158
Grasse, François Paul, comte de, 27, 146
Grayson, William, 179
Green, John, 132
Greene, Nathanael, 3, 5, 6, 27, 56, 57, 64, 70, 136, 141, 246; as president of Rhode Island society, 39
Greenleaf, William, 125
Grubb, Edward B., 228
Guardoqui, Don Diego, 113
Guerard, Benjamin, 52
Gunn, James, 179
Gustavus Adolphus VI, 252
Gustavus III, 160-61, 171

Habersham, John, 178
Habersham, Joseph, 179
Hale, Nathan, 18-19
Hall, Henry Knox, 137
Hall, Lyman, 54
Halsey, William, 252
Hamilton, Alexander, 11, 12, 23, 26, 65, 78, 92, 96, 105, 130, 139, 186, 191, 193; attendance at King's College, 127; at constitutional convention, 100, 101-2; and *Federalist Papers*, 141; as lawyer, 131; as major general, 195, 196; as Mason, 136; oration delivered at N.Y. society meeting, 75; as president general, 199; as secretary of Treasury Department, 178; social mobility of, 125; on taxation, 8, 10; as vice president general, 189

Hamilton, Alexander van Cortlandt, 255
Hampton, Wade, 229
Hancock, Winfield Scott, 238
Hand, Edward, 24, 31, 194, 195
Harding, Warren G., 238
Harmar, Josiah, 110, 114
Harrison, Benjamin, 128
Hart, John, 132
Hartley, Thomas, 179
Harvard University, 53
Haskell, Jonathan, 86
Haslet, David, 132
Hatch, Francis, 253-54
Hawkins, Benjamin, 179
Haydenbourg, baron de Closen, 169
Hayes, Rutherford B., 237, 238
Hazen, Moses, 8
Heath, William, 19, 24, 25, 104, 122, 128, 166; marriage of, 130; and organizing state societies, 38; position on society, 28, 29, 30; as principal organizer, 27-28
Hebecourt, marquis d', 111
Henry, prince of Prussia, 83-85, 101
Hereditary societies, 226, 229-30, 238-39
Hereditary succession: in French society, 156, 157; in society, 17, 19, 49-50, 52, 54, 60-61, 62, 63, 65, 71-72, 77, 188-89, 196, 199, 200, 210
Hervilly, comte d', 165
Heth, Henry, 229
Higginson, Stephen, 71
Hildreth, Samuel, 110
Hill-Physic-Keith House, 247
Historic preservation and commemoration, 233-35, 245-46
Historical documents, discovery and preservation of, 246-47
Hitchcock, Enos, 84, 86, 106, 135, 185
Hollad, Park, 125
Holten, Samuel, 71
Hoover, Herbert, 252
Hopkins, Samuel, 52, 211
Houdin, Michel Gabriel, 168
Howard, John Eager, 129, 195
Howe, Robert, 3, 31, 35
Howell, Joseph, 178
Hoyt, Harry Ramsay, 254, 256

Huger, Isaac, 128
Hughes, James Miles, 11, 192
Hull, Isaac, 212
Hull, William, 6, 31, 81, 85, 86, 102, 211
Hume, Edgar Erskine, 250–51, 252
Humphreys, David, 58–59, 63, 72, 73, 86, 97, 101, 133, 135, 179, 200–201
Hunt, Henry Jackson, 137, 228
Hunter, David, 228
Huntington, Ebenezer, 31, 48, 49, 107, 133, 190
Huntington, Jedediah, 5, 7, 15–16, 24, 129; as banker, 133; as collector of port, 178; as president of Connecticut society, 39–40
Huntington, Samuel, 4

Immigrants, 233
Imposts, 8, 9, 15, 48, 71, 78
Independent Chronicle, 51, 53
Indian Territory, 114
Indian wars, 114
Institution: amended, 76–78, 96, 188, 199, 200; amended, and French society, 156; changes in, during May 1784 meeting, 59–61, 62–64; distribution of copies of, 29, 30; draft of, 17, 18, 19, 24, 25; political import of, 25; signing of, 27; text of, 258–64
Irvine, William, 109, 162, 194
Izard, George, 212

Jackson, Amasa, 122
Jackson, Andrew, 212
Jackson, Charles, 121, 122
Jackson, Ebenezer, 122
Jackson, Henry, 30, 31, 81, 128, 177; as commander of Massachusetts regiment, 85–86, 87; as treasurer of Massachusetts society, 39
Jackson, Michael (Colonel), 122
Jackson, Michael (Lieutenant), 122
Jackson, Simon, 122
Jackson, William, 98, 102, 135, 170, 209; and lobbying for half pay, 216–17; as secretary general, 190

Janson, Charles William, 206
Jay, John, 53, 139, 191, 194
Jefferson, Thomas, 16, 49, 52, 53, 55, 58, 60, 65, 245, 256; on abolition of society, 94–95, criticisms of society, 56–57, 190–91; and medals, 72–73; opinion of, on Armstrong, 12; as secretary of state, 178; and solicitation of funds for University of Virginia, 208; and statements about society, 73; and U.S. Military Academy, 198
Joffre, Joseph Jacque Césaire, 241, 256
Johnston, Albert Sidney, 228
Johnston, George Doherty, 229
Johnston, Peter, 124, 214
Johnston, Robert, 132
Jones, Catesby, 253
Jones, Jacob, 212
Jones, William, 131, 210
Judiciary, federal, society's members in, 179

Kalb, Baron Frederick de, 150, 158, 166
Kearney, Stephen W., 238
Kentucky, 209–10
Kerloguen, Denis-Nicholas Cottineau de, 168
Kersaint, comte de, 166
Kilbourne, John D., 249
King, Rufus, 71, 75, 83, 167
Kingsbury, Jacob, 114
Kirkwood, Robert, 114
Knox, Henry, 5, 6–7, 10, 11, 12–13, 14, 31, 34, 42, 59, 60, 61, 70, 93, 95, 97, 121, 130, 146, 177, 195, 257; and birth of idea of society, 15, 16, 17, 19, 198; death of, 200; and dissolution of army, 23, 24; envy of success of, 37–38; and Massachusetts protests, 80, 81, 82; on national standing army, 81, 100; organizing society, 29, 30; organizing state societies, 38–44; and pressure to establish society, 24; replaced as secretary general, 189, 195–96; as secretary general, 32, 58, 64, 97; as secretary of War De-

INDEX 273

partment, 178; signature of, on certificate, 76; social mobility of, 125; style of living of, 128, 129; as vice president general, 200; as vice president of Massachusetts society, 39
Knox, Henry Jackson, 137
Kohn, Richard H., 12
Kosciusko, Thaddeus, 161
Krauel, Richard, 83

Ladd Gilman House, 247
Lafayette, Marie Joseph Paul Yves Roch Gilbert du Motier, marquis de, 30, 42, 54, 60, 146, 147, 150, 151, 152, 153, 155, 156; decoration of, in French Revolution, 164; and half pay, 217; imprisonment of, 166; and liberal movements, 163; and officers of French society, 158; as president of French society, 155, 156, 157; tour of, 212-13
La Galissoniere, marquis de, 159
La Luzerne, chevalier de, 27, 32, 148, 150, 158
Lamar, Lucius Quintius Cincinnatus, 138
Lamartine (historian), 165
Lamb, John, 178, 192
Lameth, Comte Alexandre de, 163
Lameth, Comte Charles de, 163
Land grants, 34-35, 64, 107-13
La Neuville, Lamart de Noirman de, 165
Langeron, comte de, 167
Lansing, John, 98, 100, 102
Laurens, Henry, 2
Lauzun, duc de, 166
Law, members in, 131
Lawrence, James, 212
Lawton, Mrs. James M., 230
Lee, Arthur, 97
Lee, Henry, 61, 76, 104, 128, 193, 195, 198, 211
Lee, Richard Henry, 179
Lee, William Raymond, 228
Legion of Honor, 169-70, 239, 256
Legislature, 100, 101
L'Enfant, Pierre, 31, 32, 33, 34, 42, 61, 62, 65, 140; and French society, 146-50, 153

Lemot, Frederic, 207
Lenox, David, 139, 140, 213
Levasseur, Auguste, 212
Levees, 180
Lewis, Clifford, 128
Lewis, Morgan, 132, 220
Lezay-Marnezia, marquis de, 110, 111
Lillie, John, 198
Lillie, Samuel Shaw, 137
Limited Service Pension Act, 216
Lincoln, Benjamin, 29, 39, 70, 81, 86, 104, 130, 177, 178
Lincoln, Benjamin (current member), 255
Lincoln, Elizabeth, 130
Lindsay, Ronald Charles, 252
Lingan, James H., 24
Lippitt, Charles Warren, 254
Literature, members' contributions to, 134-35
Livingston, Henry Beekman, 128
Livingston, Henry Brockholst, 128, 130, 131, 183
Livingston, Robert R., 128, 133, 163, 179, 207
Livingston, William, 98, 101, 128; on half-pay scheme, 2-3
Loomis, Lebbeus, 134
Loubet, Emile François, 241
Louis Philippe, 171
Louis XVI, 160
Lovell, Mansfield, 228
Lowell, Ralph, 252
Lubomirka, Princess, 161
Lyman, Daniel, 217

MacArthur, Douglas, 252
MacCarthy, Eugene, 159, 167
McClary, Michael, 209
McClenaghan, Blair, 138, 181
McClurg, James, 98, 100, 102
McConnell, Matthew, 181
MacDonald, Forrest, 26
Macdonough, Thomas, 212
McDougall, Alexander, 8, 9, 14, 19, 25, 34, 36, 128, 141; on army pay, 4, 5; as banker, 133; "Brutus" as pseudonym of, 10, 19; on national finance, 10; as president of New

McDougall, Alexander (cont.)
  York society, 39; social mobility of,
  125; as treasurer general, 32, 64, 97
McFarlane, James, 193
McHenry, John, 210
McIntosh, Lachlan, 40, 42, 178
McKean, Thomas, 128, 138, 140
McKinley, William, 235, 238
Maclay, William, 178
Madison, James, 9, 10–11, 48, 99,
  182, 183
Manning, William, 196–97
Marietta, Ohio, 110, 209
Marine officers, 121
Marlatic, Comte, 111
March, Peyton C., 242
Marshall, George C., 252
Martin, Alexander, 98, 100, 102
Martineng de Gineste, baron de, 170
Mary, Queen, 251
Maryland society, 209; and amended
  institution, 77; organizing, 43–44
Mason, John M., 138
Massachusetts: death of opposition to
  society in, 70; protests in, 80–81,
  82–83; reactions to society in, 59;
  society condemned in, 51–52
Massachusetts Centinel, 64
Massachusetts society, 120–21, 209;
  and amended institution, 78; and
  investment of funds, 186; organizing, 38–39; and social position of
  members, 128
Matthews, George, 179
Maupin, Armistead Jones, 249, 254
Maxwell, Hugh, 31
Medal(s): badge, 19; conversion of, to
  decoration, 27; for heroes of Revolution, 72; new conception of, 32–
  34; sent to French leaders, 27
Medal of Honor, 239
Meigs, Return Jonathan, 131
Members and membership: ages of,
  121; children of, named after Cincinnatus, 137–38; children of,
  named after compatriots, 137; college men, 126–27; criteria for, 26,
  121–22, 210, 226–28, 254; foreign,
  26, 30, 32, 61, 62; and geographic
  mobility, 130; honorary, 26, 62,
  138–40, 211–12, 237–38, 252–53,
  256; induction of, 75; and intermarriages, 130; and local attitudes,
  122–23; as Masons, 136; motives
  for, 122–23; occupations of, 125,
  129–30, 131–36; officer ranks represented in, 121; original, numbers
  of, 120; and praise of fellow revolutionaries, 137; of presidents,
  237–38, 252, 256; of state troops,
  41–42, 122; successor, 210; transfer of, 61; in twentieth century,
  250, 253, 254–55; and wealth,
  128–30
Memoirs of the American War
  (Heath), 27
Metcalf, Bryce, 250
Meunier, Jean Nicholas de, 73
Michaelis (British officer), 48
Middleton, John, 128
Mifflin, Thomas, 96, 97, 189, 193
Military emigrations, 167–68
Military Order of the Loyal Legion,
  229
Military titles, use of, 76
Miller, Colonel, 28, 29
Mirabeau, Boniface, 154
Mirabeau, comte de, 94, 154, 155,
  157, 170, 245, 256
Mirabeau, vicomte de, 162
Mobility, of members: geographic,
  130; social, 124–28
Modern Chivalry (Brackenridge),
  205
Monarchy, 36, 83–85, 99, 101–2, 194
Monroe, James, 85, 135, 179, 211,
  216, 237
Montmorency-Laval, duc de, 167
Moore (Major), 12
Morgan, Daniel, 193
Morgan, Edmund S., 247
Morgan, George, 113
Morgan, William, 63
Morison, Samuel Eliot, 247, 252
Morrell, George Webb, 228
Morris, Gouverneur, 8, 9, 10, 11, 12,
  128, 138
Morris, Lewis, 128
Morris, Lewis IV, 130–31
Morris, Robert, 9, 30, 71, 98, 101,
  133, 138, 139; as speculator, 181;
  on taxation, 8; on union of cred-
  itors, 10
Morris, William Walton, 128

INDEX 275

Mott, Gershom, 238
Moultrie, William, 40, 50, 131
Mourning, protocol for, 188
Moylan, Stephen, 54, 55, 178
Muhlenberg, John, B. G., 41, 179
Murray, Lieutenant, 252
Museums, 247, 248-49

Napoleon, 168-69
Nason, Lucius Quintius Cincinnatus, 137
National executive, choosing, 99-101, 102
National Society of Children of the American Revolution, 229-30
National Society of the Daughters of the Revolution, 229
National society meetings: date of, 24; frequency of, 18, 25, 62, 209, 219; locations of, 236; of May 1784, 56, 58-65; 1787, 92, 93, 95-97, 98; successor members at, 210
Naval officers, 114, 121, 212
Nelson, Paul David, 12
Newburgh, N.Y.: men at, as founding nucleus of society, 6; Washington's headquarters at, 5-6
Newburgh Addresses, 1-2, 12, 13, 14, 35
Newhall, Ezra, 125
New Hampshire Gazette, 43, 52, 65, 71, 99
New Hampshire society, 56, 209, 232; and amended institution, 77, 78; organizing, 43
New Jersey society, 121, 209; and amended institution, 77, 78; and investment of funds, 185-86; organizing, 38, 39
Newman, Samuel, 121
New York Daily Advertiser, 82
New York Journal, 191-92
New York society, 209; and amended institution, 77, 78; honorary membership in, 211-12; organizing, 38, 39; and political influence, 191-93; 1786 ceremony of, 74-75
Nichols, John Taylor Gilman, 254
Nicholson, Samuel, 114
Nicola, Lewis, 5, 84, 135
Nivelle, Robert Georges, 242

Noailles, duc de, 30, 163, 164
Noailles, vicomte de, 190, 240
North, William, 31, 82, 86, 129
North, William Augustus Steuben, 137
North Carolina, opposition to society in, 71
North Carolina society, 232; and amended institution, 77; collapsing of, 200; organizing, 42

Observations on a late Pamphlet entitled Considerations upon the Society or Order of the Cincinnati (Moylan), 54-55
Ogden, Aaron, 133, 211, 218, 219; as president general, 219-20
Ogden, Mathias, 8, 9
Ohio, 209
Ohio Company, 34, 107, 109-10
Ohio settlement schemes, 110-13
Ollone, comte d', 240, 242
Olmsted, George, 249
Olney, Jeremiah, 84, 178
Olyphant, David Washington Cincinnatus, 138
O'Moran, Jacques, 166
Order of the Cincinnati in France (Gardiner), 241
Order of the Divine Providence, 53, 55
Order of Liberty, 16-17
Orders, European, 32-33, 53, 54, 63, 76, 239
Ordre Americain de Cincinnatus en France, L' (Contenson), 241
Ordre americain de Cincinnatus en France, L' (Girardot), 171
Osgood, Samuel, 51

Paca, William, 138, 179
Paine, Thomas, 57
Paper money, 2, 79, 106
Parchment Roll, 32
Paris, W. Francklyn, 239
Parker, Daniel, 181
Parker, Josiah, 179
Parrish, John, 179
Parry, Lewis, 252
Parsons, Samuel Holden, 70, 80, 103, 109, 111, 112

Pasler, Margaret, 194
Pasler, Rudolph, 194
Paterson, John, 31, 39, 87, 121
Peale, James, 134, 181
Pendleton, Nathaniel, 98, 179
Pennington, William Sanford, 131
Pennsylvania, and funding of army, 4–5
Pennsylvania mutiny, 35, 36–37, 38
Pennsylvania society, 75–76, 209; and amended institution, 77; and land grants, 109; organizing, 41; and social position of members, 128
Pennypacker, Isaac, 250
Perkins, Lafayette, 137
Perouse, comte de La, 159
Perrot, A. M., 170
Perry, Matthew C., 238
Perry, Oliver Hazard, 212
Pershing, John, 242
Pétain, Marshal, 242
Pettengill, Joseph, 31
Phelon, Patrick, 114
Piatt, William, 114
Pickering, Timothy, 14, 28, 34, 107, 108, 122, 140, 179
Pierce, Benjamin, 124–25
Pierce, Franklin, 125, 237
Pierce, Henry Dearborn, 137
Pierce, John, 25, 178
Pierce, John, Jr., 74
Pierce, William, 98, 101, 102
Pike, Zebulon, 211
Pinckney, Charles Cotesworth, 96, 100, 104, 127, 128, 129–30, 170, 195, 210, 218; as lawyer, 131; as president general, 199–200, 208, 209; as vice president general, 199
Pinckney, Charles Cotesworth (current member), 255
Pinckney, Thomas, 127, 128, 131, 178–79, 218; as president general, 219
Pinckney, Thomas (current member), 255
Pintard, John, 192, 193
Platt, Richard, 134, 183–84
Pleville-le-Pelley, Vice-admiral, 169
Plumb, J. H., 247
Poirey, Joseph Leonard, 168

Polish members, 161
Polish Order, 53, 55
Polk, William, 178
Poniatowski, King Stanislaus, 161
Ponteves-Giens, marquis de, 170
Ponteves-Giens, vicomte de, 159, 160
Pontgibaud, chevalier de, 150
Popham, William, 220–21
Porcelains, Cincinnati, 76
Posey, Thomas, 114, 207–8
Prade, comte de la, 159, 167–68
Presidents, U.S.: membership of, in society, 237–38, 252, 256; titles of, 179–80
Princeton commencement, 48
Provence, comte de, 167
Prussia, 161
Publications, historical, 246
Purple Heart, 33
Putnam, Israel, 121
Putnam, Rufus, 6, 14, 31, 87, 107, 109, 110–11, 130, 136, 215; as Mason, 136; and Ohio Company, 34

Quesne, marquis du, 240
Quincy, Josiah, 53

Randall, Blanchard, 253
Randall, Thomas, 133
Randolph, Edmund, 52, 55, 92, 98, 100, 179
Reagan, Ronald, 256
Reed, John, 114
Reeves, Enos, 134
Revolution's Godchild (Davis), 246
Rhode Island, opposition to society in, 52
Rhode Island society, 209, 219, 230–31; French members of, 240–41; and investment of funds, 185; 1786 meeting of, 79–80; organizing, 39
Ribbons, 231
Rice, Oliver, 125
Richmond, Christopher, 12, 17, 28, 29, 36, 37
Roberts, Lucius Quintius Cincinnatus, 137
Rochambeau, comte de, 27, 146, 147,

INDEX

148, 149, 150, 151, 153, 155, 156, 158, 160; imprisonment of, 166; medal sent to, 19
Roche, Edward, 131
Rochefontaine, chevalier de, 168
Rogers, Horatio, 228
Roosevelt, Franklin, 252
Rose, John, 161-62
Rosenthal, Baron Gustavus H. de, of Livonia, 161-62
Rostaing, marquis de, 163
Rouerie, marquis de La, 32, 149, 153, 163
Rouvray, marquis de, 163
Rule of 1854, 227, 230, 232, 254
Russia, 161, 167

Saige, Gerard Le, comte de La Villèsbrunne, 256
St. Clair, Arthur, 35, 40, 41, 56, 57, 112, 114
Saint Simon, marquis de, 167
Saltonstall, Leverett, 253
Sargent, George Washington, 137
Sargent, Winthrop, 57-58, 60, 61, 63, 64, 109, 110, 112, 114, 126
Sarreck, comte de Custine, 166
Savage, Edward, 181
Sawyer, Frederick Augustus, 137
Sawyer, Gamaliel Bradford, 137
Schofield, John M., 238
Schuyler, John, 120, 230
Schuyler, Philip, 168, 181
Scioto Company, 110-11, 183
Scott, John Fulton Reynolds, 253
Scott, Joseph Warren, 221
Scott, William, 8
Scott, Winfield, 212
Segond, chevalier de, 159
Ségur, comte de, 155, 156, 158
Ségur, marquis de, 147, 148, 153
Sever, James, 114
Sevier, John, 108
Shaw, Samuel, 7, 16, 24, 31, 42, 76, 126, 179
Shays's Rebellion, 79, 86-87
Shepard, William, 87
Sherman, William T., 238
Sherrill, Henry Knox, 252
Shy, John W., 247
Siemering, Rudolph, 235

Simons, John, 229
Smallwood, William, 40, 43
Smith, Colonel, 62, 63
Smith, Israel, 114
Smith, John Spear, 247
Smith, Page, 247
Smith, Peregrine, 188
Smith, Samuel, 129
Smith, Sylvanus, 125
Smith, William S., 59, 61, 130, 192, 195
Society of the Cincinnati: associations, 245-46, 255; birth of, in mind of Knox, 15, 16, 17; controversy over, 43, 48-54, 55-57, 58-59, 64-65; as creditor, 10; criticism of, 71-73, 94-95, 114-15; criticism of, in France, 154-55; decline of, 205, 206, 208-9; favorable opinions of, 54-55, 57-58; financial status of, 249; foreign contributions to, 51, 62; foreign members of, 160-62, 171; and friendship, 17, 186, 255, 257; functions of, 122, 140-42, 255; growth of, 73, 254-55; headquarters, 247-49 (*see also* Anderson House); leadership of, in twentieth century, 249-51, 253-54; membership figures, 232; mission of, 232-33; museums associated with, 247, 248-49; name, origin of, 18; officers, election of, 31, 32; official birthday of, 25; and old-boy network, 126; original images of, 19; original structure and functions of, 15, 16, 17-19; political usefulness of, and dispersing of army, 23-24; and politics of 1790s, 190-97; as pressure group, 17; presidents as honorary members of, 237-38, 252; publications of, 246, 247; rebirth of, 226-44; and research, 249, 254; scope of, 26; spread of knowledge of, 38, 48. *See also* Members and membership; National society meetings; *specific names;* State societies
Sons of the American Revolution, 229
Sons of the Revolution, 229
South Carolina, opposition to society in, 52

South Carolina society, 209; organizing, 40–41
Spaight, Richard Dobbs, 98, 105
Spanish territory, 113
Spear, Edward, 114
Speculators: contributions of, to charitable funds, 139; members as, 133–34, 181–85; state societies as, 182
Stack, Edward, 167
Stacy, William, 136
Stafford, John, 125
Stagg, John, Jr., 127, 178, 182, 206
Stanton, Colonel, 241
Stark, John, 121
State(s): equality of, 100, 101; establishment of new, and prohibition of society's members, 53; and funding of army, 4–5, 6; politics, members in, 131–32; society funds to, 62, 63, 77
State Department, society's members in, 178–79
State societies: and awards for academic excellence, 246; charitable funds of, 17–18, 74 (*see also* Charitable funds); collapsing of, 200, 209; date of meetings of, 24, 255; and education, 187–88; frequency of meetings of, 18, 62, 255; and historic preservation and commemoration, 245; and historical documents, 246–47; and historical publications, 246; meetings of, 74–75, 186–87, 255; organizing, 38–44; and political influence, 191–93; revival of, 230–32; and rules for admission, 210; social interaction among, 221; as speculators, 182.
See also specific state
State troops, 41–42, 122
Stedingk, count von, 160–61, 171, 240
Steuben, Friedrich Wilhelm Augustus von, 24, 29, 31, 93, 102, 121, 168; and birth of society, 15, 16; bringing opponents into society, 139; criticism of, 50; as de facto president, 31–32; death of, 200; decoration of, 33, 181; and land grants, 108, 111, 113; as Mason, 136; military manual of, 135; on national standing army, 81; on New England Army, 82–83; as president of New York society, 191, 192; and Prince Henry of Prussia, 83, 84, 101; and 1786 New York society ceremonial, 74, 75; and state societies, 38, 40; style of living, 129
Stevens, Ebenezer, 184, 191
Stevens, John Austin, 229
Stevens, Hazzard, 228
Steward, Charles, 212
Stewart, T., 12
Stewart, Walter, 11, 13, 30, 37, 181
Stiles, Ezra, 139–40
Stone, Rufus Putnam, 137
Storey, Moorfield, 241
Stretch, L. M., 55
Stuart, Harold Leonard, 254
Suffern, Bailli de, 163
Sullivan, James, 43
Sullivan, John, 31, 40, 56, 79, 121, 131, 179; mutiny of, 35, 37
Sullivan, John (current member), 255
Sumner, Jethro, 42
Swartwout, Bernardus, 24
Swedish members, 160–61, 171
Symmes Purchase, 111–12
Szatmary, David P., 86

Taft, William Howard, 238
Talbot, Silas, 114
Talleyrand, 162
Tallmadge, Benjamin, 112, 142, 190, 195
Tallmadge, William, 142
Tammany Hall, 192–93
Tannehill, Adamson, 213, 214
Taxation, 8, 9, 10, 25; on whiskey, 193
Taylor, Zachary, 237, 238
Temple of Virtue, 11, 13, 24
Ternant, Chevalier Jean de, 158
Thatcher, Henry Knox, 228
Theodore, comte de Lameth, 171
Thomas, William S., 239, 250

INDEX

Tilton, James, 40, 59, 132, 178, 190
Titcomb, Jonathan, 87
Tousard, Anne-Louis, 168
Tousard, chevalier de, 198
Townsend, Edward Davis, 228
Traversay, marquis de, 160, 167
Treasury Department, society's members in, 178
Truman, Harry S., 252
Trumbull, John, 55, 122, 134, 135, 181, 207
Trumbull, Jonathan, 64, 77, 131, 179
Truxton, Thomas, 114, 133
Tucker, Thomas Tudor, 179
Tupper, Benjamin, 87, 102, 109, 111
Tupper, Benjamin, Jr., 130
Turner, George, 96, 97, 126

Union, political state of, 78, 79
United States Military Academy, 197-98
University of Virginia, 208

van Buren, Martin, 12
van Cortlandt, Philip, 7, 8, 31, 128
van Cortlandt, Pierre, 128
van Rensselaer, Jeremiah, 128, 179
van Rensselaer, Nicholas, 128
Varick, Richard, 192
Varnum, James Mitchell, 39, 79, 110, 112, 131
Vergennes, comte de, 147, 148
Verplanck House, 24-25
Villeverde, comte de Renaud de, 163
Vinson, Frederick M., 252
Vioménil, baron de, 148, 165, 167, 170
Virginia, opposition to society in, 52, 58
Virginia Military District, 112
Virginia society, 121, 200, 207-8, 209, 232; organizing, 41
Vose, Colonel, 28, 29

Wadsworth, Jeremiah, 80, 133, 157, 179, 194

Walker, Benjamin, 39, 65, 186
Walpole, Horace, 147
War Department, society's members in, 178
War of 1812, 211-12
Warren, James, 94
Warren, Mercy Otis, 38, 94, 123, 125, 128, 205
Warren, William, 242
Warren, Winslow, 236-37, 250, 251
Warrington, Lewis, 212
Washington, George, 11, 128, 237; on amended institution, 65, 71; and army conspiracy, 12, 13; and army pay, 2, 3, 4, 6, 26; birthday of, 180; chevrons established by, 33; and constitutional convention, 93, 94, 96; as crowned head, 84, 99; death of, 198; desiring abolition of society, 58, 60, 65; on democratic societies, 190; and dissolution of army, 23, 24, 29-30; and French society, 151-52, 153, 160; involvement, in society, 42-43, 55-56, 93-94; 95, 96, 198-199; knowledge of treatment of army of, 1, 2, 6; as Mason, 136; at May 1784 meeting, 59-61, 64; and monarchy, 85, 194; and parchment copy of institution, 27; and "Polish Order," 53; portraits of, 181; position on society, 29; as president, society's support of, 107; as president general of society, 31, 58, 64, 92, 96-97, 188, 189; signature on certificate, 76; social mobility of, 124; society's loyalty to memory of, 206-7; statues of, 206-7; at Temple of Virtue meeting, 13-14; and Whiskey Rebellion, 193
Washington College, 207, 208
Wayne, Anthony, 41, 114, 188-89, 214
Wayne, William, 236
Webb, Alexander Stuart, 228
Webb, Samuel Blachley, 31
Webster, Noah, 55
Weedon, George, 41, 93
Western Reserve, 112
Whiskey Rebellion, 193
White, Walton, 59

Whiting, John, 31
Wilkinson, James, 113
Willet, Marinus, 232–33
William and Mary, College of, 208
Williams, Otho, 61, 64, 97, 178
Wilmer, Richard Hooker, 253
Wilson, James, 139, 179
Wilson, Woodrow, 238

Witherspoon, John, 48, 127, 139
World War I, 241
Worth, William J., 238
Wylly, Richard, 178

Yates, Robert, 98, 100, 102, 105

Zeigler, David, 37, 112

www.ingramcontent.com/pod-product-compliance
Lightning Source LLC
Chambersburg PA
CBHW032034150426
43194CB00006B/271